Jurisdiction to Tax Corporate Income Pursuant to the Presumptive Benefit Principle

Series on International Taxation

VOLUME 70

Series Editors

Prof. Ruth Mason, University of Virginia School of Law
Prof. Dr Ekkehart Reimer, University of Heidelberg

Introduction & Contents

The Series on International Taxation deals with a wide variety of topics in the global tax arena. The authors include many of the field's leading experts as well as talented newcomers. Their expert views and incisive commentary have proven highly useful to practitioners and academics alike.

Objective

The volumes published in this series are aimed at offering high-quality analytical information and practical solutions to international tax practitioners.

Readership

Practitioners, academics and policy makers in international tax law.

Frequency of Publication

2-3 new volumes published each year.

The titles published in this series are listed at the end of this volume.

Jurisdiction to Tax Corporate Income Pursuant to the Presumptive Benefit Principle

A Critical Analysis of Structural Paradigms Underlying Corporate Income Taxation and Proposals for Reform

Eva Escribano

Wolters Kluwer

Published by:
Kluwer Law International B.V.
PO Box 316
2400 AH Alphen aan den Rijn
The Netherlands
E-mail: international-sales@wolterskluwer.com
Website: lrus.wolterskluwer.com

Sold and distributed in North, Central and South America by:
Wolters Kluwer Legal & Regulatory U.S.
7201 McKinney Circle
Frederick, MD 21704
United States of America
Email: customer.service@wolterskluwer.com

Sold and distributed in all other countries by:
Air Business Subscriptions
Rockwood House
Haywards Heath
West Sussex
RH16 3DH
United Kingdom
Email: international-customerservice@wolterskluwer.com

Printed on acid-free paper.

ISBN 978-94-035-0640-1

e-Book: ISBN 978-94-035-0644-9
web-PDF: ISBN 978-94-035-0652-4

Printed in the United Kingdom.

Table of Contents

Forewords

Eva Escribano's outstanding new book is the result of her doctoral dissertation written and defended within the PhD Program in Law of Universidad Carlos III de Madrid. Its "scientific" structure is exactly how, in my opinion, a doctoral dissertation ought to be. First, some hypotheses are made. Second, those hypotheses are tested in a real practical case and finally, in light of the experiment run, very interesting policy proposals are formulated. It is particularly interesting that Dr. Escribano adopts a "bottom-up" approach in studying the profit shifting phenomenon, whose public awareness has arisen since 2013 thanks to the ambitious Organisation for Economic Co-operation and Development (OECD) Base Erosion and Profit Shifting (BEPS) project. Especially after the financial crisis of 2008, various stakeholders have started to look from a different perspective at multinationals' strategies which made possible the shifting of profits from high-tax countries to jurisdictions with lower or no taxes on certain items of income. In a time where states were cutting their public services due to budget constraints, the large discrepancy existing between the location where multinational enterprises (MNEs) report profits and that of their physical presence was no longer tolerated. Nor was it acceptable that MNEs were significantly accessing and exploiting States' infrastructures, goods and services thus realizing huge amount of profits without remitting their fair share of taxes.

Dr. Escribano starts her dissertation by asking some questions and testing them in a real case: What is the role of and to what extent did "tax connecting factors" contribute to the profit shifting phenomenon? Contrary to the OECD approach to profit shifting, which is widely considered to be unduly narrow, Dr. Escribano asks what role the following three paradigms have played in the ability of companies to shift their profits out of the jurisdictions where they conduct economic activities: the separate-entity approach along with the arm's length standard, corporate tax residence and the definition of source of income (with particular emphasis on the permanent establishment concept). As I mentioned above, Dr. Escribano adopts a so-called bottom-up approach whereby all those questions are tested in a real case study that revolves around the multinational group Apple. Chapter 2, where Dr. Escribano empirically demonstrates, through the Apple case, that profit shifting is a really troublesome phenomenon, is the most interesting one. Dr. Escribano's amazing research answers very difficult technical questions such as: Where should Apple's foreign income be regarded as being generated? Which country has the right to tax? Could it be argued that a substantial portion of Apple's foreign income is generated by subsidiaries organized in Ireland? Should Apple remit most of its taxes in the United States (US) where almost all of its R&D activity takes place? How significant is customer market in value creation? By evaluating the pros and cons of the abovementioned tax connecting factors in the light of the Apple case, Dr. Escribano is able to formulate very useful proposals for all stakeholders involved in the profit shifting phenomenon. Everyone involved, from government officials, tax authorities, legal scholars, and practitioners will advance their knowledge of the profit shifting phenomenon and BEPS more generally by reading Eva Escribano's excellent book.

Prof. Reuven S. Avi-Yonah
Irwin I. Cohn Professor of Law
University of Michigan

As is widely known, base erosion and profit shifting has been a central concern in international taxation for the past years, placing the taxation of multinational groups at the forefront of the public discussions and coinciding—not by accident[1]—with the problems generated by the global financial crisis. This particular context helped to politically legitimize the work carried out by the OECD in its BEPS Action Plan, which culminated in the conclusion of the Multilateral Convention to Implement Tax Treaty Related Measures to Prevent Base Erosion and Profit Shifting last November 24, 2016, which has already been signed by eighty-seven jurisdictions and came into force after the deposit of the fifth instrument of ratification, acceptance or approval.

It is undoubtedly surprising that the BEPS reports have not been preceded by an effort on the part of the OECD to explain the reasons why profit shifting ought to be regarded as a concern in the first place and, above all, why traditional criteria around the notions of residence and source should be modulated in order to comply with what Eva Escribano calls the "BEPS mantra," i.e. "... in order to more closely align the allocation of income with the economic activity that generates that income."[2] Indeed, it has been simply impossible to find throughout the countless pages of the reports that are part of the project any thorough analysis on the international tax policy reasons that would justify the abandonment or modulation of the traditional criteria used to allocate

1. As Herzfeld, M. "The Case Against BEPS: Lessons for Tax Coordination," 21(1) *Florida Tax Review*, 2017, p. 4 states "The Global Financial Crisis of the Late 2000s Provided Both an Incentive and a Means of Addressing These Concerns"; *see also* pp. 18 ss.
2. In this respect, the OECD *Action plan on base erosion and profit shifting* (2013), available at: https://www.oecd.org/ctp/BEPSActionPlan.pdf, does not only define the expression "*economic activities that generate that income*" but also alludes to the same idea in different (and confusing) ways. E.g. "*Economic activities creating those profits*" (p. 10), "*economic activities*" in general (p. 11), "*relevant substance*" (p. 13), "*economic activities that produce that income*" (p. 19), etc.

taxing rights between residence and source in favor of the new mantra, according to which taxing rights ought to be allocated to the territories where economic activities giving rise to income take place.

In this respect, it is worth pointing out that the own use of the expression "profit shifting" presupposes a highly questionable premise: the fact that the taxation of the business profits originally corresponds to the State where the economic activities giving rise to it take place, while the taxpayer manages to "shift" them somewhere else. A premise that, due to its significance, deserves to be better explained, as jurisdictions where multinational group's profits have been shifted to, may lawfully argue that transfers of taxable bases have occurred by satisfactorily complying with the—still sacred—tax residence criteria in place, which, paradoxically, have not been called into question by the BEPS Action Plan. If profit shifting is now perceived as a concern is because the traditional jurisdictions of residence are increasingly witnessing how a great part of the profits derived by what they consider to be their "own" multinational groups are being shifted to other jurisdictions by making use of tax schemes that seem to lawfully respect the current legal—and very well-established—tax connecting factors.

What seems to have truly happened is that a change of paradigm has ultimately been placed on the table, precisely right after the OECD expressly stated that the BEPS Action Plan was "not directly aimed at changing the international standards on the allocation of taxing rights on cross border income."[3] A change of paradigm that, in my opinion, has not been sufficiently discussed nor been preceded by a careful assessment of its potential repercussion and effects. First of all, because it is far from clear which could be the rationale to assign the power to tax to the jurisdiction in which the economic activity takes place, irrespective of which is the jurisdiction of residence of the entity. Second, because nobody knows what the BEPS mantra exactly means in technical terms, due to the fact that there are many and diverse potential ways to pinpoint the jurisdiction where economic activities are taking place depending on the factors that we consider as adequate to do so (e.g., employees, tangible assets and volume of sales). Third, because if one looks at the Multilateral Convention, the only amendment that appears to be—somehow—aligned with such change of paradigm is the redefinition of the permanent establishment concept, which has served to lower the threshold allowing the source jurisdiction to tax the business profits of non-resident taxpayers, although the ultimate result of such amendment is not necessarily aligned with the place where the economic activities take place (whatever this means). Last but not least, because we should question the effects that may derive from the attribution of taxing rights to the jurisdiction where the economic activities are taking place and whether this may imply the retrieval of the taxable bases by the jurisdictions of residence or else the expansion of the taxing rights of the jurisdictions of source.

This is precisely why the kind of thesis written by Eva Escribano is important, even if more research is needed in this area. Because it goes well beyond the technical analysis of the specific proposals suggested by the BEPS Project and instead brings up

3. *See* OECD, *Action Plan on Base Erosion and Profit Shifting*, OECD Publishing, Paris, 2013, available at https://doi.org/10.1787/9789264202719-en, p. 11.

more far-reaching tax policy discussions that tend to remain hidden under—allegedly—purely technical debates which, on the contrary, involve relevant tax policy decisions. In this sense, it is praiseworthy to try to identify a guiding principle that serves to provide a rationale to the allocation of taxing rights,[4] even though her proposal on the "presumptive benefit principle" may be disputable, somehow ambiguous and, above all, far from reaching the necessary multilateral recognition and consensus, at least for the time being. In any event, as the supervisor of the thesis, my role is not to judge it, as others have already done so when awarding it with a Summa Cum Laude qualification and the 2018 European Academic Tax Thesis Award of the European Association of Tax Law Professors and the European Commission.

Nevertheless, I believe it should be highlighted that Eva Escribano's thesis comprises an excellent diagnosis of the underlying problems of the international tax system, which has been unable to adapt to the changes that the information and communication technologies in the 1980s, and the subsequent increasing digitalization of the economy,[5] which gave rise to the so-called fourth industrial revolution,[6] have triggered in both the economy and the behavior of multinational groups. It is certainly not easy to try to apply the benefit principle to global entities with decentralized structures that do not need to maintain a physical presence in the territories where they carry out their economic activities, a scenario that severely compromises the potential design of new tax connecting factors that are both coherent and theoretically well funded. Her diagnosis, based on the analysis of one of the most remarkable cases of the last years, allows us to confirm the problems derived by a set of asymmetric and uncoordinated tax residence tests that too often rely on formal factors, the dissatisfaction generated by the separate-entity approach along with the inherent limitations of the arm's length standard and, lastly, the shortcomings of the permanent establishment concept, which remains firmly anchored in the notion of fixed place of business.

This concerns well-known issues that have, however, never been directly dealt with, opting instead for an indirect approach to their solutions, which we fear they will ultimately end up being unsatisfactory. In this regard, the only set of measures—of all envisaged in the BEPS Action Plan—that truly have an impact on the determination of the tax connecting factors are those of Action 7 (related with the changes to the definition of permanent establishment to prevent its artificial circumvention), and this is particularly shocking considering that the definition of the tax connecting factors appears to be critical in the profit shifting strategies. It is true that the proposal on the limitation on benefits clause, resulting from Action 6, is somehow contributing to introduce some nuances in the own definition of tax residence, as it ultimately confirms both the insufficiency of this criterion and the impossibility to reach a greater coordination in this respect beyond the treatment of dual resident entities. In the light

4. As Avi-Yonah, R & Xu, H. H. "Evaluating BEPS," 10 (1) *Erasmus Law Review*, p. 4 suggested writing that "The Benefits Principle Should Be Reconsidered."
5. The belief that traditional rules do not work properly in the new economic scenario is certainly widespread, as rightly noted by Graetz, M "The David R. Tillinghast Lecture: Taxing International Income: Inadequate Principles, Outdated Concepts, and Unsatisfactory Policies," 54 *Tax Law Review*, 2001, 261.
6. Vid. Schwab, K. *The Fourth Industrial Revolution*, Crown Business, New York 2017.

of the results of the BEPS Action Plan, one may conclude that it has led to the adoption of a set of defensive rules that are, once again, solely aimed at both closing up the most evident breaches derived by the profit shifting strategies followed by multinational groups and raising tax revenues. This being so, the proposed solutions merely attempt to strengthen the traditional principles by patching up current rules,[7] thus disappointing those who advocated for a reflection about a new set of international taxation rules that can accommodate a more globally connected economy. The OECD has therefore missed the chance to try to build consensus on the new principles that may help articulate a new international tax system that better adjusts to the characteristics of today's economy, thus renouncing to provide truly long-term solutions to the observed issues.

The lack of progress in Action 1, intended to address the tax challenges of the digital economy, and the main assumptions of the 2019 public consultation document,[8] shows how difficult is to reach an agreement on the principles that ought to guide the distribution of taxing powers. Indeed, the document itself recognizes that jurisdictions had different views on the question of whether, and to what extent, the challenges of the digital economy should result in changes to the international tax rules, as some of them perceived the need to change existing nexus and profit allocation rules, while others believed that no action was needed beyond addressing BEPS issues.[9] As the instinctive response to these challenges has not been to revise the rules to better adapt to the new business environment but rather to tweak their application based on the principles from which those rules have been derived,[10] the reformulation of the PE concept based on the new notions of significant economic or digital presence will hardly provide a satisfactory solution, as an even more complex issue—that related to the attribution of profits—will remain unresolved.

The lack of a prior consensus at the level of the principles in relation to the challenges posed by the digital economy is likely to seriously compromise the potential definition of the appropriate rules to allocate taxing rights, precisely in the area that better illustrates the limited results of the BEPS Action Plan. This is probably the reason why some relevant jurisdictions (including the United States with its recent tax reform) and the European Union have suggested or even adopted unilateral measures that show, once again, the difficulties to overcome the—still in force—categories in international taxation, despite their manifest aging and incapacity to resolve the new problems. This is why the adoption of the Multilateral Instrument and the changes it will prompt in the tax treaty network will not be able to hide the limited results derived from the BEPS Action Plan, which should at least serve as a starting point to new—and

7. *See* Avi-Yonah, R. & Xu, H. "Evaluating BEPS" cit. p. 6.
8. *See* OECD *Addressing the Tax Challenges of the Digitalisation of the Economy*, 2019, available in http://www.oecd.org/tax/beps/public-consultation-document-addressing-the-tax-challenges-of-the-digitalisation-of-the-economy.pdf.
9. *See* OECD *Addressing the Tax Challenges of the Digitalisation of the Economy*, cit. p. 11 with references to the Interim Report.
10. *See* Báez, A and Brauner, Y. *Withholding Taxes in the Service of BEPS Action 1: Address the Tax Challenges of the Digital Economy*, IBFD 2015, p. 4, available at https://www.ibfd.org/sites/ibfd.org/files/content/WithholdingTaxesintheServiceofBEPSAction1-whitepaper.pdf.

wider—discussions on the reform of an international tax system that is, paraphrasing Jethro Tull, too young to die but too old to deal with new concerns. Further academic research, as that conducted by Eva Escribano, will be much needed in the context of these new discussions. In particular, I hope and wish this thesis serves as a point of departure for a brilliant and promising academic career, even in a university system as the Spanish one, whose lack of resources severely compromises the future of the young generations.

Juan Zornoza
Full Professor in Tax Law
Universidad Carlos III de Madrid

List of Abbreviations

ALS	Arm's Length Standard
AOA	Authorized OECD Approach
AOE	Apple Operations Europe
AOI	Apple Operations International
ASI	Apple Sales International
ATO	Australian Taxation Office
B2B	Business to Business
B2C	Business to Consumer
BEPS	Base Erosion and Profit Shifting
C+	Cost Plus Method (Transfer Pricing Method)
CCCTB	Common Consolidated Corporate Tax Base
CFC	Controlled Foreign Corporation
CIT	Corporate Income Tax
CSA	Cost-Sharing Arrangement
CUP	Comparable Uncontrolled Price (Transfer Pricing Method)
DAE	Dependent Agent Enterprise
DAPE	Dependent Agent—Permanent Establishment
DBCT	Destination-Based Corporate Tax
DEMPE	Development, Enhancement, Maintenance, Protection and Exploitation
EBITDA	Earnings Before Interests, Taxes, Depreciation and Amortization
EU	European Union
GAAR	General Anti-avoidance Rule
ICT	Information and Communications Technology
IP	Intellectual Property
IRC	(US) Internal Revenue Code

IRS	(US) Internal Revenue Service
LOB	Limitation on Benefits
MAP	Mutual Agreement Procedure
MCs	The OECD, UN and US Model Conventions
MNC	Multinational Company
OECD MC	OECD Model Convention
OECD TPG	OECD Transfer Pricing Guidelines
OECD	Organisation for Economic Co-operation and Development
PE	Permanent Establishment
PE-State	State in Which a Permanent Establishment Arises
PIT	Personal Income Tax
POB	Place of Business
POEM	Place of Effective Management
POI	Place of Incorporation
R&D	Research and Development
RP	Resale Price (Transfer Pricing Method)
SAAR	Specific Anti-avoidance Rule
SMC	Small and Medium-Sized Company
TNM	Transactional Net Margin (Transfer Pricing Method)
TPS	Transactional Profit Split (Transfer Pricing Method)
UK	United Kingdom
UN MC	United Nations Model Convention
UN	United Nations
US MC	United States Model Convention
US	United States
VAT	Value-Added Tax

List of Figures

List of Tables

Acknowledgments

This book is based on a doctoral dissertation written under the supervision of Prof. Dr. Juan Zornoza (Full Professor in Universidad Carlos III de Madrid). My first words of gratitude must go to him. For giving me a vote of confidence when I was an undergraduate student, for believing in this seemingly daring project when I first suggested it and for his guidance along this long path.

All paths have a beginning and mine started in Madrid but inexorably accelerated in Paris. Between 2011 and 2012 I had the privilege to join the Centre for Tax Policy and Administration (CTPA) within the Organisation of Economic Cooperation and Development (OECD) as a junior researcher for some months. My stay there coincided in time with the conception of the ambitious Base Erosion and Profit Shifting Project (BEPS), which intended to reconsider some of the most fundamental rules governing corporate income taxation in cross-border scenarios. My experience within the OECD not only allowed me to become more familiar with international taxation, but largely inspired me to think ahead legislation and standards in force and devote our talent and efforts to figure out new out-of-the-box policies that better adapt to new times and further improve social well-being. It is fair to say that I would have never focused my attention on tax policy and this thesis would have never been conceived as it is if it was not for my experience there. I therefore wish to thank Richard Parry and Ben Dickinson, heads of the CTPA's Global Relations Division and the Tax and Development Program respectively, along with their teams, for relying on me and letting me contribute to their different streams of work.

This thesis was written between June 2013 and June 2017. During that period of time, I was fully integrated as lecturer and researcher in the Tax Law Department of Universidad Carlos III de Madrid, whose members I would like to thank for their warm welcome and continuous support. However, I may not have had the chance to write this thesis and join the University if it were not for the funding I received from the University Faculty Training Grant (Beca para la Formación del Profesorado Universitario) awarded by the Spanish Ministry of Education for the period 2013-2017. I take this opportunity to applaud the existence of public scholarships that are awarded on a competitive basis, recognizing the effort of young talents and further providing them with unique opportunities to initiate a professional career. The need for them is critical in societies that aspire to ensure equal opportunities and break social barriers, most notably in times of crisis.

During the time I was writing the thesis, I had the privilege to make four research stays at three renowned research centers in the field of international taxation: the International Bureau of Fiscal Documentation (Amsterdam, July-August 2013), the Wirtschaftsuniversität Wien (Vienna, July-August 2014) and the Max Planck Institute for Tax Law and Public Finance (Munich, July-August 2015 and June-August 2016). I wish to express my gratitude to their directors and members, not only for providing me with a spot within their centers where I could peacefully concentrate and write, but also for the stimulating discussions I maintained with many of them. My special thanks to Prof. Dr. Wolfgang Schön, director of the Max Planck Institute for Tax Law and Public Finance, for his particular confidence on this project and the generous scholarship granted by his Institute that allowed me to spend two fruitful summers in Munich and write half of this book within its premises.

Although PhD students work as hard as we can to make contributions original, we cannot forget about the masters whose work have inspired us all along the way. There are indeed some papers that have particularly enlightened and stimulated my research, and many of them were written by Prof. Avi-Yonah (University of Michigan). I therefore wish to thank him not only for inadvertently inspiring me in the process of conceiving and writing this thesis but also for generously accepting to write a foreword to this book.

This thesis was defended last September 6, 2017 in Universidad Carlos III de Madrid (Spain) before a panel composed by Prof. Dr. Yariv Brauner (University of Florida), Prof. Dr. Alfredo García Prats (Universidad de Valencia) and Prof. Dr. Andrés Báez Moreno (Universidad Carlos III de Madrid). I wish to thank them for their comments and bright observations, as they have been of immense value in the process of converting that thesis in the book you are now holding in your hands. I also would like to thank Prof. Dr. Alice Pirlot (University of Oxford) and Prof. Dr. José M. Castro Arango (Universidad Externado de Colombia) for agreeing to become international reviewers of the thesis and writing such exhaustive reports (which were necessary to obtain the international doctorate mention) in such a short period of time.

I would also like to thank the European Commission and the European Association of Tax Law Professors (EATLP) for awarding this thesis with the European Academic Tax Thesis Award 2018, an award that chooses the best doctoral or postdoctoral thesis on issues of comparative, European and/or International Tax Law submitted in a European University throughout the precedent year. I feel deeply honored and overwhelmed to receive this award from the hands of colleagues I so much admire. Special thanks to Prof. Dr. Gutmann (chairman of the Academic Committee of the EATLP) and Adam Zalazinski (European Commission) for their kind words during the award ceremony that took place in Zurich last June 2018. Memories from that day will always remain in my heart.

Finally, I want to express my deepest gratitude to the persons that are truly part of my life.

To my family. In particular to my parents, Lola and Antonio, for your endless love, for raising me according to the values of effort and responsibility and for becoming living examples for me in so many facets of life.

To my husband, Pablo. For your overwhelming generosity, patience and day-to-day support. I would have never made it without you. I love you very much.

To my daughter, Vera. This book was made with a great deal of sacrifice, perseverance and courage. I will do my best to pass on what I have learnt from this experience to you when you grow up.

To my friends. For patiently listening to me in my worse moments and for always filling me with hope and optimism.

This small group of persons deserve to be labeled as co-authors of this piece of work, as their unconditional love and support have granted me the necessary strength and determination to accomplish this task, if not satisfactorily, at least safe and sound.

CHAPTER 1

Introduction

§1.01 BACKGROUND

International corporate income tax (hereinafter "CIT") rules have been in the eye of the storm for the last decades mainly due to the outcomes they produce. In particular, these rules have come under harsh criticism for giving rise to an evident misalignment between the territories where companies carry out their economic activities and the territories where they ultimately report the profits generated by them for tax purposes. Throughout the present thesis, this phenomenon will be referred to as "profit shifting."

This phenomenon has been corroborated by numerous economic studies carried out in the United States (hereinafter "US") over the last decade. Despite using different methodologies, they all arrive at the same conclusion. In 2008, the US Government Accountability Office issued a report which demonstrated that the top leading foreign locations of activities of US-based businesses (in terms of sales, value added, employment, compensation, physical assets and net income) barely captured taxable profits.[1] In 2011, Clausing found a large discrepancy between the physical operations of US MNCs' affiliates abroad and the locations in which they reported their income. She identified the top ten locations in terms of affiliate employment (in order: UK, Canada, Mexico, China, Germany, France, Brazil, India, Japan and Australia) and realized that such list barely matched the list of top ten locations in terms of affiliate gross profits (in order: the Netherlands, Luxembourg, Ireland, Canada, Bermuda, Switzerland, Singapore, Germany, Norway and Australia).[2] In 2013, Keightley compared the profits reported by American firms abroad with measures of real economic activity in those locations, concluding that significant shares of profits were being reported in "tax preferred" or "tax haven" countries and that such shares were disproportionate to the location of the firm's business activities (e.g., where the firm hired workers and made

1. US Government Accountability Office (2008): Effective tax rates are correlated where income is reported, p. 1.
2. Clausing, K. (2011), pp. 1580-1581.

investments).[3] In addition, he was able to demonstrate that the discrepancy between the location of profits and the location of business activities had increased over time.

In view of this, the Organisation for Economic Co-operation and Development (hereinafter "OECD") launched the ambitious Base Erosion and Profit shifting (hereinafter "BEPS") project in 2013 with the endorsement of the G20. The initial report sought to raise public awareness of this phenomenon by bringing forward a number of studies and data indicating an increasing segregation between the location where actual business activities and investment take place (using indicators as sales, workforce, payroll and fixed assets) and the location where profits are ultimately reported for tax purposes,[4] finally concluding that profits were indeed reported in jurisdictions where such activities were scanty or simply nonexistent.[5]

The BEPS Project automatically regarded profit shifting as a troublesome phenomenon that ought to be addressed and mitigated. To this end, the BEPS Action Plan endeavored to identify its causes[6] and finally provide remedies for it by means of domestic and international instruments.[7] In particular, Action 11 of the project ultimately put into motion a number of methodologies and techniques precisely intended to monitor this phenomenon and the expected (positive) impact that the implementation of the measures resulting from the Project would have in this regard.[8]

§1.02 HYPOTHESIS

The primary goal of the BEPS project led by the OECD was to mitigate profit shifting opportunities by providing domestic and international instruments "aiming at better aligning rights to tax with real economic activity" (the "BEPS mantra").[9]

The reading of the BEPS report and its subsequent Action Plan, discussion drafts and final reports left us however with a curious overall impression. Throughout the hundreds of pages dedicated to the description and identification of the phenomenon, its diagnosis and measures to mitigate it, we saw no trace whatsoever of any sound tax

3. Keightley, M.P. (2013).
4. The report provides a general overview on the data and studies regarding the existence and magnitude of the problem. *See* OECD (2013): Addressing base erosion and profit shifting (hereinafter "BEPS report"), pp. 15-24.
5. BEPS report, p. 20.
6. The breakdown of identified causes along with their respective brief description may be consulted in the BEPS Action Plan.
7. This was in fact the first and foremost objective of the whole project, *see* BEPS report, p. 21: "the main purpose of that plan would be to provide countries with instruments, domestic and international, aiming at better aligning rights to tax with real economic activity" and BEPS Action Plan, pp. 13 and 18. The final measures resulting from the BEPS project are comprised in the thirteen final reports that may be found in the OECD website: http://www.oecd.org/ctp/beps-2015-final-reports.htm (last accessed on January 10, 2019).
8. In the OECD (2013): Action plan on base erosion and profit shifting (hereinafter "BEPS Action Plan"), the OECD committed itself to establish methodologies to collect and analyze further data on the matter by means of Action 11 of the Action Plan. The result of this course of action is the OECD (2015): Final Report on BEPS Action 11—Measuring and monitoring BEPS.
9. BEPS report, pp. 15, 20 and 51 and BEPS Action Plan, pp. 11, 18, 19 and 20-21.

policy reason that would justify why this phenomenon ought to be regarded as troublesome in the first place.

As for the diagnosis of the phenomenon, as we read the BEPS Action Plan, we soon realized that the scope of the project was unduly narrow and thus intrinsically limited to perform the aforementioned task satisfactorily.[10] Hence, we decided to embark on a path parallel to that of the OECD by means of the present thesis with the intention of conducting an alternative research study irrespective of political constraints and as free as possible of prejudices.

The immediate feeling of dissatisfaction that arose in us after reading the first papers published in the course of the BEPS project was due to the intuition that the diagnosis of the causes allowing this phenomenon to happen was probably correct but surely not complete.

We instinctively assumed that tax connecting factors necessarily had to play a predominant role in the profit shifting phenomenon (i.e., the ability of companies to shift their taxable profits out of the jurisdictions where they conduct economic activities and instead book them in the jurisdictions of their choice). Tax connecting factors are the rules that identify the taxpayers that become subject to a State's tax jurisdiction, hence linking either the relevant person or an item of income to a certain territory. There are four main sets of rules that can arguably fall into this category in the context of corporate income taxation:[11] rules governing the corporate/shareholder relation for tax purposes, the tax treatment of related parties within a corporate group, corporate tax residence and the definition of source of income for corporate tax purposes.

Companies are not real persons but mere legal fictions to which domestic legislations confer a legal status analogous to that enjoyed by natural persons. While the fiction was originally conceived for private law purposes, the impact it should have in the fiscal sphere is to say the least dubious. Therefore, the first question that needs to be addressed is how States should treat companies for income tax purposes. In this context, States may treat the company either as a separate taxpayer—distinct from its shareholders—whose income becomes taxable in its own hands at the time it is perceived by means of a CIT or else, as a fiscally transparent vehicle whose profits would ultimately flow to their shareholders and become taxable in the hands of the latter.

Once States choose to remain faithful to the legal fiction for income tax purposes and thus impose a CIT at the level of the company, the second question that arises is how States should treat those integrated in groups. In this context, they may recognize the corporate group as a whole, thus ignoring the transactions carried out between its members and merely looking at its overall outcomes, or else regard the group members as separate taxpayers. In this latter case, States should be prepared to address the transfer pricing risks that the adoption of this approach would entail. For example, by adjusting the conditions of intra-group transactions in a way that the tax base of the

---

10. Escribano, E. (2017).
11. Vann, R.J. (2010), p. 293. According to Vann, these rules allocate rights among countries over international business income derived from corporations.

entity concerned includes the profits it would have obtained if the transaction had occurred with an unrelated entity by virtue of the arm's length standard (hereinafter "ALS").

The third question that needs to be answered concerns the way States confer the tax residence status to companies for the purposes of their respective CITs. Indeed, CITs borrowed from personal income taxes (hereinafter "PITs") the ability of the taxpayer to reside in a certain jurisdiction, so States had to conceive corporate residence tests revealing a relation between the company and the State analogous to that of individuals and their residence State. They addressed the challenge of defining such nexus individually at the domestic level and the matter was never brought to any international forum to be discussed. As a result, we find today a great number of heterogeneous corporate residence tests of distinct nature and pursuing diverse goals.

In parallel, States tend to establish the thresholds and/or requirements according to which a non-resident company would become subject to tax in their territories. In this context, the permanent establishment (hereinafter "PE") concept merits a special mention. Although the clause finds its roots in the Prussian domestic tax legislation of the nineteenth century, it soon made its way in the discussion forum of the League of Nations and subsequently, in its first model tax convention.[12] Since then, it has succeeded to become the most characteristic threshold allowing source taxation of business profits by antonomasia and is present in the vast majority of tax treaties worldwide.

The way States respond to the aforementioned questions in their respective domestic tax legislations and tax treaties ultimately determine the territory where the profits obtained by a company will be ascribed for tax purposes. In this context, it has become a widespread tendency to impose CITs and further regard companies as opaque tax subjects, separate and autonomous from both their own shareholders and the related parties belonging to its group. In addition, States tend to confer the tax residence status mostly to companies incorporated in accordance with their domestic legislations or else managed from their territory and further rely on the PE threshold to determine the circumstances under which the profits of a non-resident company would be subject to tax therein.

There are various reasons that led us to suspect, at first glance, that the current configuration of this sort of rules may largely explain the misalignment between that location where economic activities take place and that where profits are booked for tax purposes.

First, the very nature of these rules makes them prone to potentially generate the perceived misalignment. In particular, when they do not seem to rely on factors revealing the presence of a substantial economic activity in the territory concerned, as it is clearly the case in the overwhelming majority of corporate residence tests.

Second, we have reasons to believe that the responses made by the States to the aforementioned questions were not the result of a process of conscientious reflection

12. Economic and Financial Commission for the League of Nations (1923): Report on Double Taxation.

on the meaning[13] and the policy goals of each decision but were rather made either by inertia or by merely following the lead of neighboring States or extrapolating principles from other fields (e.g., PiTs or, worse still, private international law).[14]

Third, States began to take a position on these matters between the nineteenth and the beginning of the twentieth centuries and have barely deviated from their original positions ever since.[15] This is in spite of the fact that the global political, economic and business context has undergone an infinite number of far-reaching changes over the course of these decades.[16] In the face of this, States have traditionally reacted by adhering to the main pillars of their respective CITs[17] and then proceeding to describe how a modem transaction or problem might be shoehorned into that regime.[18]

In conclusion, it may be inferred from the aforementioned that the perpetuation of paradigms originated in a radically different context and whose inception was not based on a profound reflection is thus likely to be a source of endless problems. In particular, we believe these paradigms play a key role in the perceived phenomenon of segregation between the location of economic activities and that where profits are ultimately reported for tax purposes.

---

13. Schoueri, L.E. (2015), p. 692: "division of income among source and residence was not based on an economic reason, i.e. economic allegiance, but rather on a practical solution where imbalances were foreseen and expected to be corrected through a (hardly verifiable) equilibrium of investment flows among countries."
14. Bird, R. (2002).
15. Tanzi, V. (1998), pp. 338-339: "traditional national policies or institutions, to a large extent, still reflect the closed economy environment and thinking that existed when they were first developed."
16. McLure makes a very illustrative comparison between the context where these principles arose and today's in McLure, C.E. (Jr.) (2001), pp. 333-334. For example, the international trade prevailing in the first half of the twentieth century consisted primarily on tangible products and occurred mostly between unrelated parties, communications were relatively slow, capital was relatively immobile, intangible assets were relatively unimportant and the US was the undisputed leader in terms of politics and economics. By contrast, today's trade increasingly consists of services and digitized goods or services, while 60% of the global transactions are intra-group (Burke, J. (2011), p. 614). Further, the twenty-first century economy can be broadly characterized by the great advances in transports and communications, the key role played by intangible assets and a distinct political scene where power is increasingly spread, mostly between the US, the European Union and the emerging economies.
17. *See* Tillinghast, D.R. (1996), p. 524: "the existing body of international tax rules, as reflected both in national law and in treaties, is based in large part on the supposition that international trade consists of the physical shipment of tangible goods or the physical movement of persons to perform services at different locations. The challenge posed by the development of the Internet and related means of communication is that in many cases that is simply no longer true," and Graetz, M.J. (2001), p. 262: "many of the core concepts used to implement that structure—concepts such as permanent establishment, corporate residence, and arm's length pricing-date from a time when airplanes were first becoming a regular means of travel, and when the 'wireless' was a relatively new instrument of communication."
18. Graetz, M.J. (2001), pp. 264 and 270.

§1.03 OBJECTIVES AND STRUCTURE OF THE THESIS

Having regard to the series of hypothesis set forth in the previous section, we intend to pursue the following main objectives by means of the present thesis:

- Empirically demonstrate and evaluate the profit shifting phenomenon (i.e., the increasing ability of companies to shift their taxable profits out of the jurisdictions where the relevant economic activities take place and instead book them in the jurisdictions of their choice) by means of a real case study and further provide a new tax policy rationale (the presumptive benefit principle) that would help sustain the repudiation of this phenomenon while contributing to overcome it (Chapter 2).
- Assess whether corporate income taxation is consistent with the presumptive benefit principle and is therefore well equipped to confront the profit shifting phenomenon. In particular, we intend to confirm our hypothesis according to which the fundamental tax connecting factors underlying CITs (i.e., the rules identifying the corporate taxpayers that become subject to a State's tax jurisdiction, hence linking either the relevant person or an item of income to a certain territory) are not aligned with the aforementioned principle and are thus intrinsically prone to generate profit shifting opportunities (Chapter 3).
- Submit a number of policy proposals both at the domestic and treaty level to ensure a better consistency between corporate income taxation and the presumptive benefit principle. These proposals will explore either abandoning the fundamental paradigms underlying CITs or merely altering their design and configuration (Chapter 4).

To this end, the present thesis will be divided into three substantive chapters, thus excluding those concerning the introduction and general conclusions.

Chapter 2 intends to empirically demonstrate the existence of the profit shifting phenomenon by means of a real-life case: the multinational company (hereinafter "MNC") Apple. To this effect, we will provide a comprehensive and detailed overview on the economic presence of Apple throughout the world. In particular, we will seek to identify Apple's shareholders, directors and managers, activities concerning research and development (hereinafter "R&D") and manufacturing, employees and final customers; and further locate them, to the extent possible, on a map. Subsequently, we will cross-reference this information with the location of the group's tax bases so as to illustrate the profit shifting phenomenon in a single graphic. Once this is done, we will try to identify and break down the fundamental rules and strategies that have contributed to this outcome in the specific case of Apple. This will allow us to assess and measure the specific impact that rules (mostly US domestic rules) other than the paradigms here under review may have in this regard before embarking on the analysis of Chapter 3. Subsequently, we will propose a specific guiding principle that aims to provide both a tax policy rationale (the presumptive benefit principle) that may support the discourse of rejection towards the profit shifting phenomenon and, at the same time, a new policy guideline whose observance may help counteract it. We will finally propose a very specific and targeted use of this new proposed guideline in the framework of CITs.

Chapter 3 seeks to evidence the severe inconsistency between three paradigms that have been underlying CITs since their origin and the presumptive benefit principle, reason why CITs inherently tend to trigger profit shifting outcomes. The paradigms we are referring to are the separate-entity approach and the ALS, corporate tax residence and the PE threshold. Throughout this chapter we will: (a) reflect on the genesis and originary meaning and purposes of these paradigms; (b) briefly describe how they tend to be translated into legal provisions by analyzing common patterns followed by States; and (c) assess their (in)consistency with the presumptive benefit principle and the profit shifting risks they tend to pose. This exercise will not only enable us to test our hypothesis but also to reach further conclusions that may be useful when the time comes to reconsider the objective, scope and/or legal configuration of these paradigms.

Chapter 4 will depart from the confirmation of our hypothesis and other far-reaching conclusions reached in Chapter 3 to further advocate for some proposals *de lege ferenda* to ensure a better consistency between corporate income taxation and the presumptive benefit principle and thus mitigate the undesirable profit shifting outcomes. Proposals will explore both the direct abandonment of these paradigms and their amendment. We will equally assess whether the outcomes derived from the OECD/G20 BEPS project may be deemed to have a significant impact in this regard.

§1.04 BRIEF NOTES ON THE METHODOLOGY

The methodology used in the research varies between chapters.

In Chapter 2, we limit ourselves to collect, locate and present information concerning the Apple group on two different levels: the economic (value-adding activities and other relevant business indicators) and the tax level (allocation of the group's taxable bases). To do so, we will mostly rely on a number of comprehensive and trustworthy reports and memoranda resulting from the investigation carried out by the US Senate on the group's tax planning strategy back in 2011. For a greater consistency, we will use the fiscal year 2011 as a common benchmark so that we only cross-reference relevant data pertaining to the same year.

For its part, the objective of Chapter 3 is to identify common patterns on how States typically draft their tax connecting factors in the context of corporate income taxation. To this end, we will make use of a number of comparative studies, along with academic publications, legislation and case law relating to a variety of domestic tax regimes of an undetermined number of States. The sample of States is thus not limited, so we shall be free to make reference to the laws of any State insofar it is relevant for the purposes of our research. Throughout this chapter, we will frequently refer to the OECD, UN and US Model Conventions (hereinafter "the MCs") so as to get an idea of the variety of clauses that may be present in the actual tax treaties in the global network. In particular, we will allude both to prior versions (2014, 2011 and 2006 versions respectively) and current ones (2017, 2017 and 2016 respectively) so as to better assess the impact that recent proposed changes to tax treaties (mostly those derived from the BEPS project) may have for the purposes of our thesis.

In Chapter 4, we intend to provide a set of tax policy proposals. To this effect, we will sometimes make reference to the domestic tax rules of some States we believe serve as a useful example or else submit our own original proposals, some of them inspired by ideas previously advocated by either scholars or international organizations (with a particular emphasis on those made by the OECD within the BEPS project).

Lastly, we would like to bring attention to a structural problem we had to deal with when writing the thesis. As anticipated in the previous two sections, we focus on three main paradigms commonly underlying CITs throughout the thesis: the separate-entity entity approach along with the ALS and the definitions of corporate tax residence and PE. The problem comes with the fact that we analyze these three paradigms from three different perspectives. First, we will very briefly assess the role they play (if any) in the tax planning strategy deployed by Apple (Chapter 2). Second, we will study the origins and supposed rationales behind these paradigms and further demonstrate their contribution to the profit shifting phenomenon perceived in the Apple case (Chapter 3). And third, we will put forward a number of proposals concerning the three paradigms in the light of the presumptive benefit principle (Chapter 4). Naturally, this approach gives rise to risks of repetition of conclusions and profusion of references to other sections throughout the text. This may become annoying for certain readers, particularly for those that go through the whole text at once and in an orderly manner. Nonetheless, we accept the aforementioned risks for the sake of clarity and readability, as we prefer to be clear and repetitive rather than confusing. Further, this approach ensures that readers adequately understand the content of each section or chapter autonomously without having to read the whole text. To this end, we will also draw a number of preliminary conclusions at the end of every chapter and certain particularly relevant sections.

Before concluding the present section, we believe it is appropriate to make a brief comment on the citation style we will use to ensure a better understanding of the references. Those used in the footnotes introduced throughout the document will be solely comprised by the author's last name, the initial of his/her first name, the year of the publication and the number of the page or page rank where the idea or quotation may be found. Complete information on the publication concerned (including its title, editorial, etc.) will be provided in the References section.

CHAPTER 2

The Profit Shifting Phenomenon Unrevealed and the Presumptive Benefit Principle as an Equitable Tax Policy Guideline to Counteract It

The present chapter intends to achieve two main objectives.

First, it seeks to demonstrate and assess the profit shifting phenomenon (section §2.01). That is, the increasing ability of companies to shift their taxable profits out of the jurisdictions where the relevant economic activities take place and instead book them in the jurisdictions of their choice. We will try to provide empirical evidence revealing the existence and severity of this phenomenon in the case of the Apple group and the fundamental reasons giving rise to it (section §2.01[A]). We will later identify the most common stance of the international community towards this phenomenon and whether it is generally perceived as a concern that ought to be addressed (section §2.01[B]).

Second, we will propose a specific guiding principle that aims to provide both a policy rationale that may support the discourse of rejection towards the profit shifting phenomenon and, at the same time, a new policy guideline whose observance may help counteract profit shifting risks (section §2.02). To this effect, we will call for the recovery of a long-standing principle: the benefit principle. Nevertheless, we will advocate for a very peculiar understanding of this policy guideline that largely deviates from its conventional sense. The expression "presumptive benefit principle" will be coined precisely to refer to this suggested revised version of the traditional principle (section §2.02[A]). Subsequently, we will propose a very specific and targeted use of this proposed new guideline in the framework of corporate income taxation (section §2.02[B]).

§2.01 THE STARTING POINT: PROFIT SHIFTING AS A REAL BUT POLITICALLY UNDESIRABLE GLOBAL PHENOMENON

[A] Profit Shifting Phenomenon Unrevealed and Fundamental Causes Giving Rise to It (Apple Case)

[1] Empirical Evidence Revealing the Profit Shifting Phenomenon (Apple Case)

Beyond the studies that have already been published on the matter, we chose to expose the profit shifting phenomenon (i.e., the increasing ability of companies to report their taxable profits in jurisdictions other than those that host their economic activities) by our own means and using a real-life case.

Although we tend to believe that profit shifting opportunities are available for almost every sort of company, from the small to the multinational ones,[19] it is undeniable that risks are considerably higher in the context of multinational companies (hereinafter "MNCs"), particularly those that better embody the features that characterize the twenty-first century business models.

This is precisely why we decided to focus on the worldwide renowned MNC Apple. Even though Apple is primarily dedicated to the design, manufacturing and sale of tangible goods (a conventional business model), it heavily relies on Intellectual Property (hereinafter "IP") and manages to satisfactorily exploit the opportunities offered by technology in order to reach new clients and interact with them. The increasing importance of IP as a value-driver and the use of technology are precisely regarded as the fundamental features of today's business environment.[20]

This preliminary study intends to reveal whether profit shifting arises within this specific case and, if so, assess the extent of the phenomenon. To this end, we chose to collect certain data regarding this MNC that could provide us a complete image of its global situation from both a business and a tax perspective. First, we sought to identify and locate the group's most significant value-adding activities and other relevant managerial and business activities on a world map. Second, we raised data concerning the geographical distribution of the company's global tax base across the world. The ultimate objective of this preliminary study was no other but to discern whether there is a certain degree of correlation between the business and the tax presence of the group in the world or, on the contrary, profit shifting is indeed real.

We identified nine indicators we believe represent some of the most relevant factors of the company's daily life and value chain, from central management and innovation to distribution and final consumption of its products and services. The choice of these indicators is far from random. We believe they are all relevant for the

19. Throughout the present thesis, and particularly in Chapter 3, it will become apparent that certain paradigms underlying corporate income taxation are prone to give rise to profit shifting opportunities that may easily be exploited by small and medium-sized companies (hereinafter "SMCs") too.
20. BEPS report, p. 47.

purposes of this research, as they usually play a role when it comes to the discussion of whether or not a company is (or should be) liable to tax or not in a particularly territory. On one hand, current tax connecting factors make a direct reference to the presence of some of them within the territory concerned. Let us take for instance the shareholders (residence tests based on ownership or limitation on benefits (hereinafter "LOB") clauses),[21] the company direction (residence tests based on effective management),[22] R&D (transfer pricing assessment),[23] manufacturing (PE concept and transfer pricing assessment)[24] and sales activities (PE concept).[25] On the other hand, some other factors (in particular the workforce and the market) are expected to play soon a more significant role after the reconfiguration of the tax connecting factors as a result of the BEPS project[26] or the proposals put forward by the European Union (hereinafter "EU") (e.g., the Common Consolidated Corporate Tax Base (hereinafter "CCCTB"))[27] or the academia.

The nine indicators used in the following charts are listed below together with the source of the data and their corresponding year. For a greater consistency, we used the fiscal year 2011 as a common benchmark wherever possible. The reason why we chose this period was the difficulties we confronted when it came to collect the relevant data regarding Apple and the fact that a great amount of the data that was of interest to us was contained on the reports resulting from the investigation carried out by the US senate on the group's tax planning strategy back in 2013 and such data dated precisely from year 2011:[28]

(a) The first two indicators correspond to the ownership and direction of the company:
   - Corporate shareholders. We did our utmost to disclose the identity and residence of Apple's shareholders, although the access to the relevant data has proven to be particularly troublesome. In fact, the only reliable data may be found in the website of NASDAQ (the American stock exchange where Apple is listed), which provides very little information and confined to its institutional ownership, which accounts for 61.54% of

21. Chapter 3 section §3.02[A][1][c].
22. Chapter 3 section §3.02[A][1][b].
23. Chapter 3 section §3.01[C].
24. Chapter 3 sections §3.01[C] and §3.03.
25. Chapter 3 section §3.03.
26. For example, the BEPS project has reinvigorated the "market factor" as an element that, on its own, should trigger taxing rights in favor of the market State. *See* Escribano, E. (2015), p. 11: "the market, a historically despised factor, seems to come back to life. The first thing that strikes us is precisely the constant references to the market jurisdiction is both the draft and the final report, a fact that seems to reflect the desire of many OECD member countries to bring the source threshold closer to where the customers are."
27. For example, the CCCTB would distribute the taxable profits derived by a corporate group among the territories where it has its assets, workforce and sales. *See* EU Commission (2011): Proposal for a Council Directive on a Common Consolidated Corporate Tax Base (CCCTB), pp. 14 and 49.
28. The main conclusions of the hearing were included in the Memorandum on "Offshore profit shifting and the US tax code—part 2 (Apple Inc.)" submitted before the US Senate—Permanent Subcommittee on Investigations.

the total ownership (a total sum of 2,869 holders).[29] Its top ten institutional shareholders, who jointly account for approximately 25% of Apple's entire shareholding,[30] are all US-incorporated.

However, as it was rightly pointed out by Sanchirico, we cannot simply presume that the so-called US MNCs are in fact entirely (or almost entirely) owned by US investors.[31] Such assumption would be based on a long-held belief, the so-called home country bias, that is, the fact that investors tend to hold a disproportionate share of their equity portfolio in home country stocks.[32] This tendency is partly explained by rational factors such as tax advantages, transactions costs, governance issues, information asymmetry and foreign exchange but also by a sense of "familiarity," which leads to an irrational overconfidence in domestic stocks for the sole reason that the name and business of the domestic company would ring a bell to the potential investor.

In the recent times, it has been pointed out that the aforementioned factors have been losing relevance over time,[33] so it could be expected that the "home country bias" effect may have weakened in recent years. Indeed, numbers seem to support this hypothesis: the percentage of foreign holding of US equities has risen from 8.9% to 14.1% in the period 2006-2017 (12.2% in 2011, the year we are taking as a benchmark).[34]

On top of that, there are reasons to believe that such average foreign ownership share of US equity may not be representative of the foreign ownership share of large US multinational enterprises (MNEs) like Apple. On the contrary, this percentage will tend to be higher in these cases. The reason is that, of all the relevant factors contributing to the so-called home country bias, the only ones that seem to remain current (namely governance issues, information asymmetry or the "familiarity" bias) do not have a significant impact in the case of world-renowned MNCs.[35] This being said, and departing from the absence of trustworthy data on

29. https://www.nasdaq.com/symbol/aapl/ownership-summary (last accessed to data on January 10, 2019).
30. Vanguard Group Inc., BlackRock Inc., Berkshire Hathaway, State Street Corp, FMR LLC, Northern Trust Corp, Geode Capital Management LLC, Norges Bank, Invesco LTD and Bank of New York Mellon Corp. *See* https://www.nasdaq.com/symbol/aapl/institutional-holdings (last accessed to data on January 10, 2019).
31. Sanchirico, C.W. (2015).
32. Sanchirico, C.W. (2015). The author refers to various investigations (most notably the one conducted by Kenneth French and James Poterba in 1991), which empirically prove this bias.
33. Sanchirico, C.W. (2015), p. 222.
34. US Department of the Treasury (2017): Foreign portfolio holdings of US securities, B-3 (exhibit 2, first row of data).
35. Sanchirico, C.W. (2015), p. 274. Regarding the first factor (governance issues), it should be noted that US MNCs are usually publicly listed companies in US stock exchanges and, as such, they are subject to extensive disclosure requirements and minority-protecting corporate laws-. Accordingly, opacity and some other risks commonly faced by foreign investors do not play a key role in the case of MNCs. In relation to the latter two (information asymmetry and "familiarity" bias), MNEs are so named precisely because they spread their commercial presence all over the world, as the present section will intend to demonstrate in the particular case of

Apple's ownership, both the arguments and the data provided above strongly suggest that the "home country bias" should not be strong in the case of Apple and thus the average 12.2% percentage of foreign-owned US equities in the year 2011 should be significantly higher in this case. In the light of this, it would be reasonable to assume that around 20% of Apple's equity is likely to be owned by investors based in countries other than the US.

- Direction and management of the corporation. According to the company's bylaws, its board of directors shall be comprised by five to nine people,[36] who regularly meet in Cupertino,[37] at least four times a year, for the strategic direction and management of the company. Although there seem to be distinct management layers for each of the operating segments to better adapt to the specificities of each market,[38] the company is ultimately run from the US.[39] The percentages that will be shown in the tables below correspond to estimates provided by a study.[40]

(b) The following four indicators represent some of the key stages in the value creation process of its products and services. The first of them identifies the location of the R&D activities, probably the most decisive activities in the supply chain of technology companies like Apple, since they are the ones that can make the difference with competitors. The next two indicators correspond to the manufacturing stage: the origin of Apple's principal component suppliers and the location of the facilities in charge of the assembly of the components. Lastly, the fourth one intends to show the worldwide distribution of the firm's employees:

- R&D activities. The investment in R&D may be either direct, by financing its own R&D activities that eventually result in innovations that may be

---

Apple. Consequently, the wide geographical expansion of these kinds of companies leads to the perception of familiarity by potential foreign investors.

36. Article 2.2 Apple Inc.'s bylaws. Available at: https://corporate.findlaw.com/contracts/formation/by-laws-apple-computer-inc.html (last accessed on January 10, 2019). The directors, as of November 2018, are Tim Cook (CEO), Arthur Levinson (Chairman), James Bell, Al Gore, Robert Iger, Andrea Jung, Ronald Sugar and Susan Wagner. This information should be up to date in: http://investor.apple.com/corporate-governance.cfm (last accessed on January 10, 2019).
37. The principal executive offices are located in One Apple Park Way, Cupertino, California. *See* Apple Inc.'s 2018 Annual Report (form 10-K), front page and Memorandum on "Offshore profit shifting and the US tax code—part 2 (Apple Inc.)" submitted before the US Senate—Permanent Subcommittee on Investigations, p. 30.
38. The operating segments include Americas (both North and South America), EMEA (Europe, India, Middle East and Africa), Greater China (China, Hong Kong and Taiwan), Japan and Rest of Asia Pacific (Australia and those Asian countries not included in the previous segments).
39. Memorandum on "Offshore profit shifting and the US tax code—part 2 (Apple Inc.)" submitted before the US Senate—Permanent Subcommittee on Investigations, p. 30: "Apple's offshore affiliates operate as one worldwide enterprise, following a coordinated business plan directed by Apple Inc."
40. Dedrick, J., Kraemer, K.L., Linden, G. (2011), p. 228.

registered for greater protection,[41] or indirect, in cases where Apple disburses fees to third parties in exchange for licenses to use or commercially exploit their IP or directly acquires the technology developed by others.[42] As a result, the company currently holds a significant number of patents and copyrights and has registered or applied to register other numerous patents, trademarks and services marks.[43]

There is no accurate official data regarding the location of Apple's R&D activities. However, several official sources suggest that the vast majority of R&D activities take place within US soil. In fact, Apple's head of Tax Operations revealed in the course of the US Senate investigation on the company's tax planning in 2011 that around 95% of Apple's R&D was conducted in the US, mostly by Apple Inc.'s in-house engineers in California.[44] On the other hand, Apple admitted that 1% of Apple's R&D was conducted in Ireland by the company's local subsidiaries.[45] A surprisingly low percentage considering that the Irish subsidiaries own around the 60% of Apple's IP economic rights since the 1980s by virtue of cost-sharing agreements (hereinafter "CSAs").[46]

The absence of comprehensive information on the location of the company's R&D activities obliges us to resort to estimations once again. A closer look into the US Patent and Trademark Office website reveals the existence of several trademarks and 8,104 registered patents under Apple Inc.'s name[47] while the European Patent Office has 6,555 registered patents where the applicant is Apple Inc.[48] A quick glance at a random

41. This is the case for the iPod, as its software was developed in-house and Apple does not have to pay any license or royalty fee on each unit sold. *See* Dedrick, J., Kraemer, K.L., Linden, G. (2009).
42. Apple Inc.'s 2018 Annual Report (form 10-K), p. 6.
43. Apple Inc.'s 2018 Annual Report (form 10-K), p. 6.
44. Memorandum on "Offshore profit shifting and the US tax code—part 2 (Apple Inc.)" submitted before the US Senate—Permanent Subcommittee on Investigations, p. 28.
45. Memorandum on "Offshore profit shifting and the US tax code—part 2 (Apple Inc.)" submitted before the US Senate—Permanent Subcommittee on Investigations, p. 28.
46. The arrangements are described in the Memorandum on "Offshore profit shifting and the US tax code—part 2 (Apple Inc.)" submitted before the US Senate—Permanent Subcommittee on Investigations, pp. 25 et seq. *See also* Testimony of Apple Inc. submitted before the US Senate—Permanent Subcommittee on Investigations, pp. 3 and 11. Some of the arrangements are included within the Exhibits used in the hearing on "Offshore profit shifting and the US tax code—part 2 (Apple Inc.)," p. 58. Chapter 2 section §2.01[A][2] will later make reference to them.
47. US Patent and Trademark Office website: http://patft.uspto.gov/netacgi/nph-Parser?Sect1=PTO2&Sect2=HITOFF&p=1&u=%2Fnetahtml%2FPTO%2Fsearch-bool.html&r=0&f=S&l=50&co1=AND&d=PTXT&s1=%22apple+inc%22.AANM.&Page=Prev&OS=AANM/%22apple+inc%22&RS=AANM/%22apple+inc%22 (last accessed to data on January 10, 2019). A non-exhaustive list of Apple's trademarks is provided in its website: http://www.apple.com/legal/intellectual-property/trademark/appletmlist.html (last accessed on January 10, 2019).
48. European Patent Office website: https://register.epo.org/smartSearch?searchMode=smart&query=apple+inc (last accessed to data on January 10, 2019).

sample of forty registered patents[49] is enough to realize that the vast majority of its inventors (96%) are in fact based in the US, while only 4% of them were located elsewhere (Israel, United Kingdom (hereinafter "UK") and China in the sample). Out of the total of 171 inventors based in the US, 99% were based in the State of California while only 1% worked from other states (Florida), thus corroborating the numbers provided by Phillip Bullock.

- Component providers. Back in the 1980s and 1990s, Apple used to manufacture its own products in-house, both in California and Cork (Ireland). However, in response to the severe financial difficulties it experienced in the late 90s, the company restructured its operations and internationalized much of its activities to third-party companies.[50] Nowadays, Apple keeps outsourcing most of its activities concerning manufacturing, assembly, transportation and logistics to third party enterprises all over the world, primarily in Asia but also in Europe and the US, being some of them sole-sourced suppliers.[51] The company only keeps limited manufacturing activities in-house, maintaining facilities for this purpose in the US and Ireland (Cork).[52] Every year, Apple provides an official supplier list, which comprises its top annual suppliers, who represent the 98% of expenditures for materials, manufacturing and assembly of Apple's products.[53] Data exposed in the tables below and broken down by operating segments derive from this list. This time, we will use updated data from 2018, as the supplier's list corresponding to 2011 is not available anymore in Apple's website.
- Assembly facilities. Once the components are manufactured, they are assembled in the facilities specifically intended for this purpose. According to unofficial sources, Apple's products are assembled in China (eight assembly facilities), Brazil (one), Ireland (one) and the US (one).[54] We

49. The sample is comprised by forty patents that were randomly chosen from the US Patent and Trademark Office (twenty patents) and the European Patent Office (twenty patents). The analysis of the sample was conducted in November 2018.
50. Memorandum on "Offshore profit shifting and the US tax code—part 2 (Apple Inc.)" submitted before the US Senate—Permanent Subcommittee on Investigations, pp. 18-19.
51. Apple Inc.'s 2018 Annual Report (form 10-K), p. 5.
52. Apple Inc.'s 2015 Annual Report (form 10-K), p. 18. According to the report, some Mac computers are still manufactured by Apple in the US and Ireland (Cork). The latest annual report does not provide any more the location of Apple's own manufacturing facilities. In addition, the A5 series of microprocessors, used for iPhones and iPads, are built in Austin, Texas (US), according to the memorandum on "Offshore profit shifting and the US tax code—part 2 (Apple Inc.)" submitted before the US Senate—Permanent Subcommittee on Investigations, p. 30.
53. Apple Inc.'s 2018 Supplier List. Available at: https://www.apple.com/supplier-responsibility/pdf/Apple-Supplier-List.pdf (last accessed to data on January 10, 2019).
54. Apple used to provide this information in its website back in 2016 but right now, the data derive from unofficial sources. They are however consistent with the information we collected in 2016 from the website. *See* https://www.google.com/maps/d/u/0/embed?mid=1HLNviMZaf3mKCSxMymMhh-xwMMo&msa=0&gl=us&hl=en&ie=UTF8&t=p&ll=-3.81666561775622e-14%2C0&spn=152.144101%2C298.828125&z=1&output=embed (last accessed on January 10, 2019).

will use this information in the tables below, as we could not access to that corresponding to 2011.

- Workforce. The group itself reveals annually the total amount of full-time equivalent employees as of the month of September in its 10-K Annual Report (132,000 as of September 2018).[55] Although the latest 10-K reports reveal the rapid growth in the number of Apple employees worldwide over the years (the group employed 60,400 people in 2011 the year we are taking as a benchmark), they do not disaggregate the amounts by jurisdictions or geographical areas so we can only rely on estimates again.

  During the investigation conducted in the US Senate during 2013, the group revealed that, out of its back then 80,000 employees, 52,000 were in the US (65%)[56] while 2,452 (3%) were in Ireland.[57] On the other hand, Apple asserts it currently employs 22,000 employees in European countries (i.e., 16.7% of the total).[58] If we extrapolate the aforementioned proportions to year 2011, we will get some of the data we need for our tables below. That is: out of the 60,400 employees worldwide, we would assign 39,260 to the US (65%) and 10,086 to Europe (16.7%, out of which, 1,812 would be assigned to Ireland, corresponding to the 3%).

(c) The next two indicators represent the final stages of the process: distribution and insertion of the products on the market:

- Distribution channels. The seventh indicator refers the distribution of the firm's products and services. Apple resorts to direct and indirect distribution channels, each representing, respectively, around 25%-30% and 70%-75%.[59] Among the direct channels we find its own retail stores (the so-called Apple Stores), and its website and online platforms (e.g., App Store, Mac App Store, iTunes Store, iBooks Store, Apple Music). The indirect distribution channels comprise cellular network carriers, wholesalers, retailers and value-added resellers.

  In the tables below, we will merely make reference to the location of its own retail stores (the "Apple Stores"), as there is no reliable official information regarding the rest of the channels. Therefore, we will disaggregate the official data provided by Apple's website regarding the location of its stores[60] by geographical areas. Once again, we will use

55. Apple Inc.'s 2018 Annual Report (form 10-K), p. 6.
56. Memorandum on "Offshore profit shifting and the US tax code—part 2 (Apple Inc.)" submitted before the US Senate—Permanent Subcommittee on Investigations, pp. 17-18.
57. Memorandum on "Offshore profit shifting and the US tax code—part 2 (Apple Inc.)" submitted before the US Senate—Permanent Subcommittee on Investigations, p. 25, footnote 103.
58. https://www.apple.com/uk/job-creation/ (last accessed to data on January 10, 2019, numbers provided are updated to May 2018).
59. This is the average proportion derived from the statistics provided by the latest Apple Inc.'s Annual Reports (form 10-K), from 2013 to 2018.
60. The complete list of 473 Apple Stores with their respective addresses is available in the company's website. http://www.apple.com/retail/storelist/ (last accessed to data on January 10, 2019).

updated data of 2018, as we did not have access to the information corresponding to 2011.

- Market. Apple's market is comprised of final customers, SMCs and government and educational entities, and no single customer accounted for more than 10% of net sales in recent years.[61] Apple has managed to win a very competitive position in the global market. The increasing popularity and success of its products has enabled it to progressively gain new customers worldwide.[62] The tables below will display the market share in each given geographical area as of 2011.[63]

(d) The last indicator pinpoints the regions where Apple's global earnings (to be more precise, earnings before interests, taxes, depreciation and amortization (hereinafter "EBITDA")) are attributed for tax purposes, thus identifying the regions which would be in principle entitled to tax them. In view of the difficulty of accessing accurate and reliable data from primary sources (e.g., the annual accounts of the corresponding group's subsidiaries) we used data for the year 2011, since the documentation resulting from Apple's hearing before the Senate provides very comprehensive information regarding such tax period,[64] while the updated data remains largely beyond our reach.

The total amount of EBITDA obtained by the Apple group within the fiscal year 2011 reached USD 34.2 billion,[65] of which 30% were reported in the US (USD 10.2 billion)[66] while 70% were reported abroad (USD 24 billion). Oddly

61. Apple Inc.'s 2018 Annual Report (form 10-K), p. 4 and forms 10-K pertaining to previous years.
62. In fact, net sales in operating segments other than the Americans have grown from USD 2.5 billion to USD 153.5 billion from 1999 to 2018. *See* Apple Inc.'s 1999-2018 Annual Reports (form 10-K).
63. The disaggregated data of net sales per operating segment is provided in Apple Inc.'s 2011 Annual Report (form 10-K), p. 30. Its page 27 specifies that the expression "net sales" in the 10-K form covers the revenue from the sale of hardware, software, digital content and applications, peripherals and service/support contracts. However, we found a couple of problems, as Apple's 2011 10-K did not use the same operating segments as now. For example, the Asia Pacific segment included Greater China at that time, and there was a separate Retail segment. In order to get the data corresponding to current operating segments, we proceeded as follows. As information on the net sales conducted solely in China in 2011 was provided in Apple's 2011 Annual Report, p. 74 (USD 12.4 billion), we subtracted that amount from the total net sales conducted in Asia Pacific (USD 22.59 billion). Therefore, the Chinese segment ended up with USD 12.4 billion while the Asia Pacific segment kept USD 10.12 billion. Finally, as there was a separate Retail segment with USD 14.13 billion, we apportioned this amount among the different operating segments based on the number of Apple stores located in each one of them.
64. Information on the location of Apple's EBITDA for the fiscal year 2011 is provided in the Testimony of Prof. Shay on "Offshore profit shifting and the US tax code—part 2 (Apple Inc.)" submitted before the US Senate—Permanent Subcommittee on Investigations, p. 8, in Apple Inc.'s 2011 Annual Report (form 10-K), p. 62 and in the Memorandum on "Offshore profit shifting and the US tax code—part 2 (Apple Inc.)" submitted before the US Senate—Permanent Subcommittee on Investigations, pp. 21 and 25 (footnote 102).
65. Testimony of Prof. Shay on "Offshore profit shifting and the US tax code—part 2 (Apple Inc.)" submitted before the US Senate—Permanent Subcommittee on Investigations, p. 8, Apple Inc.'s 2011 Annual Report (form 10-K), p. 62 and Sullivan, M. (2012), p. 777.
66. Please note that this quantity, for unknown reasons, differs in the Memorandum on "Offshore profit shifting and the US tax code—part 2 (Apple Inc.)" submitted before the US Senate—Permanent Subcommittee on Investigations, p. 29, according to which the EBITDA reported in the US in 2011 amounted to USD 11 billion.

enough, 64% of the global EBITDA earned by Apple was reported in Ireland (USD 22 billion),[67] representing 92% of the EBITDA reported out of the US, a very significant proportion when compared with other significant jurisdictions, for example, the 0.6% reported in Japan and UK (USD 150 and 155 million respectively),[68] the 0.29% of Luxembourg (USD 70 million)[69] and the 0.002% of Spain (USD 0.4 million).[70]
We cannot however ignore that Apple also contributes (albeit indirectly) to generate greater tax revenues in many States across the world by contracting out certain steps of the value-added process with a great amount of third-party companies (e.g., manufacturers, assemblers). Payments for such contributions will necessarily be at arm's length and will contribute to increase the domestic tax bases of such companies and by extension their tax liabilities in their corresponding jurisdictions, although such payments are not expected to be truly significant, as Apple generally keeps a very lucrative margin (prices of some of the Apple's products nearly triple their manufacturing costs).[71]

Finally, we superimposed the data corresponding to the aforementioned nine indicators so as to analyze whether there is indeed some sort of correlation between the economic and the tax presence of this MNC around the world.

---

67. *See* Memorandum on "Offshore profit shifting and the US tax code—part 2 (Apple Inc.)" submitted before the US Senate—Permanent Subcommittee on Investigations. It reveals that most of which were reported by ASI (pp. 21 and 25—footnote 102). This quantity kept growing to USD 36 billion in 2012 according to p. 29. Page 40 reveals that 84% of Apple's non-US operating income in 2011 was booked in ASI. For its part, AOI, the holding company, received USD 6.4 billion in dividends from its low-tier affiliates according to p. 36. For a more comprehensive overview of ASI and AOE's financial information from 2003 to 2014 *see* European Commission Decision on State Aid implemented by Ireland to Apple (August 30, 2016), pp. 24-25.
68. *See* Memorandum on "Offshore profit shifting and the US tax code—part 2 (Apple Inc.)" submitted before the US Senate—Permanent Subcommittee on Investigations, pp. 34 (Japan) and 40 (UK). Further information on the UK affiliates (Apple Retail UK Limited and Apple UK Limited) may also be found in the official UK Registry of Companies: https://beta.companieshouse.gov.uk/company/04996702/filing-history and https://beta.companieshouse.gov.uk/company/01591116 (last accessed on January 10, 2019).
69. Please note the 2011 EBITDA of the Luxembourgish subsidiary (Itunes S.à.r.l.) could not be found. Instead, we use its 2011 "Earnings Before Taxes" (profit/loss of the company according to its commercial balance sheet) after its conversion to US dollars. *See* the leaked tax ruling by Luxembourg Administration regarding the aforementioned company on p. 7, available at www.icij.org. Its net turnover, however, exceeds USD 1 billion (*see* the leaked tax ruling on p. 19).
70. El País: "La declaración de impuestos le sale a Apple a devolver en España," May 20, 2012 https://elpais.com/economia/2012/05/20/actualidad/1337547016_498517.html (last accessed on January 10, 2019).
71. Forbes: "The $ 1,250 iPhone XS Max costs Apple $ 450 to make, nearly a 200% profit margin," September 27, 2018 https://www.forbes.com/sites/jeanbaptiste/2018/09/27/the-1250-iphone-xs-max-costs-apple-450-to-make-nearly-a-200-profit-margin/#3b981c6a4966 (last accessed on January 10, 2019).

Figure 1 Distribution of Apple's Relevant Economic and Tax Data among the Operating Segments (2011)[72]

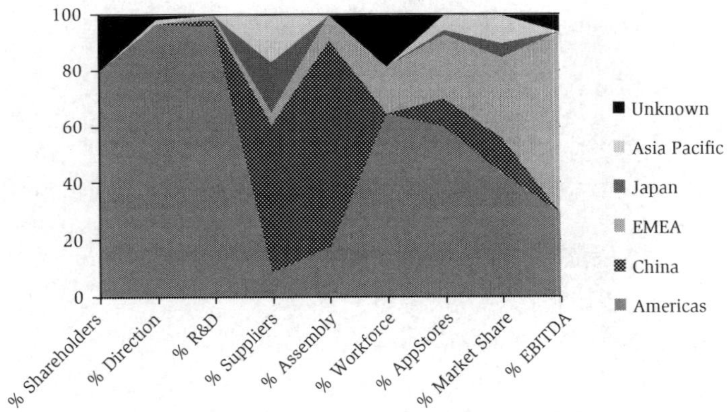

	% Shareholders	% Direction	% R&D	% Suppliers	% Assembly	% Workforce	% AppStores	% Market Share	% EBITDA
Americas	80.00	97.00	96.07	9.30	18.18	65.00	60.32	43.80	30.00
China			2.25	51.77	72.73		9.92	12.32	
EMEA			1.69	4.53	9.09	16.70	22.82	28.82	64.00
Japan			0.00	17.75	0.00		1.59	5.05	
Asia Pacific		1.50	0.00	16.65	0.00		5.36	10.01	
Unknown	20.00	1.50	0.00	0.00	0.00	18.30	0.00		6.00
Total	100.00	100.00	100.00	100.00	100.00	100.00	100.00	100.00	100.00
	Est (2011)	Est	Est	R (2018)	UN (2018)	Est (2011)	R (2018)	R (2011)	R (2011)

Figure 1 graphically displays the contribution of each one of the separating segments to Apple's global value chain in its different stages. The American segment enjoys a greater prominence in the stages of management and R&D while it keeps the vast majority of Apple's employees and retail stores within its domain. For its part, it may be easily observed that the Chinese segment plays a critical role in the production stages, since it provides the majority of the components for Apple's devices and is predominantly in charge of its final assembly. Its market share in 2011 was still modest although it doubled from 2011 to 2015.[73] The EMEA region hardly contributes to the innovation and production stages but appears to be a significant market for Apple in terms of retail stores and volume of net sales. Nonetheless, two-thirds of Apple's worldwide taxable profits ended up in this region. Finally, Japan and Asia Pacific share a similar profile, as each one supplies around 15%-20% of components and keeps a modest market share around 5%-10%.

However, this figure cannot be properly understood in the absence of the following one. On this occasion we displayed separately the information concerning just two jurisdictions that play a critical role: US and Ireland.

72. Operating segments (Apple Inc.'s 2018 Annual Report (form 10-K), p. 25): Americas (both North and South America), EMEA (Europe, India, Middle East and Africa), Greater China (China, Hong Kong and Taiwan), Japan and Rest of Asia Pacific (Australia and those Asian countries not included in the previous segments). Estimations are marked as "Est."; real data are marked as "R"; and unofficial data are marked as "UN."

73. *See* the 10-K forms corresponding to such years.

Figure 2 Distribution of Apple's Relevant Economic and Tax Data Broken Down into Two Jurisdictions: US and Ireland (2011)[74]

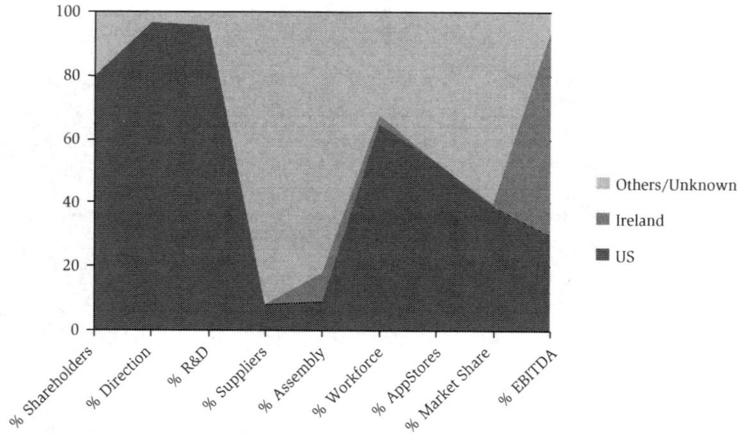

	% Shareholders	% Direction	% R&D	% Suppliers	% Assembly	% Workforce	% AppStores	% Market Share	% EBITDA
US	80.00	97.00	96.07	8.08	9.09	65.00	53.17	39.00	30.00
Ireland	0.00	0.00	0.00	0.12	9.09	3.00	0.00	1.00	64.00
Others/Unknown	20.00	3.00	3.93	91.80	81.82	32.00	46.83	60.00	6.00
Total	100.00	100.00	100.00	100.00	100.00	100.00	100.00	100.00	100.00

Figure 2 confirms that the US, the country where the group was born and is still headquartered, represents the greater relative weight within the American segment, which was discussed above. Ireland, for its part, does not contribute whatsoever to the management of the multinational group nor its R&D activities[75] and barely contributes to the production process with a small manufacturing facility in Cork (in charge of a line of specialty Mac computers for sale in Europe)[76] and one component providers out of a total of 817.[77] The insertion of Apple products in the Irish market is very modest, since there are no Apple stores in its territory and its market share scarcely represents 1%. In this context, it is surprising to see how this jurisdiction could capture nothing less than 64% of the group's global EBITDA in 2011: a total amount of USD 22 billion.

74. The sources of the information concerning the US and Ireland coincide with those already noted above. Information on the market share of these countries is available in the Testimony of Prof. Shay on "Offshore profit shifting and the US tax code—part 2 (Apple Inc.)" submitted before the US Senate—Permanent Subcommittee on Investigations, p. 8 and Memorandum on "Offshore profit shifting and the US tax code—part 2 (Apple Inc.)" submitted before the US Senate—Permanent Subcommittee on Investigations, p. 8.
75. According to the information supplied by Apple, employees of ASI and AOE conducted "less than 1%" of Apple's R&D in 2013. As the information is neither accurate nor reliable we decided to trust our own estimations, derived by the study of the sample we referred to above. In our sample, none of the inventors of the patents under review was located in Ireland, in Memorandum on "Offshore profit shifting and the US tax code—part 2 (Apple Inc.)" submitted before the US Senate—Permanent Subcommittee on Investigations, p. 28.
76. Memorandum on "Offshore profit shifting and the US tax code—part 2 (Apple Inc.)" submitted before the US Senate—Permanent Subcommittee on Investigations, p. 25.
77. https://www.apple.com/supplier-responsibility/pdf/Apple-Supplier-List.pdf (last accessed to data on January 10, 2019).

As Shay noted, this would mean that each one of Apple's Irish workers would be generating USD 9 million per year compared to the average of USD 576,000.[78] On the other hand, jurisdictions other than the US and Ireland only captured 6% of the group's global EBITDA despite greatly contributing to the value creation process (they manufactured more than 90% of the components and assembled 82% of the products) and representing a substantial share of its market (47% of Apple stores and 60% of the market share).

In view of these facts, Ting concluded that such outcome defies common sense since "the locations of real economic activities—such as R&D and sales—are detached from the locations of profits" with the result that "a disproportional amount of income was booked in the Irish subsidiaries that have relatively few employees and activities."[79]

Although the ultimate tax burden imposed over Apple's global tax base is not a key element for the purposes of our diagnostic analysis, we will provide a very brief overview on the matter. Access to the reliable data on the final CIT burden borne by each of the members of the Apple group was very arduous. Regrettably, we cannot depart from the official consolidated amount of CIT paid globally in 2011 by the Apple group since this quantity remains unknown. What is in fact public is the provision the Apple group stipulated for income taxes in the 2011 fiscal year: a total amount of USD 8.2 billion.[80] However, there are good reasons to believe that the amount of the provision may be quite far from the total amount actually paid. First, because The New York Times, albeit omitting its sources, quantified the total CIT paid by the Apple group in 2011 at USD 3.3 billion.[81] Second and more importantly, because a gap of 45%-70% is commonly appreciated between the tax provisions made by Apple and the total amount of taxes paid in the country.[82] Hence, it does not seem unreasonable to conclude that the actual total amount may be closer to USD 3.3 billion than to USD 8.2 billion.

The next question that arises is in which jurisdictions the group members actually paid their CITs and in which amount. According to the aforementioned provision for 2011 income taxes, out of the total USD 8.2 billion, 6.9 referred to federal income taxes (i.e., US CIT) while 0.6 referred to foreign taxes. With respect to the US, Apple filed with the Internal Revenue Service (hereinafter "IRS") a tax return which quantified the

78. Testimony of Prof. Shay on "Offshore profit shifting and the US tax code—part 2 (Apple Inc.)" submitted before the US Senate—Permanent Subcommittee on Investigations, pp. 8 and 9. The first amount is the result of dividing the EBITDA allocated in Ireland (USD 22 billion) by the number of employees working in this jurisdiction (2,452) in 2011. The second amount is the result of dividing the global EBITDA obtained by Apple in 2011 (USD 34.2 billion) between the total number of employees worldwide (59,000).
79. Ting, A. (2014), p. 45.
80. Apple Inc.'s 2011 Annual Report (form 10-K), p. 62.
81. New York Times: "How Apple sidesteps billions in taxes," April 28, 2012 https://www.nytimes.com/2012/04/29/business/apples-tax-strategy-aims-at-low-tax-states-and-nations.html (last accessed on January 10, 2019).
82. Memorandum on "Offshore profit shifting and the US tax code—part 2 (Apple Inc.)" submitted before the US Senate—Permanent Subcommittee on Investigations, p. 39. The table depicts how Apple reports much higher provisions for US federal tax on its annual report than the tax that eventually pays. The gap was 47% in 2009, 69% in 2010 and 64% in 2011.

total US tax paid in 2011 at USD 2.5 billion.[83] However, as regards the CIT burden on subsidiaries belonging to the group in jurisdictions other than the US, the difficulties in gaining access to the data significantly increase. Although the provision for foreign taxes anticipated in the 2011 10-K Form was equal to USD 600 million, the data collected suggests the amount may be significantly lower. For example, Apple paid a total amount of CIT of USD 20.2 million in the UK[84] and USD 13 million in Ireland,[85] while paying zero in Germany, France[86] and Spain[87] for the 2011 fiscal year. For its part, the Luxembourgish subsidiary, iTunes s.à.r.l. estimated a total CIT charge of USD 22 million for 2011 (the reliability of the provision is, once again, at best doubtful) (Figure 3).[88]

83. Memorandum on "Offshore profit shifting and the US tax code—part 2 (Apple Inc.)" submitted before the US Senate—Permanent Subcommittee on Investigations, p. 39.
84. *See* https://beta.companieshouse.gov.uk/company/04996702/filing-history (for Apple Retail UK Limited), https://beta.companieshouse.gov.uk/company/01591116 (for Apple UK Limited) and www.duedil.com for both (last accessed on January 10, 2019). While the annual accounts of the former indicate it paid GBP 8.8 million of CIT in 2011, the accounts of the latter states it paid GBP 5.5 million. Once converted to US dollars, the sum of both makes USD 20.2 million.
85. In 2011 ASI paid a total amount of USD 10 million, while AOE paid USD 3 million and AOI did not pay any CIT to any national government at least in the period 2008-2013. *See* Memorandum on "Offshore profit shifting and the US tax code—part 2 (Apple Inc.)" submitted before the US Senate—Permanent Subcommittee on Investigations, pp. 21 and 23, Testimony of Prof. Harvey Jr on "Offshore profit shifting and the US tax code—part 2 (Apple Inc.)" submitted before the US Senate—Permanent Subcommittee on Investigations, p. 4. However, the main reason of Apple's exiguous tax liabilities in Ireland may be found in the ambiguous Irish PE profit attribution rules (which do comply with the ALS) along with the beneficial tax rulings signed between ASI and AOE with the Irish tax authorities, which were declared as illegal State Aid by the European Commission precisely for not following the ALS as derived from the own State Aid Law. *See* European Commission Decision on State Aid implemented by Ireland to Apple (August 30, 2016), pp. 24-25 and Mason, R. (2017).
86. Memorandum on "Offshore profit shifting and the US tax code—part 2 (Apple Inc.)" submitted before the US Senate—Permanent Subcommittee on Investigations, p. 40.
87. Although Apple Retail Spain multiplied its sales in Spain by 14 (from 5 million to 76 million), the company carried forward losses from previous years and got a refund from the Spanish Tax Treasury. *See* El País: "La declaración de impuestos le sale a Apple a devolver en España," May 20, 2012 https://elpais.com/economia/2012/05/20/actualidad/1337547016_498517.html (last accessed on January 10, 2019).
88. *See* the leaked tax ruling by Luxembourg Administration regarding the aforementioned company on p. 3, available at www.icij.org The estimated CIT is EUR 19,867,165.

Figure 3 Relationship Between EBITDA and CIT Paid Globally, in the US, Out of the US and in a Sample of Jurisdictions (2011)[89]

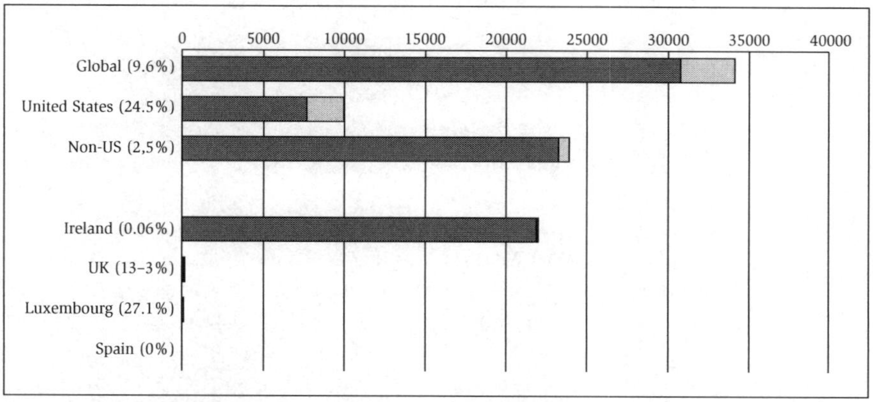

	Global	US	Out of the US	Ireland	UK	Luxembourg	Spain
EBITDA	34.2	10.2	24	22	155	70	0,4
CIT	*3.3 (Unofficial)*	2.5	*600 (Provision, probably much lesser)*	13	20	*22 (Estimation)*	0
Ratio EBITDA/CIT	9,6%	24,5%	2,5%	0,06%	13,3%	27,1%	0%

Besides the concerns that the significantly low tax burden on Apple's worldwide tax base may arise; our attention will focus on the underlying problem behind: a seemingly widespread phenomenon that is commonly referred as "profit shifting." Profit shifting may be defined as the (increasing) ability of companies to book their profits for tax purposes in jurisdictions (most probably low-tax jurisdictions) other than those where they carry out their economic activities (most probably high-tax jurisdictions).

[2] Fundamental Causes Making Profit Shifting Possible (Apple Case)

The causes allowing profit shifting to happen are multiple and varied. However, the ones behind the Apple's tax planning are rather specific and therefore should be identified and assessed separately from those of a more structural nature.

The analysis of the tax planning strategy followed by Apple along with the most relevant applicable rules allowed us to conclude that Apple managed to book their profits in jurisdictions where economic activities are virtually nonexistent by fully and scrupulously complying with the tax laws of the States involved, without traces of any

89. EBITDA is represented by the horizontal bars in their entirety, while the part of it that would correspond to the CIT paid is represented in light grey. In cases where there is no information of the CIT actually paid, the estimation or provision is provided in italics. All amounts are expressed in million dollars.

sort of abusive behavior[90] This suggests that the profit shifting phenomenon is not a problem of tax compliance but rather a problem of rules.[91]

As for the rules that ought to be blamed, it may be concluded that the predominant sources of profit shifting in the case of Apple can be found in the following two groups of rules:

(a) Specific US tax domestic provisions. This group encompasses:
   - The US regime on CSA.[92] This regime essentially enables Apple to book in Ireland an enormous amount of the profits obtained from its sales out of the US without requiring the transfer of any sort of genuine activities to such territory.

     Apple Inc., and two Irish subsidiaries (Apple Sales International —hereinafter "ASI" and Apple Operations Europe—hereinafter "AOE") signed CSAs by which they agreed to share the R&D costs of Apple's IP in exchange for sharing the profits derived by such IP worldwide:[93] while Apple Inc. (which continues to be the sole owner of the legal rights to Apple's IP) keeps the rights to manufacture/ have manufactured, sell and distribute Apple products in the "Americas" operating segment, the two subsidiaries get the entitlement to manufacture/ have manufactured, sell and distribute Apple products in territories other than the Americas.[94] To calculate their respective contributions to support the R&D costs of Apple's IP, each party paid a portion of the total costs upon the portion of product sales that occur in their respective regions.

     The point is that intangible assets are characterized precisely by their potential to generate profits that are disproportionally much higher than the costs incurred in their development. Therefore, the Irish subsidiaries get the entitlement to perceive a huge amount of profits derived from the exploitation of the company's IP in exchange for a ridiculously low prize. Indeed, the average ratio between ASI's EBITDA and the amount of the costs incurred was 15 to 1 in the period 2009-2012.[95] Such a tempting

90. Ting, A. (2014), p. 45 and Testimony of Apple Inc. submitted before the US Senate —Permanent Subcommittee on Investigations, p. 1. For his part, Shay did not adopt a position on the legal correctness of Apple's tax position. *See* Testimony of Prof. Shay on "Offshore profit shifting and the US tax code—part 2 (Apple Inc.)" submitted before the US Senate—Permanent Subcommittee on Investigations, p. 7.
91. This is also implicitly recognized by the own OECD, *see* BEPS report, p. 5.
92. OECD TPG, paragraph 8.3.
93. The arrangements are described in the Memorandum on "Offshore profit shifting and the US tax code—part 2 (Apple Inc.)" submitted before the US Senate—Permanent Subcommittee on Investigations, pp. 25 et seq.
94. *See* the explanation put forward by the company regarding the CSAs in the Exhibits used in the hearing on "Offshore profit shifting and the US tax code—part 2 (Apple Inc.)," p. 99. The "Americas" segment includes North/South/Central America and the Caribbean.
95. Memorandum on "Offshore profit shifting and the US tax code—part 2 (Apple Inc.)" submitted before the US Senate—Permanent Subcommittee on Investigations, p. 29. According to p. 25 (footnote 102) of this report, although both ASI and AOE participate in the CSAs, most offshore earnings end up in ASI. The ratio was 6.6 in 2009, 13.3 in 2010, 15.71 in 2011 and 18 in 2012.

ratio inevitably makes the agreement commercially unjustifiable from the perspective of the ALS, as it is hard to believe that Apple Inc. would have entered into these CSAs with an independent third party.[96] However, the US regime on CSAs operates as a safe harbor that cannot be challenged on the grounds of the ALS, thus shielding the parties from ulterior transfer pricing adjustments.[97]

– The ineffectiveness of the Controlled Foreign Corporations (hereinafter "CFC") regime. A number of provisions bear the greatest responsibility for rendering the US CFC regime virtually ineffective and thus thwarting the possibility of imposing US taxation on a great part of the offshore income perceived by the Irish subsidiaries.

An effective tax transparency regime could potentially result in the taxation of the certain types of income obtained by offshore subsidiaries by the time of its perception and thus before its potential repatriation to the parent's territory. The US CFC regime[98] does not however apply to the case at hands by virtue of two sets of rules: the check-the box rules and the own exceptions provided by this regime. Consequently, Apple Inc. avoided including in its tax base USD 44 billion perceived by its Irish CFCs that qualify as Subpart F income and would have otherwise been subject to US taxation in accordance with the CFC rules.[99]

As for the check-the-box rules, they allow eligible domestic and foreign entities to elect to be taxed as partnerships (transparent entities whose income flows to their shareholders in which hands is taxed) or companies (opaque separate entities subject to tax) for federal tax purposes.[100] Apple checked the box of a number of its offshore subsidiaries,[101] the main objective being to make all the transactions conducted among these disregarded subsidiaries disappear[102] and, by extension, the payments giving rise to Subpart F income.

96. Ting, A. (2014), p. 45 and Testimony of Prof. Shay on "Offshore profit shifting and the US tax code—part 2 (Apple Inc.)" submitted before the US Senate—Permanent Subcommittee on Investigations, p. 9: "the appropriate way to test the reality of the Apple arrangement is to ask whether Apple would have entered into this cost sharing arrangement if Apple's Irish affiliates had been unrelated (...) To answer yes strains credulity."
97. Brauner, Y. (2010), pp. 561 and 566.
98. Subpart F of the US IRC. *See* https://www.law.cornell.edu/uscode/text/26/subtitle-A/chapter-1/subchapter-N/part-III/subpart-F (last accessed on January 10, 2019).
99. Such estimation was made in respect of income earned by in the period 2009-2012 by AOE, AOI, ASI, Apple Distribution International and Apple Singapore. *See* Exhibits used in the hearing on "Offshore profit shifting and the US tax code—part 2 (Apple Inc.)," p. 105 and Memorandum on "Offshore profit shifting and the US tax code—part 2 (Apple Inc.)" submitted before the US Senate—Permanent Subcommittee on Investigations, p. 32.
100. For more information *see* Mullis, K. (2011).
101. For an almost complete list of Apple's subsidiaries (22) that were disregarded by virtue of the check-the-box provisions *see* the Exhibits used in the hearing on "Offshore profit shifting and the US tax code—part 2 (Apple Inc.)," pp.75-77.
102. Since e paying and recipient entities would not be considered as separate entities any more but rather part of the same company.

The repeal of the check-the-box rules would however not ensure the applicability of the CFC rules to Apple's subsidiaries, since Apple could still resort to the own exceptions provided by the CFC regime.[103] We are particularly referring to the so-called CFC look-through rule,[104] the "same country exception"[105] and the "manufacturing exception."[106]

(b) Rules that mirror structural paradigms historically underlying CITs. We are referring to the so-called tax connecting factors (i.e., the rules that link a taxpayer or an item of income to a certain tax jurisdiction), which have traditionally been configured around the notions of residence and source. There is no doubt that the outcome of Apple's tax planning strategy is in part attributable to the effect of the current definitions of residence and source:

- Residence. Apple successfully exploited a mismatch in the definition of corporate residence in the US and Ireland to make three of the Irish subsidiaries (Apple Operations International—hereinafter "AOI," ASI and AOE) stateless and thus not subject to unlimited taxation in any jurisdiction.[107]

  Such outcome was achieved thanks to the fact that the three subsidiaries were incorporated in Ireland but managed and controlled from the US, therefore falling out of the scope of the respective domestic tax residence tests adopted by such States (the Irish management and control test and the American incorporation test).[108]

103. All these options are explored in Memorandum on "Offshore profit shifting and the US tax code—part 2 (Apple Inc.)" submitted before the US Senate—Permanent Subcommittee on Investigations, pp. 14-16 and 36-37.
104. Section 954 (c)(6) IRC. This rule grants an exclusion from Subpart F taxation for certain passive income received from a related CFC under certain circumstances.
105. Section 954 (c)(3) IRC. It shields from taxation the dividends and interests paid to the CFC by a related CFC as long as they are both organized and operating in the same foreign country (Ireland in this case) and the latter has a substantial part of its assets used in the trade or business of that same country.
106. Section 954 (d)(1)(A) IRC. It stipulates that a certain type of Subpart F income would be exempted from CFC taxation as long as the CFC itself were a manufacturer and added substantive value to the goods.
107. AOI did not pay any CIT to any jurisdiction at least during the period 2007-2011, besides the taxes paid as a non-resident in France (*see* the Exhibits used in the hearing on "Offshore profit shifting and the US tax code—part 2 (Apple Inc.)," p. 84). For its part, ASI, despite not being a tax resident in Ireland, it filed tax returns during the period 2009-2013 (at least) as an operating company therein, paying USD 10 million in 2011, an extremely low amount if compared with the total income perceived by such company (USD 22 billion) (*see* footnote 101 of the Memorandum on "Offshore profit shifting and the US tax code—part 2 (Apple Inc.)" submitted before the US Senate—Permanent Subcommittee on Investigations, p. 24). Lastly, AOE only paid taxes on the income derived by the sales conducted in Ireland and the total amount of tax paid in 2011 barely reached USD 3 million (*see* the Testimony of Prof. Shay on "Offshore profit shifting and the US tax code—part 2 (Apple Inc.)" submitted before the US Senate—Permanent Subcommittee on Investigations, p. 9).
108. *See* Memorandum on "Offshore profit shifting and the US tax code—part 2 (Apple Inc.)" submitted before the US Senate—Permanent Subcommittee on Investigations, pp. 21-25. Greater detail on the Irish tax residence rules may be found in http://www.oecd.org/tax/automatic-exchange/crs-implementation-and-assistance/tax-residency/Ireland-Tax-Residency.pdf (last accessed on January 10, 2019), while the explanation of the US test may be found in

However, recent amendments made to the Irish tax legislation could already have had an impact on Apple's tax planning. First, the new anti-mismatch rule provided that an Irish-incorporated company would be treated as tax resident in Ireland provided that, by reason of a mismatch of residence rules with a treaty-partner State, it is not deemed to be resident in none of the two States.[109] Apple's subsidiaries are likely to be affected by it, as it started to apply retroactively in January 1, 2015 to companies incorporated before its entry in force. However, Ting warned that Apple could easily circumvent the anti-mismatch rule by simply shifting the place of central management and control of their three subsidiaries from the US to: (i) another country with whom Ireland does not have a tax treaty in force, or (ii) a low-tax jurisdiction which considers the company as resident therein, as that would prevent them from being stateless and therefore the rule would not apply.[110] Even if Apple manages to circumvent the aforementioned provision, its subsidiaries would still be captured by the new Irish POI test, which is expected to apply retroactively to companies incorporated before its entry in force (January 1, 2015, the case of the Irish subsidiaries) from December 31, 2020 onwards.[111] As a consequence of the aforementioned, the Irish tax reform will surely make the three subsidiaries tax resident in Ireland sooner or later.

Beyond the specific peculiarities of the Apple case, the emergence of these issues ultimately reveals that the way corporate tax residence tests are often configured along with the asymmetric positions followed the different States seem to give rise to profit shifting risks.

- Source. Apple managed to structure its transactions in their market jurisdictions in a manner so as to minimize its tax liabilities in such jurisdictions.

  ASI had the rights to manufacture, have manufactured, distribute and sell the products patterned after Apple's IP in all operating segments except for the American by virtue of its CSA with Apple Inc. Accordingly, it acquired the products from the manufacturers and subsequently resold them to the distribution companies (Apple Distribution International and Apple Singapore), in charge for distribution in EMEA and Asia Pacific respectively) for a price significantly higher than the one it paid for the goods.[112] Once the distribution subsidiaries acquired the goods, they managed the sales in their respective territories mostly through retail

http://www.oecd.org/tax/automatic-exchange/crs-implementation-and-assistance/tax-residency/United-States-Tax-Residency.pdf (last accessed on January 10, 2019).

109. Section 23A of the Taxes Consolidation Act, as amended by the Finance Act 2013.
110. Ting, A. (2014b), pp. 238-239 and 242.
111. Section 43 of the Finance Act 2014 reformed section 23A of the Taxes Consolidation Act 1997.
112. Memorandum on "Offshore profit shifting and the US tax code—part 2 (Apple Inc.)" submitted before the US Senate—Permanent Subcommittee on Investigations, p. 36.

subsidiaries,[113] with whom they signed the so-called commissionaire arrangements.[114] These arrangements do not involve any transfer of ownership: they merely entitle the retail subsidiaries to act as "commissionaires" of the principal (the relevant distribution subsidiary) and thus sell the goods in their respective jurisdiction in its own name but on behalf of the principal in exchange for a small commission.

The advantage of resorting to the aforementioned arrangements is that they guarantee keeping the tax bases of the retail subsidiaries to the minimum, as they will generally comprise merely the small commissions they receive for their services.[115] Such outcome stands irrespective of whether the retail subsidiary is treated as an agent PE of the principal or not by the local tax administrations. Both approaches would be virtually neutral from a tax perspective as long as the group manages to keep functions, assets and risks in the hands of the distribution companies, since the only item of income that would be theoretically attributable to the retail subsidiary would be the commission, whose amount would be equally calculated in accordance with the ALS either under Article 7.2 (as a PE) or 9 (as a related company) of the tax treaties in force.[116] This means that the recent amendments introduced to Article 5.5 of the 2017 OECD Model Convention (hereinafter "OECD MC") that were intended precisely to target "commissionaire arrangements"[117] will not have a genuine impact in cases like this.

Beyond the specific strategy followed by Apple to minimize its taxation in their market jurisdictions, there is a further problem of a policy nature: the PE concept is often unable to deal effectively with many of today's business models, including some used by Apple. For example, Apple distributes its popular devices through its official website and ships them

113. But also with third-party resellers and directly with Internet customers.

114. *See* OECD (2015): Final Report on BEPS Action 7—Preventing the artificial avoidance of permanent establishment status, pp. 15-27 for a brief description and explanation on the functioning of these arrangements. Apparently, Apple was one of the first MNCs to deploy commissionaire structures to distribute its products in the different market jurisdictions back in the 80s. *See* New York Times: "How Apple sidesteps billions in taxes," April 28, 2012 https://www.nytimes.com/2012/04/29/business/apples-tax-strategy-aims-at-low-tax-states-and-nations.html (last accessed on January 10, 2019).

115. Such commission remunerates their collaboration in the distribution and sale of Apple products to customers. Its amount is generally not disclosed and may vary from country to country. However, the 2010 annual accounts of one of the Spanish retail subsidiaries revealed that it received a 1% commission on sales in Spain for its services. *See* El País: "Apple factura en Irlanda el 99% de sus ventas en España," March 16, 2011 https://elpais.com/economia/2011/03/16/actualidad/1300264382_850215.html (last accessed on January 10, 2019).

116. Dziurdz, K. (2014), p. 136: "if the dependent agent is an associated enterprise of the principal, the dependent agent must be treated as an independent enterprise under article 9 and the principal's dependent agent PE must be treated as a separate and independent enterprise under article 7(2). This means that both vis-à-vis the dependent agent and the dependent agent PE the profits must be attributed at arm's length."

117. OECD (2015): Final Report on BEPS Action 7—Preventing the artificial avoidance of permanent establishment status, pp. 16-27.

to the consumer's home (offline e-commerce) and, at the same time, sells digital content through its online platforms (e.g., App Store, iTunes, etc.) (online e-commerce).[118] The truth is that the PE concept in its present form does not properly cover any of these business models. As for the former, Apple can sell its products online without having a fixed place of business (hereinafter "POB") within the market jurisdiction beyond those explicitly excluded from the scope of the clause (e.g., storage facilities).[119] As for the latter, it becomes even more evident that no fixed POB is required in order to sell goods or provide services electronically. The absence of PEs in the jurisdictions where Apple conducts its online sales prevents them from taxing the profits derived from such sales that could be hypothetically attributed to that PE. This ultimately reveals that the inherent limitations of the PE concept seem to produce the effect of segregating taxable profits from the economic activities that generate it.

A preliminary assessment on the causes of profit shifting in the case of Apple ultimately reveals that the roots of this phenomenon seem to be deeper than it may appear at first glance. Indeed, it appears that that profit shifting is, to a certain extent, the result of the erratic and misguided legal configuration of certain structural paradigms upon which CITs have historically been built, most notably the notions of tax residence and source. We will delve deeper into the profit shifting risks arising from these paradigms later in Chapter 3.

[B] Profit Shifting as a Global Concern

We have good reasons to believe that the case of Apple is certainly not unique and that we are rather facing a widespread phenomenon.[120] It is equally clear that the profit shifting phenomenon (i.e., the increasing ability of companies to report their profits for tax purposes in jurisdictions other than those that host their economic activities) is regarded globally as a problem that ought to be addressed as a matter of urgency.

In 2013, the G20 mandated the OECD to lead the project today known as "BEPS."[121] The description of the "BEPS" phenomenon was followed by the promulgation of the two general objectives that the project wished to pursue. The first objective was the elimination of double taxation without giving rise to double

118. *See* the definition and differences of both types of e-commerce in OECD (2015): Final Report on BEPS Action 1—Addressing the tax challenges of the digital economy, p. 55.
119. Article 5.4 of the MCs explicitly excludes from the scope of the PE provision certain places of business where only preparatory and auxiliary are carried out.
120. Its observance was indeed the trigger of the BEPS project. *See* the reference to multiple studies in BEPS report, pp. 15-24 and Chapter 1 section §1.01. In addition to this, the OECD has designed very sophisticated methodologies and tools aimed at better measuring the profit shifting phenomenon during the course of the BEPS project, *see* OECD (2015): Final Report on BEPS Action 11—Measuring and monitoring BEPS.
121. *See* BEPS Report and BEPS Action Plan.

non-taxation opportunities[122] while the second and primary objective was to provide domestic and international instruments aiming at better aligning rights to tax with "real"[123] "actual"[124] economic activity (hereinafter the "BEPS mantra"). Later on, the Action Plan confirmed this intention: "existing domestic and international tax rules should be modified in order to more closely align the allocation of income with the economic activity that generates that income."[125]

We should add at this point that, although the origin of the BEPS project is inevitably linked to the OECD, the project has globalized just as the economy to which it intends to adapt. This means that the objectives set by the BEPS project are not only shared by a "club of rich"[126] but by a much wider and heterogeneous group of States. The BEPS Inclusive Framework currently gathers 124 States,[127] which are equally committed to accomplish the "BEPS mantra" by means of the actions suggested by the project.[128]

Almost in parallel, the re-establishment of the link between "taxation and where economic activities take place" was also identified as one of the four main objectives and five key areas for action of the Action Plan adopted by the Commission for a fair and efficient corporate tax system,[129] following the dictates of the Member States and the European Parliament.[130] Later on, the Commission insisted on the need to ensure the accomplishment of aforementioned goal in the context of its work on taxing the digital economy.[131]

---

122. BEPS report, pp. 1 and 53.
123. BEPS report, p. 51.
124. BEPS report, pp. 15 and 20.
125. The document, however, does not only not define the expression "economic activities that generate that income" but also alludes to the same idea in different (and confusing) ways. E.g., "Economic activities creating those profits" (BEPS Action Plan, p. 10), "economic activities" in general (BEPS Action Plan, p. 11), "economic activities that produce that income" (BEPS Action Plan, p. 19) or even "relevant substance" (Action plan p. 13). What is more, in the context of transfer pricing, the alleged objective is to align transfer pricing outcomes with "value creation," i.e., that the taxable bases should end up wherever the value creating activities occur (BEPS Action Plan, pp. 20-21).
126. *See* Clifton, J.; Díaz-Fuentes, D. (2011) to witness its evolution from "club of the rich" to a more global institution.
127. http://www.oecd.org/tax/beps/inclusive-framework-on-beps-composition.pdf (last accessed to data on January 10, 2019).
128. *See* the scope and degree of the commitment of the non-OECD States that comprise the Inclusive Framework towards the BEPS project in OECD (2017): Inclusive framework on BEPS: progress report July 2016-June 2017.
129. *See* EU Commission (2015): Communication from the Commission to the European Parliament and the Council: a fair and efficient corporate taxation in the European Union: Five key areas for action, pp. 6 and 8-10. *See also* the timeline suggested to accomplish the different goals of the Action Plan: https://ec.europa.eu/taxation_customs/sites/taxation/files/resources/documents/taxation/company_tax/fairer_corporate_taxation/tax_timeline_new.pdf (last accessed on January 10, 2019).
130. EU Commission (2015): Communication from the Commission to the European Parliament and the Council: a fair and efficient corporate taxation in the European Union: 5 key areas for action, p. 9: "there has been a growing demand from the European Parliament, Member States and stakeholders to address this issue and ensure that profits generated in the EU are taxed at the place where the actual activities take place."
131. *See* EU Commission (2017): Communication from the Commission to the European Parliament and the Council: a fair and efficient tax system in the European Union for the Digital Single

It is however noteworthy that none of these organizations has provided a single solid reason why profit shifting should be indeed regarded as a concern or, in other words, why corporate profits should be taxed wherever economic activities take place. Rather, they merely suggest that this was always the underlying tax policy principle behind corporate income taxation. Such idea was explicitly asserted by the European Commission,[132] although it could also be inferred from the discourse of the OECD, since the use of the expression "profit shifting" seems to depart from the premise that profits originally correspond to a State (wherever the economic activities giving rise to it take place) while the taxpayer manages to "shift" them somewhere else.

Nevertheless, both organizations fail to provide the genuine policy reason(s) behind their categorical rejection of the profit shifting phenomenon. In the light of the absence of an explicit principle that adequately justifies why profit shifting should be a concern, we will subsequently propose a specific tax policy guideline that aims to provide both a consistent theoretical rationale that may help sustain the discourse of rejection towards the profit shifting phenomenon and, at the same time, a new guideline whose observance may help counteract profit shifting risks (section §2.02).

§2.02 THE PRESUMPTIVE BENEFIT PRINCIPLE AS AN EQUITABLE TAX POLICY GUIDELINE TO IDENTIFY THE TAXPAYERS OF CORPORATE INCOME TAXES AND MITIGATE PROFIT SHIFTING RISKS

In the present section we will propose a new tax policy principle that serves both as a theoretical basis for the repudiation of the profit shifting phenomenon and as a useful guideline whose compliance may contribute to make corporate taxpayers to book their profits in the jurisdictions where they carry out their economic activities.

[A] The Notion of Presumptive Benefit Principle

In the present section we intend to explore the role that the benefit principle could (in our view, "should") play in the context of income taxes together with its advantages

Market, p. 7, EU Commission (2018): Proposal for a Council Directive laying down rules relating to the corporate taxation of a significant digital presence, pp. 1-2 and EU Commission (2018): Proposal for a Council Directive on the common system of a digital services tax on revenues resulting from the provision of certain digital services, pp. 1-2.

132. This may be inferred from the recurring use of the word "re-establishing" in relation to the link between taxation and economic activities (*see* EU Commission (2015): Communication from the Commission to the European Parliament and the Council: a fair and efficient corporate taxation in the European Union: 5 key areas for action, pp. 6 and 9). *See also* EU Commission (2017): Communication from the Commission to the European Parliament and the Council: a fair and efficient tax system in the European Union for the Digital Single Market, p. 7 ("the underlying principle for corporation tax is that the profits should be taxed where the value is created") and also EU Commission (2018): Proposal for a Council Directive laying down rules relating to the corporate taxation of a significant digital presence, pp. 1-2 and EU Commission (2018): Proposal for a Council Directive on the common system of a digital services tax on revenues resulting from the provision of certain digital services, pp. 1-2 ("the current corporate tax rules are built on the principles that profits should be taxed where the value is created").

and inherent limitations. Lastly, we will make a brief reference to the specific role that the ability to pay principle may perform in this scenario and further explain why we believe both principles should not be regarded as mutually exclusive but rather compatible and complementary, as they cover their respective shortcomings.

The benefit principle is one of the most common (and oldest) justifications for the imposition of taxes, although its meaning has significantly varied throughout history.[133] Originally, its proponents argued that taxpayers ought to contribute to government in proportion to the benefits obtained from government institutions and programs.[134] At first, such proportion had to be assessed on an individual basis, so taxes would be justified if a correlation existed between its amount and the value of the specific benefits provided by the sovereign to each of its citizens (individual quid pro quo approach). For example, in the context of Rousseau's social contract theory, the imposition of taxes on citizens was regarded as justified insofar the tax revenues contributed to serve the general will and thus provided benefits for each of the members of the community individually considered, most notably the effective defense of his/her person and property.[135] This view only stands today in very limited scenarios.[136] Later on, the emerging understanding that all taxes collected corresponded to all State services (as a whole) rapidly spread. Thus, the individual quid pro quo approach switched to a "general" quid pro quo approach between the government and its citizens according to which there should be a global equivalence between government services and government levies.[137]

This old benefit theory has greatly evolved towards more modern views where the correlation between the amount of the tax due and the value of the benefits provided by the government to the taxpayers (either individually or collectively considered) has ceased to be the key consideration. Conversely, they all depart from the premise that the tax liability ought to be calculated in proportion to the taxpayer's

133. Vogel, K. (1988d) and Dodge, J.M. (2004).
134. Dodge, J.M. (2004), p. 2.
135. Vogel, K. (1988d), pp. 26 and 35. We are referring to the period between the end of the eighteenth and the beginning of the nineteenth century. Along the same lines, Montesquieu defined taxes as "a portion that each subject gives of his property in order to secure or enjoy the remainder (...) in other to fix such revenues, both the needs of the State and the citizens must be taken into account" (translation made by the author). The original version in French reads: "les revenues de l'État son tune portion qui chaque citoyen donne de son bien pour avoir la sureté de l'autre, ou pour en jouir agréabelement (...) pour bien fixes ces revenus, il faut avoir égard aux necessities de l'État et aux necessities des citoyens" (Montesquieu, C.L. (1747), book XIII, chapter I). According to Kelsen, a country would be entitled to tax the income and wealth of its residents or citizens whose rights to the protection and services provided by the State are matched by their duties to the State, among which is the duty to pay taxes. *See* Kelsen, H. (1946), p. 75.
136. The "old" benefit theory has been cabined off to government activities that involve citizen use of government property, facilities and services (e.g., highway tolls, hunting and fishing licenses, tuition at educational institutions, etc.). *See* Dodge, J.M. (2004), p. 3.
137. *See* Vogel, K. (1988d), pp. 28, 32 and 35 and Buchanan, J.M. (1960), p. 19: "there should exist a quid pro quo relationship between government and all individuals together." According to him, taxation would only be justified to the extent an equivalence between government services and the tax payments made by individuals, collectively considered, exists.

ability to pay and regard income taxes as a compensation for the contribution made by the State to the production and protection of the relevant income.

We will now briefly depict three of the most prominent renovated versions of the benefit principle. First, according to the "expanded version of the traditional benefit principle," the taxpayer's well-being (ability to pay) is the proper index for measuring the benefits he/she receives from the government.[138] This idea can also be traced back to Adam Smith, as he stated that the subjects of every State ought to contribute towards the support of the government "in proportion to their respective abilities; that is, in proportion to the revenue which they respectively enjoy under the protection of the State."[139] Second, the "partnership theory" or "economic version of the benefit principle" regards taxes as a "share" that a government is entitled to get from the profits of an enterprise just as if it were a "partner" or "investor" in exchange for contributing to the business by means of a public investment.[140] Third, according to the "entitlement theory," a State would be entitled to tax the profits originated within its borders insofar as it has economically contributed to the production of such profits and thus ought to be compensated for such contribution.[141] Our proposed revised version of this

138. Dodge, J.M. (2005), p. 399: "the new benefit principle (...) holds that the proper index for measuring the benefits received from government by an individual taxpayer is the taxpayer's economic well-being, that is, how well taxpayers do in the market economy, because government, by providing security, law and infrastructure (in the broad sense) enables the market economy." *See also* Dodge, J.M. (2004).
139. Smith, A. (1776), p. 639. Although he has been credited with the earliest reference to the ability to pay theory, his words imply he does not really provide a brand new standard, as it seems to rely once again on benefit grounds (Kaufman, N.H. (1988), p. 157 and Musgrave, R.A. (1959), p. 92) to the extent he seems to depart from the next two assumptions. First, that a person having twice as much property is expected to receive twice as much protection by the State and therefore ought to pay twice as much for such protection. And second, that the protection of property was the only purpose and responsibility held by the government. The four experts of the League of Nationals seemed the share Smith's approach in their 1923 influential report: "the ability-to-pay principle is more comprehensive than the preceding (benefit) theory because it includes what there is of value in the benefit theory. So far as the benefits connected with the acquisition of wealth increase individual faculty" (*See* Economic and Financial Commission for the League of Nations (1923): Report on Taxation, p. 18).
140. Dodge, J.M. (2005), pp. 444 et seq. According to Dodge, this theory "is based on the notion that government should share in national income (...) because government, by supplying infrastructure in the broad sense (physical infrastructure, national and domestic security, a capitalism enabling legal system and regulatory structure), 'earns' a share of the GDP" (Dodge, J.M. (2004), p. 19). This theory is barely distinguishable from the "expanded" version of the traditional benefit theory.
141. The entitlement theory is usually associated to Peggy Musgrave, who contended that the source State should be entitled to tax income originating within its borders because it is the State where the "income-generating activity" take place and thus the one that economically contributes to the production of income. *See* Musgrave, P.B.; Musgrave, R.A. (1972), p. 71 and Musgrave, P.B. (1984), pp. 228-246. McLure argues that entitlement to corporate tax revenue exists "any time a firm avails itself of the productive resources or the market of a nation, that is, if it has an economic presence in the nation" (McLure, C.E. (Jr.) (2000), p. 6:4). Subsequently, he highlights the three main differences between the traditional benefit principle and the entitlement theory. First, the former concentrates on the benefits provided by the government to business while the latter is based on economic benefits (e.g., the benefits of exploiting a market). Second, the latter is preferred in cases in which the tax base is calculated departing from the profits obtained by the company. Third, the latter supports a higher level of corporate income taxation than the former.

long-standing principle and its utility for the purposes of this thesis is more aligned with this latter theory, as will become apparent throughout this section.

We believe that the benefit principle is particularly useful and appropriate when the time comes to identify the members of the community that ought to contribute to the financial support of the government.[142] It would thus justify the imposition of a tax burden on persons who find themselves in a position to effectively benefit from the relevant public goods, services and infrastructures provided by the State concerned, as this fact makes them the most suitable candidates for assuming the responsibility to financially support the maintenance of such services.[143] The reason is obvious: it seems only fair that those enjoying (or in a position to do so) the benefits funded by a State should contribute to their financial support.

This fact does not only justify on theoretical grounds the imposition of a tax burden on this group of persons, it also underlines the mutual "quid pro quo" commitment between the State concerned and its respective taxpayers.[144] That is, on one hand taxpayers are likely to feel part of the community and thereby understand and accept the reason why they ought to contribute to its preservation and development, in fact they will generally be able to witness first-hand the correlation between their economic effort and the quantity and quality of the public goods, services and infrastructures. On the other hand, the State would feel committed towards its own community of taxpayers and endeavor to provide the highest possible quality of services and infrastructures, just as if they were its clients. This sense of engagement between the taxpayer and the State concerned is prone to prevent the so-called secret tax revolt referred to by Vogel,[145] that is, the increasing predisposition of normal responsible citizens—who would normally be incapable of stealing—to conceal taxable transactions to reduce its tax liabilities.

142. Musgrave, R.A. (1959), p. 62: "the benefit principle has the advantage of providing for a simultaneous determination of public services and tax shares."
143. Schanz, G. (1892), pp. 372-373: "every person who is economically tied to this community, that is every person who would benefit from the obligations of the commune being fulfilled, also shares the responsibilities (...) the inhabitants who, by necessity, are provided with internal and external security, roads from transport, sanitation, educational establishments, and are engaged with economic and cultural affairs, need to be taken account of just as much as those who live outside the community but who depend on the former for the protection of their property and who share in the consumption of the community's efforts in the form of value increases, profit and safe revenues" (free translation by Harris, P.A. (1996), p. 276). *See also* Kemmeren, E.C.C.M (2001), p. 520: "to assess whether a sufficient point of connection for the assignment of tax jurisdiction is present, a link should be made between the territory principle with the direct benefit principle, i.e. taxation should be considered as a contribution for benefits provided to an individual through state activities."
144. In cases where the right to vote is tied to the obligation to pay taxes (e.g., this is the case for American citizens that reside abroad but still predominantly retain their right to vote in federal elections), this "quid pro quo" commitment is even more acute, as the taxpayers do not only have a voice in what concerns the fate of their country but also directly bear the economic consequences of their political participation (this would be consistent with the "no taxation without representation" motto). *See* Mason, R. (2015), pp. 189-190 and Staudt, N.C. (2002).
145. Vogel, K. (1988d), p. 22.

The benefit principle acquires particular significance in cross-border scenarios, where it relates to the "inter-nation equity" principle, as coined by the Musgraves.[146] This principle calls for an equitable division of the international tax revenue between the countries that are somehow involved in its generation.[147] A way to determine whether a State has participated to some extent in the generation of a particular item of income is precisely by establishing whether its infrastructures and public services have effectively or potentially contributed to its generation. If the answer is positive, inter-nation equity would theoretically entitle the State to impose a tax burden on the taxpayer who has economically benefited from its services.[148] Conversely, inter-nation equity would be violated if the country providing the public services comes away "empty-handed" while a country that did not provide any public goods "gets the lion's share of the tax revenue."[149] This principle does not differ much from the motto proposed by the four economists in their 1923 report: "the individual's whole faculty should be taxed only once, and that liability should be divided among the tax districts according to his relative (economic) *interests* (allegiance) *in each.*"[150]

The aforementioned considerations suggest that the benefit principle should ideally inspire the rules that identify the community of taxpayers of each State.[151] This means that the principle should underlie the tax rules that ultimately identify the

---

146. Musgrave, P.B.; Musgrave, R.A. (1972). As rightly noted by Gadžo, S. (2018), p. 206: "taxing claim of each State must be justified (legitimized) not only vis-à-vis the taxpayer—as a matter of domestic constitutional order—but also vis-à-vis other States, as members of international community, being a matter of public international law."
147. Escribano, E. (2015), p. 7 and Kaufman, N.H. (1988), p. 156: "the rules governing the extent of a country's competence to tax are essentially an international matter. Internation equity (...) must provide the foundations for an equitable international tax system." Ultimately, this doctrine intends to provide a justification for country's right to tax vis-à-vis other countries (Gadžo, S. (2016), p. 188).
148. Musgrave, P.B.; Musgrave, R.A. (1972), p. 71: "a country should be entitled to charge for the cost of public services which it has rendered to the foreign investor." Vogel, K. (1988c), p. 398: "the only valid legitimation, therefore, can be derived from benefit aspects (...) usually it is the state of source that has provided most or all of the benefits relevant for production of the income (...) without this State's economic opportunities the income normally would not have been generated." Schön, W. (2009), p. 77: "under this principle, the allocation of taxing rights between the countries involved should correspond to the relative amount of public goods provided by these jurisdictions to the overall profit of the enterprise." Vogel, K. (1988c), p. 398: "the only valid legitimation, therefore, can be derived from benefit aspects (...) usually it is the state of source that has provided most or all of the benefits relevant for production of the income (...) without this State's economic opportunities the income normally would not have been generated."
149. Rust, A. (2010), p. 86. This last case is very well illustrated with an ironic example put forward by Gadžo, who makes reference to a popular Monty Python's quote ("to boost the British economy I'd tax al foreigners living abroad") to later explain that any layman would condemn such practice considering the "lack of benefits that foreigners living outside United Kingdom receive from the State, thus making the taxation uncalled-for" (Gadžo, S. (2016), p.1).
150. Economic and Financial Commission for the League of Nations (1923): Report on Taxation, p. 20. The bracketed words were inserted by Kaufman, N.H. (1988), p. 197, as she believed that by "interests" the experts meant "economic allegiance." The first model tax convention drafted by this Commission of Experts precisely intended to generate a division of the cross-border income that would approximate that which would occur if each country's economic interest in the income could be quantified using an economic allegiance analysis (Kaufman, N.H. (1988), p. 200).
151. Kaufman, N.H. (1988), p. 188.

taxpayers that would become subject to a State's tax jurisdiction (i.e., the "tax connecting factors").[152]

Of course, the problem arises when the times comes to determine whether a State's services and infrastructures have effectively contributed to the generation of a taxpayer's income. Undoubtedly, it seems to be increasingly troublesome, not to say impossible, to identify the particular benefits a taxpayer receives from each specific government in today's globalized economy.[153] In view of these difficulties, it does not seem reasonable for connecting factors to demand a case-by-case empirical demonstration of the effective use and enjoyment of the State's public services by the taxpayer and a correlation to its subsequent realization of profits.[154] On the other hand, these evident technical obstacles should never result in a complete disregard of the benefit principle.

We believe in a halfway solution between facing the practical difficulties derived from the adoption of the benefit principle and its outright disregard. Our proposed renovated version of the benefit principle, hereinafter referred as "presumptive benefit principle," serves precisely as a compromise solution that ensures compliance with benefit considerations while overcoming some of the most relevant challenges and limitations of the traditional understanding of the principle.

The presumptive benefit principle would demand the tax connecting factors to rely on certain *indicia* or factors whose presence in the territory concerned is visible and easily ascertainable and further allows us to assume that the taxpayer is in a position to (effectively or potentially) use and enjoy the State's services and infrastructures. This approach has the virtue of avoiding the technical difficulties above referred while ensuring that the benefit principle still plays a role in the identification of the community of taxpayers of a State. In our view, the reliance on assumptions and hypothesis[155] is preferable to a complete omission of the benefit principle. In the same vein, we should remember a very illustrative statement made by Barna back in 1945: "even the setting-up of untested explicit hypothesis concerning benefit accrual is preferable to omission altogether."[156] The choice of the relevant factors would be up to

152. Indeed, the benefit principle has traditionally served as the main tax policy justification for the exotic approach followed by the US that consists on imposing taxation on the worldwide income of their citizens irrespective of their actual State of residence. We will briefly come back to this discussion later in Chapter 4 section §4.02[B][3][a].

153. Schön, W. (2009), p. 75: "nowadays a business located in country A may well be supplied from country B, selling final products to Country C. It seems to be more and more unfeasible to identify the benefits a company has received from a specific government or a defined market as compared to benefits received from other governments or markets."

154. Hongler, P.; Pistone, P. (2015), p. 21: "evidently, if one tries to allocate income to a jurisdiction with a direct and precise link to the benefits obtained, it seems impossible to achieve a perfect result."

155. Tillinghast also makes the benefit principle rest on mere presumptions: "all individuals and legal entities that benefit (or may reasonably presumed to benefit from their connecting with the US) should share in the burden of supporting the nation through taxes." *See* Tillinghast, D.R. (1984), p. 242.

156. Barna, T. (1945), p. 3. He added that "it is impossible to speak of the burden of taxation without considering, at the same time, the benefits from expenditure made out of such taxation." Buchanan shares his view, as he believes that the traditional difficulties derived by the benefit principle should not be deterrent and that the benefit principle "should not be left out" of the

the State concerned and would largely depend on the nature of each income tax. We will later refer to the ones we suggest for CITs in section §2.02[B][2] and further, in Chapter 4 we will try to translate these ideas into manageable and pragmatic rules.

Notwithstanding the evident utility of the proposed presumptive benefit principle, it also shows notable deficiencies, as it is inherently unable to provide certain responses when it comes to the imposition of taxes. Most notably, it will not serve to measure the extent of the tax liability in income taxes, that is, the calculation of the tax base and the decision on the relevant tax rate.[157] The reason is that there is no reliable proportionality between the amount of income arising from a certain economic activity and the amount of public goods that could have contributed to generate such income.[158] For example, it may well be the case that a company whose activity is heavily reliant on public infrastructures is unable to be profitable while, on the other hand, a company whose activity does not require the use of any public service whatsoever may be in a position to make huge profits. However, this does not preclude States from potentially use the conventional benefit principle for the calculation of taxes (other than income taxes), such as "casual taxes" or "user charges," i.e., taxes paid in direct exchange for a specific public service provided by the State or the transfer of the right to use a particular public domain. In these cases, the tax amount would generally be a fixed sum ("poll tax") that tends to depart from the cost of the service or the value of the right to use the public domain.[159]

If one interprets the benefit principle as a strict quid pro quo exchange between the government and the individuals (either from a global or an individual point of view), the principle is prone to show further notable deficiencies.[160] In the first place, it poses an important technical one, as there does not seem to be a precise manner to impute the shares of the common benefit from public services to specific persons.[161]

---

theoretical framework justifying taxation. *See* Buchanan, J.M. (1960), p. 22. On the other hand, there are many skeptical voices despising the utility of principles guiding the allocation of taxing rights, the benefit principle among them. *See* for example Schön, W. (2009), p. 93: "the outcome of the game is truly open and one should not look for the holy grail of a natural allocation of taxing rights."

157. Georg von Schanz stated that the benefit theory should only serve to determine the group of people liable for tax. Once this group is identified, the degree of the tax liability may be fixed on the basis of other rules and the benefit principle should not play any role in this regard. Schanz, G. (1892), p. 374 (free translation by Harris, P.A. (1996), p. 277). In the same vein, *see* Schön, W. (2009), p. 76, Vogel, K. (1988d), p. 57 ("a standard for measuring individual tax burdens, however, cannot be derived from this kind of reciprocity (...) the theory of justification of taxation cannot, therefore, provide and answer to the question how to shape a just tax rate") and Kaufman, N.H. (1988), p. 158 ("a decision to implement a tax based on benefit theory does not mandate the selection of a specific tax base or a particular rate structure").
158. Schön, W. (2009), pp. 75-76: "even if the use of public goods by a taxpayer may bear some relationship with the size and nature of the business (the use of public infrastructure, the education of workers or the protection of intellectual property), the final outcome—the profit-bears no such relationship," McLure, C.E. (Jr) (2000b), pp. 1288-1289 and Báez Moreno, A. (2015), p. 270.
159. Buchanan, J.M. (1960), p.12 and Mill, J.S. (1848), p. 622.
160. Buchanan, J.M. (1960), p. 13.
161. Dodge, J.M. (2005), p. 399, Buchanan, J.M. (1960), pp. 13-14, Schön, W. (2009), p. 76 and Báez Moreno, A. (2015), pp. 270-271.

Second, when it comes to the identification of the public services concerned, it should be borne in mind that a significant portion of public funds may be intended to finance the "general welfare" (i.e., services of a very vague and general character) which does not provide precise, quantifiable and individualized benefits to individuals and groups of persons.[162] And third, one should take into consideration that public revenues do not generally serve solely to defray public services, they may also be used to further distribute goals by shifting wealth between the different social classes.[163]

We do not think the strict quid pro quo approach is either ethically acceptable in the present times or practicable when it comes to the imposition of income taxes. So, while acknowledging the risks and challenges identified in the previous paragraph, we believe none of them would affect the role we intend to attribute to the presumptive benefit principle as a guideline underlying tax connection factors. In the first place, there is no need to individualize or quantify the specific benefits to specific taxpayers. With regard to the second and third observation, the fact that tax revenues are used to cover services of general character or for wealth redistribution purposes does not preclude us from using the presumptive benefit principle the way we intend to do.

In a nutshell, we could say that we do not adhere to the traditional strict conception of the benefit principle but rather call for the use of this presumptive benefit principle as a general guideline for the purposes of identifying the community of taxpayers of a certain State, in line with the postulates of the aforementioned "entitlement theory."

Lastly, we intend to briefly note the role that the ability to pay principle can perform in this scenario and further explain why both can coexist and complement each other.

As opposed to the benefit principle, the ability to pay principle is inherently unable to guide us in the identification of the taxpayers that ought to become subject to a certain State's tax jurisdiction.[164] For example, it is unable to indicate which part of the income should be taxed in which State in a cross-border scenario.[165] This being so, the ability to pay principle will not come into play until the benefit principle first fulfills its function and identifies the community of taxpayers that "belongs" to the State concerned.[166]

Once the community of taxpayers has been properly identified (e.g., in benefit terms), inter-individual equity is tasked to ensure equal treatment at the domestic

162. Buchanan, J.M. (1960), pp. 13-14. He believes that the first reason is merely a technical challenge (that could eventually be overcome under certain circumstances) while the second one constitutes a theoretical (even ethical) rejection of the benefit principle. Schön states that the supposed benefits obtained by a taxpayer from the procurement of public goods and services are often not observable (Schön, W. (2009), p. 76).
163. Schön, W. (2009), p. 76.
164. Musgrave, R.A. (1959), p. 63 ("it does not tell us just how the tax burden is to be distributed. Worse still, it disregards the expenditure side of the problem") and Zornoza Pérez, J. (2013), p. 5.
165. Vogel, K. (1988c), p. 398 ("if the tax claims of the two States collide in such ways, sacrifice theory cannot give preference to taxation by either State") and Mössner, J.M. (2006), p. 505.
166. Kaufman, N.H. (1988), p. 164: "(it) takes for granted that the government has properly identified its taxpayers."

level[167] between the specific taxpayers belonging to such community.[168] In general terms, the ability to pay principle is regarded as a common yardstick of equality in tax matters, meaning that it would determine which taxpayers should be deemed to be in an equal economic position. This being so, inter-individual equity would demand that taxpayers in an equal economic position (e.g., same ability to pay) should be subject to the same amount of tax.[169] This generally involves the measurement of the tax liability of each specific taxpayer, in particular the calculation of the tax base (total amount that is subject to taxation)[170] and the election of the relevant tax rate (when applied to the tax base, it indicates the amount of tax to pay).[171] With regard the former, the ability to pay principle has generally served as a basis to grant tax exemptions for a certain minimum of income that corresponds to the amount that the citizen would be expected to need to effectively meet his/her basic needs. With regard to the latter, it has traditionally been used to advocate for progressive tax rates in cases in which States wish to redistribute wealth by means of their income tax systems.

The usefulness of the ability to pay (and by extension the inter-individual equity) principle begins and ends with the measurement of the taxpayer's tax liability, i.e., the tax base and the applicable tax rate.[172] And this is precisely the most relevant (and maybe sole) contribution of the principle.[173] Beyond this, it seems to lose its meaning.[174]

---

167. Kaufman, N.H. (1988), p. 164: "inter-individual equity in taxation is primarily a domestic issue."
168. Schanz, G. (1892), pp. 9-10: "tax basis and tax rate are two different subjects (...) tax liability is made dependent upon an economic relation: after the circle of taxable persons has been determined (...) society may say: each person economically bound to me is taxed (...) to exonerate the economically weak (...) according to a progressive system." (free translation by Vogel, K. (1988), p. 219).
169. Kaufman, N.H. (1988), pp. 156-157: "inter-individual equity concerns the nature and extent of an individual responsibility to support the government financially and the relative amount of each individual's obligation to do so in relation to the obligations of other individuals." *See also* Mössner, J.M. (2006), p. 505.
170. Dodge, J.M. (2005), p. 449: "although the ability to pay norm often is said to be imprecise in its implementation, it prescribes the defining characteristics of an income tax base, although the extent of this prescription may be debated." The common assumption is that the amount of income regularly obtained by a person is the best measure of his/her ability to pay.
171. Kendrick argues that the principle gives rise to three different theories of taxation: the equal, the equal-proportional and the least-sacrifice theory. According to the first one, taxes would be laid in such a manger that the sacrifices of all taxpayers are equal. As regards the second one, the tax amount would bear an equal proportion to the respective taxpayers' incomes. Lastly, the third one would advocate for a system in which taxes would be laid first on the incomes of the very rich, and only when these incomes are reduced to the level of the rich, then the rich would be taxed, and so on. *See* Kendrick, M.S. (1939), p. 95.
172. Kaufman states that inter-individual equity merely addresses the content of the tax base and the rate structure. Kaufman, N.H. (1988), p. 166. Gadžo argues that this standard merely serves the purpose of "quantifying, in monetary terms, the duty of a person to contribute to the society" (Gadžo, S. (2016), p. 182).
173. In the same vein, *see* Schön, W. (2009), p. 73: "ability to pay helps to define the cake but it does not help to slice it."
174. Vogel argued that the primary goal of all the German advocates for the sacrifice theory was to introduce a progressive income tax and, once this was achieved, the theory lost its "moral impact." In particular, and contrary to the benefit principle, it does not serve to provide a basic justification for taxation. *See* Vogel, K. (1988d), pp. 30-31.

[B] The Application of the Presumptive Benefit Principle in Corporate Income Taxation

In the present section we intend to determine the specific manner in which the presumptive benefit principle could effectively be observed in corporate income taxation.

The recognition of the "corporate fiction," i.e., that a company is a separate legal person for tax purposes independent from its shareholders (Chapter 3 section §3.01[A]), theoretically implies the recognition of its faculty to have its own ability to pay (independent and separate from that of its shareholders) and to use and enjoy the public benefits provided by the State (equally independent from the use and enjoyment by its shareholders).[175] This being so, if CITs were to be guided as any other income taxes by the (presumptive) benefit and the ability to pay principles, their regulation should theoretically regard the ability to pay of the company per se, as well as the benefits used and enjoyed by the own company, regardless of the situation of its shareholders.

To this effect, we will first determine which of the public benefits defrayed and provided by the States are susceptible to be used and enjoyed by companies (section §2.02[B][1]). Second, we will ascertain how tax connecting factors may in fact regard such use and enjoyment in practice (section §2.02[B][2]).

[1] Public Benefits That Are Susceptible to Be Used and Enjoyed by Companies

Jurisdictions may allocate their funds to a great number of varied ends. Of all the benefits they may potentially provide to their subjects,[176] only some of them are susceptible to be used and enjoyed (either directly or indirectly) by these legal fictions.[177] We will now proceed to classify such benefits into the next groups:

(a) Major public infrastructures. This category encompasses infrastructures related to transportation (e.g., road and/or railway network, airports and airways, harbors, canals, bridges, tunnels, pipelines, etc.) and communication (e.g., telecommunication networks of all sorts).

175. Marian, O. (2013), p. 1626: "The underlying assumptions (...) are that the corporation is the true beneficiary of government-created public goods, and that the corporate entity is a truly separate being from the individuals involved with it."

176. Fleming, J.C. (Jr.); Peroni, R.J.; Shay, S.E. (2002), p. 90, Avi-Yonah, R. (1997), p. 520 and Pinto, D. (2003), pp. 17-23.

177. Marian, O. (2013b), p. 474: "corporations, just like individuals, benefit from government-created public goods, and it is therefore justifiable that they pay for them." A study carried out in the US in the 1990s estimated that 13.8% of the state-local public expenditure directly or indirectly benefited businesses. The estimation covered the totality of expenditure programs specifically aimed at businesses (e.g., agricultural and water transportation terminals) as well as a proportionate apportionment of the so-called prorated programs (e.g., public buildings, legislative and financial administrations) and "joint" or "shared" expenditures (police and fire, transportation, etc.). *See* Oakland, W.H., Testa, W.A. (1996), pp. 8-9.

(b) General public policies which require financial support. This category refers to policies that entail the adoption of political measures, frequently accompanied by a significant economic investment. These policies seek diverse objectives, as the fostering of legal certainty (provision of a legal framework along with a system which ensures its compliance), a conducive business environment (e.g., the adoption of measures to keep exchange rates stable and interest low, boost the confidence of both business and consumers, ensure a safe and transparent financial system, etc.)[178] and a stable social order along with a just society (assistance for the most deprived, wealth redistribution system) among many others.

(c) Provision of general services for the community. This is the case for services of a general character and scope which tend to benefit all members of the community, including companies. E.g., water and energy supply, police and fire protection, judiciary system, postal service, waste disposal and recycling services, public safety, national security, military protection, etc.

(d) Provision of services targeted for individuals with an indirect benefit for companies. These services are directly enjoyed by individuals but produce positive externalities to companies. E.g., education and healthcare greatly contribute to a healthy and educated workforce[179] or market of customers.

[2] Factors Relying on the Assumption of Use and Enjoyment of Public Benefits by the Company

Once it has been ascertained that companies have the ability to use and enjoy a great number of public benefits under conditions equivalent to individuals, the next question that arises is which situations may allow us to assume that the corporate taxpayer would find itself in a position to access and presumably use and enjoy such public benefits in line with the considerations exposed in section §2.02[A]. As noted above, the tax legislator should identify the *indicia* whose presence in the territory concerned is visible and easily ascertainable and further allow us to make the aforementioned assumption.

The following two sections precisely intend to identify such *indicia* upon which the relevant tax connecting factors should later rest. The selected indicia should lead us to presuppose an effective or, at least, potential benefit by the company from the services and infrastructures provided by the State concerned in accordance with the presumptive benefit principle.

---

178. Graetz, M.J.; O'Hear, M.M. (1997), p. 521 quoting T.S. Adams "a large part of the cost of Government is traceable to the necessity of maintaining a suitable business environment."

179. For example, Marian suggested that AOI (company that belongs to the Apple group) could be viewed as benefiting from some form of public good in the US, as its skilled labor force. *See* Marian, O. (2013b), p. 474.

[a] The Performance of a Physical Economic Activity in the Territory Concerned

As a matter of fact, it seems that a company would only find itself in a position to use and enjoy the State's services and infrastructures to the extent that it has a significant presence in its territory. More precisely, we could reach such conclusion insofar as the company is effectively carrying on an economic activity within its borders. Taxing a company's profits on these grounds may be regarded as justified on the assumption that the sole presence of economic activities within a sovereign territory generally entails the enjoyment of the public services and infrastructures provided by the State concerned.[180] Let us think of a company that maintains a manufacturing facility, a warehouse and various stores in the territory of a State through which it produces, distributes and eventually sells its own products. These facts alone allow us to presume that the company is likely to be using most, if not all, the services we enumerated in section §2.02[B][1]. This being so, if tax connecting factors relied on factors related to the presence of a relevant economic activity within the territory, taxation would not be based on an actual, self-evident and demonstrated effective enjoyment of public benefits: it would rather be based on certain *indicia* implying that such enjoyment is very likely to have occurred.

[b] The Access to the Market of Customers of the Territory Concerned Through Remote Means

The question arises as to whether this assumption should be extended to economic activities that do not entail a physical presence in the territory concerned and still allow the company to reach its market.

This is a particularly topical question; as the past few decades have witnessed an unparalleled advance in communications, technology and transportations resulting in an undeniable increasing ability to reach new markets without the need to maintain a physical presence in the territory concerned. It is now entirely possible to either provide services remotely (e.g., cloud computing, e-mails, videoconferences) or conduct sales by remote means (e.g., websites, smartphone "apps," etc.). Let us think

180. The Musgraves concluded that a State should be entitled to tax the income resulting from activities taking place within its borders. *See* Musgrave, P.B.; Musgrave, R.A. (1972), p. 71. This way, the practical implications of the territoriality principle would not differ much from those derived from the presumptive benefit principle. *See* Brown, F.B. (2011), p. 591: "the economic nexus basis for sourcing is best understood as a surrogate for the benefits principle -that is, the location of economic activities is where the taxpayer receives government benefits that justify a source tax" and p. 608: "numerous public benefits arise from government services that are provided in countries where taxpayers conduct income-producing activities." He then enumerates some of the most common benefits that a company may derive from the States where its economic activities take place. *See also* Vann, R.J. (2003), p. 145: "if we think of source taxation in terms of benefit theory, then the place where the relevant activity of the payer is based has some claim if the income recipient is relying on institutions in that place" and McLure, C.E. (Jr) (2000), p. 6:12, footnote 14: "most of those costs (governmental costs from which a company obtains benefits) are probably related to production or distribution."

for example of a company that uses a website to reach the market of a certain State and confines itself to buying the products from foreign providers and having them delivered right to its customers' homes.

It is clear that the scope of benefits that would be within the company's reach in these circumstances would be more limited in cases in which it is not physically present in the State. For example, the company would rarely be in the position to enjoy general public services as the police/fire protection or the water supply.[181] However, we believe the company would still be likely to benefit to a greater or lesser extent of many other of the services and infrastructures enumerated in section §2.02[B][1], either directly or indirectly.[182]

In all the abovementioned scenarios, the host State would be after all providing a market for the company. It is an incontestable fact that business profits only arise where supply and demand meet.[183] However, the relevant question for the purposes of this section is whether we may infer from the presence of a considerable market of customers in a certain territory that the State has contributed financially to build this market and further make it possible the relevant transaction that would ultimately give rise to the profit. Our response is positive, and we will now proceed to explain why.

In the first place, the existence of a potential market of well-educated, healthy and prosperous customers is clearly not a random spontaneous event, but rather the consequence of diverse circumstances including, *inter alia*, their hard work and efforts, the socio-economic context in which they operate and a number of policies and services promoted (and defrayed) by their government over the years to foster their general well-being, access to education and healthcare, economic prosperity, labor

181. McLure, C.E. (Jr.) (2000), pp. 6:5-6:6: "it seems that in this world most of the public services that benefit business firms (...) do so only if the firm has a physical presence in the country." Pinto, D. (2003), p. 21: "many of the services described earlier (e.g., police and fire protection) (...) would only be available and relevant in the case where such businesses maintain a physical presence in source countries."

182. Schön, W. (2018), section 1: "economic allegiance does not require any more the taxpayer's physical presence, it is sufficient to command significant digital presence in order to penetrate the market and to benefit from the public goods which a country provides."

183. This fact alone (beyond benefit considerations) has frequently served as an argument to justify the tax claim of the market jurisdiction. *See* Devereux, M.; de La Feria, R. (2014), p. 11: "it is from sales that profits are generated, without sales there would be no income to tax." The four experts responsible for the first MC also acknowledged the importance of this factor: "the oranges upon the trees in California are not acquired wealth until they are picked, and not even at that stage until they packed, and not even at that stage until they are transported to the place where demand exists and until they are put where the consumer can use them" (*See* Economic and Financial Commission for the League of Nations (1923): Report on Double Taxation, p. 23). *See also* Schoueri, L.E.; Galendi, R.A. (2017), which refer to Kirchhoff's theory to conclude: "if an individual derives income, this is due both to her/his personal effort and to the existence of the market: it would be a waste of effort if there was not a market where one could act." Along the same lines, *see* Hongler, P.; Pistone, P. (2015), p. 33: "a strict understanding of the principle of origin according to which only individuals on the supply side can create value ignores the fact that the demand side is also value creating. For a mere economic perspective, the inputs (i.e. the supply) and the outputs (i.e. the demand) of an enterprise lead to value creation and could guide as a principle of income allocation." Lastly, Schön argues that "it cannot be disputed that the existence of a customer base in a territory, leading to the transfer of financial means from the customers to the taxpayer, forms a strong economic allegiance" (Schön, W. (2009), p. 92).

protection, etc.[184] There is no doubt that companies are likely to obtain greater profits from States whose citizens are safe, healthy, have their basic needs met and further enjoy a considerable purchasing power, circumstances that are to a certain extent due to public investments.

Second, the presence of an attractive market of potential customers in a territory does not on its own lead to sales. A framework that is conducive to electronic trade and remote transactions is as necessary as the market itself, and this framework is equally the result of the proper functioning of public infrastructures, services and policies. An appropriate infrastructure of telecommunications and supply of energy would ensure high-quality internet access; an extensive transport network together with a fast and efficient postal service would enable a quick and guaranteed delivery of the products; an appropriate legal framework supported by an efficient and reliable judicial system would enable the protection of IP rights, the enforcement of payment in the context of electronic transactions and the protection of both business and customer's rights and interests among others; and lastly, waste disposal and recycling services would enable the proper disposal of the packaging materials.[185] In scenarios in which the company confines itself to selling digital content through a website, the response would greatly differ, as the only public services that would still be at its reach would be certain infrastructures (mostly telecommunication network and supply of energy), the legal framework and the judicial system.

The abovementioned examples reveal that a company trading remotely with customers residing in a State without being physically present in its territory would still be in a position to use, enjoy or, at least, indirectly benefit from the State's services and infrastructures. This assumption has served certain scholars to justify the legitimate demand of market jurisdictions to tax the profits that companies derive from the remote sales or provision of services with their residents,[186] while the argument has not historically convinced the OECD, at least before the advent of the BEPS project.[187]

---

184. *See* Fleming, J.C. (Jr.); Peroni, R.J.; Shay, S.E. (2002), p. 91 and Brown, F.B. (2011), pp. 609-610: "the market in any country could not exist without the necessary physical, economic, and legal infrastructure, and this is largely a result of governmental functions. And by accessing a country's market through the sale of goods and services, a taxpayer is benefiting from these governmental activities, thus justifying a (...) tax" and p. 619: "a portion of the income should be assigned to that country even without the taxpayer's actual presence in the country."
185. Pinto, D. (2003), pp. 21-23, Hongler, P.; Pistone, P. (2015), p. 22, Cockfield, A. (2003), p. 3, Gadžo, S. (2016), p. 227, McLure, C.E. (Jr.) (2000), pp. 6:6 and 6:13 ("sellers of digitized content would have nor market in a country lacking basic telecommunications infrastructure or whose population lacks computer skills"), Brown, F.B. (2011), p. 611 ("one would be unable to spend and consume income within a given country in the absence of the governmental services that support physical, legal, and economic infrastructure as well as public safety") and Schön, W. (2018), section 6 ("the existence of a market requires a customer base but also some means of communication as well as a legal infrastructure—to enforce contracts—and depending on the distribution channels also a specific technical infrastructure—from motorways to data highways. As the sellers or providers of services benefit from the existence of these factors, they should pay for it").
186. This has clearly been the case in the context of destination-based corporate tax proposal (*see* Devereux, M.; de La Feria, R. (2014), p. 13: "countries where consumers reside provide services that are complementary to the consumption of their residents" and Avi-Yonah, R. (2000), pp. 1670-1675) and the sales factor of formulary apportionment systems (*see* Durst, M.C. (2014): "the market for goods and services within a country is a kind of natural resource

[3] Interim Conclusions

It is an undeniable fact that the number of benefits within the reach of the company and the extent of its effective or potential use are expected to be greater when the company physically performs an economic activity in the State concerned than in cases in which the company reaches its market through remote means.[188]

At this stage we should recall that some tax connecting factors operate as all-or-nothing rules that merely identify the taxpayers that should belong to the community of a certain State, while not getting involved in the quantification of its tax liability.[189] This being so, the reduced degree of enjoyment of public benefits would not be taken into account in the form of a reduced tax liability. This fact should make governments thoroughly reflect on the advisability of extending the presumptive benefit assumption to remote economic activities and thereby making tax connecting factors rely on it.

In our opinion, the assumption should stand considering the great amount of public benefits that companies would presumably be in the position to enjoy while conducting remote economic activities in a certain market jurisdiction.[190] However, it may be appropriate for tax connecting factors to give, where possible, more relative

located within the country's borders, and income from the exploitation of that resource should be apportioned at least in part to the country's tax base"). *See also* Vogel, K. (1988c), p. 401: "taxation by the sales State must be considered under the aspect of inter-nations equity as well. It cannot convincingly be denied that providing a market contributes to the sales income at least to some extent as providing the goods does. There is no valid objection therefore against a claim of the sales State to tax part of the sales income." Vann R.J. (2003), p. 145: "if we think of source taxation in terms of benefit theory, then the place where the relevant activity of the payer is based has some claim if the income recipient is relying on institutions in that place (...) It gives a claim to the place of sale in the business context in the sense of the location of the buyer (...) Such a justification (...) will be based on some measure of benefit from the institutions in the jurisdiction." *See also* Skaar, A.A. (1991), pp. 559-560, McLure, C.E. (Jr.) (2000), pp. 6.5-6.6, Gadžo, S. (2016), p. 227 and Tadmore, N. (2012), p. 5. On the other hand, Schön notes that there may be other options to grant taxing rights to the market jurisdiction on benefit grounds beyond income taxation (e.g., user fees, indirect taxes, etc.), *see* Schön, W. (2018), section 6.

187. OECD (2003): Are the current treaty rules for taxing business profits appropriate for e-commerce? Final report, p. 14: "(the Technical Advisory group) therefore rejected the suggestion that the mere fact that a country provides the market where an enterprise's goods and services are supplied should allow that country to consider that a share of the profits of the enterprise is derived therefrom (...) they do not regard an enterprise which may have access to a country's market as necessarily 'using' that country's infrastructure and, even if that were the case, they consider that such mere use of a country's general infrastructure would be too incidental to the business profit-making process to consider that a significant part of the profits are attributable to that country."
188. Pinto maintains a divergent opinion, as he believes that the amount of public benefits that may be accessed by companies could be "equally (if not more)" relevant in an electronic commerce context. *See* Pinto, D. (2003), p. 19.
189. This is the conclusion we reached back in Chapter 2 section §2.02[A].
190. McLure, following the "entitlement theory" (equivalent to the presumptive benefit principle and already referred to in Chapter 2 section §2.02[A]), argues that entitlement to tax corporate profits exists "any time a firm avails itself of the productive resources or the market of a nation" (McLure, C.E. (Jr) (2000), P. 6:4).

weight to *indicia* revealing a physical economic activity in the relevant territory than to those that do not.[191]

§2.03 PRELIMINARY CONCLUSIONS

In section §2.01[A] we collected relevant data on the economic and tax presence of the Apple group across the globe so as to demonstrate the existence and seriousness of the profit shifting phenomenon by our own means and throughout a real-life example. Figures 1 and 2 evidenced a clear lack of correlation between the location of the tax bases and the location of the indicators revealing the presence of a significant activity (either managerial, value-adding or commercial) in the region concerned. In particular, data concerning Ireland constituted the clearest evidence of profit shifting, as this jurisdiction surprisingly captured 64% of the group's global EBITDA in 2011 while not contributing whatsoever to the management of the group nor its R&D activities, barely participating in the production process (with just one component supplier and one assembly facility) and representing merely 1% of Apple's worldwide market.

From the reading of section §2.01[A][2] it may be inferred that the transfer of profits carried out by Apple to jurisdictions with no business activity does not result from breaches to the letter or the spirit of the laws. On the contrary, as declared by Apple itself and recognized by those who have examined its case in depth, its tax planning strategy fully complies with the tax laws of the countries involved and does not fall into abusive behaviors. This being the case, it seems that profit shifting is not a problem of tax compliance but rather a problem of rules, as the own OECD came to recognize. On the question of which specific rules ought to be blamed in the particular case of Apple, we identified two major groups. The first group comprises two very specific regimes that pertain to the US domestic tax legislation (the regimes on CSAs and CFCs along with the check-the-box provisions) while the second group involves rules that reproduce two fundamental structural paradigms underlying CITs: residence and source. The preliminary assessment of this latter group of rules ultimately suggests that the profit shifting phenomenon may be, to some extent, the result of the misguided and out-of-date legal configuration of such paradigms. Chapter 3 will later delve deeper into these concerns.

There are good reasons to believe that profit shifting is a global and widespread phenomenon that goes well beyond the case under review. It is equally clear that there is broad political consensus on the fact that this phenomenon is troublesome and ought to be addressed and mitigated as a matter of urgency (section §2.01[B]). However, the same international organizations (OECD and EU) that have recently opened fire on profit shifting, have failed to provide solid policy reasons to uphold and justify their belligerent attitude towards it. In other words, they fail to explain in tax policy terms why corporate profits ought to be taxed wherever the company carries out its economic activities.

191. In fact, the proposals that will be exposed in Chapter 4 will take this observation into account.

In the light of this, we intended to put forward a specific tax policy guideline that aims to provide both a consistent theoretical rationale that may help sustain the discourse of rejection towards the profit shifting phenomenon and, at the same time, a new guideline whose observance may help counteract profit shifting risks (section §2.02). To this effect, we called for the recovery of a long-standing principle (the benefit principle) but advocated for a very peculiar understanding of this policy guideline that largely deviates from its conventional sense ("the presumptive benefit principle") (section §2.02[A]). In a nutshell, we argued that the presumptive benefit principle should ideally guide the determination of a State's community of taxpayers, so it should inspire the tax rules that ultimately identify the taxpayers that would become subject to a State's tax jurisdiction (the "tax connecting rules"). These rules should not demand a case-by-case demonstration of the effective use and enjoyment of the State's public services by the taxpayer, but rather rely on certain *indicia* whose presence in the territory concerned is visible and easily ascertainable and further allows us to assume that the taxpayer is in a position to (effectively or potentially) use and enjoy the State's services and infrastructures. Subsequently, we intended to determine the specific manner in which the presumptive benefit principle could be complied with in the context of corporate income taxation, as we noted that the observance of such principle may help prevent and mitigate profit shifting risks (section §2.02[B]). To this end, we first identified the public services and infrastructures that are susceptible to be used or enjoyed by companies as such (section §2.02[B][1]) and further devoted to identifying a number of *indicia* whose presence in the territory of a State allowed us to assume that the company finds itself in a position to use/enjoy such public benefits (section §2.02[B][2]). In short, a genuine alignment of corporate income taxation with the presumptive benefit principle would necessarily require tax connecting factors to rely on the aforementioned *indicia*.

CHAPTER 3

Three Fundamental Paradigms Underlying Corporate Income Taxation Are Inconsistent with the Presumptive Benefit Principle and Tend to Inherently Trigger Profit Shifting Risks

Throughout the present chapter we will explore whether corporate income taxation is already aligned with the presumptive benefit principle and is therefore well equipped to confront the profit shifting phenomenon.

Our hypothesis is that rules identifying the corporate taxpayers that become subject to a State's tax jurisdiction and thus ought to pay CITs therein (i.e., the "tax connecting factors") are not consistent with the aforementioned principle. In other words, we tend believe that they contribute to make it possible for taxpayers to book their tax bases in jurisdictions other than those where they presumably derive their public benefits (i.e., to say, wherever they perform their economic activities, either physically or remotely).[192] In particular, we will devote our attention to three main paradigms whose configuration ultimately answer to the question of which State is entitled to tax the profits of which company. These paradigms have been underlying CITs worldwide almost from their inception: the separate-entity approach along with the ALS (section §3.01), the definition of corporate tax residence (section §3.02), and the definition of source for tax purposes with a particular emphasis on the PE concept (section §3.03).

We will examine their respective origins, reflect on their supposed rationales and briefly describe how they tend to be translated into legal provisions by analyzing common patterns followed by States. However, our main goal is to demonstrate that

192. We exposed this hypothesis back in the introductory chapter and further confirmed our suspicions in Chapter 2 section §2.01[A][2] in the Apple case.

they are inconsistent with the presumptive benefit principle (Chapter 2 section §2.02) and have thus become fundamental sources of profit shifting risks, in the sense that they enable, to a greater or lesser extent, corporate taxpayers to detach taxable profits from the jurisdictions where they derive their public benefits and instead book them in the jurisdiction of their choice. In other words, we intend to evidence that they all play a significant role in situations as that in illustrated in Figures 1 and 2 (Chapter 2 section §2.01[A][1]).

During our analysis, we will make reference to both domestic tax legislations and bilateral tax treaties. In this latter case, we will use the OECD MC and the OECD Transfer Pricing Guidelines (hereinafter "OECD TPG") as the primary points of reference, although references will also be made to the United Nations Model Convention (UN MC) and the United States Model Convention (hereinafter "US MC") where appropriate. It should be noted that this chapter will assess both the previous and the updated versions of these soft law instruments (i.e., 2014-2017 OECD MC, 2010-2017 OECD TPG, 2010-2017 UN MC and 2006-2016 US MC). The decision to also consider the contents of the preceding versions is based on three main reasons. The first one is that the case study (Chapter 2 section §2.01[A]) we used to reveal the problem is based on data as of 2011 and is thus a consequence of the preexisting legal framework at that time. If the intention is to diagnose the causes of such problem, it seems coherent to look at the legal framework then in effect. The second reason is that there are around 3,500 tax treaties currently in force that are largely based on prior versions of the MCs and it will take decades to renegotiate them to update them to the latest versions, despite the (limited) effects of the Multilateral Convention to Implement Tax Treaty Related Measures to Prevent BEPS.[193] The last reason is that we intend to evaluate later in Chapter 4 whether certain amendments introduced to these latest versions of the MCs and the OECD TPG and the outcomes derived from the BEPS project (in particular those affecting transfer pricing and PE rules) are more consistent with the presumptive benefit principle and will thus contribute to effectively narrow the gap between the economic and the tax presence of the companies throughout the world.

193. This process may be relatively quicker for the signatories of the Multilateral Convention to Implement Tax Treaty Related Measures to Prevent Base Erosion and Profit Shifting, which intends to swiftly implement tax treaty measures derived from the BEPS project while saving their signatories from the burden of bilaterally renegotiating their treaties. *See* the text of the Convention: http://www.oecd.org/tax/treaties/multilateral-convention-to-implement-tax-treaty-related-measures-to-prevent-BEPS.pdf (last accessed on January 10, 2019). Potentially, the Multilateral Instrument may update up to 1200 tax treaties to the latest 2017 OECD MC (*see* http://www.oecd.org/tax/treaties/multilateral-instrument-BEPS-tax-treaty-information-brochure.pdf, last accessed to data on January 10, 2019) but we have reasons not to be so optimistic. First, because the number of signatories is still modest (*see* http://www.oecd.org/tax/treaties/beps-mli-signatories-and-parties.pdf last accessed on January 10, 2019). Second, because signatories are entitled to opt for reservations and optional provisions, and thus the resulting changes to their respective treaties—also subject to the position expressed by their counterpart-are likely to reflect only some of the amendments introduced to the 2017 OECD MC (*see* http://www.oecd.org/tax/treaties/mli-matching-database.htm last accessed on January 10, 2019).

§3.01 THE SEPARATE ENTITY APPROACH AND THE INHERENT LIMITATIONS OF THE ARM'S LENGTH STANDARD MAY ENTAIL PROFIT SHIFTING RISKS

In this section we will depart from the general treatment of companies as taxable entities separate from their respective shareholders in the context of both stand-alone companies and companies integrated in corporate groups or multinationals (section §3.01[A]). We will first raise the question of whether the separate entity approach effectively contributes to the possibility of shifting profits to selected jurisdictions (section §3.01[B]). As the answer is positive, we will then proceed to analyze whether the ALS, which was originally intended to counteract the profit shifting risks that the separate entity approach poses, effectively accomplishes its original mission or, on the contrary, still allows taxpayers to shift profits to jurisdictions other than those where business activities are taken place (section §3.01[C]).

[A] The Recognition of Companies as Separate Legal Subjects for Income Tax Purposes

Companies are not real persons in the traditional sense of the word. However, at a certain time of history, domestic legislations began to confer them a legal status analogous to the one enjoyed by natural persons, comprised by a variety of rights, duties and obligations.

In order to understand the *raison d'être* of companies it is important to first become acquainted with the context in which they were born.[194] After the industrial revolution, the volume of trade between nations soared. However, trade was a risky and capital consuming business at that time, frequently requiring the amalgamation of personal fortunes. This being so, there was a growing need to regulate the manner in which capital was invested and the rights of the investors. It is in this context that registered companies began to spring up in the domestic legislations of many jurisdictions,[195] rapidly becoming a regular vehicle through which most investments were conducted. Its success was largely due to the concession of limited liability of its members, which provided a significant incentive to invest in businesses, particularly those involving greater risks.[196]

The nature of companies may be analyzed from a legal and an economic standpoint.[197] From a legal perspective, a company is a sort of legal fiction or abstraction which receives a treatment analogous to that received by a natural person. This being so, legislations generally grant them certain powers and obligations similar to those of natural persons, namely, the capacity to own property, pursue legal actions,

194. For further information on the historic origins of corporations *see* Couzin, R. (2002), pp. 11 et seq. and Harris, P.A. (1996), pp. 40-41.
195. For example, the incorporation of companies was first regulated in the UK in 1844 by the Joint Stock Companies Act.
196. Couzin, R. (2002), p. 11.
197. Harris, P.A. (1996), pp. 42-46.

be sued, enter into contracts in their own name, etc. It should be emphasized that their legal personality remains distinct and separate from the personality of its members and is thus subject to a different statutory regime. The so-called separate entity theory erects a wall between the companies and their respective shareholders: a wall whose role is to maintain rights and duties at both levels in separate levels. For example, from a legal perspective, the debts of a company are not debts of a shareholder,[198] income perceived by a company is generally not considered as income of the shareholder either, and legal responsibility that may be held by the company is usually not extended to its shareholders. The "separate entity theory" equally applies to companies whose shares are held by other companies, in a way that companies pertaining to the same corporate group are deemed to be (and thus treated as) separate persons.

From an economic viewpoint, the relationship between companies and their shareholders is not so straightforward. Companies and shareholders may well be regarded as economically independent or as economically integrated (i.e., as an economic single entity).[199]

In the case of widely held companies, a separation of ownership and control is often perceived. The majority of their shareholders resemble more to a lender than to an entrepreneur, since they abdicate their power to run the company in favor of a board of directors or other similar body and merely expect a given return on capital invested, whether in the form of dividend or capital gain. This being so, it is not the shareholders but the board of directors who decide when and in what amount dividends are distributed to shareholders, and for this reason widely held companies and their respective shareholders may be perceived as economically independent.

On the other hand, there is no such separation between ownership and control in the case of closely held companies (e.g., family business) or wholly owned or nearly wholly owned subsidiaries pertaining to the same MNC. In this case, the role of shareholders resembles more the role of an entrepreneur, as they are likely to take decisions on the management, strategy and corporate structure of the company and, most importantly, decide whether and under what conditions dividends are distributed and thus perceived in their personal capacity. As a consequence of all this, as long as there is no clear boundary between ownership and control, companies and their shareholders (whether individuals or companies) may be regarded as economically integrated and thus forming an economic single entity.

Once the nature of the company has been analyzed from both a legal and an economic standpoint, it is time to consider how companies are usually treated for income tax purposes. Since PITs began to emerge nearly two hundred years ago, income perceived by companies was almost invariably included within the ambit of income taxes. At this point, a distinction should be made as to how income derived by a company is ultimately taxed.[200]

198. Pursuant for the aforementioned privilege of limited liability, shareholders are not required to contribute any more to the debts of a corporation than the amount of capital with respect to the shares held.
199. This is the distinction made by Harris. *See* Harris, P.A. (1996), pp. 43-46.
200. These two approaches are analyzed by Harris, P.A. (1996), pp. 50-54 and Lang, M., Staringer, C. (2014). It should be noted that the preference for either of them is a mere policy decision,

On one hand, countries may decide to treat the company as a separate taxpayer, distinct from its shareholders, whose income becomes taxable in its own hands at the time it is perceived.[201] Today this is the general tendency, since the overwhelming majority of countries have CITs in place which impose the tax at the level of the company.[202] According to Harris, this option is particularly convenient for widely held companies because, as it has been exposed above, they may be seen as economically autonomous from their owners.

On the other hand, countries may decide to treat the company as fiscally transparent, in a way that results in the attribution of its profits to the shareholders behind it. Therefore, the profits would flow from the entity who legally perceives them to its owners, becoming taxable in the hands of the latter in proportion to their shareholdings.[203] Under this approach, companies are regarded as mere conduits for income tax purposes. This approach is less common and is usually reserved for closely held or wholly owned entities whose owners handle the management of the entity, since the company and the shareholders are more economically integrated, as it was noted above. The most characteristic example of a transparency regime is the CFC regime, one of the cornerstones of Apple's tax planning scheme (Chapter 2 section §2.01[A][2]).

Although the coexistence of both approaches would seem a priori advisable (i.e., two-level taxation for portfolio investment and transparent taxation for controlling shareholders), domestic tax regimes rarely establish this sort of split approach.[204]

[B] The Separate Entity Approach in the Context of Corporate Groups and the Profit Shifting Risks Posed by Transfer Pricing Manipulation

The following question would be whether the fact of belonging to a corporate group is considered relevant when it comes to the taxation of a company. Or in other words, whether companies integrated in groups are treated differently than stand-alone companies for income tax purposes. There are two main approaches countries may take in this regard. On one hand, they may choose to treat the different members of the groups separately, thus remaining faithful to the abovementioned "separate-entity

although countries tend to assess some of the criteria exposed below when making such decision. Furthermore, certain countries allow taxpayers to choose whether a foreign entity should be considered as transparent or taxable, *see* previous Chapter 2 section §2.01[A][2] on the US check-the-box rule and Lang, M., Staringer, C. (2014), p. 38 (the case of South Korea).

201. Harris, P.A. (1996), pp. 50-51.
202. According to the IFA General Report on qualification of taxable entities, all branch reports confirmed that there is a corporate income tax in place in their respective jurisdictions. *See* Lang, M., Staringer, C. (2014), pp. 23 et seq.
203. According to Harris there are two main methods to implement this approach in practice: the partnership or pass-through method and the full taxation of capital gains. *See* Harris, P.A. (1996), pp. 52-53.
204. Schön explains why the split approach is rarely in place in domestic tax legislations. The first reason could be that, in practice, it would be hard to draw a borderline between controlling and non-controlling shareholders. The second reason is the danger to introduce "sudden" leaps within the continuum of possible arrangements. *See* Schön, W. (2009), p. 108.

approach." On the contrary, they may opt to recognize the corporate group as a whole, thereby ignoring the transactions between the group members and merely looking at outcomes for the overall group[205] precisely due to the (aforementioned) economic integration they enjoy.

While the first approach has become mainstream, as it will be discussed further below, the latter one has not yet enjoyed an equivalent impact. Out of the total of thirty countries that participated in the research on group regimes headed by the International Fiscal Association in 2004, twenty had a group regime in place, although the majority of the remaining ones concluded that the adoption of such regimes was desirable.[206] However, the scope of such regimes is generally quite limited, since the recognition of corporate groups for income tax purposes has rarely transcended national borders, remaining instead in the domestic level.[207] As a consequence, consolidation measures are generally confined to resident companies[208] and, at most, the domestic PEs of non-resident companies,[209] with the only exceptions of Denmark, France and Italy, whose regimes also covered non-resident subsidiaries.[210]

Notwithstanding the above, the "separate-entity approach" is certainly the most widespread approach at the transnational level. This is in part due to the fact that the MCs, without exception, depart from the recognition of each company as a separate subject for income tax purposes.[211] This being so, tax treaties would deter States from adopting group consolidation regimes (unless they explicitly allow them) and would thus encourage them to treat each company separately and further calculate its tax base on the basis of the profits reflected in its accounts,[212] irrespective of whether it belongs to a corporate group or not.

The problem comes with the fact that the separate-entity approach enables corporate groups to significantly reduce their overall tax burden. This is so because it makes it possible for corporate groups to effectively shift taxable profits to selected

205. The most paradigmatic example is the CCCTB Proposal, *see* EU Commission (2011): Proposal for a Council Directive on a Common Consolidated Corporate Tax Base (CCCTB).
206. Masui, Y. (2004), p. 26.
207. Masui, Y. (2004), pp. 53 et seq.
208. Vann identifies two reasons that may explain why consolidation measures are not generally extended to non-resident companies. The first one is that allowing non-resident companies to utilize the rules opens up the potential for manipulating tax jurisdiction rules (e.g., a rule that allow a tax-free transfer of assets between group members may lead to an asset effectively being withdrawn from the tax jurisdiction by a transfer from a resident to a non-resident company). The second one is that group approaches blatantly contradicts the separate-entity approach followed by tax treaties and, as group regimes with transnational effects may be contrary to tax treaties, countries opt to avoid potential conflicts. *See* Vann, R.J. (2003), pp. 133 et seq. and Masui Y. (2004), p. 26.
209. The IFA general report revealed the general trend of jurisdictions affected by EU Law to extend the scope of their regimes to the domestic PEs of non-resident corporations, particularly after the year 2000. *See* Masui, Y. (2004), pp. 54 and 58-62.
210. These group regimes are described in Masui, Y. (2004), pp. 54-57.
211. Both the OECD and the UN MCs adopt this approach. The Preface of the OECD TPG states "OECD member countries have chosen this separate entity approach as the most reasonable means for achieving equitable results and minimizing the risk of unrelieved double taxation."
212. Oestreicher, A., Spengel, C., Koch, R. (2011), pp. 5-6. This paper confirms that all EU Member States tax their corporations individually and oblige them to determine their taxable income separately.

jurisdictions, in which the level of taxation is low and the level of economic activity (if any) may be equally low. As entities within the same group are not constrained by the market forces, they simply need to manipulate the conditions of its intra-group transactions in a way that results in the transfer of profits to subsidiaries resident in such jurisdictions.[213] Naturally, this leaves the door open for companies to shift their taxable profits out of the jurisdictions that provide the services and infrastructures from which they benefit, thus generating outcomes inconsistent with the presumptive benefit principle.

[C] The Arm's Length Standard as a Widespread Corrective: Its Strengths and Weaknesses in Terms of Profit Shifting Risks

Naturally, countries have developed various tools in order to minimize or eliminate the risk of profit shifting in corporate groups via transfer pricing manipulation. Domestic legislations and tax treaties have been relying for a long time in the so-called ALS,[214] which intends to make adjustments to the conditions of intra-group transactions in a way that the tax base of the entity concerned includes the profits it would have obtained if the transaction had occurred with an unrelated entity. Accordingly, the ALS may be regarded as a legal fiction (it leads to treat two related parties "as if" they were unrelated) which embeds and builds upon other fictions (the companies are fictitious themselves).[215]

The current wording of Article 9.1 of the 2017 OECD MC serves as an example of the legal configuration of the ALS:

> Where a) an enterprise of a Contracting State participates directly or indirectly in the management, control or capital of an enterprise of the other Contracting State, or b) the same persons participate directly or indirectly in the management, control or capital of an enterprise of a Contracting State and an enterprise of the other Contracting State, and in either case conditions are made or imposed between the two enterprises in their commercial or financial relations which differ from those which would be made between independent enterprises, then any profits which would, but for those conditions, have accrued to one of the enterprises, but, by reason of those conditions, have not so accrued, may be included in the profits of that enterprise and taxed accordingly.

213. Avi-Yonah believes that transfer pricing manipulation is "one of the simplest ways to avoid taxation" and "one of the most common techniques of tax avoidance," *see* Avi-Yonah, R. (2007c), p. 1. This risk should not be underestimated, since intra-group transactions represent today around 60% of the worldwide transactions according to, for example, Owens, J. (2005), p. 99 and Burke, J. (2011), p. 614.
214. It has been argued that the ALS has become a sort of "internationally accepted principle." *See* for example BEPS report, p. 36 and Avi-Yonah, R. (2007), pp. 102 et seq. For his part, Brauner regards the ALS as the "heart, spirit and the foundation of the current international transfer pricing regime," *see* Brauner, Y. (2008), p. 96.
215. Petrucci, R. (2016), p. 10.

The fundamental function of the ALS is to reduce the leeway corporate groups would otherwise enjoy to manipulate internal prices and to shift profits between jurisdictions, thus preventing groups from "opting" for the allocation of a profit to a jurisdiction of their own choice.[216] From a theoretical perspective, the ALS should be capable of fully preventing profit shifting derived from transfer pricing manipulation, as the adjustments in the tax base of the related parties should in principle eliminate the incentive of MNCs to manipulate their respective transfer prices to allocate profits in selected jurisdictions and thus reduce their overall tax burden.[217] In other words, the ALS should contribute, to some extent, to prevent companies from diverting their taxable profits out of the jurisdictions where they carry out their economic activities and are thus presumably benefitting from public services and infrastructures.

In practice, however, the ALS has proven to be far from infallible in the accomplishment of the aforementioned task. The OECD itself came to recognize that multinationals have been able to "use and/or misapply those rules [the ALS] to separate income from the economic activities that produce that income and to shift it into low-tax environments,"[218] implicitly admitting that the ALS was inherently troublesome in this regard insofar its mere use was prone to lead to these undesirable outcomes. At this stage, it is necessary to ask ourselves why, how and to what extent the ALS fails to prevent MNCs from shifting income away from the jurisdictions where the economic activities are located.

The fundamental flaw of the ALS (or in other words, the main reason behind its inability to satisfactorily fulfill its mission) lies in the ALS itself. That is, the basic failure of the ALS lies in its own nature. Being the ALS an eminently subjective parameter,[219] it makes it possible to equally advocate for the compatibility of two different transfer prices—significantly distant from each other—with the ALS. Navarro considers that the mandate imposed by the ALS is very broad and frequently generates a sort of "grey area" within which taxpayers and tax administrations may move freely and legitimately.[220] He warns that this constitutes a decisive advantage for resourceful taxpayers which may structure their transfer pricing assessment so as to "push the limits" of the ALS and thus get the most convenient pricing within the wide price range demanded by the ALS.[221] On the contrary, less-privileged taxpayers may lack the resources to perform a transfer pricing assessment as solid and convincing.

216. Schön, W. (2010), p. 232.
217. In fact, the ALS has undeniably played a key role in the prevention of profit shifting to jurisdictions. Brauner recognizes that transfer pricing rules are a "necessary component of any international income tax law" and that such legislation "stops MNEs from easily avoiding of significantly reducing taxation by shifting profits to low or no tax jurisdictions." *See* Brauner, Y. (2008), p. 86.
218. BEPS report, p. 19.
219. However much it is based on an economic and supposedly objective analysis. In fact, Wittendorff recognizes that: "the arm's length principle requires subjective, entity-specific valuation, while fair value requires subjective, market-based valuation." *See* Wittendorff, J. (2016), p. 353.
220. Navarro Ibarrola, A. (2016), pp. 57-58.
221. Vann states that the transfer pricing methodology, based on functions, assets and risks, "has been manipulated in practice to allow diversion of profits to low-tax jurisdictions." *See* Vann, R.J. (2010), p. 313.

This structural problem becomes apparent in the next two considerations we will refer to below, which we believe to largely explain why the ALS has been in practice unable to impede the shift of profits to jurisdictions which lack any kind of economic activities. These two considerations are: the asymmetries generated by the choice of the transfer pricing method and the way the inherent complexity of the ALS in practice lead to a two-speed system.

In the first place, we will provide a general overview of the most common methods used for transfer pricing purposes and afterwards we will proceed to argue why the possibility to freely choose any of them generates profit shifting risks.

Transfer pricing methods are used to establish whether the conditions imposed between associated enterprises are consistent with the ALS.[222] Both the OECD and the United Nations (hereinafter "UN") recommend the same five methods,[223] which tend to be the most widespread in the domestic legislations of countries following the standard. These methods are divided into two categories. On one hand, we have the traditional transaction methods, which are comprised by three different methods: the comparable uncontrolled price (hereinafter "CUP"), the resale price (hereinafter "RP") and the cost plus method (hereinafter "C + ").[224] These methods used to take precedence over the other two, although recent updates to the OECD TPG have abandoned this preference by introducing the so-called best method rule.[225] However, they are still regarded as the "most direct means" of establishing whether the conditions agreed by the parties comply with the ALS.[226] As it may be deduced from their respective wording, the characteristic feature of these methods is the fact that they are usually applied on a transaction-by-transaction basis, as they seek comparable prices or margins from uncontrolled transactions.[227] The fact that they generally assess each transaction separately makes them more precise, therefore leading to a relatively narrower range of acceptable prices under the ALS.

222. 2017 OECD TPG, paragraph 2.1.
223. *See* 2017 OECD TPG, Chapter 2 and UN (2013): Practical manual on transfer pricing, Chapter 6.
224. (a) CUP method: it compares the price charged for property or services transferred in a controlled transaction to the price charged in a comparable uncontrolled transaction in comparable circumstances. (b) RP method: it begins with the price at which a product purchased from an associated enterprise is resold to an independent enterprise, and then such price is reduced by a gross margin which appropriately represents the amount a reseller would seek to cover its operating expenses plus the remuneration for the functions performed. (c) C + method: it begins with the costs incurred by the supplier in a controlled transaction for property transferred or services provided to an associated purchaser, and then an appropriate cost-plus markup is added, a mark-up that should be calculated on the basis of the functions performed by the supplier. *See* their respective descriptions in 2017 OECD TPG, paragraphs. 2.14, 2.27 and 2.45.
225. *See* the 1995 OECD TPG, paragraph 3.2; and the current version on 2017 OECD TPG, paragraph 2.2.
226. 2017 OECD TPG, paragraph 2.3.
227. The OECD TPG literally states that "ideally," the ALS should be applied on a transaction-by-transaction basis, but this is only true in the case of the traditional methods. *See* 2017 OECD TPG, paragraph 3.9.

On the other hand, we have the transactional profit methods, which integrate the transactional net margin (hereinafter "TNM") and the transactional profit split (hereinafter "TPS") methods.[228] As noted above, these methods could only be applied in a subsidiary manner until very recently. Nowadays, its use is particularly recommended either in cases where each of the parties makes valuable and unique contributions in relation to the controlled transactions or where the parties engage in highly integrated activities or either in cases where there is no or limited reliable information on third parties.[229] Unlike the traditional ones, the profit methods do not usually assess transactions separately but rather use general parameters taken by comparable uncontrolled enterprises in order to arrive at the transfer pricing outcome.[230] As the ratios and indicators used for these purposes may vary considerably, the use of these methods ultimately leads to a wider range of prices that could arguably be in accordance with the ALS.[231]

Once the two categories of transfer pricing methods have been briefly outlined, we will proceed to explain why the choice of the method tends to become a new instrument for profit shifting, thus thwarting the original intent of the ALS. To prove this point, we will make a special reference to transactions involving intangibles, since the choice of method in this context is particularly troublesome.

The ALS has been harshly criticized for its inability to control tax-motivated transfer pricing with respect to the shifting of income from intangibles.[232] This sort of profit shifting phenomenon has acquired considerable importance in the last decades, as intangibles have become increasingly relevant in today's business models. The OECD recognized at the time the BEPS Action Plan was published that the ALS had been unable to prevent MNCs from carrying profits associated with the transfer and use of such intangibles to jurisdictions other than those where value-added activities were located.[233] This was precisely the case of Apple, where the conclusion of the CSAs (supposedly within the sphere of the ALS) between the parent and a number of subsidiaries enabled the group to attribute the vast majority of the profits derived by Apple's IP to the subsidiaries incorporated in Ireland, a territory where no significant

228. (a) TNM method: it examines the ratio between the net profit and an appropriate base (e.g., costs, sales, assets) that a taxpayer obtains from a transaction. (b) TPS method: it first aggregates the profits obtained from the controlled transactions in which the parties engage and then proceeds to split those combined profits between the different parties in accordance with an "economically valid basis" that approximates the division of profits that would have been anticipated and reflect in an agreement made at arm's length. *See* 2017 OECD TPG, paragraphs 2.64 and 2.114.
229. 2017 OECD TPG, paragraph 2.4.
230. Vann states that profit methods tend to aggregate transactions, thus leading to the "relaxation of the transactional requirement" even though the first stage in the analysis is transactionally based. *See* Vann, R.J. (2003), p. 168.
231. Navarro warns against the high degree of subjectivity this method entails, indicating this is its most significant disadvantage. *See* Navarro Ibarrola, A. (2016), p. 30.
232. Schoueri believes this is the "principal weakness" of the ALS. *See* Schoueri, L.E. (2015), p. 699.
233. The OECD/BEPS project devoted one of its fifteen action items to the application of transfer pricing rules to intangibles. One of the objectives of this action item was to ensure "that profits associated with the transfer and use of intangibles are appropriately allocated in accordance with (rather than divorced from) value creation." *See* BEPS report, p. 20.

economic activities were taking place.[234] The ALS cannot however be blamed entirely for this outcome insofar the American regime on CSA can hardly be categorized as consistent with the ALS itself. The reason is that this domestic regime ultimately gives rise to situations such the one illustrated by Apple, where a company (ASI) got to earn disproportionally amounts of income in return for its cost sharing payment (an average ratio EBITDA/cost of 15:1) at the expense of Apple Inc., which would have hardly entered into an agreement like this with an unrelated party.[235]

As one of essential features of intangibles is precisely their uniqueness and singularity,[236] a comparable product may hardly be found in the market. This fact generally makes the CUP method unsuitable in cases where intangibles are somehow involved. A second essential feature of intangibles is the fact that they may potentially generate income that is disproportionally higher that the costs incurred in their development. This renders the C+ method considerably attractive to taxpayers, as well as any other pricing method based on costs, such as the American regime on CSA itself.[237] The preference of this method may be easily explained by means of an example that reflects a very common tax planning scheme. Entity A, resident in a high-tax jurisdiction, incorporates a subsidiary (A') in a low-tax jurisdiction and injects a considerable amount of capital into it. A' is highly capitalized and yet, it lacks significant human and material resources, reason why it may be regarded as a "cash box." The parent company uses A' to create and exploit an intangible asset, whose legal owner is from the beginning (and never ceases to be) entity A'. This being so, A' is responsible for the management of the property and the supervision of the outsourced functions. At the time it perceives the returns generated by the intangible, A' proceeds to remunerate the different entities for the functions performed on a cost-plus basis, meaning that the price would cover the costs incurred by the service supplier plus a markup that appropriately reflects the functions performed. However, these amounts, while being compliant with the ALS, are insignificant when compared to the overall profit obtained by reason of the intangible.[238]

The abovementioned example only works to the extent that the group manages to contractually separate intangibles from functions, which is one of the tax planning

234. Chapter 2 section §2.01[A][2].
235. As it was previously stated in Chapter 2 section §2.01[A][2], the American rule on CSA effectively allowed ASI, one of Apple's Irish subsidiaries, to become entitled to substantial profits derived by the exploitation of Apple's IP in exchange for a very low price (the ratio earnings/costs reached 15:1 in 2011 and 18:1 in 2012) and without requiring the transfer of any sort of genuine activities to Ireland. In fact, according to our own estimations based on the selected sample of Apple's registered IP, no R&D activities are being conducted within this territory at all. In this particular case, however, the outcome was not due to the choice of method but rather to the US domestic regulation on CSAs, which operate as a safe harbor and thus prevent the application of transfer pricing adjustments. The inconsistency between this CSA and the ALS has been noted by Ting, A. (2014), p. 45 and the Testimony of Prof. Shay on "Offshore profit shifting and the US tax code—part 2 (Apple Inc.)" submitted before the US Senate—Permanent Subcommittee on Investigations, p. 9.
236. Brauner, Y. (2008), pp. 87-92 and 134.
237. *See* Chapter 2 section §2.01[A][2].
238. OECD (2014): BEPS Action 8 deliverable: guidance on transfer pricing aspects of intangibles, paragraph 6.42. This sort of tax planning scheme is also described and commented in Yuan, J.; Liu, R.; Chan, H. (2015), p. 5 and Navarro Ibarrola, A. (2016), p. 250.

potentials of the ALS according to Wittendorff.[239] This way, the group may be able to place valuable intangibles in low-tax jurisdictions while retaining functions in high-tax jurisdictions. As a consequence of this, while the high-taxed entity would be ascribed a routine return for the functions performed on a cost-plus basis, the low-taxed entity, by contrast, would be ascribed the residual profits, which includes the entire organization return caused by the economies of integration. Considering the above, Wittendorff believes that the ALS ultimately creates, albeit unintentionally, an incentive to relocate intangibles which are in substance developed and managed from a high-tax jurisdiction to a low-tax jurisdiction.[240]

The OECD has acknowledged the risks posed by the abovementioned transfer pricing methods, at least in respect of transactions involving intangibles. Therefore, it has been recently promoting the TPS option over the other ones in the context of the BEPS Project.[241] The new OECD approach regarding the application of the ALS to intangibles will be examined and evaluated in-depth in Chapter 4 section §4.02[A], while the present section will only refer to some of the risks that the use of this method may entail.

In general, TPS method is less likely to generate profit shifting opportunities than the traditional ones, particularly with respect to intangibles. However, as it was noted above, these methods are based on ratios and indicators that may vary considerably, thus potentially leading to a wide range of prices that could be deemed to be at arm's length. This means that both tax Administrations and taxpayers may "play" with the different indicators to move within such wide range in the desired direction. The result is more likely to benefit those who are better equipped to formulate the most convincing and solid transfer pricing analysis, as it was already noted above.

Leaving aside the tax arbitrage caused by the choice of the transfer pricing method, it is time to move on to the second consideration we wished to put forward, which is the way the complexity of the ALS leads in practice to a two-speed system.

Complexity seems to be inherent in the very nature of transfer pricing[242] and, regrettably, this runs—once again—in favor of those who are better equipped, in terms of resources, to figure out a convincing transfer pricing assessment. Complexity is thus detrimental to less-privileged taxpayers but also to Tax Administrations, whose resources may rarely equal those of MNCs.[243] This places Tax Administrations at an insurmountable disadvantage when the time comes to perform the comparability analysis and apply the ALS, a disadvantage that is compounded by the fact that MNCs

239. He identifies this risk in the interpretation of the ALS resulting from the 1995 OECD TPG, and therefore welcomes the contribution of the BEPS Project in this area. *See* Wittendorff, J. (2016), p. 332.
240. Wittendorff, J. (2016), p. 332. Avi-Yonah and Benschalom equally believe that "the porosity of current transfer pricing rules creates an artificial tax incentive to locate profits in low-tax countries, both by locating real economic activities in such countries and by shifting profits for tax purposes towards low-tax locations," *see* Avi-Yonah, R.; Benshalom, I. (2011), p. 373.
241. BEPS report, pp. 20-21 and OECD (2014): BEPS Action 10: Draft on the use of profit splits in the context of global value chains, paragraphs 33 et seq.
242. Avi-Yonah and Benschalom consider that the system is "absurdly complex." *See* Avi-Yonah, R.; Benshalom, I. (2011), p. 376.
243. Navarro Ibarrola, A. (2016), p. 59.

enjoy superior information.[244] As could not be otherwise, the problem is greatly exacerbated in the case of developing countries.[245]

Beyond the particular profit shifting risks that the ALS poses, there are more structural problems concerning the application of the ALS that will be briefly outlined here: its inability to capture the so-called synergy rents, the considerable administrative burden it imposes and the legal uncertainty it generates.

In the first place, various scholars understand that the ALS is "inherently flawed" because it treats the members of a MNC as separate entities rather than "inseparable parts of a single unified business,"[246] thereby obviating the real raison d'être of MNCs: the "internalization theory."[247] According to this theory, corporate groups, due to its own organization, manage to internalize transactions costs and thus increase its efficiency in achieving economies of scale, raising capital advertising products, protecting valuable intangibles, etc.[248] The result is that MNCs are able to enjoy higher margins of profits than those obtained by comparable enterprises that are not integrated in groups. Such extraordinary margins are referred to as "synergy rents" and the ALS as it currently stands is unable to take them into account (as they would not have arisen if unrelated parties had conducted such transaction) and thus soundly allocate them between the entities involved.[249] This means that the allocation of these rents decided by the taxpayer cannot be legitimately challenged by any jurisdiction involved, at least on the grounds of the ALS.[250]

In the second place, the application of the ALS triggers an immense administrative and compliance burden for both taxpayers and Tax Administrations. This becomes visible in the huge industry of lawyers, accountants and economists that has emerged to assist corporate groups in their transfer pricing planning and compliance.[251] Third and lastly, the application of ALS has effectively leaded to an unbearable degree of legal

244. Problems related to information asymmetries between taxpayers and Tax Administrations are considered by the OECD, particularly in context of hard-to-value intangibles. *See* OECD (20015): Final Report on BEPS Actions 8-10—Aligning transfer pricing outcomes with value creation, pp. 109-112.
245. OECD (2014): Two-part report to G20: Developing working group on the impact of BEPS in low income countries.
246. 2017 OECD TPG, paragraph 1.6.
247. This is the opinion shared by Vann, Avi-Yonah and Schoueri among others. *See* Vann, R.J. (2003), p. 139, Schoueri, L.E. (2015), p. 698 and Avi-Yonah, R. (2007c), p. 25.
248. Avi-Yonah, R. (2007c), p. 25.
249. Schoueri argues that the ALS, as it currently stands in the OECD and the UN Model Conventions, is incapable of dealing with synergy rents and that this failure cannot be corrected by way of an ambulatory interpretation of the ALS. *See* Schoueri, L.E. (2015), pp. 698 and 711-713. Zornoza Pérez and Navarro Ibarrola stated in their comments to the changes proposed by Actions 8-10 of the BEPS Project that "it is virtually impossible that transactions exclusively undertaken by MNEs—and hence transactions that independent parties would not undertake—may respect the ALP." *See* OECD (2015): Comments received on Public Discussion Draft: BEPS Actions 8, 9 and 10: Revisions to Chapter I of the OECD TPG (including risk, recharacterisation and special measures), p. 511.
250. Schoueri, L.E. (2015), p. 714.
251. Avi-Yonah, R.; Benshalom, I. (2011), p. 376. For his part, Brauner is equally critical of the industry that revolves around transfer pricing compliance: "transfer pricing has created from scratch a large, economically wasteful industry which exists only to serve the need to supply these particular valuations." *See* Brauner, Y. (2014b), p. 627.

uncertainty, frequently depriving both taxpayers and countries of the possibility to foresee the likely revenue outcome in a transfer pricing case. Avi-Yonah expresses concern over the possibility that potential investors may feel discouraged for the inability to forecast the tax burden on their potential international ventures and thus choose not to invest.[252]

This section has analyzed some of the fissures that may be appreciated in two well-established paradigms (the separate-entity approach and the ALS) with the intention to prove how such fissures may potentially be exploited by taxpayers to shift profits to jurisdictions where little or no relevant activities are taking place. This view is shared by many scholars as Vann, who held that "virtually all problem areas in tax treaties could be traced to corporate groups and the separate taxation of the companies in the group."[253] Now we will proceed to introduce the next two paradigms that will be covered in the next two sections.

Once we depart from the general recognition of a company as a separate legal subject for tax purposes, it is time to identify the jurisdiction or jurisdictions that would be in principle entitled to tax its income. Such determination is largely based on the specific domestic tax legislations of the respective jurisdictions pursuant to their own tax sovereignty, without forgetting the limitations that could eventually be imposed by international treaties in place (if any). Each jurisdiction enjoys a great degree of freedom to define their respective "jurisdictional connections," that is, the criteria used to connect the material element of the taxable event with the scope of a State's taxing power.[254] It is equally true, however, that jurisdictions have exercised their respective powers in a quite uniform way; and virtually all of them have followed, although with nuances,[255] the notions of residence and source taxation.[256]

As in the case of individuals, corporate taxpayers are generally taxed in two different ways: as residents or as non-residents of the jurisdiction concerned for their income sourced therein.[257] On one hand, a resident company is usually taxed on its worldwide income, regardless of its origin, given its strong nexus with the State. On the other hand, a non-resident corporation is commonly subject to source taxation on the income that is considered to be sourced in the State concerned. Two levels of taxation are generally distinguished at this point. First, when the non-resident company has a PE in the territory of a State such State usually imposes taxes on the (worldwide) profits that are considered attributable to it, reaching a level of taxation comparable to that borne by residents.[258] Second, when the non-resident company lacks a PE in the territory of a State, it is generally liable to tax just for the specific items of income that

252. Avi-Yonah, R. (2007c), p. 26.
253. Vann, R.J. (2003), p. 133.
254. Schindel, A., Atchabahian, A. (2005), p. 28.
255. In the next sections we will refer to some of these nuances.
256. As it may be inferred from the general report on the 2005 IFA subject on residence and source. *See* Schindel, A., Atchabahian, A. (2005), p. 28 ("basically, source and domicile (residence, nationality) are the traditional jurisdictional principles").
257. Couzin, R. (2002), pp. 2 et seq. and Lang, M., Staringer, C. (2014), p. 24.
258. In fact, in tax treaty scenarios, Article 24 of the 2017 OECD MC forbids States to grant a less favorable tax treatment to permanent establishments than to resident enterprises. The same holds true for US whose domestic legislation lacks a concept of permanent establishment but

are deemed to be sourced in such State, for example dividends, interests and royalties paid by residents therein.

The next two sections will cover the way both residence and source have been defined (at the domestic and the tax treaty level) and will try to discern whether they, somehow, may potentially generate profit shifting opportunities.

§3.02 CURRENT CORPORATE TAX RESIDENCE TESTS ARE NOT ALIGNED WITH THE PRESUMPTIVE BENEFIT PRINCIPLE AND TEND TO GENERATE PROFIT SHIFTING RISKS

This section seeks to discern whether the way corporate residence is currently defined is somehow aligned with the presumptive benefit principle. In essence, the question on the table is whether the definition of corporate tax residence contributes to make taxpayers book their taxable profits in the jurisdictions where they presumably enjoy public benefits (i.e., wherever they carry out their economic activities, either physically or remotely) or else facilitate its shift to the jurisdiction(s) of their choice where no relevant business is occurring. Or in other words, whether corporate tax residence as currently defined contributes to widen the gap between the economic and the tax presence of companies in jurisdictions, as previously detected through the Apple case in Chapter 2 section §2.01[A].

Further, we will try to prove that corporate residence tests are not the fruit of a thorough reflection in policy terms and tend to rely on factors that are increasingly inappropriate and whose application generates a high degree of dissatisfaction in the States.

To this end, we will devote the first two sections to the critical analysis of corporate tax residence in the domestic level while the latter two sections will analyze the implications from the perspective of tax treaties. First, we will evaluate the most common residence tests used by the jurisdictions in their respective CIT regulations (section §3.02[A]). Second, we will analyze whether the lack of coordination in the definition of corporate tax residence may eventually exacerbate the abovementioned risks (section §3.02[B]). Third, we will study the role played by domestic residence tests when a company intends to access the benefits provided by a tax treaty and will analyze the function performed by LOB provisions in this context (section §3.02[C]). Finally, we will critically analyze the way jurisdictions deal with dual residence of companies in tax treaties (section §3.02[D]).

[A] Domestic Corporate Tax Residence Tests: A Comparative Overview and Some Considerations

The present section is divided into two parts. In the first part we will briefly outline the content and features of the most widespread tests used by jurisdictions to assign tax

still makes a similar distinction between income effectively connected with a US trade or business and income which is not.

residence to a company along with their respective (alleged) rationales. Additionally, we will evaluate to what extent the different categories of tests effectively enable corporate taxpayers to book their profits in jurisdictions where no relevant economic activities are being carried on (in other, jurisdictions other than those where the companies presumably derive their fundamental public benefits). In the second part, we will draw some interim conclusions.

[1] Most Common Criteria Used to Confer Corporate Residence for Domestic Tax Purposes: Alleged Rationale and Profit Shifting Risks

By the time jurisdictions started to treat legal entities as separate persons distinct from their owners and furthermore chose to impose income taxes on them, it became necessary to determine the cases in which they would become subject to taxation. Such determination was made by reference to certain criteria that denoted a particular connection between the corporate taxpayer and the jurisdiction concerned.

Naturally, income taxes in force at that time had been conceived for individuals. And such taxes were largely built upon the notion of residence of the relevant individual taxpayer.[259] In this context, corporate taxpayers inherited, by analogy, the ability to reside in a certain jurisdiction for income tax purposes. For example, in countries as the UK there was certainly no other option, as the British courts were required to apply the Income Tax Acts enacted in the mid-nineteenth century to companies long before the introduction of a statutory corporate tax residence test in 1988. In the meantime, they had to live with an Act that established the taxation of profits arising or accruing to "any person residing in" the UK and therefore strive to adjust the notion of "residence" to make it compatible with companies.[260]

In this context, jurisdictions extrapolated the notion of individual tax residence to companies in very different ways, and they did so either by introducing statutory residence tests or by the progressive development of a case law doctrine.

While theoretical economics literature tends to regard residence as the place where the owner of the capital resides,[261] tax legislators have traditionally resorted to different criteria whose outcome may not be necessarily consistent with the economists' view. Hereinafter we will proceed to classify the most common tests currently used to attribute the status of tax resident to companies in four general categories. The following sections will cover all four categories: (i) tests relying on the creation of the company and its seat, (ii) tests relying on its governance, (iii) test relying on the residence of its shareholders and (iv) tests relying on the location of its business activity.

Although the analysis will be conducted separately for each category of tests, it is important to first note that most countries combine various approaches, as Table 1 and Figure 4 in section §3.02[A][1][e] will show.

259. Maisto, G. (ed.): (2010) and Schindel, A.; Atchabahian, A. (2005).
260. Couzin, R. (2002), pp. 28-33 and Loomer, G.T. (2015), p. 102.
261. Devereux, M.; de La Feria, R. (2014), p. 6.

[a] Tests Relying on the Creation of the Company and Its Registered Seat

All tests comprised in this category are of a purely formal nature. Some of them choose to focus on the moment of legal birth of the company. For example, under the place of incorporation (hereinafter "POI") test a company would be deemed to be tax resident in a certain jurisdiction provided that it is incorporated in accordance with the domestic legislation of such jurisdiction. On the other hand, as companies are generally required to indicate a legal seat (e.g., registered office or statutory seat) in their bylaws at the time of registration, some criteria choose instead to confer the tax residence to all companies whose legal seat is located within the territory concerned.

Both tests were effectively borrowed, albeit not explicitly, from private international law.[262] Indeed, they have been compared to the individual's place of birth or citizenship,[263] to the extent that they all refer to factors pertaining to the inception of the respective taxpayer while completely disregarding their subsequent evolution and development.

[i] The Rationale Behind Them

Despite being the most widespread type of tests to establish corporate tax residence, as section §3.02[A][1][e] will later indicate below, the rationale behind its use, surprisingly, remains a mystery.

Undoubtedly, formal tests offer high functional advantages.[264] They do not require an interpretative effort of any kind; their application is univocal and straightforward and therefore the outcome is easily predictable. As a consequence, they entail, at least *a priori*, a high degree of legal certainty for both taxpayers and tax administrations. And perhaps more importantly, formal tests rarely distort taxpayer's economic behavior, if ever.[265] Therefore, we may come to the conclusion that this option would be the most efficient one from an economic standpoint, meaning that it would not *a priori* affect the allocation of productive resources conceived by the corporate taxpayer.

Besides these utilitarian arguments, there do not seem to be clear and solid policy reasons behind the appropriateness of taxing companies on these grounds.[266] In this regard, it has only been argued that the POI test would be consistent with the purpose of CITs only to the extent that these are regarded as "fees for the benefits of incorporation," among which we could mention the granting of limited liability, the

262. Couzin, R. (2002), p. 31.
263. Loomer, G.T. (2015), p. 104.
264. A comprehensive explanation of the virtues of these tests may be found in Marian, O. (2013), pp. 1620-1625.
265. Marian, O. (2013b), p. 473.
266. Loomer attempted to shed some light on the reasons behind the decision of Canada and the UK to introduce the POI test (in 1961 and 1988 respectively) once their respective tests based on the decision-making of the company were already consolidated. He concludes that "the policy foundations of the corporate tax were likely not given much consideration in the course of adopting the incorporation test, and perhaps the best explanation for its adoption in Canada and the United Kingdom was a desire for a clear, simple residence rule." *See* Loomer, G.T. (2015), pp. 108-109.

transferability of interests, the centralization of management, etc.[267] However, this argument is weak and does not always stand, as there may be cases in which companies may achieve all benefits of incorporation with little or no corporate tax consequences.[268]

[ii] The Potential Profit Shifting Risks They Pose

It seems evident that formal tests do not ensure that the Residence State of a company is that providing the public services and infrastructures from which the company is presumably benefiting as the presumptive benefit principle would require. Quite the contrary, they do not require a strong nexus between the company and the jurisdiction concerned[269] but rather content themselves with a tenuous link that merely makes reference to a number of factors of a mere bureaucratic nature. Factors that are, besides, within the direct control of the taxpayer. This certainly raises serious profit shifting risks, leading to the already well-known phenomenon of "residence electivity,"[270] since taxpayers are in the position to simply "select" the jurisdiction in which they wish to incorporate the company or establish its registered office and, by extension, the jurisdiction in which they aspire to make its entity subject to tax.[271]

This being so, the most straightforward—and rudimentary—way to initiate a tax planning scheme would be the incorporation of a company in a low-tax jurisdiction or a tax haven.[272] In fact, De Broe notes that countries applying formal tests and having beneficial tax regimes effectively "attract companies that are set up to enjoy the tax benefits but that do not necessarily have a genuine nexus with that country (letter box,

267. Avi-Yonah, R. (2004), pp. 1205-1206. This idea seems equally present in Shaviro's discourse, where he refers to the US taxation imposed upon foreigners incorporating a company in the US as "a fee for US incorporation" and then continue to enumerate some of the advantages of being incorporated in the US, as being subject to securities law regimes or the enjoyment of an easier trading on US capital markets. Besides, he points out that some companies may consider that the US incorporation "brands them legally, reputationally, and otherwise as real company with high standards." In the case of certain industries (defense contracting or airlines) the incorporation in the US may be "legally or politically necessary, or at least advantageous" (Shaviro, D. (2011), pp. 130-132). Schön argues that "entities owe their very existence and internal governance structure to the legal order of the country of incorporation" (Schön, W. (2009), p. 91).
268. This would be the case of the US as a result of the check-the-box regulations. *See* Marian, O. (2013b), p. 476.
269. As De Broe notes: "the application of such a formal criterion does not ensure that the company is subject to comprehensive tax liability in the country with which its economic nexus is closest." Further, he even challenges the POI test from the perspective of the ability to pay principle: "The question may be raised whether the incorporation test is in accordance with the ability to pay principle." *See* De Broe, L. (2009), pp. 99-100. We cannot agree with this latter assertion, since the compliance with the ability to tax principle is better measured by reference to the extent of the tax liability.
270. Shaviro, D. (2011).
271. Marian, O. (2013b), p. 479: "the fact that our tax laws ask us to treat a mailbox in Ireland as a foreign corporation is an insult to intelligence."
272. *See* Desai, M.A.; Dharmapala, D. (2010), p. 728, where the authors detected that tax haven incorporations rose to 10% of US incorporations in the period 2005-2009 and peaked at 30% in 2008.

base companies performing holding activities, conduits ...)."[273] However, this option is naturally not as optimal as it may seem in the beginning, partly because operating in such territories may be troublesome due to the lack of an adequate legal framework and the difficulties to raise capital and also because such arrangement is likely to be dismantled through anti-avoidance measures,[274] which will be later covered by section §3.02[A][2][c].

However, the opportunities for "residence electivity" are not exhausted with the decision to incorporate a company in a certain jurisdiction. Besides, domestic tax legislations may allow the inbound and outbound migration of companies, that is, the domestication of companies incorporated elsewhere and the expatriation of a locally incorporated company. The study of such options goes far beyond the scope of this research and cannot be comprehensively examined. However, the case of the US may serve as an illustrative example of how these options could operate in practice.

Shaviro conducted a research in the US that intended to discern whether the cases of domestication and expatriation of companies were noteworthy and thus contributed to further aggravate the issue of "residence electivity."[275] As regards the first scenario, he noted with surprise that it was relatively common and desired by certain companies for non-tax reasons. Furthermore, many states specifically provide for the "domestication" of foreign entities and the procedures tend not to be burdensome. For example, the procedure for reincorporating a company in Delaware is as simple as filing a certificate of corporate domestication and a certificate of incorporation.[276] One notable example is the multinational News Corporation, an Australian company which reincorporated in Delaware in 2004.[277] As regards the opposite scenario, as could not be otherwise, he observed that the US did not precisely favor the way out of the country. Once a company has been incorporated in the US, the only way to escape its status as US resident is by being genuinely purchased by new owners.[278] For example, this occurred back in 1988, when Chrysler, the US automaker, was acquired by Daimler, a German company, and later become DaimlerChrysler, a company resident in Germany for tax purposes.[279] Although one may think that the barriers imposed by the US Internal Revenue Code (hereinafter "IRC") may be sufficient to discourage the emigration of companies, the next data is revealing: from 1988 to 2009 the percentage (for all US M&A deals) in which the acquirer was a foreign company located either in a tax haven or an exemption country more than doubled.[280]

It is clear that the US does not treat homogenously the cases of inbound and outbound corporate migration: while in the first case they simply demand the

273. De Broe, L. (2009), p. 101.
274. Zornoza Pérez, J. (2013), p. 15.
275. Shaviro, D. (2011), pp. 108 and 128-136.
276. Brauner, Y. (2009), p. 866.
277. Shaviro, D. (2011), p. 108.
278. Section 7874 of the US IRC. Besides, Article 1.4 of the 2016 US MC provides that the Contracting States may continue to tax its "former citizen or former long-term resident" in accordance with its domestic laws notwithstanding the other provisions of the Convention.
279. Shaviro, D. (2011), pp. 101-102 and 133: "opting out of the US corporate residence is therefore costly unless one actually wants to engage in meaningful cross-border M&A."
280. Desai, M.A.; Dharmapala, D. (2010), pp. 730-731.

submission of a document, in the second case they require a genuine acquisition by a foreign entity. Although we cannot infer a general trend from the particular policy followed by the US, it would be reasonable to expect equally disparate treatments in other jurisdictions.[281]

[b] Tests Relying on the Corporate Governance

Overall, these tests tend to confer the status of tax resident to companies which are somehow managed from their respective territories. Contrary to the first category, these are eminently substantive and applied on a case-by-case basis. And naturally, it is necessary to monitor their fulfillment with certain frequency, as the place of management of a company may be subject to changes.

The fact that the precise wording varies significantly from one State to another[282] complicates the task of drawing some general defining lines. However, De Broe noted in his study that the eight jurisdictions applying this criterion did so in a relatively homogenous manner by means of the following three-step analysis:[283]

- Identification of the relevant management activities.[284] As there may be a great number of decision-making bodies and persons with autonomous decision-taking powers within a company, he distinguished three different levels of management: strategic, day-to-day and "shop floor" management. The first one refers to the general policy decisions that affect the long-term course of the business of the company. The second one alludes to the decisions that intend to implement the strategic guidelines and manage the daily progress of the business. Lastly, the third one refers to the immediate supervision of the day-to-day operations. It is in this first part of the analysis where the disparities between jurisdictions are more profuse.[285]
- Identification of the persons who perform the relevant management activities.[286] There is a general tendency, observed by De Broe, to depart from the

281. For instance, exit taxes are expected in outbound scenarios.
282. De Broe analyzed the definition of corporate residence in the legislation of 8 civil law jurisdictions and concluded that all of them contained a factor based on the decision-making of the company. However, the terms varied significantly: principal (management) establishment and seat of management or administration (Belgium), effective seat (France), center of chief business management (Germany), place of management (Italy), place of effective management (Spain and Switzerland). On the other hand, the Netherlands employs a factual-based test in which the place of effective management plays a decisive role. *See* De Broe, L. (2009), p. 102, footnote 14. For his part, Avery Jones explained the way common law judge-based rules (originally from the UK although followed by other common law countries) have traditionally used criteria equally based on the governance of the company to determine tax residence, only they call their test "central management and control." *See* Avery Jones, J.F. (2009), pp. 121-161.
283. De Broe, L. (2009), pp. 102-119.
284. De Broe, L. (2009), pp. 102-107.
285. For example, the Netherlands, Belgium, Spain and France among others tend to opt for the first approach while Germany and Switzerland opt for the second. On the other hand, jurisdictions as Austria and Italy do not follow consistently a unique approach.
286. De Broe, L. (2009), pp. 107-114.

assumption that companies are effectively managed by those who have been entrusted with management in conformity with the respective domestic company legislation (and when appropriate, their bylaws). This being so, company legislation typically establishes a single-tier management structure where the board of directors tends to be the corporate body responsible for management functions[287] although there may be exceptions.[288]

Notwithstanding the above, tax administrations and courts do not generally forgo the opportunity to verify whether the body appointed by the corporate legislation for the management of the company (e.g., the board of directors) effectively exercises in practice the mandated functions.[289] They may do so by means of a substance over form approach through which they examine all the relevant and objectively ascertainable facts of the case in order to discover who is de facto managing the company in lieu of the ones theoretically entrusted with such responsibility. Such analysis would eventually lead to the identification of the so-called de facto managers, which will be usually the ones to be taken into account for the purposes of the application of the corporate residence rule.

The abovementioned substance over form analysis may potentially point at the shareholders as the de facto managers of the firm. Although there is nothing preventing this from actually happening, one should always perform the analysis with due consideration. This is so because, as mentioned before, one cannot confuse the general powers of the shareholders (e.g., the right to appoint and dismiss the directors) with management powers. This becomes particularly tricky in the case of subsidiaries belonging to corporate groups.[290] Tax administrations and courts generally depart from the recognition of the subsidiary as a legal entity distinct from its shareholders and subject to a separate and autonomous management. It is generally believed that the fact that the board of the subsidiary behaves in conformity with the economic

287. This is the case for all the 8 countries surveyed. However, smaller companies may only have one or more managing directors. *See* De Broe, L. (2009), p. 107.

288. For example, the legislation of certain jurisdictions establishes for certain types of companies a two-tier management structure comprised by the board of directors plus a supervisory board whose functions include the advice and supervision of the board of directors (De Broe, L. (2009), p. 107). This could be the case for Austria and Germany (*Aktiengesellschaften*), the Netherlands (*structuurvennootschappen*), France (*sociétés anonymes*) and Italy (*società per azione*). Equally, the legislation of certain jurisdictions allows (or even specifically establishes) shareholders to somehow get actively involved in the management of the company even though, as a matter of principle, shareholders do not enjoy management powers (De Broe, L. (2009), p. 108). This would be case for France (the bylaws of French companies may provide that management decisions are to be approved by the shareholders), Belgium (the shareholders may vote, on request by the board, on the modification of the company's object, its dissolution and certain changes of the bylaws) or Germany and Austria (their shareholders may pass resolutions with specific orders to be followed by the directors).

289. De Broe, L. (2009), pp. 109-114.

290. De Broe, L. (2009), pp. 110-114: "the more difficult question is from what point the involvement of shareholders (and in particular shareholders and parent companies) in the management of the company shifts the management from the level of the board or managing directors of the subsidiary to the level of the shareholders."

interests and overall objectives of the group to which it belongs does not imply that they are not effectively performing management functions.[291] However, it may be rightly concluded that the de facto managers of the subsidiary are in fact its shareholders, but only insofar as they "usurp the management powers of the board of directors and frequently and constantly make the management decisions on their own order."[292]

- Localization of the relevant management activities. The last step of the analysis typically requires the determination of the place where the management activities are in substance made, regardless of the place where they are prepared, implemented, executed or communicated.[293]

  Once again, tax administrations and courts usually depart from a general assumption, according to which relevant management decisions are made in the meetings regularly held by the corporate body appointed to that effect (e.g., the board of directors).[294] However, this does not prevent administrations and courts from rebutting the presumption by applying a substance over form approach that may eventually lead to a different conclusion. This would be the case if the directors limit themselves to approving in their meetings decisions that were made elsewhere by the de facto managers. The test is wrongfully applied by certain jurisdictions that allude to criteria that bears no relation to the location of the decision-making, as for example the place of shareholders meetings (to the extent that they are not deemed to be de facto managers), the residence of the directors, the localization of assets or the place where the main activities of the company are carried out.[295] For its part, the Gibraltarian rule steps aside from the general trend by explicitly conferring the tax residence to companies whose management and control is exercised

291. Couzin, R. (2002), P. 96.
292. De Broe, L. (2009), p. 113. This situation is illustrated in a case brought before the British House of Lords in 1959. A parent company resident in the UK had three wholly owned subsidiaries operating in Kenya. The evidence showed that these subsidiaries were resident in Kenya and had their respective separate board of directors. However, it was in fact established that none of the boards ever made any decisions and simply stood aside in all matters of importance. Consequently, the Court reached the conclusion that the central management and control of the subsidiaries was effectively exercised by the parent board, regardless of whether this fact could be found to be contrary to the subsidiaries' bylaws: "the business is not the less managed in London because it ought to be managed in Kenya." *See* the Decision by the House of Lords of the United Kingdom, 1959, "Unit Construction Co. Ltd v. Bullock (Inspector of Taxes)."
293. With the only exception of jurisdictions following the day-to-day management approach, in which case relevance is given to the place where the strategic management is implemented in the form of day-to-day managerial decisions. *See* De Broe, L. (2009), p. 115.
294. De Broe, L. (2009), p. 115.
295. The Spanish tax administration and courts and tend to presume that the residence of the directors of a company is equivalent to the place where the meetings of the board take place and, by extension, the place were management decisions are in substance made. The residence of the directors is therefore considered not only as a valid indicator in the determination of the place of management but frequently the decisive one. *See* for example the judgment by the Spanish High National Court (Audiencia Nacional), April 21, 2005. Additionally, De Broe found more case law in this regard in Belgium, France and Switzerland. *See* De Broe, L. (2009), p. 116.

outside Gibraltar provided that the persons in charge of managing the firm are ordinarily resident in Gibraltar.[296]

[i] The Rationale Behind Them

The original rationale behind these criteria may be inferred from the UK case law of the second half of the nineteenth century. The study of this case law turns out to be particularly interesting for two main reasons. The first one is that residence rules based on the governance of the company developed earlier in the UK than in civil law countries[297] and the second one is that, unlike legislators, courts have the duty to explain the considerations that substantiate their positions, which allows us to witness first-hand the original raison d'être of this category of tests.

Two cases argued and decided together in the UK in 1876 set the pace for subsequent judgments in the country. We are referring to *The Cesena Sulphur Co Ltd v. Nicholson* and *The Calcutta Jute Mills Co Ltd v. Nicholson*.[298] Both companies were incorporated in the UK and had most of their directors in the UK, while their business operations were carried out wholly abroad (in Italy and India respectively) where their assets were situated and their respective managing directors and the majority of their shareholders had their residence (74% and 64% respectively).[299] In order to settle the case, the court began disregarding the POI as a decisive factor, since it was regarded as "insufficient" to establish residence therein. Then, the court departed from a private international law rule laid down in an 1846 Act that established that a court would have jurisdiction insofar the dependent "dwells or carries on his business" within the court's area. Huddlestone B., following previous judgments in private law matters, stated that the rule referred to the place where "the real trade and business is carried on" or "le centre de l'enterprise."[300] At this point, and against all odds, the Court considered these companies as UK residents for tax purposes on the grounds that this expression ought to be interpreted as "place of intellectual control of the business,"[301] namely, the place where the central management and control is found instead of the place where the

296. http://www.oecd.org/tax/automatic-exchange/crs-implementation-and-assistance/tax-residency/Gibraltar-Residency.pdf (last accessed to data on January 10, 2019).
297. Avery Jones, J.F. (2009), p. 121.
298. Judgment by the High Court (Exchequer Division), 1876, "The Cesena Sulphur Co Ltd v. Nicholson" and "The Calcutta Jute Mills Co Ltd v. Nicholson."
299. Avery Jones, J.F. (2009), pp. 130-131.
300. Judgment by the High Court (Exchequer Division), 1876, "The Cesena Sulphur Co Ltd v. Nicholson" and "The Calcutta Jute Mills Co Ltd v. Nicholson."
301. Avery Jones, J.F. (2009), p. 129.

productive operations were taking place.[302] This approach was later reinforced in the leading case De Beers[303] and progressively consolidated in subsequent cases.

The British courts law always expressed their preference for the highest level of control at the expense of the day-to-day management, as one may easily infer from the terminology used by several judgments: the "paramount authority,"[304] the "head and brain"[305] or "the superior and directing authority."[306] Lord Halsbury advocated this position by saying that, even though the company in question dealt with land, goods and clients in another territory, "the person who governs the whole commercial adventure (and) makes the profits by his skill or industry, however distant may be the field of his adventure" is the person who is trading.[307]

Be that as it may, tests based on the place where the corporate decisions were made, either in the form of the expression "place of effective management" (hereinafter "POEM") or the "central management and control," became the fundamental tests in common law countries[308] and were rapidly incorporated in civil law countries along with formal ones.

Similarly, it has been argued by a few scholars that the use of these tests would be consistent with one of the policy purposes traditionally attributed to corporate income taxation (at least in the US): the control over managers that accumulate substantial power and the restriction of potential abuses of power.[309] This being so, subjecting a company to CIT in the jurisdiction from which their managers effectively exercise their powers would fulfill the aforementioned purpose.[310] Additionally, this

302. Avery Jones includes an excerpt of the judgment in which Huddlestone B. explained his position: "No doubt the manufacturing part was done in Italy, and the company might have found sulphur in another country, and carried on the manufacturing part of the business in that other country, but the administrative part were carried on at the place from which all the orders flowed, where officers and agents were appointed and recalled, where their powers were granted and revoked, where whatever money was sent was received, and where the dividends were declared and were payable." *See* Avery Jones, J.F. (2009), p. 136.

303. Decision by the House of Lords of the United Kingdom, 1905, "De Beers Consolidated Mines Ltd. v. Howe (Surveyor of Taxes)," where Lord Loreburn stated that "a company resides, for the purposes of income tax, where its real business is carried on... I regard that as the true rule; and the real business is carried on where the central management and control actually abides." In a subsequent decision by the House of Lords, Viscount Sumner argued that the term resident was "exceedingly unsuited" to describe a legal entity and "the only analogy that is really possible between a person and a company is that of carrying on business at a place." *See also* the Decision by the House of Lords of the United Kingdom, 1928, "Egyptian Delta Land and Investment Co. Ltd. V, Todd (Inspector of Taxes)."

304. Decision by the House of Lords of the United Kingdom, 1912, "American Thread Company v. Joyce (Surveyor of Taxes)."

305. Decision by the House of Lords of the United Kingdom, 1895, "San Paulo (Brazilian) Railway Company Limited v. Carter (Surveyor of Taxes)."

306. Decision by the House of Lords of the United Kingdom, 1953, "Union Corporation Limited v. Commissioners for the Inland Revenue."

307. Decision by the House of Lords of the United Kingdom, 1895, "San Paulo (Brazilian) Railway Company Limited v. Carter (Surveyor of Taxes)."

308. Avery Jones, J.F. (2009), pp. 138-139.

309. Avi-Yonah has traditionally defended the maintenance of the corporate tax on the grounds that it assists in curbing undesirable power accumulations by corporate management. *See* Avi-Yonah, R. (2004) and Avi-Yonah, R. (2007b), p. 383. These arguments were, however, firmly repealed by Brauner in Brauner, Y. (2008b), pp. 602-617.

310. Marian, O. (2013b), p. 477.

choice would also be consistent with the fact that companies are increasingly entrusting their board of directors with the responsibility to oversee the company's tax planning strategies and further ensure that it obeys the relevant tax legislation.[311]

[ii] The Potential Profit Shifting Risks They Pose

Residence tests based on corporate governance do not guarantee either that the resulting Residence State of a company is that presumably supplying the public benefits to that company. In other words, it is fair to say that these tests are not aligned with the presumptive benefit principle either. What is more, these tests are just as susceptible to manipulations as the previous ones, thus turning into common tools for profit shifting.

In the first place, companies may easily transfer their board meetings to a jurisdiction of their choice, to the extent that it provides a residence test based on the place where the company is effectively managed and controlled. Similarly, they may incorporate subsidiaries in other jurisdictions and make them liable to tax therein for their worldwide income insofar as they manage to keep in such jurisdiction an ostensibly independent board of directors.[312] This being so, taxpayers can easily capture the residence status of the jurisdiction that best fits their needs.

Unlike what happens with formal tests,[313] the very nature of this category of residence tests especially favors subsequent shifts of corporate residence. As a matter of principle, jurisdictions relying on these tests accept that any transfer of managerial functions would effectively cause the end of the residence status in their country,[314] since anti-avoidance rules would rarely apply to the extent that the transfer is genuine. Indeed, the effective transfer of management functions to a foreign jurisdiction of choice in order to capture a tax residence status therein is not rare. The phenomenon started in the UK right after the judgment on De Beers.[315] And more recently, Voget revealed that 6% of a sample of 140 MNCs relocated their headquarters essentially for tax reasons in the period 1997-2007.[316]

As a result of the abovementioned, one could come to the conclusion that tax residence migration tend to be easier in jurisdictions relying on tests based on the effective management of the company than in others following formal tests, as evidenced by the abovementioned example regarding the US.[317] For this reason, we

311. As fostered by the OECD itself, *see* OECD (2015): Principles of corporate governance, pp. 45 and 47.
312. Decision by the House of Lords of the United Kingdom, 1959, "Unit Construction Co. Ltd v. Bullock (Inspector of Taxes)."
313. *See* the case of the US in Chapter 3 section §3.02[A][1][a].
314. Shaviro, D. (2011), p. 138.
315. Decision by the House of Lords of the United Kingdom, 1928, "Egyptian Delta Land and Investment Co. Ltd. V, Todd (Inspector of Taxes)." As a curiosity, this company appointed a foreign board in 1907, just one year after De Beers.
316. Voget, J. (2010). On the other hand, Marian did not find significant studies proving a causative correlation between the adoption of these tests and real migration of corporate headquarters, *see* Marian, O. (2013b), p. 477.
317. *See* Chapter 3 section §3.02[A][1][a].

could say that the substantive nature of these tests has not prevented them from eventually becoming another "tax-planning device"[318] insofar they still allow companies to select their country of residence at will.[319]

More recently, these tests have been facing new challenges related to the information and communications technology (hereinafter "ICT"). As rightfully identified by the OECD back in 2001, the availability of technologies such as videoconferencing renders unnecessary any physical meeting of persons in one particular place to hold discussions and make decisions:[320] telephone and internet enable each director to state his/her point of view and participate in the decision-making process without being physically present at a certain place.[321] This further exacerbates the tax planning opportunities outlined in the previous paragraph.

In case decisions are taken during a videoconference held by managers located in different jurisdictions, it may well occur that no jurisdiction claims the residence status of the company or, on the contrary, that all or many of them simultaneously do so, being difficult or even impossible to distinguish a solely dominant place of management.[322] In such situations, taxpayers may take precautions not to trigger an unwanted change of residence status.[323]

And besides the particular challenges posed by the internet, global business may have a managing director "constantly on the move" that may make decisions while flying over the ocean or while visiting the branches of the company in different continents.[324] Similarly, it may well be the case that the meetings of the board of directors may be held in different places throughout the year on a rotational basis, with the consequent difficulty of discerning the one that should prevail for the purposes of applying the residence tests.[325]

318. Arnold, B.J. (2003), p. 1564.
319. The British Inland Revenue itself recognized this reality back in 1981, acknowledging that the test had "become artificial with the passage of time and technical innovation" and that it had "enabled companies to arrange a residence for tax purposes which may bear little relation to the seat of the company's operations." *See* British Inland Revenue (1981): Company residence: a consultative document, paragraph 2.
320. *See* in general OECD (2001): The impact of the communications revolution on the application of "place of effective management" as a tie breaker rule (Discussion Draft) and particularly its pages 8 and 9. Although the draft revolves around the concept of POEM as envisaged in the OECD Model Convention, most of its considerations apply equally to domestic tests based on the same criteria.
321. Rivier, J.-M- (1987), p. 75.
322. Chan provides a complete overview of the challenges and risks that technologies bring when it comes to the interpretation of the central management and control test that is in place in Australia. *See* Chan, C. (2014) and Hughes, D. (2013), pp. 164-171.
323. Hughes provides practical advice on how to maintain the non-residence status and thus avoid the UK residence in a scenario characterized by a profusion of information technologies. For instance, he states: "it would be highly advisable that directors did not call into board meetings from the UK, but instead where necessary, attended the board meeting held abroad in person." Similarly, he provides advice with respect of the use of different means of communication, as fax, email, smartphone communication, telephone, videoconferencing, etc. *See* Hughes, D. (2013), pp. 164-171.
324. OECD (2001): The impact of the communications revolution on the application of "place of effective management" as a tie breaker rule (Discussion Draft), p. 9.
325. According to the guidelines provided by the UK Government, the HMRC will not review the residence status of companies in which the board of directors meets regularly overseas but

We can therefore conclude that, even though these tests are of a substantive nature, they still confer the taxpayer a certain degree of freedom to select its country of residence irrespective of the real ties it may have with such country. Additionally, challenges related to the ICT may further increase such freedom of choice, not to mention the complex interpretation issues it may cause and the consequent risks of either companies with multiple tax residences (and double taxation) or stateless companies.

[c] Tests Relying on the Residence of the Corporate Shareholders

These factors confer the status of tax resident to companies whose shareholders controlling the voting power of the company are residents of the jurisdiction concerned. This approach is rather exceptional and can only be seen in very few countries as Australia (when it is applied jointly with the "carry on business" test that will be analyzed in the next section) although countries as Greece and the Netherlands tend to take it into consideration when applying the POEM test.[326]

In Australia, the term is interpreted so as to require an "actual" control of the voting rights and not merely the holding of those rights, meaning that the test would only be considered satisfied when shareholders actually exercise such control and not in cases the shareholders abstain from voting at the general meeting.[327] Additionally, the resident shareholders must have actual control over 50% of the voting power for the rule to be applied.

[i] The Rationale Behind Them

Originally, this test came up in common law countries in a context in which locally owned companies appointed foreign board of directors in order to avoid the already well-established "central management and control" principle.[328] It was in 1920 when the UK Royal Commission on the Income Tax recommended the UK legislator to introduce a rule by which companies would still be considered as tax resident in the UK insofar the majority of the voting power could be exercised in the UK. Although the UK did not follow the recommendation, other common law countries as Australia did.

Although this test originally emerged with the specific objective of closing a previously detected loophole, some scholars have further supported its appropriateness on certain policy considerations. For example, the test would be considered to be consistent with the idea of taxing companies with the purpose of reaching the pockets of its individual shareholders and thus taxing the wealth they accumulated behind

holds a "small minority of meetings, not more than one or two" in the UK in any one accounting period. *See* British HM Revenue & Customs (2014): International Manual, part INTM120150.

326. *See* the profile of the respective country: http://www.oecd.org/tax/automatic-exchange/crs-implementation-and-assistance/tax-residency/ (last accessed on January 10, 2019).
327. Dirkis, M. (2009), p. 328.
328. Avery Jones, J.F. (2009), p. 140.

corporate forms.[329] As Marian notes: "if the purpose of corporate taxation is to serve as a vehicle for taxing individuals, corporate tax residence tests should be designed to ensure that the corporate tax eventually burdens the intended individuals"[330] and clearly the best way to do is by establishing a test equivalent to that provided by the Australian legislation, as already supported by a few scholars.[331] For example, Nikolakakis introduces the expression of "substantial residence" referring to the residence of the "ultimate economic beneficiary,"[332] so it may be inferred from his words that he equates the true residence of a company with the residence of its respective shareholders.

One of the potential disadvantages this category of tests may entail is the administrative burden it may eventually pose, particularly in relation to publicly traded companies.[333] A risk that has been dismissed by Marian, who suggests that such determination could be made on a time-average basis to simplify the process.[334]

[ii] The Potential Profit Shifting Risks They Pose

This sort of residence tests is not aligned either with the presumptive benefit principle insofar as they do not contribute to book the worldwide profits of the company to the State that is presumably providing the public services and infrastructures from which it is benefiting, as such State would not necessarily coincide with that that hosts the majority of the company's shareholders.

However, these tests carry fewer risks of manipulation than the precedent ones and are thus less prone to be used for profit shifting purposes. Nonetheless, they would still be troublesome insofar the residence of the shareholders is determined by easily manipulable tests as the previous two ones. Particularly considering that the majority of the shareholders of MNCs are frequently institutional investors (e.g., investment funds),[335] which in turn tend to select their respective residence States for tax reasons.

[d] Tests Relying on the Location of the Business Activity of the Company

Although much rarer, some domestic legislations confer tax residence to companies whose main business activity is carried on within their respective jurisdiction. This is

329. Auerbach, A. J. (2006), Bank, S.A. (2007), p. 393 and Kleinbard, E.D. (2012b), p. 684. In the latter paper it is stated that "the strongest justification for the existence of a corporate income tax is that it serves as a substitute for the imposition of current tax on the firm's owners."
330. Marian, O. (2013b), p. 474.
331. Green, R.A. (1993), pp. 70-74 and Kleinbard, E.D. (2001), p. 160.
332. Nikolakakis, A. (2009), p. 916.
333. Shaviro, D. (2011), p. 415.
334. Marian argues that 87% of the aggregate value of companies traded in the US stock markets is owned by US residents and that it does not seem realistic to think that many companies would have their ownership percentages constantly moving up and down the 50% threshold. *See* Marian, O. (2013b), p. 478. On the other hand, Graetz does not think this is an appropriate solution: "linking corporate residence to the residence of its owners does not seem practical in the context of multi-tiered multinationals." *See* Graetz, M.J. (2001), p. 323.
335. As illustrated in the case of Apple, *see* Chapter 2 section §2.01[A][1].

the case for Italy,[336] Australia and, to some extent, also territorial systems as France and Costa Rica among others.[337]

The most emblematic example of this category of tests is the Italian test, which may be found in the Article 73 of the Italian Corporate Income Tax Act):[338]

> 3. For the purposes of income taxation, a company having its legal set, headquarters or main object of the activity in the territory of the State for the greater part of the tax period will be considered as resident therein (...)
>
> 4. The exclusive or main object of the activity of the resident company will be determined according to the law, the act of incorporation or the corporate bylaws in case they take the form of a public deed or authenticated private agreement. Main activity will be interpreted as the activity that is essential to directly achieve the primary goals of the company as laid down in the law, act of incorporation or bylaws.
>
> 5. In the absence of an act of incorporation or corporate bylaws in the aforesaid forms, the resident company's main activity will be determined on the basis of the activity that is effectively exercised in the territory of the State (...)

For its part, the Australian residence test is established in subsection 6(1) of the (Australian) Income Tax Assessment Act (ITAA) 1936[339]

> Resident or resident of Australia means: (...)
>
> b) a company which is incorporated in Australia, or which, not being incorporated in Australia, carries on business in Australia, and has either its central management and control in Australia, or its voting power controlled by shareholders who are residents of Australia.

Both tests confer the tax residence status to companies that are either carrying on the main object of their activity (*oggetto principale dell'attività*) or a business in general in their respective territories. However, the Australian test explicitly demands an

336. De Broe, L. (2009), pp. 118-119 and Tenore, M. (2009), pp. 530-544.
337. Back in 1984 Tillinghast found a similar rule in the domestic legislation of Pakistan, according to which any company which had more than half of its gross income effectively connected with the conduct of a trade or business in Pakistan would be regarded as tax resident therein. *See* Tillinghast, D.R. (1984).
338. The original text may be found here: http://www.altalex.com/documents/leggi/2014/07/17/tuir-titolo-ii-capo-i-soggetti-passivi-e-disposizioni-generali#61906 (last accessed on January 10, 2019).
339. http://www8.austlii.edu.au/cgi-bin/viewdoc/au/legis/cth/consol_act/itaa1936240/s6.html (last accessed on January 10, 2019).

additional requirement: the company must either have its central management and control or the residence of the majority of its shareholders in Australia.

We will start by interpreting the terms "oggetto principale dell'attività" and "business" and further ascertain which sort of activities may eventually fall under the scope of both terms. Both States advocate for a "wide" interpretation of these terms, covering both operational activities (e.g., manufacturing, trading, provision of services, etc.) and the mere management of activities, assets and stock portfolios among others (e.g., real estate management, trusts, investment funds, holdings, etc.).

The Italian Supreme Court interprets *oggetto principale* as production activities, conclusion of contracts and any other economic relations that the company maintains with third parties.[340] Antonini underlines the importance of distinguishing between the location of the activity from which the income derives and the place where tangible and intangible goods (real estate, titles, shareholding, patents, licenses, etc.) are kept, since the latter should not influence the outcome of the analysis.[341] He gives a couple of examples to illustrate his point. First, he gives the example of a company incorporated elsewhere whose primary business is the management of a couple of buildings located it Italy. In such case, he understands that the "oggetto principale dell'attività" cannot be found where the immovable are (Italy) insofar as the real business activity is the management of the buildings and it was carried out from elsewhere. The second example he gives concerns a holding company which owns a subsidiary.[342] He believes that the "oggetto principale" of the holding company is not located where the shareholdings are (the country of residence of the subsidiary) but rather in the State where the holding company is actually managing its portfolio.[343] The position defended by Antonini is the prevailing one in Italy. In a case analogous to the first example he provided, the Italian Corte di Cassazione reached the same conclusion[344] and a resolution by the Italian Tax Administration of 2003 sustained the same approach he did with regard to holding companies.[345]

On the other hand, the Australian Taxation Office (hereinafter "ATO") draws a distinction between companies with operational activities (e.g., trading, manufacturing or mining activities) and those that merely manage investment assets.[346] While the former ones would be considered to carry on a business in Australia to the extent that their "major operation activities" take place therein, the latter ones would have their business in Australia insofar their "high-level investment decisions" are made therein. This statement allows us to conclude that the term "business" is conceived by the ATO as a wide concept that integrates passive activities as the investment in property or

340. Della Valle, E. (2016), p. 5.
341. Antonini, M. (2008), p. 150.
342. Antonini, M. (2008), pp. 151-154.
343. This position is equally defended by Manzitti, A. (1998), p. 181, who believes that the "oggetto principale" of a holding company is not necessarily influenced by the residence of the companies it owns.
344. Judgment by Corte di Cassazione in December 10, 1974 (civil law case).
345. Resolution by the Italian Tax Administration, January 29, 2003, n. 18/E.
346. Australian Taxation Office (2004): Draft Taxation Ruling: "Residence of companies not incorporated in Australia—carrying on business in Australia and central management and control," paragraphs 9-12.

shares.[347] Australian courts weigh different factors when the time comes to decide whether the company is effectively carrying on a business within its soil, for example: the repetition of transactions and activities, their commercial nature, their size and scale, the existence of a profit motive, the organization and system underlying the activities, the inherent characteristics or qualities of the property deal in and the inherent characteristics of the taxpayer.[348] Also, the courts require that the company is effectively carrying on the business in the territory of Australia, thereby excluding "dormant" businesses.

This fact-based approach offers the advantages and disadvantages that are typically inherent in all substance over form approaches. On one hand, it prevents companies from declaring a business object in their bylaws (other than the genuine one) that take place in a territory other than Italy or Australia precisely to avoid the tax residence status therein. On the other hand, it gives the administrative and judiciary bodies a great power (and its consequent wide margin of discretion) to interpret the rule, with the resulting high degree of legal uncertainty.

The Italian test poses a further uncertainty as regards its interpretation due to the inclusion of the requirement that the "oggetto dell'attività" must be "principale." Should it be interpreted in a way that the activities carried out in Italy must prevail over those exercised in other States (relative prevalence) or that the Italian activities must outweigh the activities of the entire company (absolute prevalence)? Italian courts have showed their preference for the latter approach.[349] This problem has not arisen in Australia, as its domestic test merely demands the carrying on a business therein, without referring to the relative weight of the Australian business within the global business of the company.

It must be finally noted that, in both cases, the analysis departs from paper. The Italian rule specifically indicates that the assessment should start from the object of the entity as determined on the law, the act of incorporation or the bylaws. The *oggetto principale dell'attività* is presumed to be the one that may be regarded as "essential to directly achieve the primary goals of the company as laid down in the law, act of incorporation or bylaws"[350] to the extent that these sources take the form of a public deed or an authenticated private agreement. For its part, Australian courts equally

347. Kashyap, A.; Shaflender, L. (2004). p. 187 and Australian Taxation Office (2004): Draft Taxation Ruling: "Residence of companies not incorporated in Australia—carrying on business in Australia and central management and control," paragraph 40: "a company may be carrying on business (...) even if its main activity is the management of investment assets. Examples of the types of returns a company may receive from the management of its investment assets include rent, dividends, interest and royalties."
348. *See* Dirkis, M. (2009), pp. 325-327, where he exposes the most representative cases that shape the notion of "carry on business" for the purposes of the residence test.
349. Approach endorsed by scholars as Novara, considering that resident companies are, after all, subject to tax on a worldwide basis. *See* Novara, G. (1990), pp. 14 et seq.
350. Article 73.3 of the Italian Presidential Decree 917/1986, which regulates both the personal and the corporate income tax. The rule then defines the term: "per ogetto principale si intende l'attività essenziale per realizzare direttamente gli scopi primary indicate dalla legge, dall'atto constitutive o dallo statuto." This approach finds its origin in the civil doctrine according to Antonini, M. (2008), p. 149.

begin with the statutory definition of the corporate business.[351] However, as one would expect, both tests make real facts prevail in case they do not correspond to the content of the aforementioned sources.[352] Manzitti describes the Italian test as "an absolutely objective and factual criterion" despite its reference to formal factors.[353] The reason is that, ultimately, the Italian courts must focus on the activities that are "effectively exercised" in Italy.[354] The same considerations apply in the case of Australia.

Finally, a special reference should be made to jurisdictions with territorial tax systems, although they do not exactly fit in this category to the extent that the notion of tax residence is theoretically irrelevant for them. France is a paradigmatic case that may serve as an example. According to its territorial system, companies would only be subject to tax on income derived from any business carried out in France.[355] This being so, the concept of residence should theoretically be irrelevant when it comes to the taxation of a company in France. This is however not entirely true. In practice, the French system has ended up being a "mixed approach," partly due to the influence of tax treaty practice.[356] As a consequence of this, the systems departs from two general rebuttable presumptions that stand upon the very notion of residence: (i) companies having their "seat" in France would be taxable in France except with respect to the profits deriving from a PE located abroad, and (ii) a company having its seat abroad is taxable in France only if it maintains a PE in France.[357] As it can be observed, both presumptions depart from the idea that corporate profits are taxable by default in the country of residence. Furthermore, and contrary to what would happen in a pure territorial system, the burden of proof to overturn the presumption falls on the taxpayer.[358] A similar approach is equally followed by other jurisdictions as Costa Rica.

[i] The Rationale Behind Them

These tests would be entirely consistent with the presumptive benefit principle insofar as they make a company subject to tax on its worldwide income precisely in the jurisdiction where it conducts a substantial business activity and, by extension, where it is presumably using and enjoying the relevant public services. Antonini argues that the Italian test is indeed justified by the greater use by the company of the infrastructures and economic, legal and financial resources provided by the State in which it

351. Dirkis, M. (2009), pp. 325-327.
352. Antonini, M. (2008), p. 149 and Tenore, M. (2009), pp. 538-539 on the Italian rule.
353. A reference that he describes as inadequate, *see* Manzitti, A. (1998), pp. 180-181.
354. Antonini, M. (2008), p. 149.
355. Article 209.1 of the Code Général des impôts. Text available here: https://www.legifrance.gouv.fr/affichCodeArticle.do?idArticle=LEGIARTI000030059670&cidTexte=LEGITEXT000006069577&dateTexte=20141230&oldAction=rechCodeArticle&fastReqId=275759247&nbResultRech=1 (last accessed on January 10, 2019). For an explanation on how the regime works *see also* De Boynes, N. (2009), pp. 446-452.
356. De Boynes, N. (2009), p. 448.
357. These presumptions are established in administrative guidelines according to De Boynes, N. (2009), p. 448.
358. De Boynes, N. (2009), p. 448.

exercises its main business activity.[359] The benefit principle rationale has however traditionally served to justify source-based taxation instead, as we will later argue in section §3.03[B].

[ii] The Potential Profit Shifting Risks They Pose

By their very nature, this category of tests cannot lead to outcomes detached from the existence of economic activity. The reason is obvious, as they are the only ones of all the four categories that actively pursue economic activity.

Nonetheless, we should warn about certain other risks that these tests may pose. By conferring the tax residence status on these grounds, jurisdictions face the risk of distorting the taxpayer's economic behavior, as taxpayers may feel tempted to base their business decisions on tax reasons rather than on reasons of efficiency. On one hand, they may decide not to establish a business activity in an otherwise optimal jurisdiction for the simple fact that they wish to avoid the tax residence status therein. On the other hand, taxpayers may choose to bring their business in a jurisdiction which follows other categories of tests despite the fact it does not provide the perfect environment for their business in terms of workforce, infrastructures or legal system.

We should acknowledge that CITs, for their very nature, always generate distortions in the taxpayer's economic choices, such as the organizational form (the incorporation decision), the financial structure (debt/equity ratio), the dividend policy (pay-out ratio) or certain investments decisions with respect to industry, asset mix, location, risk-taking or timing.[360] However, it is equally true that the adoption of these tests may contribute to further aggravate the distorting effects of these taxes.

[e] Presence of These Tests in the Domestic Tax Legislations Throughout the World

Table 1 Criteria Used by Seventy-Three Jurisdictions to Establish Corporate Tax Residence in Their Respective Domestic Legislations (2019)[361]

	POI/RO	*POEM/CMC*	*R Shareh.*	*Business*
Andorra	X	X		
Argentina	X			

359. Antonini, M. (2008), p. 153.
360. Bird, R. (2002), p. 194.
361. POI (place of incorporation), RO (registered office), POEM (place of effective management), CMC (central management and control), R. Shareh. (residence of shareholders) and Business (location of business) Information displayed on the table is based on the most updated and comprehensive source of data in this regard, which is provided by the OECD website. *See* http://www.oecd.org/tax/automatic-exchange/crs-implementation-and-assistance/tax-residency/ (last accessed to data on January 10, 2019). Additionally, one may also consult Maisto, G. (ed.) (2009) for a number of both civil and common law jurisdictions and Ribes, A. (2012) for EU Member States.

	POI/RO	*POEM/CMC*	*R Shareh.*	*Business*
Aruba	X	X (*)	*	
Australia	X		X	X
Austria	X	X		
Azerbaijan	X	X		
Belgium	X	X		
Belize		X		
Brazil	X			
Brunei	X	X		
Bulgaria	X			
Canada	X	X		
China	X	X		
Colombia	X	X		
Cook Islands	X (*)			
Croatia	X	X		
Cyprus		X		
Czech Republic		X		
Denmark	X	X		
Estonia	X			
Faroe Islands	X	X		
Finland	X	X		
Germany	X	X		
Gibraltar		X		
Greece	X	X (*)	*	
Greenland	X			
Guernsey	X	X		
Hong Kong	X	X		
Hungary	X	X		
Iceland	X	X		
India	X	X		
Ireland	X	X		
Isle of Man	X	X		
Italy	X	X		X
Japan	X			
Jersey	X	X		
Korea	X	X		
Latvia	X			

	POI/RO	*POEM/CMC*	*R Shareh.*	*Business*
Lebanon	X			
Liechtenstein	X	X		
Lithuania	X			
Luxembourg	X	X		
Macao	X			
Malaysia		X		
Malta	X	X		
Mauritius	X	X		
Mexico		X		
Montserrat	X			
Netherlands	*	X (*)	*	
New Zealand	X	X		
Norway	X	X		
Poland	X	X		
Portugal	X	X		
Romania	X	X		
Russia	X			
Saint Lucia	X	X		
Saint Vincent	X	X		
Samoa	X	X		
San Marino	X	X		
Saudi Arabia	X	X		
Seychelles	X	X		
Singapore		X		
Slovak Republic	X	X		
Slovenia	X	X		
South Africa	X	X		
Spain	X	X		*
Sweden	X	X		
Switzerland	X	X		
Trinidad & Tobago		X		
Turkey	X	X		

	POI/RO	POEM/CMC	R Shareh.	Business
United Kingdom	X	X		
United States	X			
Uruguay	X			

(*) Comments and observations

1. Territorial systems are ignored, since tax residence is not of relevance in such context. This is the case for France[362] and Costa Rica.[363]
2. States not having CITs in place are equally omitted from the table. E.g. Bahrain, Bermuda, Cayman Islands, the Bahamas and Turks and Caicos Islands.
3. Aruba: When determining POEM, residence of shareholders may be assessed along with other criteria
4. Cook Islands: The test refers to the "head office."
5. Greece: Residence of the majority of the shareholders may also be taken into consideration in its POEM test.
6. Netherlands: When interpreting POEM, POI and residence of shareholders will be taken into account.
7. Spain: The location of a business in Spain is not a test itself but rather part of anti-tax haven deemed residence rule.[364]

362. Maisto, G. (ed.) (2009), pp. 446 et seq. and http://www.oecd.org/tax/automatic-exchange/crs-implementation-and-assistance/tax-residency/France-Tax-Residency.pdf (last accessed to data on January 10, 2019).
363. http://www.oecd.org/tax/automatic-exchange/crs-implementation-and-assistance/tax-residency/Costa-Rica-Tax-residency.pdf (last accessed to data on January 10, 2019).
364. For further details *see* Chapter 3 section §3.02[A][2][c].

Figure 4 Most Common Combinations of Residence Tests in the Seventy-Three Surveyed Countries (2019)[365]

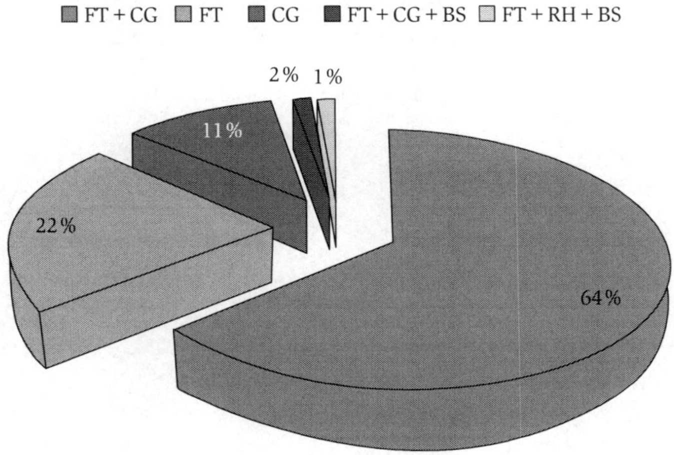

Out of the total of seventy-three surveyed jurisdictions: 90% use formal tests and 80% employ tests relying on the governance of the company, while criteria based on the residence of the shareholders and the location of the business activities are only trusted by 1.4% and 2.8% respectively. The preferred combination of rules, followed by 64% of the surveyed jurisdictions, is the one conformed by formal tests and tests based on the company decision-making. All countries apply both alternatively (if one is met the company would be deemed to be resident) except for Sweden who requires both cumulatively. Only 22% of the jurisdictions employ solely formal tests while only 11% of them choose to use solely tests based on the place where the company is effectively managed. This means that 97% of the surveyed jurisdictions rely either on both formal tests and tests based on corporate governance together or one of them, while solely 3% of them follow alternative approaches. Only 3% of the surveyed States (i.e., Italy and Australia) follow corporate tax residence tests that may be regarded as consistent with the presumptive benefit principle and are thus well equipped to prevent profit shifting from happening.

365. FT: formal tests (POI and/or registered office); CG: tests based on corporate governance (POEM or central management and control); RH: tests based on the residence of the shareholders; and BS: tests based on the location of the business activities. *See* http://www.oecd.org/tax/automatic-exchange/crs-implementation-and-assistance/tax-residency/ (last accessed to data on January 10, 2019).

[2] *Interim Conclusions*

[a] *Most Corporate Tax Residence Tests Currently in Place Were Inherited from Private International Law*

Private international law arose from the need to settle "conflicts of laws." That is, situations in which individuals or companies, as a result of their actions or transactions, expose themselves to being subject to the legislative and/or judicial jurisdiction of two or more countries. In this context, private international law serves the function of establishing which country would have jurisdiction over the individual or company to prescribe legal rules or adjudicate legal conflicts by means of the so-called connecting factors.[366]

Behrens was the responsible for drawing the conclusions from the comparative study of the connecting factors used by thirteen countries[367] to determine the circumstances under which their respective company legislation (*lex societas*) would be applicable to a given company.[368] In doing so, he classified the criteria used into three different categories: (i) factors relying on the creation of the company as a legal person, (ii) factors relying on the internal governance structure and decision-making and (iii) factors relying on the business activity of a company.

Undoubtedly these categories should sound familiar to us at this point. And a closer study of the criteria within each category[369] ultimately confirms our first impressions: they are suspiciously similar to the residence tests used for CIT purposes. Naturally, we are not alone in holding this opinion, as it is shared by some other scholars.[370] Indeed, Couzin explicitly recognized that the absence of statutory or case law definitions of corporate residence made legislators and courts seek inspiration in

366. Behrens, P. (2009), p. 3.
367. We are referring to the comparative analysis published in Maisto, G. (ed.) (2009), which covered a total of 13 countries: Australia, Austria, Belgium, Canada, France, Germany, Italy, Netherlands, South Africa, Spain, Switzerland, UK and US.
368. Behrens, P. (2009), pp. 3-27.
369. The first category encompasses POI, place of registration, registered office or statutory seat as defined in the articles. The second one covers the "nerve center" of the company, the place of principal administration/center of management, the place of most important decisions, the place of implementation of the most important decisions and the place where the controlling organ of the company is located (board meetings and shareholders' meetings). Lastly, the third category includes criteria such as the principal POB, the principal place of activities and the place "d'exploitation." *See* Behrens, P. (2009), pp. 7-10.
370. De Broe stated that: "in most countries all or some of the tests applied for corporate tax purposes are identical or similar to those applied for private international law purposes," *see* De Broe, L. (2009), p. 97. In the same vein, Couzin argued that the "the adaptation of connecting factors [from private international law] theretofore limited to natural persons to incorporated companies by means of analogy become the touchstone in the explication of corporate residence for income tax purposes." However, he finally concluded that income taxation had "produced rather than inherited" a generally accepted meaning of corporate residence. *See* Couzin, R. (2002), p.21. Similarly, Van Daele stated that: "if we compare the criteria used by various countries to determine the applicable company law, on the one hand, and the criteria used to establish a country's taxing jurisdiction, on the other hand, it appears that there are many occasions where they coincide." *See* Van Daele, J. (2011), p. 195.

the field of private international law, which had already developed a methodology, vocabulary and approach.[371]

This being the case, the next question would be whether the resemblance of these criteria is merely superficial or, on the contrary, their interpretation is equally homogeneous. De Broe believes that the interpretation of the terms in both areas of law "very much converges."[372] This is particularly true in the case of common law countries. We should recall at this point that the British courts of the nineteenth century that gave birth to the "central management and control" test departed, in their reasoning, from a rule of private international law and followed the ideas previously expressed in judgments in private law matters,[373] as section §3.02[A][1][b] exposed above. For their part and as a general rule, civil law countries tend not to be carried away by the case law in private international law when it comes to the interpretation of the residence tests.[374]

This reality would not be worrying per se if not were for the fact that tax law and private international law respond to different rationales.[375] It is true that both legal orders share the common purpose of connecting cases having a foreign element with a certain country on the basis of a connection with the latter.[376] However, the ultimate function performed by both legal orders and their respective connecting factors differs significantly: while private international law intends to identify the "proper law" of a company for the purposes of applying it in a legal dispute before a court, tax law aims at identifying a connection (between a country and a person or item of income) that triggers a tax liability, or more specifically, an unlimited tax liability when it comes to residence-based taxation.[377]

---

371. Couzin, R. (2002), p.21. The inspiration is certainly undeniable in the case of the formal tests. Couzin recognized that the POI test for tax purposes "effectively, although not explicitly, borrowed from the private international law the definition of domicile." More recently, Loomer stated that "for the purposes of private international law, a corporation's domicile is considered to be the country of its incorporation." *See* Couzin, R. (2002), p. 31 and Loomer, G.T. (2015), p. 104.
372. De Broe, L. (2009), p. 97. On the contrary, Behrens believes that the convergence merely occurs in the surface, while "their precise meaning is context-dependent and may therefore be quite different." *See* Behrens, P. (2009), p. 27.
373. In the case "The Cesena Sulphur Co Ltd v. Nicholson," the seed of the "central management and control" test, the court referred in multiple occasions to judgments pertaining to the area of private international law. *See* Judgment by the High Court (Exchequer Division), 1876, "The Cesena Sulphur Co Ltd v. Nicholson" and "The Calcutta Jute Mills Co Ltd v. Nicholson" and Avery Jones, J.F. (2009), p. 134, where an excerpt of it may be found.
374. Two exceptions should be highlighted. The first one is Austria, where the interpretation of "centre of business direction" (term used in its tax legislation) and "seat of administration" (term used in private international law) is quite uniform. In the case of Italy, the interpretation of the main activity test is again quite homogeneous. *See* Simader, K. (2009) and Tenore, M. (2009).
375. In the same vein, Van Daele states that: "it is important to emphasize that connecting factors serve a different purpose from private international law and work according to a different mechanism regarding the taxation of companies." *See* Van Daele, J. (2011), p. 194. In the same vein, *see* Behrens, P. (2009), p. 26: "it is important to understand the different function fulfilled by connecting factors in this context (corporate taxation) as opposed to the private international law context."
376. Sachdeva, A.M. (2014), p. 3.
377. Behrens, P. (2009), pp. 26-27.

Once we have understood the purpose underlying private international law when it comes to the identification of the proper *lex societas*, it is easier to appreciate the appropriateness of its connecting factors. In the case of the POI test, for example, it is only natural that a company is governed by the laws of the country of incorporation, to the extent that it is ultimately a creature of such laws and its existence is necessarily linked to them.[378] As regards the factors relying on the governance and the business of the company, it is argued that one of the objectives of company laws it the protection of the creditors, and these factors lead to point at the country in which the company is more closely linked and by extension, where such creditors may be presumably located.[379]

While these connecting factors may make some sense in the field of private international law if we bear in mind its specific purposes and rationale, we cannot say the same in the context of tax law. In other words, the mere extrapolation of terms from private international law to tax law without taking into consideration the different functions performed by each legal order constitutes a manifest error. And most importantly, it reveals that the gestation process of current tax residence tests lacked a serious reflection on the particular objectives, specificities and needs of tax law. Consequently, some scholars have recently pleaded, albeit belatedly, for a true reconsideration of current tax residence tests which finally contemplates the particularities and purposes of tax law.[380]

[b] The Implementation of New Residence Tests Has Generally Been Motivated by the Desire of Closing the Loopholes of Previous Tests Rather Than by Clear Policy Purposes

The analysis of the origins and rationales of the respective residence tests has led us to conclude that jurisdictions have usually incorporated new residence tests to their respective legislations or jurisprudence with the aim of remedying the shortcomings and deficiencies of the preexisting tests.

For example, the decisions by the British House of Lords that planted the seeds of the "central management and control" test back in the nineteenth century came up with this new test as a reaction against formal tests, which they had despised for being

378. Behrens, P. (2009), p. 8.
379. Behrens, P. (2009), pp. 8-10.
380. For example, Behrens stated that "international taxation cannot easily borrow from international law (...) it must develop the relevant notions according to its own principles and policies." *See* Behrens, P. (2009), p. 27. Van Daele shared his view, but he also brought forward additional arguments from an EU Law perspective. In a nutshell, he noted that the interaction of the criteria from both legal orders caused a distortion to regulatory competition, in a sense that tax consequences appear as soon as one wants to relocate a business in order to pursue a more suitable company legislation. He finally suggested the use of different criteria in both fields of law "in order to enhance the mobility of companies, without tax issues deterring companies from choosing the company law that best serves the enterprise's business needs." *See* Van Daele, J. (2011), p. 195. Nonetheless, we also found dissenting opinions. Sachdeva, for example, advocated for the convenience of using conflict of laws jurisprudence in international tax matters and used an example some US judgments that followed this approach. *See* Sachdeva, A.M. (2014).

"insufficient." In fact, the leading case De Beers expressly asserted that, in the absence of a "central management and control" test a company "might have its chief seat of management and its centre of trading in England under the protection of English law, and yet escape the appropriate taxation by the simple expedient of being registered abroad and distributing its dividends abroad."[381] More recently, it has even been argued that this test works "as an anti-avoidance provision,"[382] a view we do not share and furthermore regard as problematic.[383]

Ironically, there was a movement in the opposite direction a few decades later. Some common law countries with an already well-established case law on the "central management and control test" amended their respective legislations to introduce the POI test.[384] The reason behind this decision is that the governments were concerned about tax avoidance through the manipulation of central management and control.[385]

Similarly, tests based on the residence of the company's shareholders equally arose with this same objective. Australia, the only surveyed jurisdiction which currently follows this approach, adopted this test in a context in which locally owned companies were appointing foreign boards of directors in order to avoid the "central management and control" test. This being so, Australia decided to follow the advice of the UK Royal Commission on the Income Tax, which recommended the introduction of

381. Decision by the House of Lords of the United Kingdom, 1905, "De Beers Consolidated Mines Ltd. v. Howe (Surveyor of Taxes)." *See* Chapter 3 section §3.02[A][1][b], where the origins of this category of tests are explained.
382. In 2013 Hughes defended that the British central management and control test "operates primarily as an anti-avoidance provision to prevent companies from manipulating their residence status." *See* Hughes, D. (2013), p. 3. With respect to the Spanish rule on POEM, Martínez Giner states that "(its) purpose is to prevent international tax avoidance when companies when companies are incorporated under foreign law with registered offices abroad but carry on their activities in Spain where they have their place of effective management" while Carmona argues that it allows to "attract the tax residence of entities that have been illegitimately delocalized." *See* Martínez Giner, L.A. (2009), p. 766 and Carmona Fernández, N. (2007), p. 137. For its part, the explanatory notes of the Bill to amend the Australian Income Tax Assessment Act explicitly said this criterion ensured that "a number of companies incorporated outside Australia whose sole or principal business is located in Australia" were taxable as residents.
383. In our opinion such argument should be dismissed, since the rule lacks the traditional components of anti-avoidance rules (e.g., tax saving, artificiality, business purpose, valid economic reasons, existence of other legal or economic non-tax consequences, etc.) and instead presents itself as regular connecting factor with the sole purpose of assigning tax residence status under certain circumstances. Besides, such understanding may be troublesome to the extent it may potentially lead to misleading interpretations of the rule that go beyond its scope.
384. For example, Canada did so in 1961 and the UK in 1988.
385. In the case of the UK it is more evident. It was explicitly stated in the International Manual published by the HMRC that the incorporation rule was added to deal with so-called nowhere companies, being incorporated in the UK but managed and controlled in a State that does not use management and control as a residence test. *See* the British HM Revenue & Customs (2014): International Manual (https://www.gov.uk/hmrc-internal-manuals/international-manual/intm120050 last accessed on January 10, 2019). In the case of Canada, the official reason was not so clearly disclosed, but Pyrcz and Loomer believe it is the same. *See* Pyrcz, O.A. (1973) and Loomer, G.T. (2015), p. 108 ("the most cogent explanation is that the government was concerned about tax avoidance through the manipulation of central management and control"). Arnold described the central management test resulting from De Beers as a new "tax planning device." *See* Arnold, B. J. (2003), p. 1560.

this test as a way to counteract this widespread practice.[386] Lastly, although not explicitly mentioned, it would be reasonable to conclude that the introduction of residence tests relying on the location of the business activity of the company equally responds to the same purpose.

The analysis of these residence tests also reveals the increasing tendency to rely on factors much less mobile and more difficult to manipulate. A tendency that culminated with the adoption by some countries of tests based on the residence of the shareholders and the location of the business activity. This tendency is also visible in the special anti-avoidance rules that will be described below in section §3.02[A][2][c].

Nevertheless, beyond the perceptible objective of overcoming the deficiencies and weaknesses of preexisting residence tests, it seems that a serious reflection on the policy purposes that each one of the tests could accomplish was missing.

[c] Current Residence Tests Are Often Criticized for Leading to Jurisdictions in Which the Company Is Not Sufficiently Connected from an Economic Point of View: A "Flaw" That Tends to Be Corrected by Means of Anti-avoidance Rules

We should first acknowledge that, as a matter of principle, there are not residence tests that are better than others. Each one of them simply serves a different policy purpose.

Therefore, if we follow the POI test because we regard our CIT as a fee for the benefits of incorporation,[387] we should not be bothered by the fact that a group of persons decides to incorporate a company in a low-tax jurisdiction or a company previously incorporated in our country chooses to migrate. Similarly, if we choose to follow the POEM test because we believe that our CIT serves the function of preventing potential abuses of power by the managers,[388] we should not be concerned by the fact that a company genuinely transfers its board of directors out of our territory. In both cases, we should respectfully accept the outcome of our own residence tests: that the company concerned would effectively cease to be tax resident in our jurisdiction. And, as long as we truly believe in the logic behind our own rules, these practices should not pose any problem.

The problem is that, generally speaking, most jurisdictions do not seem satisfied with the logical outcomes of their respective residence tests. And, in our opinion, the motive is that jurisdictions adopt these tests without really knowing, understanding and accepting their supposed rationale. Instead, they believe these tests per se ensure a "sufficient relationship" between the jurisdiction concerned and the company that would become liable to tax for its worldwide income on the basis of these criteria. Or perhaps, they believe the tests contain some sort of indicia of some "deeper and less

386. *See* Chapter 3 section §3.02[A][1][c], where the origins and purposes of this test are briefly outlined.
387. *See* Chapter 3 section §3.02[A][1][a] to see the rationale that is allegedly behind the POI test.
388. *See* Chapter 3 section §3.02[A][1][b] to see the rationale that is allegedly behind the residence tests based on the governance of the company.

visible corporate trait."[389] As a consequence, they observe with surprise and disappointment that such tests may lead to a situation in which the company is tax resident in a jurisdiction in which it does not have any significant connection beyond the one explicitly stated by the residence test, i.e., the country where it was incorporated, where it has its registered office or where its board of directors meet, for example.

More specifically, jurisdictions seem to be particularly worried with the fact that the residence tests lead to consider a country in which the company does not have "economic substance" as its residence country for tax purposes. For example, the British Inland Revenue stated back in 1981 that the British residence tests had "enabled companies to arrange a residence for tax purposes which may bear little relation to the seat of the company's operations."[390] These complaints have equally impregnated multiple doctrinal articles. For instance, De Broe argues that the application of current residence tests "does not ensure that the company is subject to comprehensive tax liability in the country with which its economic nexus is closest."[391] In the same vein, Schön asserts that the application of residence-based taxation to companies which are merely incorporated under the laws of the country concerned makes little sense insofar there is no "serious economic connection" with the country.[392]

This scenario is, however, a quite plausible one. As a matter of fact, such scenario would be the natural consequence of most current residence tests. The reason is that tests followed by the vast overwhelming majority of States, by their very nature, do not specifically require an economic attachment between the company and the country concerned,[393] the only exception being the tests based on the location of the economic activity that are currently in force in Italy and Australia, which are the only ones that are aligned with the presumptive benefit principle.[394]

As many jurisdictions do not accept the outcomes of their own rules, they try to remedy this "flaw" by means of anti-avoidance rules that effectively and actively pursue the desired economic substance. In this regard, it could be said that many States aspire to achieve outcomes consistent with the presumptive benefit principle but not through the residence tests themselves but (indirectly) through the action of anti-avoidance rules. We shall confine ourselves to providing a few examples, as a thorough study of the application of anti-avoidance rules in the context of tax residence tests clearly goes beyond the scope of the present investigation. Hence, our sole purpose is to note the general tendency to rely on anti-avoidance rules as a way to correct the unwanted (albeit logical) outcomes of current residence tests.

---

389. Couzin, R. (2002), pp. 263-264. He believes that countries following traditional residence tests (as POI or POEM management) regard them as a "*signal for something else*," as he finds illogical that a country considers a company incorporated in accordance with its law as domestic regardless of where its shareholders reside, its business is managed, its profits are made, its assets are deployed and the labor of its employees is exercised.
390. British Inland Revenue (1981): Company residence: a consultative document.
391. De Broe, L. (2009), p. 99.
392. Schön, W. (2005), p. 345.
393. Loomer shares our view: "various legal meanings ascribed to corporate residence require little in the way of economic attachment to the purported home state." *See* Loomer, G.T. (2015), p. 92.
394. *See* Chapter 3 section §3.02[A][1][d].

In the first place, jurisdictions may resort to their general anti-avoidance rules (hereinafter "GAARs") to counteract the effects of the residence tests and either deny the residence status of allegedly domestic companies or extend the residence status to foreign ones. On one hand, we have the case of Germany, where the tax administration is entitled on the basis of their domestic GAAR to deny the tax residence status to companies which merely have their legal seat in Germany but do not have a "genuine economic link" with the country to the extent that the only reason behind the election of Germany as the legal seat is to obtain a tax advantage.[395]

However anti-avoidance rules would more likely operate the other way around, that is, to extend the residence status to a (formally) foreign company that is still heavily present in the jurisdiction concerned. Indeed, as Zornoza cautions, the incorporation (or migration) of a company in (to) a tax haven or low-tax jurisdiction, although optimal at first glance, is very likely to be targeted by a great number of anti-avoidance rules.[396] The IFA General report on the topic observed that, at least back in 2001, jurisdictions hardly ever used their GAARs (or equivalent unwritten principles) in these scenarios for various reasons: e.g., the difficult access to the relevant information for the purposes of the application of the rule, the recent adoption of such rules and, most importantly, the existence of other domestic provisions that specifically targeted these cases.[397]

Indeed, as noted by the IFA general report, domestic legislations have multiple specific anti-avoidance rules (hereinafter "SAARs") that may take the form of deemed residence rules or rebuttable presumptions whose application lead to the treatment of a non-resident company as resident for CIT purposes in cases in which the company is somehow still sufficiently connected to the jurisdiction concerned. Such connection is generally defined by means of criteria that are much less susceptible to manipulations. For example, the fact that the company carries on its business within the territory or the fact that most of their shareholders are resident therein. The following examples illustrate this trend.

Under the Spanish Corporate Income Tax Act, when a company resident in a low-tax jurisdiction carries on its activity in Spain it will be deemed to be tax resident in Spain unless it effectively proves that its effective management is located in the former jurisdiction and that it operates for "valid economic reasons."[398] This rule

395. In similar situations Germany has made use of its domestic GAAR, established in Article 42 of the *Abgabenordnung* (German Tax Code). *See* the judgment by the Finanzgericht Baden-Württenmerg, April 13, 2000, 3 K 235/97. Although this is the most correct way to deal with these situations, Englisch noted that some scholars advocate instead for the application of the sham rule (Article 41.2 of the *Abgabenordnung*), considering that the legal seat in Germany is a "simulated act" that has to be disregarded pursuant to such rule. We agree with Englisch on the appropriateness of using the GAAR in these scenarios. *See* Englisch, J. (2009), p. 486. The *Abgabenordnung* may be consulted here: http://www.gesetze-im-internet.de/ao_1977/index.html (last accessed on January 10, 2019).

396. *See* Zornoza Pérez, J. (2013), pp. 15-16 and for a more comprehensive insight *see* Arnold, B. J.; Dibout, P. (2001).

397. Arnold, B. J.; Dibout, P. (2001), p. 34 and more recently Van Weeghel, S. (2010), p. 28.

398. Article 8.1 of the Spanish Corporate Income Tax Act. *See* http://noticias.juridicas.com/base_datos/Fiscal/540273-l-27-2014-de-27-nov-impuesto-sobre-sociedades.html#a8 (last accessed on January 10, 2019). Martínez Giner translated the rule as follows: "the tax authorities may

applies as a rebuttable presumption and therefore it would not produce effects if the company is able to successfully prove both the location of the POEM and the "valid economic reasons" together with the "good business purpose."[399]

For its part, Italy provides a rebuttable presumption according to which a company incorporated in a jurisdiction other than Italy would be presumed to have its POEM in Italy (and thus become tax resident therein) if, at the end of the fiscal year, such company directly controls one or more companies resident in Italy and, at the same time, at least one of the next conditions is met: either (i) it is controlled (directly or indirectly) by shareholders that are resident in Italy or, (ii) it is managed by a board of directors mainly composed by members resident in Italy. Once these conditions are met, the foreign company will be treated as a resident in Italy unless it is able to demonstrate that it is not effectively managed from Italy.[400]

The US incorporated an equivalent SAAR is the IRC back in 2004. Pursuant to such rule, a foreign company would be regarded as domestic for tax purposes provided that the following three conditions are met: (i) the company directly or indirectly acquires substantially all of the properties held directly or indirectly by a domestic company, (ii) after the acquisition, at least 80% of the stock (by vote or value) is held by former shareholders of the domestic company and (iii) after the acquisition the expanded affiliated group (which includes the entity) does not have substantial business activities in the foreign country in which the entity is created or organized, when compared to the total business activities of such expanded affiliated group.[401]

The SAARs described above effectively lead to the automatic extension of the residence status to foreign companies for being "closely linked" to the jurisdiction concerned in terms of ownership and/or business activity. This being so, once the SAAR becomes applicable, the tax jurisdiction of the country would automatically cover a company that is *a priori* out of its scope, and consequently such company would be regarded as a domestic taxpayer for all legal intents and purposes. That is, the company would become subject to full tax liability on its worldwide income and additionally, would be obliged to comply with the other tax and administrative requirements to which domestic companies are ordinarily subject.[402]

presume that an entity situated in a tax-free territory pursuant to paragraph 2 of the first additional provision of the Act on Measures for the Prevention of Tax Fraud or in a tax haven, has its residence in Spain when its main assets, directly or indirectly, consist of property located in Spain or rights that are fulfilled or exercised in Spanish territory, or when its main activity is carried on in this country, unless the entity accredits that its effective management takes place in the former territory and it was incorporated and operates for valid economic reasons and good business purpose other than the simple management of securities or other assets." *See* Martínez Giner, L.A. (2009), pp. 775-778.

399. The Spanish General Directorate for Taxation held that this clause should be interpreted in the sense that there should be more reasons for the incorporation apart from securing the tax advantage.
400. Article 73.5-bis of the Italian Presidential Decree 917/1986, which regulates both the personal and the corporate income tax. This provision was introduced in 2006.
401. Sections 7874 (b) and 7874 (a) (2) (B) IRC.
402. Bardini reaches this conclusion in respect the Italian SAAR but the same applies to the remaining ones. *See* Bardini, C. (2010), p. 379.

A more unorthodox (and definitely undesirable) approach is the one recently taken by the Spanish tax authorities so as to gain the tax residency of a holding company incorporated and managed from a territory other than Spain. As the Spanish SAAR was inapplicable to the case (the territory in question was not a low-tax jurisdiction), the Administration chose to resort to the POEM test so as to conclude that the holding had its POEM in Spain on the grounds that its main assets were located in Spain and its main shareholders and main manager were tax resident therein, despite the fact that the meetings of the board of directors occurred abroad. This approach entails a genuine "deep subversion" from the legal criteria used in Spain to determine POEM.[403]

At this point, we should briefly allude to other category of rules that in substance plays an equivalent role. We are referring to CFC rules (also known as fiscal transparency regimes), which are present in a large number of domestic legislations.[404] Just as the abovementioned SAARs, CFC rules lead to the taxation of non-resident companies (CFCs) on the basis that they are "closely linked" to the jurisdiction concerned in the sense that they are effectively controlled by domestic companies.[405] However, unlike those SAARs, the CFC would not be regarded as a domestic taxpayer for all intents and purposes. That is, it would neither be taxed for its worldwide income nor be subject to the same compliance requirements as domestic companies. On the contrary, the CFC would solely be taxed provided certain conditions are met and merely on certain categories of income that are deemed to pose greater profit shifting risks, e.g., passive income.[406]

We could conclude that the existence of the abovementioned anti-avoidance and CFC rules reveals the underlying determination of some States to tax companies which, while not meeting their respective residence tests, are nevertheless sufficiently connected to their territories, either because they are controlled by residents or because they carry on a business activity therein.[407] However, instead of amending their residence tests straightaway so that they effectively require the desired degree of

403. Báez Moreno, A.; Zornoza Pérez, J.J. (2017), pp. 12-13.
404. The IFA general report on limits on the use of low-tax regimes by MNCs noted that, back in 2001, 19 countries (out of a total of 30 surveyed) had adopted or were in the process of adopting CFC rules. *See* Arnold, B. J.; Dibout, P. (2001), p. 38. The objective of these rules is to counteract tax deferral opportunities that would otherwise exist, to the extent resident companies may easily incorporate foreign companies in lower-tax jurisdictions and shift their income there, particularly passive income.
405. Bardini compares the effects of the deemed residence rule and the CFC regime in Italy and subsequently proceeds to assess their compatibility with EU Law. *See* Bardini, C. (2010).
406. For example, as a general rule, CFC regimes only apply when the CFC is subject to taxes below a certain threshold and merely subject to CFC taxation income that is more likely to be geographically mobile (e.g., dividends, interests, insurance income, IP income, insurance income). The abovementioned IFA general report on the use of low-tax regimes by MNCs is useful to compare the different approaches followed by the surveyed counties back in 2001. *See* Arnold, B. J.; Dibout, P. (2001), pp. 38-66. More recently, the OECD has published some recommendations to strengthen domestic CFC rules to effectively counteract profit shifting risks, *see* OECD (2015): Final Report on BEPS Action 3: Designing effective Controlled Foreign Company rules.
407. In this latter case, States may be regarded as indirectly pursuing outcomes consistent with the presumptive benefit principle.

linkage or "substance," they choose to resort to rules with anti-avoidance nature that help them reach the desired outcomes. In the light of this, we sympathize with the idea of introducing new residence tests which would render unnecessary the existence of such anti-avoidance rules.[408] Along the same lines, Maisto suggested the introduction of a residence test according to which a company would be deemed to be tax resident in a jurisdiction to the extent that most of its shareholders are tax resident therein,[409] as such approach would effectively render unnecessary CFC rules.[410]

[B] The Lack of Coordination in the Domestic Definitions of Corporate Tax Residence May Generate Mismatches That Could Be Used to Shift Profits

The freedom of countries to define residence and thereby select the persons who would become liable to unlimited taxation is theoretically boundless. In fact, a general overview of the domestic residence tests quickly reveals that each one follows a different approach, albeit it is possible to identify some common patterns.[411]

It seems that jurisdictions have indeed managed to keep the definition of residence under their sovereignty, squandering the opportunities to achieve a certain level of international coordination at both the tax treaty or the EU level.

With regard to tax treaties, none of the most influential model tax conventions, namely the OECD, the UN or the US ones (the MCs),[412] has suggested the introduction of a consensual definition of residence. In fact, the matter was deliberately left out of the discussion in the Commentaries on the OECD MC, which states that: "conventions (...) do not normally concern themselves with the domestic laws of the Contracting States laying down the conditions under which a person is to be treated fiscally as resident (...) they do not law down standards which the provisions of the domestic laws on residence have to fulfill in order that claims for full tax liability can be accepted between the Contracting States (...) States take their stand entirely on the domestic laws."[413]

With regard to EU Law, the conclusion does not differ, as neither positive nor negative integration has led to any sort of coordination between the Member States. Yet, there have been a few proposals in this direction. For example, Ribes and González Sánchez have called for the harmonization of corporate tax residence definitions as, in

408. In fact, we will later propose a new corporate tax residence test in Chapter 4 section §4.02[B][3] with this objective.
409. This test already exists in Australia, where it is applied in conjunction with other tests. *See* Chapter 3 section §3.02[A][1][c].
410. Maisto, G. (2014), p. 327.
411. *See* Chapter 3 section §3.02[A].
412. *See* Articles 1 and 4 of the 2017 OECD Model Convention: https://www.oecd.org/ctp/treaties/2014-model-tax-convention-articles.pdf, the 2017 UN Model Convention: http://www.un.org/esa/ffd/documents/UN_Model_2011_Update.pdf and the 2016 US MC: https://www.irs.gov/pub/irs-trty/model006.pdf (last accessed on January 10, 2019).
413. Commentary on Article 4 of the 2017 OECD Model Convention, paragraph 4.

their opinion, it would limit both tax evasion and double taxation and thus improve the economic integration in the EU.[414]

In general, asymmetries among domestic tax systems inexorably generate tax planning opportunities, a phenomenon that is commonly referred to as "international tax arbitrage."[415] The same is true with regard the disparities between the respective definitions of residence for CIT purposes, as taxpayers can easily exploit these mismatches to shift their profits to territories where economic activities take place or even make them disappear from the face of the Earth. Indeed, we already witnessed the emblematic example of Apple. Let us recall that three subsidiaries belonging to the Apple group achieved the status of "stateless" to the extent that they did not meet any of the residence tests provided by the jurisdictions with which they were somehow linked.[416] In a nutshell, as Ireland followed (at that time) solely the "central management and control" test inherited from the UK case law while the US followed (and still do) only the POI test, the subsidiaries did not meet any of these tests, since they were incorporated in Ireland but managed from the US.

Apple successfully exploited a mismatch in the residence tests of Ireland and the US. However, such disparities are not at all rare. If we go back to section §3.02[A][1][e] and consult Table 1 we could check at a glance that this same asymmetry is equally present in multiple combinations of jurisdictions. As there are fifteen jurisdictions that solely follow the POI test while nine do likewise with tests relying on the decision-making of the company, this makes a total of 135 combinations (within a sample of barely seventy-three countries) that are equally exploitable for profit shifting purposes. For instance, this same asymmetry between the domestic residence tests of Ireland and Bermuda was equally used by Google Ireland Holdings, one of Apple's subsidiaries.[417]

[C] The Elevation of the Threshold to Access Tax Treaty Benefits Reveals the Weaknesses of Domestic Corporate Residence Tests

The entitlement to the benefits provided by tax treaties is usually conditioned upon compliance with various general requirements. For the purposes of reviewing such requirements, we will make reference to the three MCs.

414. Ribes suggests the simultaneous application of two tests: POI and "effective economic integration of the company in the Sate in question." For her part, González Sánchez proposes the application of both the POI and POEM tests, although she strongly advocates for a source-based taxation system within the EU and merely maintains the relevance of the residence tests in the relationships between EU Member States and non-EU States. *See* Ribes, A. (2012) and González Sánchez, E. (2005).
415. Rosenbloom studied this phenomenon in Rosenbloom, D. (2000), where he noted that it was only natural that taxpayers seeking to keep their tax burdens to a minimum study the rules of individual countries for the purpose of turning them to their advantage: "the effort will involve a focus on differences in the applicable rules" (p. 140).
416. Chapter 2 section §2.01[A][2].
417. Kleinbard observed that Google Ireland Holdings was incorporated in Ireland while managed from Bermuda. As Ireland followed at that time solely the "central management and control" test and Bermuda provides a POI test, the consequence was that Google Ireland Holdings was stateless. *See* Kleinbard, E.D. (2011), p. 710.

[1] Departure from the Domestic Definition of Tax Residence

In the first place, Article 1 of all three models makes the application of the treaty subject to the fact that the person, either individual or legal entity, is resident of one or both contracting States. The determination of the residence status for the purposes of the tax treaty depends on Article 4 of the three MCs. The wording of Article 4.1 is almost identical in the three models except for a few details (Table 2).

Table 2 Comparison of Article 4.1 in the Three MCs[418]

OECD Model Convention (2017)	*UN Model Convention (2017)*	*US Model Convention (2016)*
For the purposes of this convention, the term "resident of a Contracting State" means any person who, under the laws of that Sate, is liable to tax therein by reason of his domicile, residence, place of management or any other criterion of a similar nature (…) This term, however, does not include any person who is liable to tax in that State in respect only of income from sources in that State or capital situated therein	For the purposes of this Convention, the term "resident of a Contracting State" means any person who, under the laws of that State, is liable to tax therein by reason of his domicile, residence, **place of incorporation**, place of management or any other criterion of a similar nature … This term, however, does not include any person who is liable to tax in that State in respect only of income from sources in that State or capital situated therein	For the purposes of this Convention, the term "resident of a Contracting State" means any person who, under the laws of that State, is liable to tax therein by reason of his domicile, residence, **citizenship**, place of management, **place of incorporation**, or any other criterion of a similar nature (…) This term ~~however~~ does not include any person **whose tax is determined in that Contracting State on a fixed-fee, "forfeit" or similar basis or** who is liable to tax in that State in respect only of income from sources in that State ~~or capital situated therein~~ **or of profits attributable to a permanent establishment in this State**

From the reading of the model provisions, we may infer a few ideas. The first one is that the models do not provide an agreed definition of residence for the purposes of its application. The second one is that all MCs make a reference to the domestic legislations of the Contracting States, which are ultimately entrusted with the function

418. Words in bold and strike-through indicate the variations from the 2017 OECD MC.

of designating which persons will be considered as "residents" for both domestic and treaty purposes. The third idea is that the models provide a non-exhaustive list of criteria that may be used by the Contracting States in order to establish the residence status of both individuals and legal entities. And finally, the fourth and last idea is that the models would only respect the domestic residence status as long as they trigger an unlimited tax liability in the State concerned.[419]

[2] Treaty Shopping and the Inclusion of LOB Provisions in Some Tax Treaties

The US was probably the first jurisdiction to consider that the requirements to access the benefits provided by a tax treaty were per se insufficient. It was believed that the sole condition of being resident in one of the contracting states allowed taxpayers to claim treaty benefits in situations that were regarded as abusive or simply "inappropriate." In particular, the US was concerned with cases in which taxpayers that were resident in third States managed to capture the benefits of a tax treaty that was not *a priori* intended for them. Or in other words, cases in which such taxpayers succeeded in "shopping" into an otherwise unavailable tax treaty.[420] Situations that are commonly referred to as "treaty shopping."

The next example will show how this outcome is quite easy to achieve. Once the taxpayer knows the State from which he expects to derive income from (the source State), a careful examination of the treaty network of such state allows him to "select" the most favorable treaty, i.e., the one that limits source-based taxation to a greater extent.[421] Once the desired treaty is selected, the taxpayer simply needs to make use of a legal entity that is resident in the State with which the source State has signed such treaty. As by the mere fact of being resident of one of the contracting states the application of the treaty is triggered by virtue of its Articles 1 and 4, the taxpayer would easily gain access to its benefits and thus minimize its tax burden at source. As a consequence of the abovementioned, residents of a third State would be able to indirectly access the benefits of a treaty that is intended to be reciprocal between two states.

Once the phenomenon of "treaty shopping" was identified as a problem, some jurisdictions began to implement measures to counteract it.[422] In this context, the US pioneered the adoption of LOB provisions in bilateral tax treaties in 1945.[423] A LOB provision may be broadly defined as a rule that imposes additional requirements

419. As Zornoza points out that "article 4(1) of the OECD Model Tax Convention (...) defines residence not by reference to the circumstances which determines it (...) but by the effect it produce, i.e. the liability to tax on a worldwide basis." *See* Zornoza Pérez, J. (2013), pp. 4-5.
420. Rosenbloom, D. (1994), p. 83.
421. Rosenbloom, D. (1983), p. 764.
422. For a comprehensive review of these measures, *see* Vega Borrego, F.A. (2003), pp. 74-146 and De Broe, L. (et.al.) (2011), pp. 384-389.
423. The first LOB may be found in the tax treaty signed between the US and UK in 1945, although the first comprehensive one did not arrive until 1989 in the tax treaty between the US and Germany. A brief review of the evolution of the US treaty policy in relation to LOB provisions may be found in Avi-Yonah, R.; Panayi, H.J.I. (2010), pp. 41-44.

beyond the residence status that must be satisfied for a person to claim the benefits under a tax treaty.[424] Its overall objective is therefore to prevent taxpayers that are not "sufficiently" linked to its residence state from enjoying the benefits of its tax treaties, e.g., conduit companies.

Although the LOB provisions originally arose in the US in the 1940s, they progressively made their way into the most influential model tax conventions[425] and gained a large number of adepts throughout the world in the subsequent decades. As a matter of fact, more than 200 bilateral tax treaties included a LOB provision as of August 2012 and the US was a party to only fifty of them,[426] as other jurisdictions as Japan and Canada[427] have equally incorporated these provisions in their respective tax treaty networks. Finally, as a result of the BEPS project it can be expected that LOB provisions will soon become more widespread in the forthcoming tax treaties.[428]

A comprehensive study of the different clauses integrated in the LOB provision clearly exceeds the scope of this research[429] so this section will limit itself to enumerate and roughly describe some of its most common clauses. In general terms, all of them intend to seek a "sufficient" and "genuine" connection between the company and its respective residence state in order to deny treaty benefits to resident companies which lack such connection. However, each one of the clauses defines such "sufficiency" and "genuineness" by means of factors and indicators of very diverse natures:

(a) Publicly traded companies test (Article 22.2.c 2016 US MC and Article 29.2.c 2017 OECD MC). A publicly traded company is presumed to be sufficiently connected to the country in which its shares are primarily and actively traded. The rationale behind this criterion is the general belief that the burden imposed by securities regulation and the corresponding exposure to public scrutiny makes publicly traded companies an anomalous (and thus unlikely)

424. Bates, J.D. (et al.) (2013), p. 395.
425. LOB provisions may be found in the US MC of 1977, 1981, 1996, 2006 and 2016, in the Commentary on Article 1 of the 2014 OECD MC (paragraph 20) since 2003 and in the Commentary on Article 1 of the UN MC (paragraphs 17-20).
426. Bates, J.D. (et al.) (2013), p. 396.
427. The inclusion of LOB provisions in the Japanese treaties was driven by a shift in its tax treaty policy under which Japan adopted a zero withholding tax rate on cross-border investment income with the intention of promoting cross-border economic activities. Naturally, such a generous offer needed to be supplemented by anti-treaty shopping measures. *See* Bates, J.D. (et al.) (2013), p. 396. For its part, Canada finds itself in a similar situation. *See* Brown, P.A. (2014), p. 742.
428. OECD (2015): Final Report on BEPS Action 6: Preventing the granting of treaty benefits in inappropriate circumstances and new Article 29 ("entitlement to benefits" added to the 2017 OECD MC).
429. For a detailed study of these clauses, *see* Vega Borrego, F.A. (2006). The LOB provision of the US MC is analyzed in the Technical Explanation accompanying the US MC. For its part, the LOB proposed by the OECD in the context of the BEPS project is commented in OECD (2015): Final Report on BEPS Action 6: Preventing the granting of treaty benefits in inappropriate circumstances.

choice for treaty shopping.[430] It has also been argued that this test may have been initially thought as a surrogate for local ownership.[431]

(b) Ownership and base-erosion tests (Article 22.2.f.i-ii 2016 US MC and Article 29.2.f 2017 OECD MC). These tests depart from the assumption that a company is sufficiently connected to its residence state if the majority of the persons who ultimately own the company are equally residents of such State. At this point, the first prong of the test (ownership) alludes to equity owners while the second prong (base-erosion) refers to lenders and others in a non-equity relationship. The logic behind these tests is that companies whose owners and lenders are resident in its same State are deemed to be sufficiently connected to such state and therefore deserve to enjoy the benefits of its tax treaties.

(c) Active trade or business test (Article 22.3 2016 US MC and Article 29.3 2017 OECD MC). A company is presumed to be genuinely connected to its resident State to the extent that it conducts an active trade or business within its territory.[432] The test applies provided that two conditions are met: (i) the company or a related person is engaged in an active trade or business in the residence State and (ii) the income from the source State emanates from such trade or business.[433] The rationale behind this test is that the conduct of a business in the residence State sufficiently reveals that there is a "good business purpose" behind the presence of a company in that state.[434]

(d) Derivative benefits test (Article 22.4 2016 US MC and Article 29.4 2017 OECD MC. By virtue of this test, treaty benefits are granted only if the tax rate to which the equivalent beneficiary is entitled under the treaty between its residence State and the source State is at least as low as the tax rate provided by the treaty between the State in which the company seeking benefits is resident and the source State.[435] Unlike previous tests, the rationale of this

430. Bates, J.D. (et al.) (2013), p. 395. In the same vein, the OECD stated that "as a general rule, because the shares of publicly traded companies and of some entities are generally widely held, these companies and entities are unlikely to be established for treaty shopping." *See* OECD (2015): Final Report on BEPS Action 6: Preventing the granting of treaty benefits in inappropriate circumstances, p. 35.

431. However, it should be noted that there may be no correlation between the place where the company is listed and the place where its owners reside. In fact, such link is increasingly weaker. *See* Jiang, Q. (2015), p. 144.

432. Naturally, this test must be assessed item by item, so treaty benefits will only be granted in relation to those items of income that effectively comply with all the required conditions.

433. Similarly, the test would also apply in cases in which the income is derived by a trade or business that the company or a related person carries on in the source State as long as the business activity in the residence state is "substantial" in relation to that of the source State. Indeed, the Technical Explanations accompanying the 2016 US MC specify that this assessment should be made with "due regard will be given to the relative size of the economies in both contracting states."

434. Bates, J.D. (et al.) (2013), pp. 396 and 399. It is evident that this test finds its origin in the doctrine of economic substance, according to which it may be presumed that a structure or transaction with economic substance is not artificially arranged for the purpose of tax avoidance (*see* Jiang, Q. (2015), p. 146).

435. Bates, J.D. (et al.) (2013), p. 400.

test is unclear,[436] although some scholars have argued that it departs from the assumption that third-country residents cannot be regarded as "shopping" a treaty to the extent that they would have been entitled to equally beneficial treaty benefits.[437]

(e) Headquarters test (Article 22.5 2016 US MC and Article 29.5 2017 OECD MC). This test grants access to treaty benefits to resident companies which function as headquarters for a multinational group provided that the multinational carries on significant businesses in various States other than the residence State and effectively derive a significant amount of income from them.[438]

(f) Discretionary relief (Article 22.6 2016 US MC and Article 29.5 2017 OECD MC). This clause authorizes the competent authority to discretionally grant benefits to resident taxpayers who fail the objective tests but still "deserve" to be entitled to such benefits. For this purpose, the competent authority must assess all relevant facts and circumstances to further determine whether the establishment, acquisition or maintenance of the resident and the conduct of its operations had "as one of its principal purposes" the entitlement to the treaty benefits.[439] If the answer is no, the benefits could be granted by virtue of this clause. The purpose behind this clause is the fact that the previous mechanical tests may not always cover all the cases in which it is considered appropriate to grant access to treaty benefits and therefore the need for a test of a more subjective nature arises. In fact, Bates notes that competent authorities, in practice, tend to apply this clause only when the taxpayer nearly qualifies under one or more of the objective clauses.[440]

[3] Interim Conclusions

Before drawing the conclusions that are more directly linked with the subject of this investigation, we would like to first share a preliminary reflection.

It seems that both the US and the OECD have been unable to accurately identify what they understand by "treaty shopping" and therefore which specific situations should fall under its scope. On the contrary, both have provided general, vague and

436. Bates, J.D. (et al.) (2013), p. 400.
437. Brown, P.A. (2014), p. 746.
438. This test was recently incorporated to the last update of the US MC in 2016 and clearly responds to the particular needs of this State since it is no secret that it hosts the headquarters of the most profitable multinationals throughout the world.
439. The memorandum of understanding between the US and the Netherlands lists a number of factors to consider when it comes to the application of the discretionary provision: (i) the date of incorporation of the company seeking benefits, the continuity of the historical business and ownership of the company, (ii) the business reasons for the company residing in its state of residence, (iii) the extent to which the company is claiming special tax benefits in its country of residence, (iv) the extent to which the company's business activity in the source state is dependent on the capital, assets or personnel of the company in the residence state and (v) the extent to which the company would be entitled to treaty benefits comparable to those afforded by the US-Netherlands treaty if it had been incorporated in the country of residence of the majority of its shareholders.
440. Bates, J.D. (et al.) (2013), p. 396.

equivocal definitions of this phenomenon[441] that potentially encompass a broad spectrum of situations ranging from purely abusive wholly artificial arrangements to bona fide arrangements with substance.[442] Furthermore, ambiguous and subjective notions as "improper" or "inappropriate" use of tax treaties[443] do not obviously contribute to clarify the contours of this phenomenon. On top of this, it seems that is not even clear whether treaty shopping should be regarded as troublesome or not in the first place.[444]

In a context in which the (supposed) problem is not clearly outlined, it is thus hardly surprising to find a very wide range of motley measures that intend to address it. The LOB provision is a ten-pages set of varied clauses of disparate natures that seem to lack a coherent and uniform purpose.[445] Instead, the provision presents a wide range of safe harbors whose satisfaction lead us to the irrefutable presumption that the resident company in question does not pose problems from a treaty shopping perspective. In a nutshell, these safe harbors draw a dividing line between what the State considers as a reprehensible access to treaty benefits and what is not. A dividing line that is arbitrary,[446] lacks a coherent rationale[447] and is merely an ad-hoc response to a phenomenon that, while perceived as troublesome, has not yet been accurately identified.

That being said, we will now proceed to formulate the conclusions that are more directly linked to this work.

441. This opinion is shared by Jiang, Q. (2015), p. 139. Such "definitions" may be found in the Technical Explanations to the US MC ("anti-treaty shopping provisions are intended to prevent residents of third countries from benefiting from what is intended to be a reciprocal agreement between two countries," in the Commentary on Article 1 of the 2014 OECD MC, paragraph 20 ("[LOB provisions] are aimed at preventing persons who are not residents of either Contracting States from accessing the benefits of a Convention through the use of an entity that would otherwise qualify as a resident of one of these States") and finally in the OECD (2015): Final Report on BEPS Action 6: Preventing the granting of treaty benefits in inappropriate circumstances, p. 9 ("treaty shopping (...) involves strategies through which a person who is not a resident of a State attempts to obtain benefits that a tax treaty concluded by the State grants to residents of that State").

442. Avi-Yonah, R.; Panayi, H.J.I. (2010), pp. 21-25.

443. These expressions appear constantly in OECD (2015): Final Report on BEPS Action 6: Preventing the granting of treaty benefits in inappropriate circumstances.

444. Scholars have generally identified five arguments against treaty shopping: (i) it defeats the purpose of tax treaties, (ii) it breaches the principle of reciprocity in a tax treaty and alters the balance of concessions, (iii) it is contrary to the principle of economic allegiance, (iv) it is a disincentive for states to negotiate tax treaties with source states and (v) it causes an undesired loss of revenues in source states. These arguments are explained and supported by Wardzynski, A. (2014), pp. 472-473. On the contrary, Avi-Yonah and De Broe provide counterarguments to each one of them in De Broe, L. (et.al.) (2011), pp. 383-384 and Avi-Yonah, R.; Panayi, H.J.I. (2010), pp. 25-30.

445. Fleming, J.C. (Jr.) (2012) and Jiang, Q. (2015), p. 139. In fact, Jiang suspects this is intentional: "the OECD has deliberately left the concept broad so as to have flexibility in developing anti-treaty shopping measures."

446. Bates, J.D. (et al.) (2013), p. 401.

447. It should be noted that some LOB clauses directly respond to the particular needs of the jurisdiction that promotes them. The best example is the headquarters test promoted by the US, as this country hosts the headquarters of a great number of multinationals. *See* Chapter 3 section §3.02[C][2].

In the first place, it can be concluded that the "problem" of treaty shopping arises as a direct consequence of the weakness of residence tests.[448] Using the words of Fleming, the first line of defense established by treaties against treaty shopping is precisely the residence status of the taxpayer in at least one of the contracting States.[449] While jurisdictions seem to trust the criteria commonly used to confer the residence status to individuals, to the extent that LOB clauses automatically regard them as qualified persons and thus entitled to treaty benefits,[450] the same cannot be said with regard to companies. Traditional corporate residence tests (particularly the formal ones), as opposed to personal residence tests,[451] do not per se guarantee a sufficient and substantive connection between the taxpayer and the relevant State.[452] This being so, jurisdictions observe that taxpayers that formally comply with the residence tests may be entitled to treaty benefits in circumstances in which they are not sufficiently attached to their residence state. For this reason, they prefer not to trust traditional residence tests as a valid and sufficient threshold to access treaty benefits.

Second, as section §3.02[A][2][c] revealed above, jurisdictions tend to counteract the dissatisfaction associated with traditional residence tests with a layer of anti-avoidance rules. This case is no exception to this trend. Instead of directly amending their respective domestic residence tests to ensure the desired level of connection between the taxpayer and the territory concerned, jurisdictions choose to require such connection by means of an anti-treaty shopping rule: the LOB provision. It is not coincidental that the LOB provision originally arose in a jurisdiction (the US) that has the weaker type of residence test (it solely relies on a POI test).[453] The introduction of the LOB provision ultimately results in the distinction between mere residents and "true residents" or "qualified residents," when only the latter deserve to be entitled to treaty benefits.

Third, jurisdictions use LOB provisions to demand a nexus between the taxpayer and the relevant territory that is stronger and more meaningful than the one required by traditional residence tests.[454] The different clauses that compose the LOB provisions seek a "sufficient" and "genuine" relationship between the taxpayer and its residence state but, as noted above, they do so by means of different factors and indicators of varied natures. However, it can be appreciated that many LOB clauses tend to rely on similar criteria to those used by the SAARs studied in section §3.02[A][2][c]. As with the SAARs analyzed in that section, LOB clauses equally tend to rely on indicators that are less susceptible to manipulations. Indicators that may be classified into two main

448. Couzin, R. (2002), p. 264: "Limitation on benefits provisions (...) reflect a perceived weakness in the residence definition." Brauner, Y. (2009), p. 901: "the background for the evolution of LOB is in the abuse of the simple corporate residence rule."
449. Fleming, J.C. (Jr.) (2012), p. 248.
450. *See* Articles 22.2.a) US MC and 29.2.a) of the 2017 OECD MC. Kemmeren, E.C.C.M. (2001), p. 260: "abusive application of tax conventions via interposing individuals currently does not seem to be the main problem."
451. Chapter 4 section §4.02[B][3][a].
452. As Chapter 3 section §3.02[A][2][c] revealed.
453. Wheeler, J.C. (2011), p. 294.
454. In the words of Brauner, "LOB politely rejects the basic corporate residence rule." *See* Brauner, Y. (2009), p. 901.

groups: those related to the location of the company's owners (publicly traded companies,[455] ownership, base-erosion and derivative benefits tests) and those related to the location of the company's business (active trade or business test).

The above considerations ultimately confirm many of the findings already set out in section §3.02[A][1]. Additionally, the analysis carried out in sections §3.02[A] and §3.02[C] allows us to reach a more general conclusion. We believe that a greater use of residence tests relying on the residence of the corporate shareholders[456] or the location of the business activity of the company,[457] as they per se demand a higher level of connection between the taxpayer and the state concerned, would in practice render LOB provisions unnecessary, as they would all lead to equivalent outcomes for the reasons explained above. In particular, the adoption of this latter sort of tests (those based on the location of a business activity in the territory concerned) would be adequate from the perspective of the presumptive benefit principle, as they would ensure that only companies narrowly linked to the State (and presumed beneficiaries of its services and infrastructures) gain effective access to the benefits of its tax treaty network.

[D] Causes and Remedies for Situations of Dual Residence of Companies in Tax Treaty Scenarios

As a consequence of the variety of residence tests that jurisdictions employ and the different ways to interpret them, a company may well be regarded as resident for domestic tax purposes in two or more jurisdictions. This situation would thus trigger the more severe case of double taxation, as all jurisdictions may potentially intend to tax the worldwide income perceived by the company.

In cases in which two of those residence States have signed a tax treaty patterned after one of the most influential model tax conventions, the issue would be *a priori* solvable. However, for the purposes of applying the tax treaty, it becomes necessary to discern which contracting State will perform the role of "residence State" and which one would eventually perform the role of "source State," as treaties allocate taxing rights on the basis that there is a residence and a source state. In this context, the Articles 4 of the MCs provide "tie-breaker" rules that serve to tip the balance in favor of one of the two contestant States. These rules have undergone significant changes in the recent updates to the three MCs, as Table 3 will subsequently show.

455. Although the fact that the shares of a company are publicly traded in a domestic stock exchange does not necessarily proves that its shareholders primarily reside therein, it has been said that this test functions as "surrogate" for domestic ownership. *See* previous section.
456. *See* Chapter 3 section §3.02[A][1][c].
457. *See* Chapter 3 section §3.02[A][1][d].

Table 3 Comparison of the Tie-Breaker Rules Envisaged in Article 4 of the OECD MC, UN MC and US MC (Precedent and Current Versions)

OECD MC	*UN MC*	*US MC*
2014	2011	2006
3. Where by reason of the provisions of paragraph 1 a person other than an individual is a resident of both Contracting States, then it shall be deemed to be a resident only of the State in which its place of management is situated.		4. Where by reason of the provisions of paragraph 1 of this Article a company is a resident of both Contracting States, then if it is created or organized under the laws of one of the Contracting States or a political division thereof, such company shall be deemed to be a resident of the first-mentioned Contracting State. In all other cases involving dual resident companies, the competent authorities of the Contracting States shall endeavor to determine the mode of application of the Convention to such company. If the competent authorities do not reach such an agreement, that company will not be treated as a resident of either Contracting State for purposes of its claiming any benefits provided by the Convention.
2017	2017	2016
3. Where by reason of the provisions of paragraph 1 a person other than an individual is a resident of both Contracting States, the competent authorities of the Contracting States shall endeavor to determine by mutual agreement the Contracting State of which such person shall be deemed to be a resident for the purposes of the Convention, having regard to its place of effective management, the place where it is incorporated or otherwise constituted and any other relevant factors. In the absence of such agreement, such person shall not be entitled to any relief or exemption from tax provided by this		4. Where by reason of the provisions of paragraph 1 of this Article a company is a resident of both Contracting States, such company shall not be treated as a resident of either Contracting State for purposes of its claiming the benefits provided by this Convention. 5. Where by reason of the provisions of paragraph 1 of this Article a person other than an individual or a company is a resident of both Contracting States, the competent authorities of the Contracting States shall by mutual agreement

OECD MC	*UN MC*	*US MC*
Convention except to the extent and in such manner as may be agreed upon by the competent authorities of the Contracting States.		endeavor to determine the mode of application of this Convention to that person.

[1] Tie-Breaker Rules Envisaged in Precedent Versions of the MCs

[a] The US Peculiar Tie-Breaker Rule: POI

First of all, we will refer to the 1996 and 2006 US MC, as their approach to the dual residence issue was entirely divergent. They did have a tie-breaker rule which tipped the balance in favor of the contracting State in which the company had been created or organized under its respective legislation. The technical explanations, however, did not provide any single argument to support the choice of the POI test. In cases in which this rule was not able to resolve the dual residence conflict, Article 4 used to entrust the competent authorities of both states with the task of reaching an agreement.

[b] The OECD and UN Tie-Breaker Rule: POEM

For their part, the solution traditionally promoted by both the OECD and the UN was the use of the POEM test as a tie-breaker.[458] This time we will not dwell on the content and interpretation of the provision nor discuss the risks it poses, since section §3.02[A][1][b] already did. Unlike the Technical Explanations to the US MC, the Commentaries on the OECD and the UN MC explicitly state the reasons behind their choice. Both state that "it would not be an adequate solution to attach importance to a purely formal criterion like registration (…) therefore paragraph 3 attaches importance to the place where the company, etc. is actually managed."[459]

[2] New Approaches to Resolve the Dual Residency Dispute

A special mention should be made to a recent trend that is visible in the treaties negotiated in the last few years and also in the updated versions of the MCs. Jurisdictions increasingly tend to leave the resolution of the dual residence issue in the hands of the competent authorities of the contracting States, although they restrict the authorities' discretionary power by enumerating some factors that must necessarily be

458. To consult the historical evolution of this rule in the models of the League of Nations and the OECD *see* Loomer, G.T. (2015), pp. 123-126.
459. Commentary on Article 4 of the 2014 OECD MC, paragraph 22 and Commentary on Article 4 of the 2011 UN MC, paragraph 8, which limits itself to copy the wording of the Commentaries on the OECD MC. This reasoning derives from an OECD report that dates back from 1958, according to Loomer, g. (2015), p. 125.

taken into account, as the POI of the company or its POEM. This shift of paradigm has been indirectly promoted by the OECD and the UN for years, since they both include in their Commentaries on their respective precedent versions of their MC an alternative version of Article 4.3 which equally refers to the mutual agreement procedure (hereinafter "MAP").[460] The reason put forward by the OECD and the UN is that the case-by-case approach is the best way to deal with the difficulties in determining the POEM that may arise from the use of new communications technologies,[461] a risk that we already noted and discussed above.[462]

It can be expected that this approach gains new adepts in the following years, since the three new versions of the MCs have incorporated MAP as a new way to resolve dual residency situations.[463] Interestingly, the OECD now proposes an amendment to the Commentaries that would lead to change the supposed justification of the rule. While the previous Commentaries justified the resort to the MAP on the grounds that the interpretation of the POEM tests was problematic, the new Commentaries on the 2017 OECD MC state that the reason behind the shift of paradigm lies in the fact that "there had been a number of tax avoidance cases involving dual resident companies."[464]

[3] Interim Conclusions

First of all, we would like to share a general reflection that is more closely related to the cause of the problem than to its remedy.

The mere fact that cases of dual residence are far from rare should make us wonder whether it may be a sign of a malfunction of the domestic residence tests. In other words, the fact that a company may be regarded as tax resident by various jurisdictions by virtue of their respective test leads us to believe that these tests may be "overshooting" and attracting companies that do not really "belong to them."[465] On the other hand, residence tests that in fact demand a substantive and strong nexus between

460. Commentary on Article 4 of the 2014 OECD MC, paragraph 24.1 (introduced in 2008) and Commentary on Article 4 of the 2011 UN MC, paragraph 10. They both suggest the same wording for Article 4.3: "Where by reason of the provisions of paragraph 1 a person other than an individual is a resident of both Contracting States, the competent authorities of the Contracting States shall endeavor to determine by mutual agreement the Contracting State of which such person shall be deemed to be a resident for the purposes of the Convention, having regard to its place of effective management, the place where it is incorporated or otherwise constituted and any other relevant factors. In the absence of such agreement, such person shall not be entitled to any relief or exemption from tax provided by this Convention except to the extent and in such manner as may be agreed upon by the competent authorities of the Contracting States." In addition to the POEM and the POI, the Commentary add a few more factors to take into account: where the accounting records are kept.
461. Commentary on Article 4 of the 2014 OECD MC, paragraph 24.1.
462. *See* Chapter 3 section §3.02[A][1][b].
463. The BEPS project has caused the shift of paradigm in the OECD MC and may also have influenced that of the UN and US MCs. *See* OECD (2015): Final Report on BEPS Action 6: Preventing the granting of treaty benefits in inappropriate circumstances, pp. 72-75.
464. Commentary on Article 4 of the 2017 OECD MC, paragraph 23.
465. Couzin, R. (2002), p. 266.

the corporate taxpayer and the jurisdiction concerned, by their own nature, would be less prone to cause overlapping attributions of residence.[466]

That being said, we will proceed to extract two main conclusions from the analysis on the way jurisdictions tend to resolve the dual residence of companies in tax treaties.

First, we should recall the scope and precise role played by Article 4.3. Its function is confined to solving cases of dual residence where the taxpayer is deemed to be resident in both contracting States by virtue of their respective domestic residence tests. This means, *sensu contrario*, that it does not deal with companies that are not resident anywhere (stateless companies),[467] primarily because the application of the treaty would not be triggered in the first place to the extent that the taxpayer is not resident in any of the contracting States.[468] As a result, we may conclude that Article 4.3 is inherently unable to deal with one of the most common profit shifting techniques, as the Apple case study revealed.[469]

Second, we have analyzed the alleged rationale behind the different policy choices as expressed in their corresponding soft law instruments in the previous sections. With respect to the use of formal tests as tie-breaker rules, the Technical Explanations to the US MC (1996 and 2006) did not provide a single justification. However, we suspect that this choice may have been motivated by mere policy interests, as the US solely employs this test for domestic tax purposes. With regard to the POEM test, the explanation provided by both the Commentaries on both the 2014 OECD and the 2011 UN MC cannot be regarded satisfactory. They do not conveniently explain why the State in which the POEM is located should win the tie-breaker test and therefore be the resident State for treaty purposes. On the contrary, they resort to the simplistic argument that POEM tests are "better" than formal tests. As far as the MAP approach is concerned, while its first alleged justification was that the POEM test was increasingly difficult to apply in practice, the OECD recently changed its position. Indeed, it now argues that the advisability of resolving the cases of dual residence on a case-by-case basis is due to the need to tackle "tax avoidance" cases involving dual resident companies.

We may therefore conclude, thus confirming the general reflection already exposed in section §3.02[A][2][b], that a careful consideration on the meaning and purpose of the residence standard is again missing. We already observed at the domestic level that jurisdictions do not seem to give serious consideration to the configuration of their respective domestic residence tests and more importantly, the respective policy purposes they intend to accomplish with them.[470] Likewise, jurisdictions do not seem to reflect on why the residence status of a company in one State should prevail over the residence status in the other contracting State for tax treaty

466. For example, the tests relying on the residence of the shareholders (Chapter 3 section §3.02[A][1][c]) or the business activity of the company (Chapter 3 section §3.02[A][1][d]).
467. *See* Chapter 3 section §3.02[B].
468. Articles 1 and 4 of the tax treaties. *See* Chapter 3 section §3.02[C].
469. *See* Chapter 2 section §2.01[A][2].
470. *See* Chapter 3 section §3.02[A][2][b].

purposes.[471] Instead, we find a conglomeration of arbitrary tie-breaker rules that do not seem to follow a thoughtful and coherent logic.

§3.03 THE PERMANENT ESTABLISHMENT THRESHOLD IS NOT AS ALIGNED WITH THE PRESUMPTIVE BENEFIT PRINCIPLE AS IT COULD BE EXPECTED AND MAY THUS TRIGGER CERTAIN PROFIT SHIFTING RISKS

Jurisdictions do not solely tax the profits earned by their resident corporate taxpayers but also tend to tax non-residents for the income deemed to be sourced in their respective territories. For example, wherever they have a PE in their territories.

The fundamental purpose of this section will be to ascertain whether the legal configuration of source—by means of the PE concept—may be regarded as aligned with the presumptive benefit principle. In other words, the question is whether the definition of PE contributes to make taxpayers book their profits in the jurisdictions where they presumably enjoy public benefits (i.e., wherever they carry out their relevant economic activities, either physically or remotely)[472] or else facilitate its shift to the jurisdiction(s) of their choice where no relevant business is occurring.

However, we will also examine the origins and supposed rationale behind the PE concept to demonstrate that it is the result of the economic context where it originally arose and responds to the particular needs and wishes of the capital exporting jurisdictions, as represented by the OECD. As a result, we intend to prove that its lack of adaptation to present times has given rise to numerous problems that tend to be addressed by means of unfortunate interpretations of the clause.

To this end, this section intends to point out the undetermined significance of source (section §3.03[A]) to later review the theoretical foundations upon which source-based taxation has traditionally been built (section §3.03[B]). Later, we will provide a general overview of the trends on how source has generally been defined for CIT purposes at both the domestic and the tax treaty level, with a particular emphasis in the PE threshold (section §3.03[C]), whose tax treatment is increasingly equivalent to that of a resident subsidiary (section §3.03[D]). Subsequently, we will analyze the most widespread modalities of PEs and assess their consistency with the presumptive benefit principle (section §3.03[E]). Lastly, some conclusions will be drawn (section §3.03[F]).

---

471. The OECD suggested back in 2001 and 2003 a few changes to Article 4.3 of the OECD MC that fell by the wayside. One of the proposals was to tip the balance in favor of the contracting State in which the company had a stronger economic nexus. In p. 12 the OECD recognized that this criterion was not at first sight aligned with the "underlying rationale for residence taxation." This is remarkable since the OECD itself does not seem to believe there is a clear and unique rationale behind residence taxation, since in the same paper it proposed a conglomerate of alternatives for Article 4.3 (e.g., POI or registration, place where the shareholders or the directors reside) that do not appear to follow a unique rationale. *See* OECD (2001): The impact of the communications revolution on the application of "place of effective management" as a tie breaker rule (Discussion Paper).
472. Chapter 2 Section §2.02[B][2].

[A] The Departure Point: The Undetermined Significance of Source

It is generally asserted that, pursuant to their own sovereignty, States would be in principle entitled to tax income sourced in their respective territories irrespective of the circumstances surrounding the person who obtain it. Yet, there does not seem to be a clear and unambiguous understanding on what "source" actually means. On the contrary, in the words of Vogel, source is unambiguous only in what it excludes: taxation based on "source" is different from taxation based on residence or citizenship.[473]

Economists have intended to shed some light on the notion of source from a theoretical perspective. In general terms, source is predominantly identified with the territory that is somehow connected to the production of the income in question or where value is added to a good.[474] However, economists have attempted to further specify this broad definition by means of two approaches: the supply and the supply-demand.[475] The first one would identify the source with the place where the production factors generating the profit are, while the second one would locate the source of the profit both where the production factors are and where the final product is used or consumed, to the extent that it regards the profit as the result of the interplay of both supply and demand.

It is precisely due to the inherent vagueness of the notion of source of income that it has traditionally been located in a variety of places,[476] e.g., where the tangible or intangible property is located[477] or used,[478] where the services are performed, where the contract is signed or executed, where the payer is located or reside,[479] where the payment is made or where the expenses are borne,[480] *inter alia*.

[B] The Theoretical Rationales Behind Source-Based Taxation

The lack of a preexisting natural concept of source confers tax legislators a considerable margin of discretion when it comes to the legal configuration of source for income tax purposes. However, there is a tendency to draft source rules in a quite homogeneous way, and the reason behind this behavior may be the fact that jurisdictions have, knowingly or unknowingly, follow patterns of source-based taxation that seem theoretically justifiable. As there is a great variety of potential justifications that may serve to legitimize the exercise of taxing rights over non-residents' income,[481] this section

473. Vogel, K. (1988), p. 223.
474. Vogel, K. (1988), p. 223.
475. Musgrave understands that there is no straightforward economic basis for choosing one approach over the other. *See* Musgrave, P.B. (1984), p. 245.
476. Kemmeren, E.C.C.M. (2001), p. 33.
477. Pires, M. (1989), p. 122.
478. Pires, M. (1989), p. 121.
479. These nexuses follow the so-called paying state principle.
480. Pires, M. (1989), p. 122.
481. An overview of the fundamental theoretical foundations for source-based taxation may be found in Pinto, D. (2003), pp. 17-46.

will merely focus on the most relevant ones: benefit principle, capital import neutrality and base erosion.

There are no commonly agreed principles that govern the share of the tax base between residence and source states. However, back in the 1960s the economist Musgrave provided a theoretical framework named "inter-nation equity" which called for an equitable division of the tax revenue between the different jurisdictions that are to some extent involved in the generation of cross-border income.[482] At this point, she suggested making use of the old principles of benefit[483] or "economic allegiance"[484] to evaluate and calibrate the appropriate level of inter-nation equity in each given case. Accordingly, it would be understood that the division of the tax base is equitable to the extent that each jurisdiction is entitled to a share of the tax revenue arising from a cross-border transaction in proportion to the supposed benefits it provided to the taxpayer.[485] Thus, a taxpayer that is granted access to these public services would owe a certain degree of economic allegiance to the provider jurisdiction that should result in a tax liability as a compensation for the costs incurred by such jurisdiction that contributed to the generation of the profit. This theoretical framework on the share of the tax base undoubtedly favors source-based taxation,[486] to the extent that it may be presumed that the State of source is the one providing most or all the benefits that are relevant for the production of the income and would thus deserve to be compensated for the costs incurred under the inter-nation equity theory.

Although the ideas of inter-nation equity, benefit and economic allegiance feature prominently among the traditional justifications for source-based taxation,[487] others have equally played a role in the literature, although to a lesser extent. This is for example the case of the principles of neutrality (particularly capital import neutrality) and base erosion.

482. For a deeper analysis on her theory, *see* Musgrave, P.B. (1963), pp. 15-22, Musgrave, P.B.; Musgrave, R.A. (1972) and more recently Kaufman, N.H. (1988), pp. 188-201. As explicitly recognized by Graetz, Musgrave's analysis has dominated the international income tax policy literature for more than three decades. *See* Graetz, M.J. (2001), p. 286.
483. Musgrave, P.B. (1963), pp. 15-16. When discussing Musgrave's theory, Vogel argued that "the only valid legitimation, therefore, can be derived from benefits aspects." *See* Vogel, K. (1988c), p. 398. We already referred to the traditional benefit principle back in Chapter 2 section §2.02[A].
484. The term was first coined by Schanz, G. (1892) and later analyzed by Griziotti, B. (1929) and Allix, E. (1937).
485. Musgrave, P.B. (1963), p. 16. Benefits as the use of public facilities and infrastructures, education and training for the labor force, a secure legal framework that protects property rights or the police/fire/defense protection, among many others. *See* Pinto, D. (2003), p. 19.
486. Vogel, K. (1988c), p. 398: "Without this state's economic opportunities the income normally would not have been generated" and Avi-Yonah, R. (1997), p. 520: "These benefits justify source-based corporation taxation in the sense that the host country's government bears some of the costs of providing the benefits that are necessary for earning the income." In the same vein, *see also* Brown, F.B. (2011), pp. 574-575, Schön, W. (2009), p. 75 and Gadžo, S. (2016), p. 190.
487. As explicitly recognized by Graetz, Musgrave's analysis has dominated the international income tax policy literature for more than three decades. *See* Graetz, M.J. (2001), p. 286. In addition, the economic allegiance theory was also embraced by the so-called four experts who drafted the first known tax model. *See* Economic and Financial Commission for the League of Nations (1923): Report on Double Taxation, P. 19.

Neutrality essentially requires that economic processes should not be affected by external factors (as taxes) since productivity would be higher provided that the production factors are distributed by the market mechanism without public interference.[488] Scholars have generally identified two dimensions of neutrality: capital export neutrality (investors should pay the same tax whether they receive income from a given investment made locally or abroad) and capital import neutrality (capital funds originating in various countries should compete at equal terms in the capital market of any country).[489] While the first option has enjoyed great support for being more economically efficient from a theoretical point of view, the second option (which tends to justify source-based over worldwide taxation) has been advocated for fostering international competitiveness. However, Gandenberger provided two strong counter-arguments that dismantled the arguments in favor of capital export neutrality,[490] thus concluding that source-based taxation was better justified in terms of neutrality.

As regards the base erosion principle, it is deemed to justify source-based taxation insofar it relates to a payment that is deductible against the tax base of the source country.[491] However, as it is frequently criticized for not providing by itself a sufficient justification for source taxation,[492] it has been argued that it should solely play a subsidiary role.[493]

[C] The Emergence of Legal Conventions to Establish Taxation at Source and the Origin of the Permanent Establishment

Departing from the non-self-defining nature of source, domestic and tax treaty rules defining the source of specific items of income could not aspire to become more than artificial legal conventions.[494] We will go through some of the most common source

488. Vogel, K. (1988b).
489. Vogel, K. (1988b), p. 311.
490. These are the two arguments he put forward. First, in a residence-based regime where the residence State's tax rates are higher than the ones imposed by the source State, a reduced after-tax profit would reduce the chance of an enterprise to finance new investments in the source State. The reason being that the enterprise has to anticipate a higher overall tax burden than its competitors from lower-tax States. Second, as the level of taxation in each State is likely to correspond to some extent to the level of public goods provided, a State providing less public benefits may have a lower tax rate than its neighboring States. This being so, if the source State has a lower tax rate than the residence State, the enterprise's decision whether or not to invest in such State may be affected by this fact. *See* Vogel, K. (1988), p. 222 citing a paper written by Otto Gandenberger back in 1983.
491. Arnold notes that this principle has traditionally served to justify the taxation of both the director's fees and the employment income derived by non-residents where they receive the income from an employer resident or a PE located in the source State. *See* Arnold, B.J. (2011), p. 66.
492. Brauner, Y.; Báez Moreno, A. (2015), p. 9.
493. Arnold, B.J. (2011), p. 66.
494. Avi-Yonah, R. (2007), p. 27: "the source of income is difficult to define (...) this problem has been partially resolved by arbitrary rules embodied in tax treaties that define the source of various categories of income." Ault, H.J.; Bradford, D.F. (1990), p. 12: "A complex series of somewhat arbitrary rules is used to establish source."

rules applicable to income obtained by companies by taking the OECD MC as a point of reference.

The legal conventions used by the OECD MC to define the source of income may be classified into two main categories.[495] The first category includes substance-based rules that intend to trace the economic source of the income, that is, the territory where the income economically arises, either where the production factors are located or used (supply-based approach) or where the production factors and the market are located (supply-demand approach). This is the option preferred for active income[496] and certain types of passive income.[497] Undoubtedly, these rules are likely to be better aligned with the principles set out in the previous section, particularly the benefit and the economic allegiance principles. On the other hand, the second category comprises formal rules that refrain from seeking the true economic source of the income and instead content themselves with an arbitrary threshold that is certain and easy to administer. This category often encompasses source rules in relation to certain types of passive income and generally refers to the territory where the income is made available and where costs corresponding to that income are incurred,[498] e.g., the jurisdiction where the payer resides.[499] They generally lack a clear policy justification[500] beyond practicability considerations, since they tend to apply in the context of passive income whose ultimate economic source is hard to discern and, even in the case it could be identified, the imposition of a tax at source would be difficult or simply impossible to enforce.[501]

Among the first category of source rules, comprising those of substantive nature, we find the concept of PE. The history of the PE is as long as the history of the tax treaties itself.[502] In fact, it was already present in the first commonly regarded tax treaty signed by Austria-Hungary and Prussia in 1899, being its immediate precedent (the

495. Distinction made by Avi-Yonah, R. (2007), pp. 42-43 and Pires, M. (1989), pp. 121-122.
496. Article 7 of the 2017 OECD MC allows the state in which the corporate taxpayer have a "permanent establishment" to tax the business profits attributable to it irrespective of the residence of the company.
497. These rules tend to follow the *situs* principle. According to Article 6 of the OECD MC, income derived from immovable property may be taxed by the jurisdiction where the property is physically located, irrespective of the circumstances of the recipient. Similarly, Article 13 of the OECD MC (paragraphs 1 and 4) states that gains derived from the alienation of immovable property or from the alienation of shares (whose value, in turn, predominantly derive from immovable property) may be taxed by the jurisdiction where the property is located.
498. Pires, M. (1989), p. 122.
499. These rules follow the so-called paying State principle and may be seen in Articles 10 (dividends) and 11 (interests) of the 2017 OECD MC. Article 10.2 explicitly allows the jurisdiction where the company paying the dividend is resident to tax it at source while Article 11.2 does the same in respect of the jurisdiction where the interest "arises," meaning the jurisdiction where the payer is resident (as Article 11.5 clarifies).
500. In the case of rules following the "paying State principle," they could arguably be justified in the base erosion principle as described in the previous section.
501. Avi-Yonah argues that the main reason behind the "paying State principle" in the case of dividends is that it would be administratively hard for a State to tax a dividend paid by a foreign corporation to a foreign shareholder whenever it considers that the income originally arose from its territory. *See* Avi-Yonah, R. (2007), p. 43.
502. Skaar, A.A. (1991), p. 71.

Bestriebsstätte) in the Prussian domestic legislation since 1845.[503] Later on, the League of Nations borrowed the concept and introduced it in the first model tax convention in history,[504] so did the OECD, the UN and the US in their respective future MCs. Over time, the PE has become an international standard that is almost invariably present in both tax treaties and domestic tax legislations.

The PE concept is consistent with the supply-based approach,[505] thus disdaining the relevance of the providing a market of goods or services. Further, it reflects the economic context in which it arose and the policy interests of the jurisdictions with greater power to influence the debate on international tax rules. It is the continued presence of these two factors what explains not only its initial success but also its perpetuation over the subsequent decades.[506]

With respect to the first factor, the PE is surely a result of the economic context where it emerged. Essentially, the clause makes source taxation of business profits conditional on a physical and stable presence of the non-resident enterprise in the host jurisdiction. Considering the economic context where the PE originally arose, where the physical presence was critical to perform any kind of business activity (including the provision of services),[507] a parameter entirely based on physical presence seemed to be a proper way to measure the degree of involvement in the economic life of the host State. Additionally, the imposition of a source-based tax by the State in which a PE is located was regarded as justified by virtue of the principles mentioned in the previous section. What is more, the degree of economic presence revealed by the fulfillment of the requirements of the PE clause lead to the presumption that the non-resident taxpayer having a PE in a jurisdiction was in fact enjoying to some extent the public benefits provided by such jurisdiction in a way that the PE clause could also be regarded as consistent with the presumptive benefit principle.[508]

---

503. Skaar, A.A. (1991), pp. 72-75.
504. Economic and Financial Commission for the League of Nations (1928): Report on Double taxation and tax evasion.
505. OECD (2003): Are the current treaty rules for taxing business profits appropriate for e-commerce? Final report, p.14: "the TAG's approach was therefore in line with the supply-based approach of considering that business profits should be viewed as originating from the location of the factors that allow the enterprise to realize business profits. It therefore rejected the suggestion that the mere fact that a country provides the market where an enterprise's goods and services are supplied should allow that country to consider that a share of the profits of the enterprise is derived therefrom."
506. Escribano, E. (2015), pp. 8-9.
507. McLure describes the fundamental features of the economic context in which international taxation was born: international trade consisted primarily of tangible products, communications were relatively slow and physical presence was generally required for the conduct of business. *See* McLure, C.E. (Jr.) (2001), pp. 333-334. Along the same lines, *see* Skaar, A.A. (1991), pp. 65-67 and Tillinghast, D.R. (1996), p. 524: "the exiting body of international tax rules (...) is based in large part on the supposition that international trade consists of the physical shipment of goods or the physical movement of persons to perform services at different locations."
508. The (proposed) presumptive benefit principle and its use for CIT purposes is explained in Chapter 2 section §2.02[B]. *See also* Skaar, A.A. (1991), p. 559: "the conventional wisdom is that an enterprise with a foreign PE has extended its activities abroad to such a degree that the benefits from this country's expenditure networks justify taxation in that country (...) a PE is merely a piece of evidence of economic allegiance." This assumption still remains in the

Above and beyond these considerations, the PE was also a policy decision that undeniably responded to the particular needs and wishes of the capital exporting jurisdictions, whose interests were (and still are) primarily represented by the OECD. Both the League of Nations and the OECD chose to give preference to residence-based taxation in their respective Model Conventions to satisfy the fiscal interests of such jurisdictions, and they did so by adopting a high threshold as the PE to minimize the chances of taxation at source.[509]

[D] The Progressive Personalization of the PE Towards the "Functional Resident"

The PE has succeeded to become the most characteristic threshold allowing source taxation of business profits by antonomasia. However, its role does not end there. Both tax treaties and, by extension, domestic tax legislations have conferred the PE a wider role that goes beyond enabling the jurisdiction where the PE is located to tax the business profits that arise from it by virtue of Article 7.[510] This section will explain why.

A PE is not a legal person but rather an economic reality. It only acquires significance from a legal point of view once the compliance with the requirements envisaged in the PE clause is verified. However, the moment a PE is deemed to exist it is automatically granted a tax treatment equivalent to that of legal persons. That is to say, while lacking legal personality, PEs do in turn enjoy a sort of "fiscal personality" that somehow equates them with legal persons for certain purposes.[511]

Further, there is a growing tendency to equate the tax treatment of PEs and resident entities for income tax purposes.[512] We will now proceed to provide various arguments that sustain this statement.

Commentary on Article 7.1 of the 2017 OECD Model Convention, paragraph 9: "it is perhaps sufficient to say that it has come to be accepted in international fiscal matters that until an enterprise of one State sets up a permanent establishment in another State it should not properly be regarded as participating in the economic life of that other State to such an extent that it comes within the jurisdiction of that other State's taxing rights." *See also* Doernberg, R.L.; Hinnekens, L.; Hellerstein, W.; Jinyan, L. (2001), p. 349 ("the permanent establishment rule was justified by the territorial theory of economic allegiance: whoever benefits from an economic community ought to pay tax to that community") and Reimer, E. (2012), p. 11 ("(the PE) is part of the broad picture of assigning substantial profits to the respective source State (...) the source State is granted the right to tax in exchange for its efforts to create, maintain an safeguard good economic conditions for foreign investors").

509. The US actively supported the adoption of the PE in the debates within the League of Nations to protect the interests of US enterprises carrying on business overseas. On the other hand, capital importing countries as the Latin-American ones, have leaded a long fight against the PE threshold, as evidenced in the 1943 Mexican Model Convention and the Andean Pact Model where the PE is merely an example of source-based taxation of business profits. For the US stance *see* Graetz, M.J.; O'Hear, M.M. (1997), pp. 1074-1089 and for the Latin-American position *see* Zapata, S. (1998), pp. 252-253.
510. In the same vein, *see* Schön, W. (2009), pp. 104-105, where this phenomenon is referred to as "the double-sided nature of the PE concept."
511. Gutiérrez de Gandarilla, F.A. (2010), pp. 22-44. The author provides powerful arguments to demonstrate that the PE has been subject to a "progressive personalization."
512. Schön believes there is an "implicit analogy" between PE and residence taxation and furthermore regards the PE as an "extension of unlimited tax liability to non-incorporated

The first and most evident reason is that the State in which the PE arises (hereinafter "PE-State") is *a priori* entitled to tax the worldwide income attributable to the PE[513] as if it were in fact an entity resident therein. In this respect, two observations should be noted. First, the PE does not solely capture active income under the scope of Article 7. As Article 7.4 of the 2017 OECD MC points out, the PE-State may equally tax other types of income (covered by articles of the MC other than Article 7) as long as they are attributable to the PE. This is the case for passive income under Articles 10, 11, 12 and 13, which may be found attributable to the PE to the extent that the underlying right or asset giving rise to such income is "effectively connected" to it.[514] Second, Article 7 of the 2017 OECD MC allows the PE-State to tax the worldwide income that may be attributable to the PE irrespective of its sources. Thus, it would be irrelevant whether its income is sourced in the State where the enterprise (its head office) reside, the State where the PE itself is located or even a third State.[515] This fact suggests that the nature of the tax liability triggered by the PE is much more closely in line with the notion of personal tax liability than with that of objective nature, the reason being that the latter one is by its own nature constrained by the territoriality principle and thus limited to sources of a particular jurisdiction.[516] In short, all these factors allow us to conclude that the tax treatment of PEs seems to be substantially equivalent to that of resident taxpayers.[517]

The analogous status of taxpayers that are resident in a State and PEs located therein is further confirmed by the methodology employed to assign profits to them, particularly after the advent of the "authorized OECD approach" (hereinafter "AOA") back in 2010.[518] In essence, the AOA puts forward the so-called functionally separate entity approach, a variation of the preexisting "separate entity approach" followed to

business units" rather than a threshold for limited tax liability. *See* Schön, W. (2009), pp. 104-105. In the same vein, *see* Vann, R.J. (2003), pp. 144-146.

513. While Article 7.1 of the 2017 OECD MC solely covers profits that are "attributable to the permanent establishment" in accordance to Article 7.2, Article 7.1 of the 2017 UN MC equally covers profits derived by sales of goods or merchandise in the PE-State, as well as profits derived by other business activities carried out in such State of the same or similar kind as those effected through the PE. This approach is referred to as "limited force of attraction rule." *See* Hirschböck, M. (2003), pp. 405-424.

514. *See* the respective PE provisos in Articles 10.5, 11.5, 12.3 and 13.2 2017 OECD MC. The income will be considered as "effectively connected" when it is possible to regard the holding (with regard to a dividend), the debt-claim (interest), the right or property (royalty) or the alienated movable property (capital gain) as "functionally connected" to the PE. A complete overview on the function and interpretation of such clauses may be found in Haller, B. (2003), pp. 227-250, where the author is critical with the lack of guidance on how to interpret "the effectively connected" criterion.

515. Schön, W. (2009), p. 104: "it is common ground that third-country income can be allocated to a PE if there is some economic connection between the third-country income and the activities of the PE, thus hypothesizing a restricted sort of unlimited tax liability for the PE in the jurisdiction where it is located."

516. Gutiérrez de Gandarilla, F.A. (2010), p. 32 and Schön, W. (2009), p. 105.

517. García Prats, F.A. (1994), p. 473. García Prats acknowledges that the tax liability imposed on PEs has been subject to a progressive "personalization," to the extent the State where the PE is located may tax on a "worldwide effectively-connected income basis."

518. This is the thesis maintained by Burgers, I.J.J. (2009). However, it should be noted that the AOA does not represent a rupture with the previous system but rather an enhancement of it. *See*

allocate profits between associated companies. In accordance with the AOA, a PE would be attributed the profits it might be expected to make, in particular in its dealings with other parts of the enterprise, "if it were a separate and independent enterprise" engaged in the same or similar activities under the same or similar conditions.

However, the application of such rule entails a major obstacle: the PE is not a "separate and independent enterprise," as it is not legally distinct from the rest of the enterprise. As noted above, the PE lacks legal personality and is therefore unable to legally own assets, assume risks, possess capital or conclude contracts. This makes it necessary to develop a previous mechanism aimed at hypothesizing the PE as a (functional) "separate and independent enterprise" distinct to the legal entity to which it really belongs. To do so, it becomes necessary to "put flesh into the fiction" by equipping the PE with the assets, risks and capital it would have if it truly were a separate entity performing the same functions.[519] The first step of the two-step analysis proposed by the AOA precisely takes care of this.[520] At this point, the OECD suggests starting by the identification of the significant people functions performed by the PE. Once identified, the AOA would first attribute to the PE the economic ownership of the assets presumably used in the functions it performs.[521] Subsequently, the AOA would attribute to the PE any risks inherent in (or created by) the PE's own significant people functions relevant to the assumption of risks.[522] Lastly, the AOA would assign to the PE the necessary capital to support the function it undertakes, the assets it economically owns and the risks it assumes.[523] Once the PE has taken the form of a functional separate enterprise distinct from the rest of the enterprise to which it belongs, the second step of the AOA comes into play. The AOA leads to the recognition of most of the dealings between the PE and the rest of the enterprise as if it were transactions between related parties.[524] And, once such dealings are recognized, they ought to be priced on an arm's length basis following, by analogy, the 2017 OECD TPG.[525] It is precisely at this point where the treatment of PEs largely equates that of associated subsidiaries.[526]

Besides, there are some minor additional arguments that similarly contribute to confirm the quasi-residence status enjoyed by the PEs. As Vann points out, the fact that

---

Bennet, M. (2008), p. 469 and OECD (2008): Attribution of profits to permanent establishments, which resulted in the amendment of the OECD MC (Article 7.2) and its Commentaries in 2010.

519. Schön, W. (2009), p. 104: "(the AOA) transforms the PE into a notional subsidiary for the purpose of tax allocation."
520. OECD (2008): Attribution of profits to permanent establishments, pp. 13-19.
521. OECD (2008): Attribution of profits to permanent establishments, pp. 15-16.
522. OECD (2008): Attribution of profits to permanent establishments, pp. 16-17.
523. OECD (2008): Attribution of profits to permanent establishments, pp. 17-18.
524. OECD (2008): Attribution of profits to permanent establishments, pp. 18-19 and Schön, W. (2009), p. 111: "the OECD's profit attribution project hypothesizes the permanent establishment as an independent unit capable of entering into notional dealings with the head office, as are regularly concluded between a parent and its subsidiary company."
525. OECD (2008): Attribution of profits to permanent establishments, p. 20.
526. In Chapter 3 section §3.01[C] we described the ALS as a legal fiction that builds upon other fictions (as companies are also legal fictions). The ALS as applied to PEs is a fiction on top of fiction (the company as if where a person) on top of fiction (a PE as if it were a company). *See* Petrucci, R. (2016), p. 10 (footnote 44).

the State where the enterprise is tax resident exempts from taxes the business profits of a foreign PE may be read as an implicit recognition of the foreign PE as a foreign taxpayer that falls under the jurisdiction of other State.[527] Additionally, tax treaties themselves tend to treat PEs and residents as interchangeable categories for certain purposes. For example, Article 15.2 of the 2017 OECD MC allows the State where the activity is performed to tax the employment income perceived by a non-resident provided that the remuneration is born either by an employer resident or a PE located in the State of the activity. Lastly, some scholars have even advocated for the amendment of Article 1 of the MCs to ensure the access of PEs to the benefits of the treaty and thus avoid the double taxation that is likely to arise in triangular scenarios.[528]

The increasingly uniform tax treatment conferred to residents and PEs is not accidental, but rather the logical outcome of legal mandates coming from both tax treaties and EU Law. In the first place, the treaty principle of non-discrimination as applied to PEs[529] seeks to ensure that a PE is not treated by the PE-State less favorably than enterprises resident in such State and carrying on the same activities. This principle is by no means demanding effective neutrality: PEs and residents may be treated differently for tax purposes just as long as the PE is subject to tax on its net profits and not at a higher rate than those of the resident.[530] Second, EU Law equally calls for neutrality of legal form in cross-border situations, thus prohibiting the unjustified discriminatory treatment between subsidiaries and PEs in objectively comparable situations.[531] Although the non-discrimination principle derived by EU Law goes certainly further than the treaty principle, it does not unconditionally grant a neutral tax treatment between PEs and subsidiaries. The main reason is that they will not always be found to be in comparable situations, as the comparability criterion will only be satisfied to the extent that PEs are taxed in a similar way to resident subsidiaries.[532]

In conclusion, even though there is an undeniable tendency to assimilate PEs to subsidiaries for tax purposes, largely inspired by the non-discrimination principles envisaged in treaties and EU Law, there are still major differences between them that should not be overlooked. First, both the PE and the enterprise to which it belongs will generally have the same creditworthiness, while parents and subsidiaries may well have a different one.[533] Second, it is impossible for a PE to guarantee the creditworthiness of the rest of the enterprise or vice versa.[534] Third, the PE does not have its own

527. Vann, R.J. (2003), p. 144.
528. García Prats, F.A. (1994), p. 481.
529. Article 24.3 of the 2017 OECD MC and 2017 UN MC (same wording) and Articles 24.2 and 24.3 of the 2017 US MC. The second sentence establishes an exception, but it only applies to PEs of individuals.
530. Panayi, H.J.I. (2013), pp. 229-230.
531. For an analysis of the ECJ case law on the matter *see* Panayi, H.J.I. (2013).
532. Panayi is critical with the fact that the ECJ only regards tax considerations when it comes to the analysis of comparability, thus omitting other regulatory differences between PEs and subsidiaries that may be of relevance. *See* Panayi, H.J.I. (2013), p. 229.
533. OECD (2008): Attribution of profits to permanent establishments, p. 18.
534. OECD (2008): Attribution of profits to permanent establishments, p. 18.

shareholders, unlike a subsidiary.[535] Fourth, parents and subsidiaries may enter into transactions with full legal effects while dealings between a PE and its home office are solely recognized for the purposes of attributing profits to the PE.[536] And lastly, the AOA may not necessarily achieve equality of outcome between subsidiaries and PEs, since PEs are likely to be more profitable, as the PE structure provides for efficient capital utilization, risk diversification, economics of scale, etc.[537]

[E] Analysis of the PE Concept in Tax Treaties in Its Respective Modalities in the Light of the Presumptive Benefit Principle

This section intends to briefly analyze the PE concept in its different modalities: the POB (also known as "basic rule"), the construction clause, the agency-PE and the service-PE. To do so, we will depart from the wording of Article 5 as drafted in the MCs. It is not the objective of this thesis to provide a thorough analysis on the content of the rule and the interpretation issues it may pose, as other scholars have already greatly contributed to its understanding.[538] On the contrary, the main purpose of the analysis, as we did before with the previous paradigms, is to ascertain whether the way the PE is drafted is aligned with the presumptive benefit principle or else allows corporate taxpayers to detach taxable profits from the jurisdictions where they perform their economic activities, either physically or remotely (and, by extension, where they presumably access their public benefits) and instead book them in those of their choice.

As a matter of principle, source is predominantly identified with the territory that is somehow connected to the production of the income in question or where value is added to a good (supply-based approach).[539] In view of the above, the PE aspired to become the translation of such ambiguous notion of source into an easy-to-administer and pragmatic rule. Thus, in principle, one would expect that the different modalities of PE would precisely represent various forms of income-generating business activities. As a consequence of the abovementioned, theoretically, the PE concept by its very nature should be, at least, partially aligned with the presumptive benefit principle: it should lead us to the territory where relevant economic activities are taking place (supply-based approach), while it may not be well-equipped to lead us to the territory providing a market of customers (demand approach).

We will subsequently try to corroborate whether the aforementioned assumptions are indeed true. We will first raise the question as to whether all the situations comprised within the current clause indeed allow us to assume the potential access to the benefits provided by the PE-State to the corporate taxpayer (sections §3.03[E][1]). Subsequently, we will ask ourselves the opposite question: are there situations beyond

535. Burgers, I.J.J. (2009), p. 73.
536. Moerer, O.; Klaver, B. (2015), p. 1590.
537. OECD (2008): Attribution of profits to permanent establishments, pp. 75-76.
538. Most importantly Skaar, A.A. (1991), García Prats, F.A. (1996) and Williams, R.L. (2014), among others.
539. Chapter 3 section §3.03[C].

those explicitly covered by the PE clause in which the potential access to public benefits by the company may be presumed? (section §3.03[E][2]).

We anticipated before that we would reserve the right to make reference to prior versions of the respective MCs (i.e., 2014 OECD MC, 2011 UN MC and 2006 US MC) where appropriate.[540] In this section we will exercise such right because we are aware that most tax treaties in place have not yet implemented the amendments proposed by the new versions of the MCs (and their update is expected to take decades),[541] and because we wish to evaluate later in Chapter 4 the impact that these latest versions will have for the purposes analyzed in the present thesis.

[1] Situations Covered by the Clause Which Allow Us to Assume (or Not) the Potential Access to Public Benefits

It has often been argued that the PE was originally conceived as a piece of evidence of the potential access by the non-resident enterprise to the public benefits provided by the PE-State, thereby justifying the imposition of taxes by the latter on the profits obtained by the non-resident taxpayer that could arguably be attributed to such PE.[542] In fact, we believe most of the scenarios covered by the PE concept allow us to assume that the corporate taxpayer would find itself in the position to potentially access the public benefits provided by the PE-State in line with the presumptive benefit principle, although the assumption is not equally strong in all the modalities of PE, as will be shown throughout this section. We will equally note some of the profit shifting risks that each of the modalities may give rise to. That is, relevant economic activities that would be doomed to be excluded from the scope of the clause, contrary to what the presumptive benefit principle would require.

[a] Fixed Place of Business

All the three most influential MCs agree on the definition of the PE as a "fixed place of business through which the business of an enterprise is wholly or partly carried on" (Article 5.1 of the MCs). Similarly, they all provide the same non-exhaustive list of illustrative examples of the kind of premises the PE clause intends to encompass:[543] places of management, branches, offices, factories, workshops, mines, oil or gas wells, quarries and other places of extraction of natural resources (Article 5.2 of the MCs). For its part, Article 5.4 of the respective MCs lists a number of business activities which shall not be considered PEs regardless of the fulfillment of the requirements established by Article 5.1. Their common feature is that they may be regarded as activities of

540. We explained the reasons behind this decision in the introduction of Chapter 3.
541. Most notably those incorporated in the 2017 OECD MC and the 2017 UN MC, resulting from the BEPS project.
542. Chapter 3 section §3.03[B].
543. The general belief is that the mere inclusion in the list does not automatically convert the place into a PE for tax treaty purposes. On the contrary, all requirements established in Article 5.1 will need to be fulfilled. *See* Skaar, A.A. (1991), pp. 113-114.

preparatory or auxiliary character, and the main reason why they are automatically excluded is that they are merely support activities that barely add value to the primary business activity of the non-resident enterprise.[544] Besides, even if they could constitute a PE, little profits would be attributable to it pursuant to Article 7 as it currently stands.[545]

It is not difficult to presuppose that a non-resident company carrying out a business activity through any of the examples of POB given by Article 5.2 would be in a position to use and/or enjoy, to a greater or lesser extent, the public services and infrastructures present in the State concerned.

[i] The Potential Profit Shifting Risks It Poses

The OECD noticed a couple of risks in the context of the BEPS project.

First, MNCs having a cohesive operating business in the host jurisdiction may easily split such activities into geographically separate places of business (under the responsibility of either the parent company or any other related party) which, on their own, qualify for the exemption envisaged in Article 5.4 of the MCs for being "preparatory or auxiliary."[546] The fact that such activities are not carried out altogether in the same POB but in separate ones would render ineffective Article 5.4.f, which solely combines the activities of a sole POB for the purposes of evaluating whether the combination effectively exceeds the threshold. This phenomenon is typically referred to as "fragmentation of activities" and eventually allows MNCs to have a substantial economic presence in a jurisdiction without incurring in tax liabilities therein.[547] Still, source-based taxation would be justified on the grounds of the presumptive benefit principle in these situations.

Second, Article 5.4 of the 2014 OECD MC presumes that all the activities listed in the paragraph are preparatory or auxiliary without admitting evidence to the contrary. This gives rise to the question as to whether such activities, in the context of certain recent business models, may play a prominent role in practice and may thus become significant in their respective value chains.[548] If that were the case, the PE clause would be automatically excluding relevant business activities from its scope and thus preventing its taxation at source.

[b] Construction PE

All the three MCs provide in their Article 5.3 a special category of PEs for building sites and construction or installation projects to the extent that they last for a certain time

544. Commentary on Article 5.4 of the 2014 OECD MC, paragraph 23.
545. Chapter 3 section §3.03[D].
546. OECD (2015): Final Report on BEPS Action 7—Preventing the artificial avoidance of permanent establishment status, p. 10. The risk was already foreseen in the Commentary on Article 5 of the 2014 OECD Model Convention, paragraph 27.1.
547. Martín Jiménez, A. (2014), p. 7.
548. OECD (2015): Final Report on BEPS Action 7—Preventing the artificial avoidance of permanent establishment status, pp. 10 and 28.

period.[549] Originally, at least in the case of the OECD MC,[550] they were integrated in the non-exhaustive list of fixed places of business provided by Article 5.2. The reason for their exclusion was that these kinds of sites and projects, by their own nature, could hardly ever comply with the permanence requirement and, besides, the OECD wished to avoid the erroneous interpretation that the places listed in Article 5.2 do not necessarily satisfy the general requirements set by Article 5.1.

The assumption of access to benefits remains valid (not to say stronger) in scenarios involving the presence of a building site or a construction/installation project in the host jurisdiction for a certain time period.

[i] The Potential Profit Shifting Risks It Poses

The OECD itself noted an important profit shifting risk related to this clause in the context of the BEPS project. Article 5.3 of the MCs is vulnerable insofar the temporal requirement may be easily circumvented by means of contract-splitting between related companies.[551] In those cases, while the economic activity may well persist for the required period, a mere contractual arrangement would be sufficient to render ineffective the clause and thus impede taxation at source. Once again, a situation where the presumptive benefit assumption could be made would inevitably fall out of the scope of the PE clause.

[c] Dependent Agent

All three MCs likewise agree that a non-resident company should be treated as having a PE in the host jurisdictions when, under certain conditions, a person (the dependent agent) is acting for it therein.[552] The rationale behind this alternative threshold may not be the benefit principle but rather the principle of equity, as it is argued that an enterprise conducting business through a separate legal person (the dependent agent) should be granted a tax treatment equivalent to that conferred to an enterprise conducting business directly in the source state by means of a fixed POB by virtue of Article 5.1.[553]

As Vogel noted, it does not seem appropriate in policy terms to regard any dependent agent as a PE of its principal. On the contrary, the PE status should be reserved to agents who, "in view of the scope of their authority or the nature of their

549. The three provisions vary considerably. The 2011 UN MC adds "assembly projects" and "supervisory activities in connection therewith" while the US MC adds the "installation or drilling rig or ship used for the exploration of natural resources." As regards the temporal requirement, both the 2014 OECD MC and the 2006 US MC demand twelve months while the UN reduces the minimum period to six months.
550. 1963 OECD MC.
551. OECD (2015): Final Report on BEPS Action 7—Preventing the artificial avoidance of permanent establishment status, pp. 11 and 42. The risk was already foreseen in the Commentary on Article 5 of the 2014 OECD Model Convention, paragraph 18.
552. *See* Articles 5.5 and 5.6 of the 2014 OECD MC, Articles 5.5, 5.6 and 5.7 of the 2011 UN MC and Articles 5.5 and 5.6 of the 2006 US MC.
553. Eisenbeiss, J. (2016), pp. 482-483 and Hoor, O.R.; O'Donnell, K. (2015), p. 932.

activity" involve their principal to a sufficient extent in business activities in the host jurisdiction.[554] At this point, each of the MCs demands different conditions pursuant to their respective policy goals.

The 2014 OECD MC and the 2011 UN MC require a person acting on behalf of the non-resident enterprise who "has and habitually exercises" in the host jurisdiction "an authority to conclude contracts in the name of the enterprise." For its part, the UN MC adds a supplementary provision, since it would still regard the agent as a PE to the extent that it habitually maintains in the host jurisdiction "a stock of goods or merchandise from which he regularly delivers goods or merchandise on behalf of the enterprise," even if it lacks the aforementioned authority to conclude contracts. Lastly, Article 5.5 of the 2006 US MC is similar to that of the OECD except for the fact that the US MC does not require the contracts to be concluded "in the name of the enterprise" but rather to be "binding" on such enterprise.[555]

The different approaches followed by the OECD/UN and the US in their respective definitions of agents are grounded in the disparate regulation of agency in civil and common law.[556]

On one hand, civil law regards the agent as a person entitled to conduct contracts that are legally binding on the principal. For a contract to bind the principal, two conditions are generally required in civil law scenarios.[557] First, the principal needs to previously grant the agent the authority to perform legal acts on his/her behalf. And second, the agent endowed with such authority needs to disclose the principal to the third party in the process of contracting. *A priori*, the contract would only bind the principal if both conditions are met. Accordingly, a commissionaire who acts in its own name (albeit for the account of the principal) would not be regarded as an agent for the purposes of civil law and would thus be unable to legally bind the principal.[558]

On the other hand, common law defines the agent in a similar way as a person who can represent the principal in such a way as to affect his/her legal position.[559] However, the abovementioned conditions are not required any more. Common law does not regulate the agency contract and furthermore regards the contract between the agent and the third party as one in fact concluded between the principal and the third party whether or not the principal is disclosed or not. As contracting "in the name" of the principal is irrelevant, such expression is unknown in common law. For

554. Vogel, K. (1997), p. 329 and Commentary on Article 5 of the 2014 OECD Model Convention, paragraph 32.
555. Curiously, the American clause is aligned with the concept of agent originally conceived by the League of Nations for the first MC: "a foreign enterprise regularly has business relations in another country through an agent established there, who is authorized to act on its behalf." *See* League of Nations (1929): Report on the Council on the work of the First Session of the Committee, p. 4. It was not until 1963 that the "in the name of" requirement was included in the OECD MC.
556. A comprehensive overview of such differences may be found in Avery Jones, J.F.; Lüdicke, J. (2014), particularly in pp. 204-209.
557. Avery Jones, J.F.; Lüdicke, J. (2014), pp. 204-205.
558. Avery Jones, J.F.; Lüdicke, J. (2014), p. 206.
559. Avery Jones, J.F.; Lüdicke, J. (2014), p. 205.

all these reasons, the distinction between agents and commissionaires does not arise in this context.[560]

Once the agent is deemed to fulfill all the requirements established in the relevant PE clause, it would be treated as a PE (Dependent Agent—Permanent Establishment (hereinafter "DAPE") and thus attributed the corresponding profits.

Lastly, brokers, general commission agents and any other agents of an independent status are not considered agents for the purposes of Article 5.5 to the extent that they act "in the ordinary course of their business."[561] The reason is clear: they should not be regarded as a prolongation of the non-resident enterprise but rather as autonomous entrepreneurs carrying out separate businesses.[562]

[i] The Potential Profit Shifting Risks It Poses

We will now proceed to analyze three profit shifting risks that relate to the agency clause.[563]

The first risk we will make reference to is more acute in the 2014 OECD MC. The most sensitive part of the clause is the one that requires the agent to have and habitually exercise an authority to conclude contracts "in the name of the enterprise." Its reliance on a mere formality (the fact that the contract is concluded in the name of the non-resident taxpayer) increases the possibilities of circumventing the rule by simply changing the literal terms of the contract. This is the reason why MNCs (Apple among them)[564] have recently switched from their previous distribution arrangements to the present "commissionaire arrangements."[565] First of all, the agent transfers to its principal its fixed assets, stock and customer base. Subsequently, and pursuant to the so-called commissionaire arrangement, the agent would be entitled to sell the non-resident's products in its own name but on behalf of the non-resident, who would never cease to be the legal owner of such products.[566] This simple restructuring effectively allows MNCs to keep the same amount of commercial activity in the host jurisdiction without technically having a PE therein to which profits would be attributable for tax treaty purposes. On the contrary, the host jurisdiction would solely

560. Avery Jones, J.F.; Lüdicke, J. (2014), p. 206.
561. Article 5.6 of the 2014 OECD MC and the 2006 US MCs and Article 5.7 of the 2011 UN MC.
562. Skaar, A.A. (1991), pp. 513-515.
563. The OECD has historically cautioned against these risks, more recently in OECD (2015): Final Report on BEPS Action 7—Preventing the artificial avoidance of permanent establishment status.
564. *See* Chapter 2 section §2.01[A][2]. Similarly, Dell converted seventeen European subsidiaries into commissionaires back in 1995 and Roche equally conducted a similar business restructuring, *see* Martín Jiménez, A. (2014), pp. 63 and 65.
565. The strategy is explained in OECD (2015): Final Report on BEPS Action 7—Preventing the artificial avoidance of permanent establishment status, pp. 15-16 and Eisenbeiss, J. (2016), p. 483.
566. OECD (2015): Final Report on BEPS Action 7—Preventing the artificial avoidance of permanent establishment status, p. 15.

be entitled to tax the small commission such agent is expected to receive for the services provided.[567]

This risk is much more limited in the 2006 US MC and the 2011 UN MCs. For its part, the US MC does not regard the formalities of the contract but rather refers to its effects ("contracts that are binding on the enterprise"). Thus, the American clause would be less likely to be circumvented by a simple contractual arrangement.[568] On the other hand, the UN provides a rule identical to that of the OECD but further complements it with an alternative provision. Such provision would regard the agent as a PE of the non-resident taxpayer to the extent that it maintains in the host jurisdiction a stock of goods or merchandise from which it regularly delivers goods or merchandise on behalf other enterprise. Once again, the reliance on a more substantive minimizes the potential profit shifting risks that may derive from the PE clause.

The second risk occurs equally in all three MCs. As they literally refer to the authority to "conclude" contracts in the host jurisdiction, a PE would solely exist to the extent that the conclusion of the contract effectively takes place in such territory. It is therefore possible for a company to substantially negotiate contracts though agents in the host jurisdiction but eventually conclude them abroad.[569] In those cases, the commercial activity would remain the same, but a mere formality would de facto prevent the constitution of the PE and the corresponding taxation at source.

The third risk also arises in all the three MCs. MNCs may attempt to "disguise" a dependent agent as an independent one for the purposes of qualifying for the exception.[570] To this end, MNCs may make use of a related party that acts (exclusive or almost exclusively) on behalf of the principal but in the guise of an independent agent acting in the ordinary course of its business.[571] Pursuant to the literalism of the article, such agent would not constitute a PE despite being substantially equivalent to a dependent agent.

[d] Provision of Services

The 2011 UN MC provides a special category of PE that refers to the furnishing of services.[572] Pursuant to such article, a non-resident enterprise would be deemed to

567. The commissionaire's service to the principal is usually remunerated at a cost-plus basis and this is the only profit that would be subject to tax in the source State. If the company succeeds to minimize the functions, assets and risks that could be attributable to the commissionaire, then a typical commission may merely amount to 5%-15% of the sales proceeds. *See* Darby, J.B. (2006), pp. 15-16 and Eisenbeiss, J. (2016), p. 484.
568. The proof is that Article 5.5 was not been amended by the 2016 update to the US MC, which intended to implement some of the recommendations derived by the BEPS project.
569. OECD (2015): Final Report on BEPS Action 7—Preventing the artificial avoidance of permanent establishment status, pp. 9-10.
570. Established in Article 5.6 of the 2014 OECD, 5.7 of the 2011 UN MC and 5.6 of the 2006 US MC.
571. This risk was also identified in the course of the BEPS project. *See* for example OECD (2015): Final Report on BEPS Action 7—Preventing the artificial avoidance of permanent establishment status, p. 10: "where the person that habitually exercises an authority to conclude contracts constitutes an 'independent agent' to which the exception of Art. 5(6) applies even though it is closely related to the foreign enterprise on behalf of which it is acting."
572. Article 5.3.b of the 2011 UN MC.

have a PE in the host jurisdiction if it engages employees or other personnel for the provision of services (including consultancy services) if such activities continue within the territory of the jurisdiction concerned for more than 183 days in any 12-months period for the same or connected projects.

[i] The Potential Profit Shifting Risks It Poses

The clause poses risks equivalent to those of the construction PE. The reason is evident. The 183-days rule may be easily circumvented by splitting the project into various contracts with related parties.[573] In those cases, the provision of services may well persist for a long period, but a mere contractual arrangement would effectively impede the application of the rule and thus the taxation of its attributable profits at source.

[e] The Probable Inconsistency Between Certain Provisions of the PE Clause and the Presumptive Benefit Principle

While the provisions dealing with the fixed POB and the construction site are undoubtedly justified on the grounds of the presumptive benefit principle, the truth is that the presence of other provisions may not be that justified.

For example, the automatic exclusion of the activities listed in Article 5.4 of the MCs from the scope of the PE clause on the basis that they are deemed to be "of a preparatory or auxiliary nature" is, strictly speaking, untenable from the perspective of the presumptive benefit principle. The reason is that all the listed activities involve the use of a physical POB in the host jurisdiction, a fact that per se allow us to assume the potential access to public benefits irrespective of the nature of the activities that the non-resident company carries out through it.

The same applies to other clauses where the PE arises behind a person or group of persons that are resident in the host jurisdiction, either natural or legal, either related or unrelated with the non-resident company. This is, for example, the case of a subsidiary providing a fixed POB through which the non-resident enterprise carries on its own business (Article 5.1 of the MCs), an individual acting as its DAPE (Article 5.5 of the MCs)[574] or a team of in-house or outsourced workers engaged by the non-resident company to provide services therein (Article 5.3.b of the UN MC). It is true that the person(s) through which the PE arises (PE-person) is presumably in the position to access the benefits provided by such State. However, as long as it is considered as tax resident in this State, it will already be subject to tax therein irrespective of its consideration as a PE. Furthermore, its tax liability will commonly encompass its worldwide income, including an arm's length remuneration for the service provided to the non-resident, whether unrelated or related with the PE-person (by virtue of the applicable transfer pricing rules following the ALS).

573. Martín Jiménez, A. (2014), p. 52.
574. Schoueri, L.E.; Günther, O-C (2011) and Article 5.7 of the OECD and US MCs and 5.8 of the UN MC.

At this point, we would like to raise two questions. The first one is whether the PE-person could be attributed any profit pursuant to the AOA beyond the arm's length remuneration received from the non-resident for its service. The profits that could arguably be attributed to the person-PE are likely to be zero or minimal.[575] The second question is whether, in case the PE-person could be attributed profits by virtue of its status as a PE, the taxation of the income obtained by the non-resident company in the PE-State may be justified in benefit terms. Considering that the State presumably providing the public benefits (the PE-State) already exerts tax jurisdiction over the person-PE for its worldwide income (including the remuneration for its service to the non-resident company), the answer is likely to be negative.

All in all, the presumptive benefit principle has led us to question the PE clause in its current form, in particular the sense of keeping the PE exemptions in Article 5.4 of the MCs as well the sense of considering the presence of PEs behind resident taxpayers that are already subject to tax in the host jurisdiction.[576] However, their withdrawal would be desirable only to the extent that States regard this rule as an instrument at the exclusive service of the presumptive benefit principle. On the contrary, when States intend to achieve other or additional policy objectives by means of the PE, this reform may not make sense any more. For example, States may wish the PE to encompass only significant value-creating activities, an approach that would be consistent with the current methodology promoted by the OECD to attribute profits to PEs.[577] This being so, Article 5.4 of the MCs should undoubtedly be kept. It may also be the case that States wish the PE to represent a considerable degree of involvement of the non-resident company in the economic life of the host jurisdiction,[578] thus justifying the distinction between dependent and independent agent (Articles 5.5 and

575. *See* the considerations on the "single taxpayer" and "dual taxpayer" approaches in Chapter 4 section §4.02[C][2][c].
576. This latter observation would also entail the revision of tax treaties so as to exclude these scenarios from the scope of Articles 5 and 7.2 and instead rely on the ALS of Article 9. The application of the AOA (most notably its first phase) could be regarded a justifiable only in cases in which the PE lacks legal personality and is thus inherently unable to own assets, assume risks, possess capital or conclude contracts, thus making it necessary to hypothesize the PE as if it were a "separate and independent enterprise." To the extent the PE materializes in these scenarios under the wing of a person (which, on the contrary, has such capacities), we could arguably conclude that Article 9 of the MC would apply and the ALS contained in such Article could therefore help to adjust (if necessary) the relevant remuneration without the need to resort to the economic analysis suggested by the AOA. In these cases, Article 9 by itself would ensure an appropriate arm's length remuneration for the subsidiary considering the functions performed, assets used and risks assumed and, by extension, an appropriate tax revenue for the host State.
577. Pursuing this objective by means of the PE would be consistent with the AOA, whose analysis departs from the identification of the "significant people functions" (*see* Chapter 3 section §3.03[D]).
578. This is actually the supposed rationale behind Article 7 (and by extension Article 5) of the OECD MC. *See* Commentary on Article 7 of the 2017 OECD MC, paragraph 11: "until an enterprise of one State has a permanent establishment in another State, it should not properly be regarded as participating in the economic life of that other State to such an extent that the other State should have taxing rights on its profits."

5.6 of the MCs)[579] as well as the possibility that a person resident in the host jurisdiction constitutes a PE of the non-resident company to which profits could be attributed.[580] This latter possibility is also typically justified on equity grounds.[581]

Be that as it may, States should reflect on the policy objective(s) they wish to pursue by means of the PE threshold. In cases where they merely seek consistency between the PE and the presumptive benefit principle, the suggestions made in the present section should be at least explored. On the contrary, in cases where States regard the PE clause as a means to achieve other or additional policy purposes,[582] they should first identify them and subsequently reflect on how best the wording of the clause may contribute to their accomplishment.

[2] Situations Beyond the Scope of the PE Clause Which Allow Us to Assume the Potential Accessibility to Benefits

The PE clause merely covers the economic activities that express themselves in the terms required in the PE clause. In particular, the PE equates physical and stable presence with taxable presence:[583] a common pattern that is obvious and visible in all the four modalities of PEs set out in the MCs. As pointed out above in section §3.03[C], requiring a physical and stable presence was perfectly consistent with the economic context in which the PE arose, where the physical presence was critical to perform any kind of business activity.[584]

However, the presence of these two requirements in today's clause automatically leads to leave untaxed all other relevant business activities which, while not complying with these two conditions, still allow us to presume that the non-resident company

579. Commentary on Article 5 of the 2017 OECD MC, paragraph 83: "such treatment (that of a DAPE) is to be limited to persons who in view of the scope of their authority or the nature of their activity involve the enterprise to a particular extent in business activities in the State concerned" as opposed to paragraph 102: "such an agent (the independent one), who represents a separate and independent enterprise, should not result in the finding of a permanent establishment of the foreign enterprise." On the contrary, such a distinction cannot be upheld in benefit terms.
580. *See* Arnold, B.J. (2011), p. 65 on the PE service of the UN MC: "a source country should be entitled to tax income from services only if the involvement of the non-resident service provider in the commercial life of the source country is significant."
581. The fact that an enterprise conducting business directly in the source jurisdiction (through a POB) should not be taxed differently from an enterprise choosing to conduct business through a separate legal person (e.g., acting as a dependent agent, providing a POB for the enterprise, etc.). *See* Eisenbeiss, J. (2016), pp. 482-483.
582. For example, those referred in the previous paragraph or in Chapter 3 section §3.03[B].
583. Escribano, E. (2015), p. 8.
584. Back then, this nineteenth century legal clause was certainly able to cover most of the significant economic activities that could take place in a nineteenth century business environment. *See* Hongler, P.; Pistone, P. (2015), p. 21: "when the benefit theory developed, and the PE definition was implemented into the OECD Model, neither the digital world nor computers existed. This could be one reason why it is argued that a physical presence is required for source taxation as there had not been any possible benefits besides physical benefits that could occur (e.g., streets, public transport, police, etc.)."

finds itself in the position to use and/or enjoy the public infrastructures or benefits provided by such State.[585]

As regards the stability and permanency requirements, the PE clause leaves out of its scope the conduction of certain activities insofar the time threshold (explicitly or implicitly) required is not reached.[586] It is true that a non-resident company conducting an economic activity in the host jurisdiction for a period of time not exceeding such threshold may well be in the position to benefit from the services provided by such State,[587] but it is equally true that shorter periods of presence are likely to result in a lower number of benefits within its reach or a reduced degree of use and/or enjoyment of them. This being so, the existence of these thresholds should not be considered as troublesome from the perspective of the presumptive benefit principle. Additionally, its use is also advised from a compliance perspective, as an excessive proliferation of PEs in different jurisdictions is undesirable. In any event, States should reflect upon the pertinence of establishing lower or higher time thresholds, waiving their advantages and disadvantages and, above all, considering the policy purposes they intend to achieve through the PE clause in order to make the decision that best fits their needs.

As regards the need to be physically present in the host jurisdiction, the PE excludes economic activities that do not any entail a physical presence in the territory however much they allow the company to reach its market of customers by the remote supply of goods and services. For example, the POB clause envisaged in Article 5.1 of the MCs is noticeably unable to capture transactions conducted through remote means, e.g., catalogue shopping via mail-order transactions or sales carried out through call centers, websites, smartphone "apps," etc. Similarly, Article 5.5 of the MCs is unable to capture agents performing remotely the very same commercial activity performed by

585. This very same question was equally put forward by Gadžo, S. (2016), p. 247.

586. Indeed, the Commentaries on the OECD MC themselves recognize that "the underlying principle in Article 5 that the presence which an enterprise maintains in a Contracting State should be more than merely transitory if the enterprise is to be regarded as maintaining a permanent establishment, and thus a taxable presence, in that State" (Commentary on Article 5 of the 2017 OECD MC, paragraph 98). As regards the fixed POB, the time threshold is not stated explicitly and the interpretation of the "permanence" criterion by domestic courts is not entirely consistent, but the Commentaries recognize that "permanent establishments normally have not been considered to exist in situations where a business had been carried on in a country through a place of business that was maintained for less than six months" (Commentary on Article 5 of the 2017 OECD MC, paragraph 28). For its part, the temporal requirement in the construction PE varies per treaty (e.g., the OECD and the US MC sets a twelve-months period while the UN MC sets a 6-months period). Lastly, the agency-PE, the clause demands the agent to "habitually exercise" its authority to conclude contracts on behalf of the non-resident enterprise (or else, "habitually maintains" a stock of goods or merchandise in the host jurisdiction under the UN MC). The Commentaries intend to shed some light on the interpretation of the term "habitually": "the extent and frequency of activity necessary to conclude that the agent is 'habitually exercising' contracting authority will depend on the nature of the contracts and the business of the principal. It is not possible to lay down a precise frequency test" (Commentary on Article 5 of the 2017 OECD MC, paragraph 98).

587. Skaar, A.A. (1991), pp. 559-560: "the circumstance that short-term business operations may accumulate substantial profits from domestic sources indicates on the contrary that the taxpayer benefits substantially from the infrastructure of the host country, even though no PE exists."

DAPEs[588] or concluding the contracts outside the host jurisdiction.[589] Lastly, Article 5.3.b of the UN MC would automatically exclude the remote provision of services. Back in Chapter 2 section §2.02, we provided numerous arguments to sustain that a company trading remotely with customers residing in a State without being physically present in its territory would still be in a position to use, enjoy or, at least, indirectly benefit from the State's services and infrastructures.[590] This fact, coupled with the undeniable increasing ability of companies to conduct business remotely,[591] makes it urgent to reconsider the scope of the PE clause so as to accommodate these situations. Otherwise, digital companies that trade with their customers by remote means (Apple itself among them) would enjoy an unjustifiable tax advantage in contrast to non-digital companies in the jurisdictions where they operate.[592]

In a nutshell, the abovementioned considerations reveal that the PE has ceased to be the only valid indicator of the potential accessibility of the non-resident company to the benefits provided by the host State.[593] The amendment of the clause appears to be necessary insofar as States wish to truly align the clause with the presumptive benefit principle and further adapt it to the new business environment.

[F] Interim Conclusions

[1] The Permanent Establishment Acts as a "Functional Resident" in Contrast to the "Vacuous Resident" Resulting from the Application of the Residence Tests

Section §3.03[D] provided numerous arguments demonstrating the increasing tendency to equate the tax treatment of PEs and resident companies for income tax purposes. The primary reason being that the PE-State is *a priori* entitled to tax the

588. Article 5.5 requires the agent to be acting physically in the territory of the State concerned, although it does not need to be resident or have a POB therein. Such interpretation may be logically inferred from the wording of the clause and is further confirmed by the Commentary on Article 5 of the 2014 OECD Model Convention, paragraph 32.
589. Martín Jiménez, A. (2014), p. 28.
590. Chapter 2 Section §2.02[B][2][b].
591. Changes in business models, communications and technology makes it increasingly possible to conduct a significant economic activity in the host jurisdiction does not express itself in the terms required in the PE clause.
592. This was revealed in a study conducted by the European Commission. In a sample of seven major digital companies and seven major non-digital companies, all US-based, it was demonstrated that the former enjoyed an average effective tax rate of 9.58% in 2011 as opposed to the 17.54% of the latter. *See* EU Commission Expert Group on Taxation of the Digital Economy (2014): Final report, pp. 54-55.
593. Skaar, A.A. (1991), p. 573: "an enterprise's connection to the soil, its PE, is no longer a reliable evidence of economic allegiance." Eisenbeiss states that "countries increasingly come to the realization that economic allegiance, and thus a justified tax claim, can exist in situations outside the scope of the current PE threshold" and that the PE "does not provide a fair allocation of taxing rights and thus violates the notion of inter-nation equity," a principle we linked with the presumptive benefit principle back in Chapter 2 section §2.02[A]. *See* Eisenbeiss, J. (2016), p. 496. In the same vein, *see* Skaar, A.A. (1991), p. 559: "a PE is merely a piece of evidence of economic allegiance."

worldwide income attributable to the PE a non-resident enterprise has within its territory.

Additionally, in situations in which the wide taxing rights of both the Residence and the PE-State are expected to collide, tax treaties tend to give precedence to the taxing rights of the PE-State over those of the Residence State. They do so by obliging the latter to either exempt the profits that are attributable to the PE or give a credit for the levied by the PE-State.[594] In other words, tax treaties tend to deny the taxing rights of the Residence State over the profits obtained by one of its residents inasmuch as they are attributable to a PE located abroad. In those cases, the PE-State would effective appropriate such profits for tax purposes.

Consequently, we could say that the PE has not only become a sort of "functional resident" with a tax status equivalent to those enjoyed by resident entities. It has further gained primacy over the taxing rights of the Residence State, at least in tax treaty scenarios. The question remains as to why this nineteenth century legal fiction promoted by tax treaties has managed to undermine the wide taxing rights traditionally enjoyed by the jurisdictions with respect to their own residents.

At this stage we should look back at the conclusions of section §3.02, particularly those laid down in section §3.02[A][2][c]. We then reached the conclusion that most residence tests are inherently unable to ensure, per se, a genuine and sufficient relationship between the corporate and the jurisdiction concerned. Domestic corporate tax residence tests followed by the overwhelming majority of States (97%) lead to attribute the status of tax resident to companies incorporated, with their registered office and/or effectively managed from their territory.[595] Thus, the fact that the residence jurisdiction coincides with that to which the company is more economically bound is left to chance. On the other hand, the PE concept does ensure a genuine and substantive connection between the PE-State and the corporate taxpayer, as section §3.03[E] revealed.

In this context, it is easy to understand in policy terms why the PE-State is (and should continue to be insofar as residence tests are not reconsidered) legitimized to tax the worldwide profits attributable to the PE of a non-resident enterprise at the expense of its Residence State.[596] In fact, one may interpret the progressive tendency to equate the tax treatment of PEs and residents (section §3.03[D]) and its strengthening over the last decades as a natural reaction to the growing weaknesses and inconsistencies of the

594. Articles 23A and 23B of the 2014 OECD MC, respectively.

595. The seventy-three countries-survey presented in Chapter 3 section §3.02[A][1][e] (*see* Table 1 and Figure 4) revealed that jurisdictions rely on formal tests (22%), governance tests (11%) or a combination of both (64%), thus representing 97% of the surveyed States.

596. Schön, W. (2018), section 1: "the existence of a permanent establishment was seen as an indication for strong and visible economic allegiance to a source jurisdiction, which was duly awarded priority vis-à-vis the competing taxing claims of the residence country." Along the same lines, Brauner believes that the US have compensated an extremely simple residence test (the POI) with a strong and far-reaching source rule (the "trade or business" test). *See* Brauner, Y. (2009), p. 867.

residence tests.[597] This is because it is increasingly difficult in a globalized world to maintain the assumption that the Residence State (i.e., where the corporate taxpayer is incorporated or managed) is the one that enjoys a closer connection to the taxpayer, while the PE is able to ensure such close connection more straightforwardly.

[2] The Unfortunate Tendency to Resort to Eccentric or Substance-Based Interpretations and Anti-avoidance Rules as a Way to Counteract the Weaknesses of the PE concept

In section §3.03[E] we concluded that the PE clause as it stands in the 2014 OECD MC is not as consistent with the presumptive benefit principle as it may be *a priori* expected to be insofar as it tends to inherently leave out of its scope many relevant business activities[598] whose presence in the territory concerned indicate that the corporate taxpayer is presumably benefiting from local public services and infrastructures.

States are well aware that a literal, strict interpretation of the PE clause prevents them taxing the profits obtained by non-residents in cases in which they have a substantial economic presence in their territories. As they do not generally seem to accept the (logical) outcome of following the literal wording of the PE concept,[599] they may choose either to force the interpretation of the preexisting rule beyond its literal meaning[600] or, conversely, amend the rule in the desired direction (the "policy approach").

At least before the arrival of the BEPS project, jurisdictions generally opted for the first approach, thus perpetuating the unfortunate habit of trying to counteract the weaknesses of rules by resorting to either eccentric interpretations, substance-over-form approaches and anti-avoidance rules.[601] We will now provide various examples for each one of these approaches, placing special emphasis on the so-called *PE-Spanish*

597. Vann, R.J. (2003), p. 148: "the taxation of PEs is nowadays best viewed as a residence-supporting concept rather than a source taxing principle." The weaknesses of residence tests were analyzed in Chapter 3 section §3.02.

598. Indeed, Martín Jiménez seems to share this opinion, as he stated back in 2014 that: "the PE may inherently produce the effect of segregating taxable income from activities that generate it" (Martín Jiménez, A. (2014), p. 9) and that "the PE was designed to tax significant activity carried on in the State of source, but it permits some relevant presence and activity taking place there go to untaxed"(Martín Jiménez, A. (2014), p. 13, *see also* pp. 45 and 54-55). Skaar equally shares this view: "rather than protecting the tax base in the source State, the PE principle has become instrumental in ensuring avoidance of source-State taxation" (Skaar, A.A. (1991), p. 559).

599. The same was true in the context of the residence rules, as Chapter 3 section §3.02[A][2][c] highlighted. Martín Jiménez provides various arguments to demonstrate the general "sense of dissatisfaction in some countries with the PE threshold in article 5 of the OECD Model." *See* Martín Jiménez, A. (2016), p. 458.

600. Martín Jiménez regards the interpretation of the PE concept by the Spanish courts as a "defensive" mechanism to some of the structures that the BEPS Project later tried to eliminate. Martín Jiménez, A. (2016), p. 458.

601. A tendency we already criticized in the context of the residence tests. *See* Chapter 3 sections §3.02[A][2][c] and §3.02[C][3].

approach[602] taken by the Spanish administrative and judiciary bodies, as it very well illustrates each one of them.

First, jurisdictions have sometimes opted for peculiar interpretations of the PE concept that go beyond either its literal wording or its supposed spirit or intention. It was the advent of the ICT and the popularization of the internet what exacerbated the pressures upon the PE concept and originated the perfect breeding ground for these unconventional practices.

The e-commerce phenomenon brought serious interpretative issues in relation to the PE, and the OECD sought to address such issues in the early 2000s in order to ensure a uniform and coordinated understanding of the term to prevent conflicts of interpretation and the subsequent unintended double taxation.[603] In the case of websites, the OECD defined them as a mere "combination of software and electronic data," rightly concluding that they were inherently unable to fulfill the first of the requirements of the PE concept, insofar an intangible property could never constitute a "place."[604] Such interpretation, albeit perfectly consistent with the literal wording of the PE concept, did not satisfy Greece, Spain and Portugal, which expressly reserved their rights not the follow this position.[605] This served as an excuse to the Spanish Central Economic-Administrative Court to regard a website as a PE and further attribute all the profits derived by the online sales to it back in 2012.[606] Similarly, India maintains that a website by its own may constitute a PE in certain circumstances.[607]

On the other hand, the OECD equally addressed the possibility of a server (i.e., the computer equipment where websites are stored) constituting a PE. In essence, the OECD came to recognize such possibility as long as two requirements were met: (i) the

602. For a general overview of the singular interpretation of the PE concept in Spain *see* Carmona Fernández, N. (2013) and Martín Jiménez, A. (2016).
603. OECD (2003): Are the current treaty rules for taxing business profits appropriate for e-commerce? Final report and Escribano, E. (2015), p. 10.
604. Commentary on Article 5 of the 2017 OECD MC, paragraph 123.
605. Back then all three included their reservations in the Commentary on Article 5. Later on, only Greece, Chile, Mexico and Portugal maintain such reservations. *See* Observations on the Commentary on Article 5 of the 2017 OECD MC, paragraph 177 and 182.
606. Resolution by the Spanish Central Economic-Administrative Court (TEAC), March 15, 2012, "Dell case." Calderón Carrero, J.M.; Martínez-Matosas, E. (2012), p. 386: "the TEAC did not accept the application of the OECD commentaries to article 5 (...) the tax authorities and the Court argued that such OECD commentaries do not apply to the case under analysis as the activities performed in Spain were economically significant (that is, trading, selling and delivering)." Martín Jiménez, A. (2016), p. 463: "the TEAC attributed relevance to the web pages for the Spanish market, which were maintained and fed by personnel in Spain (...) the TEAC finally concluded that, as the activities were significant, the commercialization of Dell products in Spain though the web page must be attributed to the activities of Dell Ireland in Spain." Later on, both High National and the Supreme Court corrected the reasoning of the TEAC, rightly concluding that a website can never constitute a "place" of business.
607. Positions of non-OECD economies to Commentary on Article 5 of the 2017 OECD MC, paragraphs 26 and 33. According to such position, India manifests that a website may constitute a PE in certain circumstances (paragraph 33) as it regards that intangible property may on its own constitutes a "place" (paragraph 26).

server should be effectively at the disposal of the non-resident enterprise[608] and (ii) activities carried out through it could not be of preparatory or auxiliary nature.[609] Again, such interpretation was perfectly consistent with the wording of Article 5. However, we believe the outcome of such interpretation is not only absurd but also contrary to the alleged spirit of the PE concept,[610] which is to provide a threshold that denotes a significant economic involvement with the host jurisdiction,[611] and also to the presumptive benefit principle. For its part, a server does not per se manifest any kind of participation in the economic life of the host State beyond the presence of a "dusty computer running in the basement of a building."[612] But these concerns did not rise at that time and, most importantly, did not prevent many jurisdictions (Austria, Germany, India, Italy, among others) from actually considering servers as PEs.[613] For their part, other jurisdictions (Brazil, Ireland, UK and the US among others) acted more wisely and categorically refused to accept the interpretation offered by the OECD.[614]

Beyond the attempts of the OECD, Brauner and Pistone have recently put forward a proposal suggesting a radical reinterpretation of the notion of fixed POB[615] so as to encompass situations that can barely qualify as fixed POBs. In particular, they call for the adoption of a multilateral protocol within the EU Member States that would coexist with their tax treaties in force. Such protocol would specify the way the PE clause of such treaties ought to be interpreted from then on: "the fixed place of business shall be deemed to exist also when the enterprise carries out business in the other Contracting State without a physical presence on the territory of such State. This situation includes cases in which the enterprise regularly concludes contracts with users in such Contracting State for an amount that exceeds XXX in a given year." This way, the expression fixed POB would equally capture situations of digital presence provided that this is significant in quantitative terms (e.g., sales volume).

The proposal suggested by Brauner and Pistone may be regarded at first sight as a quick easy-to-implement tactical solution to broaden up the scope of the PE clause. It

608. It should be noted that the taxpayer can easily circumvent this requirement by means of the so-called hosting arrangements, through which the non-resident taxpayer does not rent the server as such but an amount of disk space to store the corresponding website. *See* Escribano, E. (2015), p. 10.
609. Commentary on Article 5 of the 2017 OECD MC, paragraphs 124-130.
610. Escribano, E. (2015), p. 10.
611. *See* Chapter 3 section §3.03[B].
612. Escribano, E. (2015), p. 10. Other scholars have also strongly criticized the OECD's stand on this matter. *See* for example Cockfield, A. (2006), p. 172 and Doernberg, R.L.; Hinnekens, L. (1999), p. 7: "Servers can easily be located anywhere and their location is generally unknown and unimportant in a business transaction." In fact, Google registered a patent in 2008 that consisted on the installation of mobile data center platforms at the sea by stacking containers filed with servers and storage systems. *See* New York Times: "Google's search goes out to the sea," September 7· 2008.
613. This book provides a very complete overview on the position of a diverse group of jurisdictions regarding the server-PE, including administrative guidelines and judgments. *See* Cockfield, A., Hellerstein, W., Millar, R., Waerzeggers, C. (2013), pp. 127-131.
614. The UK submitted an explicit reservation in this matter, which still maintains. *See* Observations on the Commentary on Article 5 of the 2017 OECD, paragraph 176. The position of the other jurisdictions is well explained in Cockfield, A., Hellerstein, W., Millar, R., Waerzeggers, C. (2013), pp. 127-131.
615. Brauner, Y.; Pistone, P. (2017).

would however give rise to a number of regulatory risks that should not be underestimated. The main risk is that the proposed multilateral protocol is expected to equally affect treaties signed between Member and non-Member States. In our opinion, this would ultimately mean treaty override. Or, in other words, the unilateral imposition of an amendment to a bilaterally agreed clause after its approval that would blatantly contravene the *pacta sunt servanda* principle enshrined in Article 26 of the Vienna Convention on the Law of Treaties, being twenty-six of the twenty-eight Member States parties of this Convention.[616]

There are two main reasons why we believe this proposal would give rise to treaty override.[617] First, while the authors argue that this measure does not imply the unilateral modification of the clause but rather a reinterpretation of it, we cannot share their opinion. The interpretation of a rule involves exploring its ultimate meaning and determining its content and precise scope so as to assess its application to a specific factual situation. However, such exercise should necessarily depart from the ordinary meaning given to the terms comprised in the rule and never go beyond the possible meaning that could be attributed to such terms.[618] Going back to the case at hand, we cannot possibly argue that the new proposed stance is a clarification or specification of the expression fixed POB, as such immaterial and intangible presence would undoubtedly exceed the scope (and possible meaning) of the term "place."[619] Second, the authors suggest that the introduction of a joint EU observation to the Commentaries on the OECD MC would effectively make non-Member States treaty partners have an *ex ante* knowledge of this new standard for (re)interpretation of the expression and would therefore be in a position to "decide what measures they should take in that respect." In this sense, we believe the only natural reaction these States may have cannot be other than requesting the suspension[620] or termination of the treaty[621] by invoking the material breach of the treaty by their counterparty.

In conclusion, the proposal supported by Brauner/Pistone should not disguise itself as an "interpretative tool" as a way to justify its compatibility with treaties signed with non-Member States. Instead, the proposal should present itself as a straightforward amendment to the classic PE clause whose application should be confined, for the time being, to EU soil.

616. Romania and France are the only exceptions. *See* https://treaties.un.org/pages/ViewDetailsIII.aspx?src=TREATY&mtdsg_no=XXIII-1&chapter=23&Temp=mtdsg3&clang=_en (last accessed on January 10, 2019).
617. We presented these arguments elsewhere in Escribano, E. (2019), section 2.
618. The "grammatical interpretation" is one of the most common interpretation methodologies in Law and is also envisaged in Article 31 of the Vienna Convention on the Law of Treaties.
619. Indeed, Kofler, Mayr and Schlager argue that a domestic expansion of the PE concept so as to cover "digital presences" would contravene current Article 5 of tax treaties: "in the absence of a physical PE within the meaning of article 5 of the OECD Model, taxation of a digital presence of persons covered by a treaty would generally be barred under treaty law in relation to the respective treaty partner State or would unilaterally only be realizable through treaty override." *See* Kofler, G.W.; Mayr, G.; Schlager, C. (2017), p. 529.
620. Termination and suspension are foreseen in Article 60 of the Vienna Convention on the Law of Treaties.
621. Termination is also envisaged in Article 32 of the 2017 OECD MC, Article 31 of the 2017 UN MC and Article 30 of the 2016 US MC.

Second, a much more common approach has been the adoption of an economist or substance-based approach when interpreting the PE concept. Once again, we should refer to the so-called PE-Spanish approach, as it has become paradigmatic. First of all, it should be noted that the substance-based interpretation of the PE concept has not emerged spontaneously: it has been explicitly promoted by the OECD through the 2002 and 2003 updates to the Commentaries on the OECD MC,[622] as will be shown below. Furthermore, it may be read as a "defensive" reaction of tax administrations and courts towards the recent business restructurings carried out by MNCs with the purpose of avoiding the constitution of a PE in the host jurisdiction.[623] During the 1990s and early 2000s, many MNCs restructured the business of their subsidiaries, converting distributors into commissionaires and full-fledged manufacturers into contract-manufacturers.[624] As a result, the MNCs managed to maintain the same business activity than before whilst preventing the host jurisdiction from taxing the profits attributable to that activity.

The courts' general premise was that Spain was legitimized to tax the profits of a non-resident enterprise to the extent that there was a high degree of penetration of its economic activity in the Spanish territory.[625] In light of this, we will now proceed to provide a few examples on the impact of the Spanish substance-based interpretation of the PE concept (as it was drafted in the 2014 OECD MC and prior to the amendments triggered by the BEPS project).

In the first place, the Spanish courts followed a substance-based interpretation with regard to Articles 5.1 and 5.4 to address the fragmentation of activities in the host jurisdiction with the intention of qualifying for the "auxiliary/preparatory activity" exception (section §3.03[E][1]). In particular, they coined the expression "complex operating settlement with economic coherent" so as not to apply the PE-exceptions envisaged in Article 5.4 and thus consider the existence of a PE in Spain. In "Borax," the courts argued that Article 5.4 was not applicable because the activities carried out by the subsidiary could not be considered in isolation but rather as parts of an "established, permanent and complete business structure."[626] A similar consideration may be found in the Commentary on Article 5.4.f of the 2014 OECD MC,[627] where the

622. Martín Jiménez, A. (2014), p. 61.
623. Martín Jiménez, A. (2014), p. 68.
624. Martín Jiménez, A. (2014), p. 61. This was precisely the case for Apple, *see* Chapter 2 section §2.01[A][2].
625. Resolution by the Spanish Central Economic-Administrative Court (TEAC), March 15, 2012, "Dell case" and Martín Jiménez, A. (2014), p. 66.
626. Judgment by the Spanish High National Court (Audiencia Nacional), February 9, 2011, "Borax case" and, later on, the judgment by the Spanish Supreme Court (Tribunal Supremo), June 18, 2014, "Borax case," both applying the UK-Spain tax treaty.
627. Commentary on Article 5 of the 2014 OECD MC, paragraph 27.1: "subparagraph f) is of no importance in a case where an enterprise maintains several fixed places of business within the meaning of subparagraphs a) to e) provided that they are separated from each other locally and organizationally, as in such a case each place of business has to be viewed separately and in isolation for deciding whether a permanent establishment exists. Places of business are not 'separated organizationally' where they each perform in a Contracting State complementary functions such as receiving and storing goods in one place, distributing those goods through another, etc. An enterprise cannot fragment a cohesive operating business into several small operations in order to argue that each is merely engaged in a preparatory or auxiliary activity."

courts may well have found their inspiration. What is interesting is that the applicable treaty lacked a clause equivalent to that of the Article 5.4.f of the 2014 OECD MC, and this fact alone should have prevented the courts from combining the activities of the non-resident and further argue that such combination of activities went beyond what might be considered as preparatory or auxiliary.

Second, the Spanish courts equally followed an economic interpretation in the context of Article 5.5 of the 2014 OECD MC to counteract the effects of the so-called commissionaire arrangements. We should recall at this point that, under such arrangements, the agent is legally entitled to sell the non-residents products in its own name but on behalf of the non-resident. As section §3.03[E][1][c] warned above, such arrangements managed to circumvent one of the requirements explicitly established in Article 5.5: the conclusion of contracts "in the name of the enterprise." In this context, the courts did not accept the logical outcome of the literal wording of Article 5.5 and chose not to focus on mere contractual formalities but rather focus on the economic effects of the acts performed by the agent. And they did so by concluding that an agent acting on behalf of a non-resident conformed a PE to the extent that its acts were able to bind the principal, thereby omitting the part of the clause that specifically required the conclusion of the contracts "in the name of the enterprise."[628] Such interpretation did not come out of thin air, as the OECD itself promoted it in the Commentaries on the MC.[629] However, the Spanish courts went one step further in the controversial judgments on the "Roche Case": both the High National and the Supreme Court agreed that an agent PE exists not only where there is a person with authority to enter into contracts on behalf of a principal but also when this person "involves the foreign principal in the national market."[630] It should be noted that this approach towards the agent PE has not succeeded in all civil law States despite the global-reaching influence of the Commentaries on the OECD MC.[631]

Third, the Spanish courts equally resorted to an economic interpretation of Article 5 to presume that subsidiaries acted as PEs of their parents. It should first be noted that, as a matter of principle, tax law regards parents and subsidiaries as

628. Judgment by the Spanish High National Court (Audiencia Nacional), January 24, 2008, "Roche case," judgment by the Spanish Supreme Court (Tribunal Supremo), January 12, 2012, "Roche case" and resolution by the Spanish Central Economic-Administrative Court (TEAC), March 15, 2012, "Dell case." *See also* Martín Jiménez, A. (2014), p. 62.

629. Commentary on Article 5 of the 2014 OECD MC, paragraph 32.1: "the phrase 'authority to conclude contracts in the name of the enterprise' does no confine the application of the paragraph to an agent who enters into contracts literally in the name of the enterprise; the paragraph applies equally to an agent who concludes contracts which are binding on the enterprise even if those contracts are not actually in the name of the enterprise." The courts made explicit references to the Commentaries on the OECD MC in their respective judgments.

630. Judgment by the Spanish High National Court (Audiencia Nacional), January 24, 2008, "Roche case" and, later on, the judgment by the Spanish Supreme Court (Tribunal Supremo), January 12, 2012, "Roche case." This position has been severely criticized by Martín Jiménez, A. (2014), p. 64, who believes the Spanish courts departed from an erroneous assumption when they reached this conclusion.

631. *See* for example the judgments by the French Supreme Administrative Court (Conseil d'État), March 31, 2010, "Zimmer Ltd v. Ministre d l'Économie, des Finances et de l'Industrie," the Norwegian Supreme Court, December 2, 2011, "Dell products v. Tax East" and the Italian Supreme Court, March 9, 2012, "Boston Scientific."

independent legal entities subject to unlimited tax liabilities in their respective Residence States. This does not however preclude a subsidiary from constituting a PE of their respective parent to the extent that it effectively complies with the requirements set out in Article 5.[632] For example, the subsidiary may constitute a fixed POB insofar it makes its facilities or premises (complying with the location and duration tests) available to the parent ("right-to-use" test) through which the parent carries on its own business ("business activity" test). Similarly, the subsidiary may constitute a DAPE of the parent if has and habitually exercise the authority to conclude contracts in the name and on behalf of the parent. Nonetheless, Article 5.7 of the 2014 OECD MC[633] states that the fact that a subsidiary is controlled by a non-resident parent and the latter carries on business in the subsidiary's States "shall not of itself" mean that the subsidiary is serving as a PE of the parent company. In essence, Article 5.7 establishes that the condition of PE cannot be presumed on the basis of the economic dependence between the two companies and should instead by sufficiently demonstrated on a case-by-case basis. However, the Spanish courts have neglected the effects of Article 5.7 and the principle of legal independence of parents/subsidiaries, as they have frequently resorted to the economic dependence between them to presume that the subsidiary was effectively serving as a PE of the former without carefully assessing whether the requirements of Article 5 were effectively fulfilled.[634]

Finally, we will refer to the last of the three approaches we mentioned at the beginning of the present section. That is, the use of anti-avoidance rules to compensate the deficiencies of the PE concept.[635] We intend to demonstrate here that this approach is as troublesome as the two previous ones, albeit for different reasons.

In the first instance, we observe an overuse of terms as "abuse," "avoidance" or "artificial" when it comes to the definition of certain arrangements conducted by MNCs that essentially lead to minimize taxation at the host jurisdiction.[636] We believe it is indeed an "overuse" because some of the practices labeled as such do not technically

---

632. Schoueri, L.E.; Günther, O-C (2011), p. 69.
633. Article 5.8 of the 2011 UN MC and 5.7 of the 2006 US MC, although this last one has a slightly different wording.
634. Judgment by the Spanish Supreme Court (Tribunal Supremo), January 12, 2012, "Roche case" and judgment by the Spanish Supreme Court (Tribunal Supremo), June 20, 2016, "Dell case." Martín Jiménez is very critical with this approach, *see* Martín Jiménez, A. (2014), pp. 64, 65 and 68.
635. Martín Jiménez analyzes the appropriateness of using GAARs in the context of Article 5, arguing that Spain should have resorted to its domestic GAAR instead of adopting the abovementioned economic interpretation of the article. He does not, nevertheless, refer to the problems that domestic GAARs pose in tax treaty scenarios. *See* Martín Jiménez, A. (2014), pp. 70-71. Additionally, the OECD itself encourage the use of domestic anti-avoidance rules in tax treaty scenarios, *see* for example Commentary on Article 5 of the 2014 OECD MC, paragraph 6.2, paragraph 18 ("such abuses may, depending on the circumstances, fall under the application of legislative or judicial anti-avoidance rules") and paragraph 42.45 ("the 183-day thresholds provided for in the alternative provision may give rise to the same type of abuse as is described in paragraph 18 above. As indicated in that paragraph, legislative or judicial anti-avoidance rules may apply to prevent such abuses").
636. OECD (2015): Final Report on BEPS Action 7—Preventing the artificial avoidance of permanent establishment status.

deserve such label.[637] For example, is it reasonable to argue that the act of fragmenting the business activities of a MNC into geographically separate places (under the responsibility of different related parties) necessarily constitutes an abuse of Article 5? And similarly, is it reasonable to conclude that the commissionaire arrangements are nothing more than artificial schemes with the purpose of avoiding the constitution of a PE?

Having said this, and even considering that we are facing practices that in fact fall under the scope of anti-avoidance rules, we should further assess whether the application of such rules is technically feasible or not. In this context, we find another obstacle. As long as the MCs do not provide SAARs that may be applicable in the context of Article 5 or GAARs, there is no choice but to resort to domestic anti-avoidance rules. This leads us to the endless debate as to whether the application of domestic anti-avoidance rules in tax treaty-scenarios is compatible with the relevant treaty in place. Although the OECD wished to make it very clear that domestic anti-avoidance rules were perfectly compatible with tax treaties,[638] we very much doubt of such position[639] and rather believe that the application of domestic anti-avoidance rules is likely to lead to a treaty override.

Once the three approaches to counteract the weaknesses of Article 5 have been analyzed, we will proceed to draw a few general conclusions.

What these approaches primarily reveal is that Article 5 has become a source of endless frustration. This is so because jurisdictions seem increasingly reluctant to accept the logical outcomes derived from the literal wording of Article 5 as it stands in the 2014 OECD MC.[640] They simply realized that following literally the wording of Article 5 prevented them from taxing the profits of a non-resident enterprise in cases in which it had a very significant business presence in their territories.

As a matter of principle, we may sympathize with the general premise on which the "PE-Spanish approach" (and its respective versions in other States) is based, i.e., the fact that a non-resident enterprise should be subject to tax in the host jurisdiction in cases in which it carries on a significant business activity therein. And by extension, we may agree with the outcomes of these approaches, as they would also tend to be consistent with our proposed presumptive benefit principle. However, we believe that

637. Martín Jiménez seems equally reluctant to use the label of "artificial" in certain circumstances. He stated: "the PE (...) is a threshold designed as an exception to a general rule, taxation in the country of residence (...) so it is not easy to say that when the outcome of a structure or transaction is in line with the general rule (taxation in the state of residence) it is 'artificially avoiding the exception (taxation in the State of the PE)'." Martín Jiménez, A. (2014), p. 9. He then added that "in strict legal terms, what the taxpayers did was in line with the legal standard admitted in article 5 of the OECD Model" (Martín Jiménez, A. (2016), p. 465.

638. Particularly in Commentary on Article 1 of the 2014 OECD MC, paragraph 9.2: "these anti-avoidance rules are part of the basic domestic rules set by domestic tax laws for determining which facts give rise to a tax liability, they are not addressed in tax treaties and are therefore not affected by them. Thus, as a general rule, there will be no conflict between such rules and the provisions of tax conventions."

639. We endorse the arguments and conclusions of Zornoza and Báez in Zornoza Pérez, J.; Báez Moreno, A. (2010).

640. A tendency we already observed in the context of residence tests back in Chapter 3 section §3.02[A][2][c].

it is not acceptable to achieve this goal by the means described in the present section.[641] The reason being that all three approaches, to a greater or lesser extent, compromise the principle of legal certainty and, more generally, the respect for the rule of law. Using some of the examples above referred, we will now put forward three reasons to justify our position.

First, some of the administrative and case law doctrines above referred go beyond the possible meaning of the terms of the rule. This is for example the case of the virtual PE, as some courts understood that a website constituted a "place" for the purposes of Article 5.1 (Dell case). Further, other doctrines even constitute a direct breach of the corresponding rule they intend to interpret. Let us take as an example the omission of the "in the name of" requirement when applying the agency-PE clause (Roche and Dell) or, what is even worse, the consideration of an agent as a PE in cases in which it lacked the authority to enter into contracts (Roche case). In Borax, for example, the courts chose not to apply the PE-exceptions of Article 5.4 on the basis that they all formed part of a sole business cycle, despite the tax treaty in place did not entitle the court to do so, as it lacked Article 5.4.f of the 2014 OECD MC. Similarly, the courts presumed that certain subsidiaries were acting as PEs of their respective parents even though Article 5.7 literally establishes that such condition cannot be presumed (Roche and Dell). On a more general level, the application of domestic anti-avoidance rules in tax treaty scenarios may likewise lead to a direct breach of a tax treaty rule (and by extension the *pacta sunt servanda* principle) for the reasons previously stated.

Second, there are cases in which the courts have literally followed the wording of Article 5 but the outcome of such interpretation defeats the alleged purpose of the PE rule. This is clearly the case of the server-PE. As explained above, the PE threshold is intended to capture a significant economic involvement with the host jurisdiction, while a server does not per se manifest any kind of participation in the economic life of such jurisdiction beyond the presence of a dusty computer in the basement of a building.

Third, we have observed that the origin of the vast majority of these approaches is commonly found in the Commentaries on the 2014 OECD MC. At this point, we would like to warn against backdoor "amendments" to the wording of the MCs by means of soft law instruments. Particularly when such revisions explicitly or implicitly contradict the literal meaning of the rules they intend to interpret or clarify. Although these soft law instruments do not directly produce legal effects of any kind nor constitute authoritative interpretation materials, they undoubtedly have a great influence in administrative bodies and courts. And for this reason alone, the OECD should be more careful when drafting them to avoid undesirable outcomes as the ones referred above.

In short, all these arguments ultimately reveal that the resort to eccentric interpretations, substance-based approaches and anti-avoidances rules as a way to neutralize the dissatisfaction that Article 5 generates is dangerous, in the sense that it

641. Martin Jiménez, A. (2016), p. 458: "it is true that the response is unfortunate in the terms that are considered in this article, but it is probably not as unfounded, in substance, although not in form, as it may appear at first sight."

compromises the principle of legal certainty and undermines the system of "rule of law."[642] At this stage, the only way forward is to carefully assess the deficiencies of the PE concept as it currently stands and subsequently suggest amendments to the rule in Chapter 4.

Last but not least, attention should also be paid to the PE-Spanish approach as regards the attribution of profits to the PEs. Back in section §3.03[D] we succinctly described the methodology recently suggested by the OECD (commonly known as "AOA") as to how to apply Article 7.2 of the OECD MC to attribute profits to the PEs. The Spanish courts deviated from the orthodox approach once again, as some judgments disregarded the functional analysis required by the OECD TPG and/or the AOA report and instead departed from all the income derived from the sales in Spain with a deduction of expenses directly connected with those sales, even those obtained by a French subsidiary of the group.[643] As a result of this, the Spanish courts succeeded in bringing the profits derived from the Spanish market to the Spanish tax base by means of their peculiar interpretation of both Articles 5 and 7.2 of the treaty in place.

The position held by the Spanish courts should be once again regarded as a threat to the principle of legal certainty and the rule of law. However, the question remains as to whether the outcome reached by the Spanish court is indeed legitimate. If the response is positive, the question arises as to whether the methodology proposed by the OECD for the attribution of profits to PEs constitutes in fact an obstacle for the aforementioned goal and, if so, whether it should be reconsidered. We will equally address these questions later in Chapter 4.

Although States have traditionally dealt with the deficiencies and limitations of the PE clause by means of either anti-avoidance rules or eccentric and substance-based interpretations, we strongly opposed this approach for the reasons explained throughout this section. Instead, we advocate for the direct amendment of the PE clause in both tax treaties and domestic tax legislations.[644] As the BEPS project has fortunately chosen this same approach, we will analyze in Chapter 4 section §4.02[C] the outcomes of the project in this regard and further suggest some *de lege ferenda* proposals to ensure a

642. Along the same lines *see* Martín Jiménez, A. (2016), p. 472. He believes that the Spanish approach is a "nothing more and nothing less than a reaction that questions the current PE threshold" and such reaction "should have been undertaken using other mechanisms rather than by way of a peculiar interpretation of article 5 (...) trying to lower that threshold by interpretation obviously gives rise to a problem of uncertainty." Elsewhere, Martín Jiménez argued that the "PE-Spanish approach" transmits a wrong message internationally: the fact that the Spanish authorities and courts are aggressive and technically not very sophisticated and the fact that legal certainty is at risk when conducting transactions in Spain. *See* Martín Jiménez, A. (2014), p. 69.

643. Martín Jiménez, A. (2016), pp. 464, 466 and 468-469. *See* the Resolution by the Spanish Central Economic-Administrative Court (TEAC), March 15, 2012, "Dell case," the judgment by the Spanish High National Court (Audiencia Nacional), June 8, 2015, "Dell case" and the judgment by the Spanish Supreme Court (Tribunal Supremo), June 20, 2016, "Dell case."

644. Position shared by Martín Jiménez, *see* Martín Jiménez, A. (2014), p. 55: "this solution (the policy approach) has an advantage over others, and specially, anti-avoidance norms or doctrines: if drafted clearly and having administrability in mind, they are often much easier to apply than anti-avoidance rules or doctrines or transfer pricing legislation."

better consistency between the clause and our proposed version of the benefit principle.

§3.04 PRELIMINARY CONCLUSIONS

As evidenced though the Apple case study in Chapter 2 section §2.01[A], there is an increasing misalignment between the location where the actual business activities take place and the location where the profits are eventually reported for tax purposes (a phenomenon referred here as "profit shifting"). A phenomenon that is regarded as a global concern (Chapter 2 section §2.01[B]) and is also contradictory with the (here suggested) presumptive benefit principle (Chapter 2 section §2.02).

In order to appropriately dissect the causes giving rise to this phenomenon, we briefly mentioned the particular rules and strategies that enabled Apple to shift their profits out of the jurisdictions where the business activities took place (Chapter 2 section §2.01[A][2]). Beyond these factors, we perceived the influence of other causes of a more general and fundamental nature.

This chapter intended to confirm our hypothesis according to which corporate income taxation is not aligned with the presumptive benefit principle and thus tend to trigger profit shifting outcomes. In particular, the main purpose of this chapter was to ascertain to what extent three long-standing paradigms underlying CITs (the separate-entity approach and the definitions of residence and source for tax purposes) have effectively contributed to make it possible for taxpayers to book their tax bases in jurisdictions other than those where they presumably derive their public benefits (i.e., wherever they carry out their economic activities), contrary to what the presumptive benefit principle would require.

Besides, we also took the opportunity to examine and reflect on the origins and supposed rationales behind those three traditional paradigms so as to reach further conclusions that exceeded the main purpose of the thesis.

In the first place, section §3.01 referred to the separate-entity approach. We then observed that the separate tax treatment of companies belonging to a same group enabled taxpayers to easily shift taxable profits to selected jurisdictions (section §3.01[B]). The ALS serves as a corrective and indeed manages to minimize this risk, but it is unable to completely eradicate it (section §3.01[C]). In this regard, we argued that the ALS is far from being a mathematical parameter and instead tends to lead to a wide range of acceptable prices within which taxpayers and tax Administrations may move freely and legitimately. We noted that this fact constituted an advantage to resourceful taxpayers, as they are better equipped to push the limits of the ALS and get the price within the range that best fits their needs. Besides, we also provided evidence that transfer pricing outcomes perfectly compliant with the ALS could still entail significant profit shifting risks. The example we provided referred to the use of transfer pricing methods based on costs in scenarios involving intangibles, as intangibles may potentially generate income that is disproportionately higher than the costs incurred in their development.

Second, section §3.02 sought to discern whether the way corporate tax residence is aligned with the presumptive benefit principle or else contributes to generate profit shifting risks. After the analysis of the most common corporate tax residence tests (section §3.02[A][1]), we realized that most of them were inherited from private international law (section §3.02[A][2][a]). At this point, we warned of the risks derived by a mere extrapolation of terms from a legal order whose function and purpose had little to do with those of tax law, noting that this ultimately revealed that the gestation process of current tax residence tests lacked a serious policy assessment. We also demonstrated that, historically, the implementation of new residence tests was primarily driven by the desire of closing the loopholes of the preexisting tests rather than by clear policy purposes (section §3.02[A][2][b]). In our opinion, the fact that jurisdictions adopted residence tests without really knowing, understanding and accepting their supposed rationale and meaning resulted in the unwillingness of jurisdictions to accept the logical outcomes of their own residence test (section §3.02[A][2][c]). Particularly when the residence tests led to consider a State in which the company does not have "economic substance" as its residence State for tax purposes. While jurisdictions tended to counteract this risk by means of anti-avoidance rules, the fact remains that such scenario was indeed a quite plausible one, as the corporate tax residence tests followed by the vast majority of jurisdictions (97%), by their own nature, do not specifically require any kind of economic attachment between the corporate taxpayer and the potential Residence State. Therefore, residence tests that do not guarantee a sufficient economic bond with the State could be instrumental in tax planning schemes intended to shift profits to selected jurisdictions where no economic activities take place, contrary to what the presumptive benefit principle would require.

Ultimately, the conclusions drawn in sections §3.02[C][3] and §3.02[D][3] further confirmed those exposed above. First, we argued that treaty shopping opportunities were a direct consequence of the weakness of residence tests. In this context, anti-treaty shopping measures (e.g., LOBs) became necessary to compensate such deficiencies and further require a sufficient and substantive connection between the corporate taxpayer and the relevant State, as most residence tests were inherently unable to do so. Second, we argued in section §3.02[D][3] that the proliferation of dual residence cases was equally a consequence of the malfunction of domestic residence tests. The reason being that residence tests that do not demand a genuine and strong connection between the corporate taxpayer and the jurisdiction concerned (i.e., most of them) were more prone to cause overlapping attributions of residence.

Furthermore, section §3.02[B] revealed that that the lack of coordination in the domestic definition of corporate tax residence was likely to generate profit shifting opportunities. The most emblematic example was that of "stateless companies," i.e., companies that were not regarded as tax resident by any jurisdiction and, accordingly, were able to shift taxable profits to territories were no business activity was taking place or even make them disappear from the face of the Earth (evidenced in the Apple case study, in Chapter 2 section §2.01[A][2]). After the study of the residence tests used by a sample of countries, we observed that the same asymmetry exploited by Apple was equally present in many other combinations of jurisdictions.

Finally, section §3.03 intended to ascertain whether the definition of source for tax purposes was similarly aligned with the presumptive benefit principle. Due to its relevance, we decided to focus on the PE concept, explaining its origins (section §3.03[C]) and the significance it had acquired over the years in international tax law. Subsequently, we stated that the PE had ultimately become a sort of "functional" resident, as there was an increasing tendency to equate the tax treatment of PEs to those of resident subsidiaries (section §3.03[D]). Further, tax treaties gave precedence to the taxing rights of the PE-State over those of the Residence State, thus emptying the tax base of the latter in favor of the former (section §3.03[F][1]). A preference that could be justified by the fact that the residence tests rarely guarantee a substantive connection between the taxpayer and the territory, while the PE concept does.

Subsequently, we tried to corroborate whether the PE concept (in its different modalities) is as consistent with the presumptive benefit principle as it may be *a priori* expected to be (section §3.03[E]).

First, we raised the question as to whether all the situations covered by the scope of the clause equally signal that the taxpayer may be in the position to effectively or potentially benefit from the local services or infrastructures (section §3.03[E][1]). We concluded that some of the modalities are perfectly consistent with the aforementioned principle (e.g., sections §3.03[E][1][a] and §3.03[E][1][b]) while the existence of others may not be that justified on the grounds of this principle (section §3.03[E][1][e]). Additionally, we equally noted that several relevant economic activities are doomed to be excluded from the scope of the clause due to deficiencies in its wording, while the presumptive benefit principle would justify its taxation (section §3.03[E][1]).

Second, we wondered whether there are situations beyond the scope of the clause where the taxpayer could be regarded as a potential beneficiary of the local services (section §3.03[E][2]). We concluded that the remote supply of goods and/or services to local customers would undoubtedly fall out of the scope of the clause while its taxation would still be justified on the grounds of the presumptive benefit principle, just as we concluded in Chapter 2.

Finally, we denounced that States that showed dissatisfaction with the outcomes derived by the literal wording of Article 5 tended to counteract its limitations and weaknesses by means of eccentric or substance-based interpretations and anti-avoidance rules (section §3.03[F][2]). We strongly criticized this approach, since we believed it potentially led to compromise the principle of legal certainty and, more generally, the respect for the rule of law. On the contrary, we advocated for an amendment of Article 5 as the best way to counteract its inherent deficiencies, adapt it to the twenty-first century economic context and ultimately ensure its alignment with the presumptive benefit principle, an approach we later explored in Chapter 4.

For all the arguments presented in this chapter, we believe that these three fundamental paradigms underlying CITs (and by extension, corporate income taxation in general) are not consistent with the presumptive benefit principle and have indeed contributed, due to their inherent nature, weaknesses or lack of updating, to allow corporate taxpayers to book their profits in jurisdictions other than those where they presumably derive their public benefits (i.e., wherever they carry out their economic activities).

Chapter 4

Proposals for a CIT Reform in the Light of the Presumptive Benefit Principle

We believe the presumptive benefit principle should ideally underlie the tax rules that identify the taxpayers that would become subject to a State's tax jurisdiction (the tax connecting factors). This means that tax connecting factors should ultimately be based on factors or *indicia* revealing that the corporate taxpayer finds itself in the position to use/enjoy the State's services and infrastructures to some extent. We concluded that this assumption could be made wherever the company is effectively carrying on an economic activity within the borders of the State or else is able to access its market by remote means (Chapter 2 section §2.02[B][2]). In this context, we observed that, in general terms and except for a few notable exceptions, the presumptive benefit principle does not seem to underlie tax connecting factors present in current CITs (Chapter 3). In fact, they have occasionally become instrumental in detaching taxable profits from the jurisdictions where corporate taxpayers are in position to use and enjoy the public benefits (Chapter 2 section §2.01 and Chapter 3). This being so, we called for a reconsideration of these rules and expressed our willingness to propose a few amendments to this effect in Chapter 4. After all, as rightly noted by Bird, the presumed rationale of the CIT should govern its design.[645]

In section §4.01, we will make a preliminary evaluation of the BEPS project. First, we will first identify its objectives and evaluate their consistency with the presumptive benefit principle. Then, we will assess the theoretical scope of the Project and its suitability to reach its alleged purposes.

Subsequently, we will submit a few policy proposals both at the domestic and treaty level. Such proposals are generally intended to bring taxable profits closer to the jurisdictions where the company's economic activities are taking place and/or those that provide a market of customers, departing from the assumption that these

645. Bird, R. (2002), p. 201: "what are the implications for the design of corporate tax? That is, to what extent does the why govern the how, and just how should the tax designed be influenced by the presumed rationale of the tax being designed?"

jurisdictions are effectively or potentially providing the services and infrastructures from which the corporate taxpayer is presumably benefiting. These proposals seek to narrow the current gap (evidenced in the Apple case back in Chapter 2) between the economic and the tax presence of the companies throughout the world.

The first set of proposals are grouped in section §4.02. They all respect and maintain the current *status quo*, i.e., the maintenance of the paradigms underlying CITs under review in the present study. This means that they accept the separate entity approach, the ALS as a generally valid corrective against profit shifting risks (at least in most cases), the fact that a company should continue to be considered as resident of one State for tax purposes and be subject to an unlimited tax liability therein and, finally, the fact that the PE threshold should continue to determine whether a non-resident company should be taxed in a host jurisdiction or not. However, adaptations to these paradigms will be suggested. Some of them will be intended to enhance the corresponding legal rule in the light of the conclusions reached in Chapter 3. Most of them will though seek to ensure a better consistency with the presumptive benefit principle, as claimed by Chapter 2. In this context, we will also assess the impact of the proposals derived from the BEPS project and to what extent they may be considered as consistent with the presumptive benefit principle.

Finally, we will briefly mention two proposals that involve the departure from these three paradigms in section §4.03. The decision not to invest much efforts in these proposals lies in the fact that their implementation is today a political utopia.

§4.01 A PRELIMINARY ASSESSMENT OF THE BEPS PROJECT'S SCOPE AND OBJECTIVES

[A] The Objective of the BEPS Project and Its Apparent Consistency with the Presumptive Benefit Principle

Just as we anticipated in Chapter 2, the profit shifting phenomenon has been regarded as a global concern in recent times. In the light of this, the primary objective of the BEPS project[646] led by the OECD was indeed to provide domestic and international instruments "aiming at better aligning rights to tax with real actual economic activity" (the "BEPS mantra").[647] We then asserted that such claim could be justified precisely on the grounds of the presumptive benefit principle: a corporate taxpayer should be subject to tax wherever it carries out its economic activities insofar as it may be presumably benefiting from the services and infrastructures supplied by the host jurisdiction and thus such jurisdiction should be somehow compensated for its contribution to the generation of profits within its frontiers.[648] This means that the BEPS project would be

646. The contents of Chapter 4 section §4.01 are largely based on the ideas presented in a paper we published elsewhere (Escribano, E. (2017), p. 250—252).
647. *See* Chapter 2 section §2.01[B]. BEPS report, pp. 15, 20 and 51 and BEPS Action Plan, pp. 11, 18, 19 and 20-21.
648. Chapter 2 section §2.02.

implicitly endorsing a tax reform that is consistent with our suggested version of the benefit principle.[649]

[B] The Limited Scope of the BEPS Action Plan

As one would expect, the ambitious task entrusted to the OECD got complicated when the time came to identify the causes contributing to the so-called BEPS phenomenon and further delineate the scope of the Action Plan to counteract it.

Although the BEPS report had promised to take a holistic approach rather than ad-hoc measures and further seek imaginative and ambitious solutions,[650] the Action Plan failed to meet these expectations for the reasons we are about to explain.

At first sight, the Action Plan left us an awkward sense of *déjà vu*. The reason is that many of its Actions seem to merely dust off old OECD reports for the occasion.[651] This is for example the case of Actions 2,[652] 5,[653] 6,[654] 7[655] and 12.[656] Conclusive evidence that the BEPS Project had retrieved old measures to address the challenges identified in the report is the fact that virtually all the amendments that were introduced in the 2017 OECD MC are based on preexisting Commentaries on the OECD MC which are, in turn, the result of old OECD reports. This is particularly the case as regards the proposed changes to Articles 1.2 (application of the treaty to entities that are regarded as transparent for tax purposes),[657] 1.3 (saving clause in favor of the Residence State),[658] 4.3 (tie-breaker rule for determining the residence for treaty purposes of dual-resident persons other than individuals),[659] 5.4 (anti-fragmentation provision),[660] 5.5 (refinement of the agency-PE to address its loopholes),[661] 10.2 (the

649. In fact, final report on Action 1 explicitly endorses the benefit principle as a valid conceptual basis for the allocation of taxing rights, *see* OECD (2015): Final Report on BEPS Action 1—Addressing the tax challenges of the digital economy, pp. 24-26.
650. These guidelines may be inferred from the BEPS report, pp. 60-62. All of them were welcomed by Brauner, Y. (2014), p. 58.
651. Brauner was not mistaken when he warned against the potential risk that a tight 2-years deadline could lead the OECD to resort to the arsenal of ad-hoc measures already proposed in previous reports. *See* Brauner, Y. (2014), p. 60.
652. OECD (1999): The application of the OECD Model Tax Convention to partnerships, OECD (2011): Corporate loss utilization through aggressive tax planning and OECD (2012): Hybrid mismatch arrangements: tax policy and compliance issues.
653. OECD (1998): Harmful tax competition: an emerging global issue.
654. OECD (1986): Double taxation and the use of conduit companies, OECD (2003): Restricting the entitlement to treaty benefits, OECD (2008): Tax treaty issues related to REITs and OECD (2010): The granting of treaty benefits with respect to the income of collective investment vehicles.
655. OECD (2002): Issues arising under Article 5 (permanent establishment) of the model tax convention.
656. OECD (2011): Tackling aggressive tax planning through improved transparency and disclosure and OECD (2013): Co-operative compliance: a framework from enhanced relationship to co-operative compliance.
657. Commentary on Article 1 of the 2014 OECD MC, paragraph 5. Retrieved by Action 2.
658. Commentary on Article 1 of the 2014 OECD MC, paragraphs 6.1 and 23 and Commentary on Article 7, paragraph 14. Retrieved by Action 6.
659. Commentary on Article 4 of the 2014 OECD MC, paragraph 24.1. Retrieved by Action 6.
660. Commentary on Article 5 of the 2014 OECD MC, paragraph 27.1. Retrieved by Action 7.

need to retain the ownership of shares for a certain period of time to be entitled to reduced withholding tax),[662] 13.4 (extension of the concept of shares)[663] and X (limitation-on-benefits rule).[664]

Besides this visible lack of originality, we believe the Action Plan committed two major mistakes that thwarted the opportunity to engage in a deep reform capable of achieving the ambitious policy objectives set forth by the Report and the Action Plan.

First, the point of departure could be no other than an upfront acknowledgment that we were confronting a clear crisis of rules. While the initial report on BEPS seemed to share this view,[665] the Action Plan deviated to some extent from this approach. Without ignoring the imperative need to revise the rules, the Action Plan redirected its focus to the taxpayers once again to hold them accountable for what was happening.[666] As a result of this, the document made an inaccurate and certainly inappropriate use of certain legal terms as "artificiality" or "abuse,"[667] while referring to vague expressions as "aggressive tax planning"[668] that are devoid of any legal basis. In short, the Action Plan gave the impression that it sought to raise the standard required to the taxpayer from the mere compliance with the letter and spirit of the laws to some sort of "exemplary" behavior that would satisfy some sense of justice or morality.[669] We believe that this approach is unfortunate and prone to generate severe problems from a legal certainty perspective. Besides, it seems apparent that the majority of the cases involving renowned MNCs which gave rise to BEPS concerns (Apple is no exception)[670] do not pose problems from a tax compliance perspective, as their tax situation tend to be the natural consequence of the rules in place.

Second, a truly genuine revision of the international tax legal framework needs to be conducted necessarily without any prejudices. Even though the BEPS report

661. Commentary on Article 5 of the 2014 OECD MC, paragraph 32.1. Retrieved by Action 7.
662. Commentary on Article 10 of the 2014 OECD MC, paragraphs 16 and 17. Retrieved by Action 6.
663. Commentary on Article 13 of the 2014 OECD MC, paragraph 28.5. Retrieved by Action 6.
664. Commentary on Article 1 of the 2014 OECD MC, paragraph 20. Retrieved by Action 6.
665. BEPS report, p. 5: "While there clearly is a tax compliance aspect, as shown by a number of high profile cases, there is a more fundamental policy issue: the international common principles drawn from national experiences to share tax jurisdiction may not have kept pace with the changing business environment." In the same vein, *see* p. 28: "Beyond cases of illegal abuses, which are the exception rather than the rule, MNEs engaged in BEPS comply with the legal requirements of the countries involved."
666. This is at least what we infer from the reading of Actions 6 (prevent treaty abuse), 7 (prevent the artificial avoidance of PE status) and 12 (require taxpayers to disclose their aggressive tax planning arrangements) of the BEPS project.
667. For example, the consideration of the behaviors depicted in Action 7 as "artificial" is, to say the least, debatable.
668. An undefined expression that is present in a great part of the BEPS reports.
669. Inasmuch as the BEPS Action Plan intends to attribute some sort of legal repercussions to the behaviors covered by the expression "aggressive tax planning," it seems to demand the taxpayers to structure their business operations in a way that the consequent tax liabilities lead to a proper contribution to the public expenditure of the countries concerned.
670. Chapter 2 section §2.01[A][2] provided several arguments to sustain that the shift of profits carried out by Apple was not the consequence of breaches to the letter or spirit of the laws. On the contrary, its tax planning strategy seems to fully comply with the tax legislation of the countries involved with no trace of abusive behaviors.

promised to deliver innovative, ambitious and holistic solutions,[671] we soon discovered with disappointment that the Action Plan had pushed out of the negotiation table a few principles of notorious importance. First, the discussion on the separate tax treatment of the entities belonging to the same group (the so-called separate entity approach) together with the standard that has traditionally served as a corrective to counteract the profit shifting risks that arise in these scenarios (the ALS) was rejected.[672] Second, the discussion on the distribution of tax jurisdiction between residence and source was equally dismissed, as the Action Plan chose not to question the residence-source relationship or the traditional configuration of these principles, confining itself to "restore" taxation at both levels.[673] In a nutshell, the OECD seemed to believe in the possibility to lead a tax reform that could effectively achieve the "BEPS mantra" (i.e., "align the allocation of income with the economic activity that generates that income") without first assessing to what extent these omnipresent paradigms are responsible for the possibility to shift taxable profits out of the jurisdictions where economic activities occur and, if necessary, propose amendments to these paradigms in order to ameliorate these risks.

We have good reasons to believe that leaving these paradigms out of the scope of the project constitutes an error. In Chapter 3 we provided numerous arguments to demonstrate how the three of them have contributed, to a greater or lesser extent, to allow corporate taxpayers to book their profits in jurisdictions other than those where their economic activities take place.[674] Or, in line with the conclusions reached in Chapter 2, how they have become instrumental in enabling companies to shift their profits out of the jurisdictions where they have presumably been in the position to use, enjoy or indirectly benefit from the public services, contrary to what the presumptive benefit principle would suggest.

Even though the OECD chose not to question the convenience of maintaining these paradigms in effect nor substantially modifying their content to better achieve the ultimate objective of BEPS, it was indeed willing to introduce a few minor amendments to these standards and rules for these purposes. In particular, the BEPS Action Plan entrusted the accomplishment of the "BEPS mantra" to a specific group of Actions, most notably to Actions 6 (treaty abuse), 7 (artificial avoidance of the PE status) and 8-10 (transfer pricing),[675] and implicitly to Action 1 (digital economy).[676] These work

671. BEPS report, pp. 60-62.
672. BEPS Action Plan, p. 14: "There is consensus among governments that moving to a system of formulary apportionment of profits is not a viable way forward; it is also unclear that the behavioral changes companies might adopt in response to the use of a formula would lead to investment decisions that are more efficient and tax-neutral than under a separate entity approach." In fact, Actions 8 to 10 were precisely aimed at updating the interpretation of the arm's length standard.
673. BEPS Action Plan, p. 11: "while actions to address BEPS will restore both source and residence taxation in a number of cases (...) these actions are not directly aimed at changing the existing international standards on the allocation of taxing rights on cross-border income." Action 1 was the only exception to this rule, as we will later see.
674. *See* in special the preliminary conclusions exposed in Chapter 3 section §3.04.
675. BEPS Action Plan, p. 18. All these Actions belong to the second group of actions that are aimed at restoring the "full effects and benefits of the international standards" in accordance with the aforementioned goal.

streams gave rise to the recommendation of a few minor amendments to these paradigms which we will subsequently review in the next section along with our own proposals *de lege ferenda*.

§4.02 ENHANCEMENT OF CURRENT PARADIGMS

The BEPS project appears to be the perfect breeding ground to pursue the amendment of the paradigms underlying CITs in the light of the presumptive benefit rationale, as we believe that the BEPS project is implicitly pointing in this same direction (section §4.01[A]).

In this section we will evaluate the appropriateness and impact of the BEPS proposals, in particular those related to transfer pricing rules and the ALS (Actions 8-10, section §4.02[A]) and the PE threshold (Actions 1 and 7, section §4.02[C]). In addition, we will also consider the possibility of introducing further amendments we believe would be more appropriate and effective to enhance these paradigms and, where appropriate, ensure their consistency with the presumptive benefit principle.

[A] Proposals Within and Beyond the Arm's Length Standard

Both the separate entity approach and the ALS find themselves among the most essential paradigms underlying corporate income taxation.

In Chapter 3 section §3.01 we raised the question as to whether the separate-entity approach and the ALS are consistent with the presumptive benefit principle or, in other words, whether they contribute to ensure that corporate taxpayers book their profits for tax purposes wherever they carry out their economic activities and thus, where they potentially access the public services and infrastructures provided by the local government. We concluded back then that the separate-entity approach per se poses significant profit shifting risks via transfer pricing manipulation, but the ALS comes into play precisely to counteract such risks, although it has proven to be far from infallible in the accomplishment of such task for a number of reasons (Chapter 3 section §3.01[C]).

So, departing from the conclusions reached in Chapter 3 section §3.01, we will now proceed to analyze in section §4.02[A][1] whether the new OECD approach on transfer pricing resulting from the BEPS project is better aligned with the presumptive benefit principle in the sense that it helps bring the taxable bases closer to where the economic activities are located. Subsequently, in section §4.02[A][2], we will examine whether this new approach is compatible with the current legal configuration of transfer pricing rules following the ALS or, on the contrary, demands the amendment of the latter.

676. Action 1 was conceived as a transversal stream within the Project whose aim was to "identify the main difficulties that the digital economy poses" in international taxation (BEPS Action Plan, p. 14). However, one of its objectives was precisely to evaluate "the ability of a company to have a significant digital presence in the economy of another country without being liable to taxation due to the lack of nexus under current international rules."

[1] The Merits of the "Value Creation" Approach on Transfer Pricing Fostered by the BEPS Project and Its Apparent Consistency with the Presumptive Benefit Principle

In this section we intend to briefly describe and then critically analyze the approach chosen by the BEPS project as regards the interpretation and application of the ALS. In particular, we will evaluate whether the proposals put forward within the BEPS project are consistent with the presumptive benefit principle according to the role we attributed to this principle in Chapter 2 section §2.02. In other words, do the BEPS proposals on transfer pricing effectively contribute to place the taxable bases in the jurisdictions where the relevant economic activities take place contrary to the recent trends illustrated in Chapter 3?

In principle, the main purpose of the BEPS project was no other than to "provide countries with instruments, domestic and international, aiming at better aligning rights to tax with real economic activity."[677] As we noted in section §4.01, the Action Plan entrusted this task to a group of Actions, including Actions 8 to 10, related to transfer pricing. The document departed from the recognition that MNCs "have been able to use and/or misapply those rules (transfer pricing rules based on the ALS) to separate income from the economic activities that produce that income and to shift it into low-tax environments."[678] The word "use" indeed presupposed the implicit recognition that the ALS, in its current form and by its own nature, may give rise to transfer pricing outcomes that are not aligned with the location of the relevant economic activities. Curiously enough, the final report on Actions 8-10 deviated from the assertion made by the Action Plan, claiming that such outcomes did not derive from the "use" of transfer pricing rules but rather from their "manipulation,"[679] thus rejecting the view that the ALS was inherently troublesome in this regard. We believe the first position is more realistic, as we tried to demonstrate in Chapter 2 section §2.01[A][2] and Chapter 3 section §3.01[C] that the results derived from the application of the ALS (and perfectly consistent with such standard) may not necessarily place the relevant taxable bases wherever the relevant economic activities take place.

In this context, the Action Plan expressed its commitment to the present *status quo* and further specified the objective of the Actions related to transfer pricing regulation: ensuring that transfer pricing outcomes are aligned with "value creation,"[680] i.e., that the taxable bases should end up wherever the value creating activities occur. To this end, the Action Plan proposed to address the "flaws" of the

677. We referred to the objectives of the project in Chapter 4 section §4.01[A].
678. BEPS Action Plan, p. 19.
679. OECD (2015): Final Report on BEPS Actions 8-10—Aligning transfer pricing outcomes with value creation, p. 9: "the existing guidance on the application of the principle has also proven vulnerable to manipulation. This manipulation can lead to outcomes which do not correspond to the value created through the underlying economic activity carried out by the members of a MNE."
680. BEPS Action Plan, p. 20.

current system, especially with respect to areas that were identified as particularly risky, i.e., transactions dealing with intangible assets, risk and over-capitalization.[681]

At first sight, one may intuitively presuppose that the 2017 OECD TPG based on the ALS should be better aligned with the presumptive benefit principle than the current regulation in place, insofar as the objective of Actions 8-10 was precisely to use the ALS to bring the taxable bases wherever the "real" "value creating" economic activities take place and we believe that the presence of economic activities within a territory of a State allows us to assume that the company carrying out such activities may be in the position to effectively or potentially use the benefits provided by such State, although their potential to "add value" would not be so relevant for the purposes of the aforementioned principle.[682] The OECD assimilated value creation to the performance of functions, use of assets and assumption of risks, thereby neglecting the role that the market may arguably be considered to play in the process of value creation.[683] From the perspective of the presumptive benefit principle, this position entails the outright rejection of the assumption that a company would also be in a position to enjoy or use some of the services and infrastructures provided and defrayed by the State in which the company has its market, as we claimed back in Chapter 2 section §2.02[B][2][b].

Subsequently, we will review some of the latest developments introduced to the new 2017 OECD TPG as a result of the BEPS project.

Grosso modo, the intention of the BEPS package on transfer pricing[684] is to ensure a more significant share on the profits for the group entities which are deemed to add value. In the context of intangible assets,[685] such entities would be the ones that perform functions, use assets and/or assume risks in the development, enhancement, maintenance, protection and exploitation (hereinafter "DEMPE") of intangibles,[686] placing a greater weight in the performance of functions.[687] We will now review these three categories of activities that would deserve appropriate arm's length compensation.

681. BEPS Action Plan, p. 20.
682. Chapter 2 section §2.02[B][2].
683. Schoueri, L.E.; Galendi, R.A. (2017): "this mantra is far from being able to determine in any and every case where value is created and works rather as a formula to deny the importance of demand (market) for value creation even though, as mentioned above, taxation where consumption occurs was the very reason for the whole BEPS movement."
684. OECD (2015): Final Report on BEPS Actions 8-10—Aligning transfer pricing outcomes with value creation, along with the previous discussion drafts and interim reports published in the precedent years.
685. Defined as "something which is not a physical asset or financial asset, which is capable of being owned or controlled for use in commercial activities, and whose use or transfer would be compensated had it occurred in a transaction between independent parties in comparable circumstances." *See* OECD (2015): Final Report on BEPS Actions 8-10—Aligning transfer pricing outcomes with value creation, pp. 67 and 69-90 for a classification of the different kinds of intangibles (2017 OECD TPG, paragraphs 6.6 and 6.15—6.17).
686. OECD (2015): Final Report on BEPS Actions 8-10—Aligning transfer pricing outcomes with value creation, pp. 77-84 (2017 OECD TPG, paragraphs 6.47-6.72).
687. Navarro observes that the new parameter grants a greater weight to functions over assets and risks both in the framework of functional analysis and when the time comes to select the "most appropriate" method. *See* Navarro Ibarrola, A. (2017), p. 136.

As regards the performance of functions related to DEMPE activities,[688] the legal owner of the intangible may either physically perform all the functions through its own personnel or outsource the functions to either related or unrelated parties.[689] In case it is a related party the one who ends up performing such functions, it should be compensated on an arm's length basis considering the availability of comparable uncontrolled transactions, the importance of the functions performed to the creation of value and the realistically available options of the parties.[690] In case the performance of functions is outsourced to either a related or an unrelated party, the legal owner or any other group entity exerting control over such outsourcing would also be entitled to compensation.[691] The relative importance of each one of the functions performed in relation to DEMPE activities would greatly depend on the specific circumstances of the case.[692]

With regard to the use of assets in DEMPE activities, this may include the use of intangibles for research, development or marketing purposes (e.g., know-how, customer relations, etc.), physical assets or funding.[693] In relation to the latter, any group entity providing funding would only be entitled to a risk-adjusted return on its funding unless it also exerts control over the risks or performs other functions associated with the funded activity or asset. An entity will be considered to exert control over risks to the extent that it has the ability to both make decisions to take on, lay off or decline a risk-bearing opportunity and make decisions on whether and how to respond to the risks associated with the opportunity and further performs such decision-making functions.[694] As regards the scope of such risks, the entity will have to assume and control both the financial risk (the one that is inherent in the funding provided) and the "operational risk" (the one linked to the operational activities for which the funding is used).[695] For example, when funding is provided for the development of an intangible,

688. The nature of the "important functions" will greatly vary depending on the particular facts of the case. In the case of self-developed intangibles, such functions may include: design and control of research and marketing programs, direction of and establishing priorities for creative undertakings, control over strategic decisions regarding intangible development programs and management and control of budgets. For any kind of intangible (either self-developed or acquired), functions may include defense, protection and ongoing quality control over functions performed by related or unrelated enterprises. *See* OECD (2015): Final Report on BEPS Actions 8-10—Aligning transfer pricing outcomes with value creation, p. 80 (2017 OECD TPG, paragraph 6.56).
689. OECD (2015): Final Report on BEPS Actions 8-10—Aligning transfer pricing outcomes with value creation, pp. 78-79 (2017 OECD TPG, paragraphs 6.50-6.58).
690. OECD (2015): Final Report on BEPS Actions 8-10—Aligning transfer pricing outcomes with value creation, p. 79 (2017 OECD TPG, paragraph 6.52).
691. OECD (2015): Final Report on BEPS Actions 8-10—Aligning transfer pricing outcomes with value creation, p. 79 (2017 OECD TPG, paragraph 6.53).
692. The report provides various examples in this regard. For example, a fully developed and currently exploitable intangible may require no development at all and little or no maintenance and protection while contributions on its exploitation would acquire great significance (p. 78).
693. OECD (2015): Final Report on BEPS Actions 8-10—Aligning transfer pricing outcomes with value creation, pp. 81-82 (2017 OECD TPG, paragraphs 6.59-6.64).
694. OECD (2015): Final Report on BEPS Actions 8-10—Aligning transfer pricing outcomes with value creation, p. 23 (2017 OECD TPG, paragraph 1.65).
695. OECD (2015): Final Report on BEPS Actions 8-10—Aligning transfer pricing outcomes with value creation, pp. 81-82 (2017 OECD TPG, paragraphs 6.61-6.64).

the financier is expected to have control and make decisions concerning the development of the intangible to be entitled to get a compensation beyond a mere risk-adjusted return.[696]

Lastly, in relation to the assumption of risks related to DEMPE activities, risks may include those related to the development of intangibles (e.g., the risk that costly R&D will prove to be unsuccessful or the risk related to the timing of the investment), those related to the product itself (e.g., its obsolescence, the fact the other competitors may launch competitive products), those related to IP rights (e.g., claims of infringement) or those related to the exploitation (e.g., how well the product is received by the market).[697] The identity of the group entities assuming the risks related to DEMPE[698] will determine who will bear the consequences if the risk materializes.[699]

Once the identification of the group entities who have been deemed to add value (by either performing functions, using assets or assuming risks related to DEMPE activities) is over, the next step is to identify and determine the arm's length price and conditions of the controlled transaction.[700] To do so, it should be taken into account the level and nature of the relevant activity and the compensation received by comparable uncontrolled entities performing similar activities.[701]

Naturally, the allocation of a great share of profits to this first group of entities would be detrimental to other group entities. For example, the legal owner of the intangible,[702] despite being legally entitled to all the returns derived from the intangible, will not per se be entitled to any portion of the return resulting from the exploitation of the intangible for transfer pricing purposes other than the arm's length compensation (if any) for holding title.[703] Similarly, an entity whose role is limited to

696. OECD (2015): Final Report on BEPS Actions 8-10—Aligning transfer pricing outcomes with value creation, p. 82 2017 OECD TPG, paragraph 6.64). According to Brauner, however, the financial risk may be considerably larger than other risks, thus giving rise per se to a significant compensation: "some co-financing arrangements occur in market conditions, and such arrangements may often represent financial risks that are agreeably larger than other relevant risks in such transactions." *See* Brauner, Y. (2016), p. 123.

697. OECD (2015): Final Report on BEPS Actions 8-10—Aligning transfer pricing outcomes with value creation, p. 82 (2017 OECD TPG, paragraph 6.65).

698. The process of identifying the persons assuming risks is described in OECD (2015): Final Report on BEPS Actions 8-10—Aligning transfer pricing outcomes with value creation, p. 22 (2017 OECD TPG, paragraph 1.60).

699. OECD (2015): Final Report on BEPS Actions 8-10—Aligning transfer pricing outcomes with value creation, p. 83 (2017 OECD TPG, paragraph 6.66).

700. OECD (2015): Final Report on BEPS Actions 8-10—Aligning transfer pricing outcomes with value creation, p. 85 (2017 OECD TPG, paragraphs 6.73-6.74).

701. OECD (2015): Final Report on BEPS Actions 8-10—Aligning transfer pricing outcomes with value creation, p. 85 (2017 OECD TPG, paragraph 6.75).

702. In case it is impossible to identify the legal owner of the intangible under applicable law or governing contracts, the group entity that, based on the facts and circumstances, "controls decisions concerning the exploitation of the intangible and hast the practical capacity to restrict other from using the intangible" will be considered the legal owner of the intangible from transfer pricing purposes. *See* OECD (2015): Final Report on BEPS Actions 8-10—Aligning transfer pricing outcomes with value creation, p. 76 (2017 OECD TPG, paragraph 6.40).

703. OECD (2015): Final Report on BEPS Actions 8-10—Aligning transfer pricing outcomes with value creation, p. 76 (2017 OECD TPG, paragraph 6.42). Unless the legal owner physically performs functions related to DEMPE or controls the outsourcing of such functions to either related on unrelated parties (*see* p. 79).

the provision of funding (along with the control of its inherent financial risk), will merely be compensated by a "risk-adjusted return" to be calculated on the basis of the cost of capital or the return of a realistic alternative investment with comparable economic characteristics.[704] Neither the legal owner nor the financier would be entitled to an arm's length compensation beyond the aforementioned amounts unless they are regarded to contribute to the value-adding process in the line expressed in the previous paragraphs.

The "value creation" approach on transfer pricing rules promoted by the OECD has been welcomed by some scholars for various reasons. For example, Tavares notes that this new approach is much more consistent with contemporary economic theories that seek to identify the most significant features that contribute to the success of an enterprise, most notably the knowledge-based theory of the firm.[705] This theory can be traced back to Penrose, who suggested that the access and use of information through management decision-making is what makes a difference and creates value.[706] Later on, advocates of this theory argued that enterprises essentially learn and grow on the basis of technological and organizational knowledge.[707] Thus, firms serve as "repositories" of valuable knowledge that can be easily and "cheaply" learned through continuing association.[708] In the words of Tavares, these ideas seem to be "strikingly consistent" with the direction of the BEPS value creation approach.[709]

The OECD puts forward some mechanisms that contribute to put into effect the profit allocation process inspired by the principle of "value creation," most notably, the choice of the relevant transfer pricing method (with a particular focus on the TPS method) and a proposed new approach on CSAs.

As regards the choice of the transfer pricing method, the BEPS project chooses to promote methods that are less reliant on comparability analysis (i.e., transactional methods)[710] and most notably the TPS method in transactions involving intangibles.[711] The TPS method is found to be the most appropriate one in cases in which the business

704. OECD (2015): Final Report on BEPS Actions 8-10—Aligning transfer pricing outcomes with value creation, p. 81 (2017 OECD TPG, paragraphs 6.61-6.62).
705. Tavares argues that the "value creation" approach (reflected in a number of outcomes derived by the BEPS project, e.g., the modified nexus approach—action 5-, the activity exception to the LOB clause—action 6- and the DEMPE approach on transfer pricing—actions 8 to 10) captures the "knowledge-based" views of the firm. *See* Tavares, R.S.J. (2016), pp. 271-272.
706. Penrose, E.T. (1959).
707. Foss, N.J. (1996), p. 470: "the essential thing about the firm is not only its 'contractualness' but just as much its function as a repository of distinct productive (technological and organizational) knowledge, and as an entity that can learn—and grow—on the basis of this knowledge (...) Such knowledge stocks are associated with differential efficiencies, and are accumulated in a path-dependent way. Thus, they not only help explain why some firms realize competitive advantage while other firms do not, they also help in addressing issues relating to diversification and innovation." For more literature on the topic, *see* the footnotes in Tavares, R.S.J. (2016), p. 272.
708. Tavares, R.S.J. (2016), p. 273.
709. Tavares, R.S.J. (2016), p. 272.
710. Petrucci, R. (2016), p. 25.
711. In Chapter 3 section §3.01[C] we provided a general overview on the different transfer pricing methods.

operations are highly integrated[712] and the parties of the transaction make unique and valuable contributions (e.g., unique intangibles)[713] in such a way that there does not seem to be any reliable comparables. Be that as it may, it has been noted that the TPS method is likely to become "the rule rather than the exception for transactions involving intangibles."[714]

This method does not assess transactions separately but rather departs from the "combined profits" that arise from the relevant controlled transactions in which the related parties are engaged[715] to further split the outcome between the parties on an "economically valid basis" that approximates the allocation of profits that would have been reflected in an agreement made at arm's length.[716] It is precisely at this point that the BEPS approach comes into play, as it would promote a selection of profit splitting factors that are indeed aligned with the activities that are regarded in the final report as true "value-adding" activities.[717] Consequently, the TPS method would become instrumental in achieving the profit allocation desired by the BEPS project and, by extension, the ultimate goal of the BEPS Actions on transfer pricing (i.e., the alignment between transfer pricing outcomes and value creation).[718]

The empowerment of the transactional transfer pricing methods method, and most notably the TPS, has been applauded by numerous scholars, even before the advent of the BEPS project. In general, it is commonly regarded as a "pragmatic solution" in between transfer pricing and formulary apportionment[719] and the most dignified manner to deal with the inherent constraints of the ALS without pleading for

712. The report itself notes that all MNC seem to enjoy such integration, so it seems to be unclear how the criterion should be applied. *See* OECD (2015): Final Report on BEPS Actions 8-10—Aligning transfer pricing outcomes with value creation, p. 58.
713. The report does not provide further guidance on the significance of "unique" and "valuable" contributions, although commentators on the previous discussion draft suggested that "unique" contributions should be defined as those "that cannot be benchmarked by reference to uncontrolled transactions" while "valuable" contributions should be defined as those which are expected to yield future economic benefits. *See* OECD (2015): Final Report on BEPS Actions 8-10—Aligning transfer pricing outcomes with value creation, p. 58.
714. Brauner, Y. (2016), p. 106.
715. 2017 OECD TPG, paragraphs 2.114 and most notably 2.124-2.137.
716. 2017 OECD TPG, paragraphs 2.138-2.151. Schoueri argues that the TPS method intends to simulate the "profit split" that would have been agreed by independent parties. *See* Schoueri, L.E. (2015), p. 693.
717. OECD (2015): Final Report on BEPS Actions 8-10—Aligning transfer pricing outcomes with value creation, p. 80 (2017 OECD TPG, paragraph 6.57): "it may be necessary to utilize transfer pricing methods not directly based on comparables, including transactional profit split methods and ex ante techniques to appropriate reward the performance of those important functions."
718. OECD (2015): Final Report on BEPS Actions 8-10—Aligning transfer pricing outcomes with value creation, p. 59: "transactional profit split methods could make a contribution to achieving this aim (aligning transfer pricing outcomes with value creation)."
719. Schön describes the TPS method as a "limited fractional apportionment" and Avi-Yonah and Benshalom regards it as a "quasi-formulary" method, while Tavares argues that it is a "middle ground" between the OECD guidelines and formulary apportionment. In fact, the two only significant differences between the TPS method and a formulary solution are, on the one hand, the fact that the former departs the profit derived by a sole transaction while the latter departs from the overall profit obtained by group and, on the other hand, the fact that the former does not establish the profit split criteria (which would be established on the basis of the facts and circumstances of the case) while the latter does indeed predetermine them in the rule. *See*

its formal abandonment.[720] Schoueri regards the increasing use of this method as a piece of evidence of the failure of the ALS.[721]

The preeminence of transactional transfer pricing methods has been accompanied by the devaluation of certain traditional methods, particularly the C+ method in the context of transactions involving intangibles. The report acknowledges that compensation based on the reimbursement of costs plus a modest mark-up is not appropriate to reflect value creation.[722] For example, such remuneration is unlikely to reflect the anticipated value (or the arm's length price for) of the contributions for the entities performing R&D functions.[723] This is particularly true where significant residual profits arise (i.e., profits well above the return on capital), a scenario that may be quite common in transactions involving intangible assets, as these are precisely characterized by their potential to generate income that is disproportionally higher that the costs incurred in their development.[724]

The new approach on transfer pricing also has a significant impact on the regulation of CSAs.[725] In fact, the report intends to ensure consistency between the new guidance on CSA and the other changes introduced to the 2017 OECD TPG, particularly those related to intangibles,[726] the reason being that CSAs are commonly used for the development of intangibles. In essence, it is claimed that independent parties would only consent to enter into a CSA to the extent that they expect "mutual and proportionate benefit," meaning that they would demand the value of each participant's share of the overall contributions to the CSA to be consistent and proportionate with the participant's share of the overall expected benefits to be received.

The first step of the process entails the identification of the "true" participants in a CSA. A party of a CSA will only be considered a participant of the agreement for transfer pricing purposes insofar it has a "reasonable expectation that it will benefit from the objectives of the CSA activity."[727] Subsequently, it should be ascertained whether the value of the contribution made by the participant and its share of the

Schön, W. (2010), p. 235 and Avi-Yonah, R.; Benshalom, I. (2011) and Tavares, R.S.J (2016), pp. 273-274. Formulary apportionment is briefly mentioned in Chapter 3 section §3.01[B] and Chapter 4 section §4.03.

720. On the contrary, *see* Brauner, Y. (2016), p. 106: "(the TPS method) is somewhat widely accepted as the best way for the OECD to abandon arm's length in the transfer pricing of intangibles without losing too much face."
721. Schoueri, L.E. (2015), p. 699.
722. Navarro Ibarrola, A. (2017), p. 136.
723. The OECD argues that the C+ method will rarely be appropriate in the context of transactions involving R&D contributions, also in the context of CSAs. *See* OECD (2015): Final Report on BEPS Actions 8-10—Aligning transfer pricing outcomes with value creation, pp. 86 and 170 (2017 OECD TPG, paragraphs 6.79 and 8.26).
724. *See* the explanation and examples put forward in Chapter 3 section §3.01[C].
725. We defined CSAs back in Chapter 2 section §2.01[A][2], where we briefly explained the role that CSAs play in the Apple's tax planning scheme.
726. Brauner, Y. (2016), p. 111. OECD (2015): Final Report on BEPS Actions 8-10—Aligning transfer pricing outcomes with value creation, p. 161. The new guidance on CSA may be consulted in pp. 161-181.
727. OECD (2015): Final Report on BEPS Actions 8-10—Aligning transfer pricing outcomes with value creation, pp. 167-168 (2017 OECD TPG, paragraphs 8.14-8.18).

expected benefits derived from the CSA are in fact consistent and proportionate. This makes it necessary to make the following two determinations:

(a) Value of the contribution. Contributions made by participants in a CSAs may take many forms, such as the provision of pre-existing assets or intangibles (e.g., the contribution of a patented technology whose value must be determined at arm's length) or the performance of services (e.g., development activities).[728] The report notes that the valuation of this latter type should be based on the "value of the functions performed."[729] This being said, the report warns that a valuation based on costs plus a mark-up will not generally be appropriate, as it will not conveniently reflect the real value of the contribution.[730]
(b) Share of the expected benefits. The report first notes that a significant part of the benefits derived by the CSA may not arise immediately but rather after some time. As regards the allocation of the benefits among the participants in the CSA, it is often guided by certain "allocation keys," such as sales (turnover), profits, units used/produced/sold, number of employees and so forth.[731] As a matter of principle, the selection of the relevant factor(s) should serve to ensure a certain degree of consistency between the value of the contribution and the share of the benefits. Where participants merely provide funding, they cannot expect a benefit that goes beyond an arm's length risk-adjusted return on its funding.[732]

The new approach on CSAs confirms the trend of the new BEPS approach on transfer pricing (whose features were identified above), as it underlines once again the importance to allocate a significant portion of the taxable bases to related parties performing relevant functions considering the value of their respective contributions (whose valuation should not generally be made at cost) at the expense of those which merely provide funding or holds the legal ownership of the asset.

It seems obvious than the US regime on CSAs,[733] which plays such a significant role in the Apple's tax scheme, clearly contradicts these premises.[734] First, and above all, the US regime on CSAs does not require the participants in the CSA to have a

728. OECD (2015): Final Report on BEPS Actions 8-10—Aligning transfer pricing outcomes with value creation, p. 170 (2017 OECD TPG, paragraph 8.8.24-26).
729. To this end, the report makes a reference to the guidance in Chapters I-III, VI and VII of the 2017 OECD TPG.
730. In cases in which the difference between the value and the costs is "relatively insignificant," the value of the contribution may be measured at cost (e.g., services CSAs). On the contrary, the measurement of contributions to development CSAs at cost will "generally not provide a reliable basis for the application of the arm's length principle." OECD (2015): Final Report on BEPS Actions 8-10—Aligning transfer pricing outcomes with value creation, pp. 170-171 (2017 OECD TPG, paragraph 8.27).
731. OECD (2015): Final Report on BEPS Actions 8-10—Aligning transfer pricing outcomes with value creation, pp. 168-169 (2017 OECD TPG, paragraphs 8.19-8.22).
732. Brauner, Y. (2016), p. 123.
733. We briefly described this regime back in Chapter 2 section §2.01[A][2].
734. Brauner, Y. (2016), p. 124.

"reasonable expectation" that they would benefit from the agreement in order to be considered as "true" participants. In fact, it is clear that Apple Inc. would hardly be regarded as a potential beneficiary of such agreement in the case at hand. Second, the US regime makes the shares of the expected benefits derived from the CSA dependent upon the financial contribution made by the participant to cover the costs for developing the relevant intangible irrespective of whether they actually perform any relevant function related to this activity. As we concluded back then, these agreements do not commonly entail any sort of functional contribution in the form of the provision of services or activities. As it happens, the signature of the CSA between Apple Inc. and the Irish-incorporated subsidiaries did not prompt the transfer of any sort of R&D activities to Ireland.[735]

We started the present section with the hypothesis that the BEPS approach on transfer pricing seemed to be consistent with the presumptive benefit principle at first sight. Once the new approach and its corresponding new proposed guidance has been analyzed, we are in a better position to confirm the hypothesis. The reason is that States where the related parties are performing "significant value-adding functions" (in relation to DEMPE activities) will be better compensated with a greater share of the group's taxable base for their "indirect" contribution to the group's activities through the supply of public services and infrastructures.

Even though the new approach on transfer pricing should be welcome from a theoretical perspective for the reasons outlined above, it is evident that it will continue to be subject to manipulation. The OECD wishes to allocate taxable bases to the jurisdictions where value is deemed to be created (i.e., where significant value-adding functions are performed) and, naturally, nothing prevents MNCs to transfer employees performing such functions to the jurisdictions of their choice, thereby indirectly selecting the jurisdiction where their profits will be ultimately taxed according to the 2017 OECD TPG. Wittendorff draws attention to this risk, warning that low-tax jurisdictions with a "mild and sunny climate" will be favored over cold and rainy ones when the time comes to relocate the relevant people.[736] Naturally, this scenario is to be expected and should further be accepted, as it would nonetheless be consistent with the presumptive benefit principle. On the contrary, the lack of acceptance of this plausible scenario would denote that the reasons behind the new approach (whether the "value creation" approach endorsed by the OECD or the "presumptive benefit" principle in our case) are not transparent and sincere but rather entail a hidden agenda according to which taxation should ideally occur in high-tax jurisdictions or, to put it bluntly, in the territories of the OECD Member States.

Lastly, the question remains at to whether the new BEPS approach on transfer pricing, and particularly its expression in the form of the 2017 OECD TPG, is in fact consistent with the current legal configuration of the ALS or, on the contrary, either goes beyond its theoretical scope or leads to limit it. We will try to provide an answer to this question in the next section.

735. In the case of Apple, Apple Inc., ASI and AOE (parties of the CSA) agreed to share the R&D costs of Apple's IP in exchange for sharing the profits derived by such IP worldwide.
736. Wittendorff, J. (2016), pp. 332-333.

[2] *The Doubtful Compatibility of the "Value Creation" Approach and the Current Legal Configuration of Transfer Pricing Rules Following the ALS*

In the present section we will first raise the question as to whether the ALS is a suitable instrument to pursue the "profits follow value creation" objective as set out by the BEPS project. Second, we will evaluate whether the new proposed guidance on transfer pricing (the 2017 OECD TPG) that results from the empowerment of the so-called value creation approach is indeed consistent with the current legal configuration of transfer pricing rules following the ALS.

As regards the first question we first need to identify the supposed rationale and objective of the ALS. This matter is not free of controversy. To begin with, and to the best of our knowledge, rules that contain the ALS have never made explicit their specific purpose. This means that we can only infer the presumable purpose of the rule from its literal wording and from the effects of its application. In this context, it is commonly argued that two alternative principles seem to underlie the ALS: either ability to pay or anti-avoidance. We will now proceed to analyze whether we can consistently uphold any of these theories.

As a matter of principle, the ALS intends to ensure equal tax treatment between independent and dependent parties to further avoid the creation of tax advantages in favor of the latter that would distort competition.[737] As Schoueri suggests, behind such rationale we may find the principles of ability to pay and equity.[738] The reason is that dependent parties enjoy a de facto power to misprice their transactions to reduce their overall tax liabilities and transfer pricing legislation precisely intends to re-establish equality among taxpayers by allocating income according to their ability to pay irrespective of such power.[739] According to Navarro, however, the application of the rule does not always generate outcomes that may be deemed as consistent with the aforementioned goal.[740] First, related and unrelated parties can hardly be considered to be in a comparable situation, as their situation is not equivalent neither from an economic nor an organizational perspective.[741] Second, even if we considered that both types of entities are in a comparable situation, the ALS can never be considered to grant homogeneous tax treatment between them to the extent that its application necessarily entails the imposition of additional (indeed quite significant) compliance and administrative costs to the former group of entities in relation to the latter.[742]

The other most common rationale that is supposedly behind the ALS is the anti-avoidance purpose. The reason is that the practice commonly followed by related

737. 2017 OECD TPG, paragraph 1.8: "the arm's length principle provides broad parity of tax treatment for members of MNE groups and independent enterprises. Because the arm's length principle puts associated and independent enterprises on a more equal footing for tax purposes, it avoids the creation of tax advantages or disadvantages that would otherwise distort the relative competitive positions of either type of entity."
738. Schoueri, L.E. (2015), pp. 695-696.
739. Schoueri, L.E. (2015), p. 695.
740. Navarro Ibarrola, A. (2016), pp. 59-61.
741. Navarro Ibarrola, A. (2016), p. 60.
742. Hamaekers, H.M.A.L. (1998), pp. 297-298.

parties to "misprice" their transactions is often labeled as "abusive."[743] Navarro equally rejects this stance for various reasons.[744] First, the ALS does not make any reference to criteria that are traditionally used in the context to anti-avoidance rules, e.g., artificiality, valid commercial reasons, the existence of a tax saving or the existence of results beyond such tax saving. This being so, transfer pricing rules following the ALS could potentially apply irrespective of any of these considerations. Second, the fact that the application of transfer pricing rules may lead to counteract the avoidance of taxes solely indicates that this is indeed one of the probable consequences of their application, it does not have to be necessarily its purpose.[745] And finally, the fact that MNCs shift profits to low-tax jurisdictions by means of their transfer pricing policy is not, on its own, indicative of an abusive behavior. Otherwise, this would imply the equation between the existence of a tax saving and the existence of abuse, an approach that is inadmissible.[746] All these considerations suggest that the anti-avoidance purpose should not be regarded as the rationale and justification of the ALS.

As a consequence of the aforementioned, it seems that none of these traditional rationales is consistent with neither the literal wording nor the final outcome of the ALS. On the contrary, Navarro concludes that the ALS lacks a specific objective and is merely a legal convention that serves as a pattern to attribute profits to related parties.[747] This means that the application of the ALS should be conducted in an "aseptic way," i.e., assigning the profits to the relevant related parties as if they were unrelated, irrespective of any further consideration deriving from the supposed rationale(s) behind the ALS.[748] Otherwise, States may feel tempted to deviate from the possible meaning of the transfer pricing provision precisely to satisfy its supposed objective.[749]

This being said, one may interpret the fact that the OECD entrusts the ALS with the task of aligning its outcomes with value creation in the context of the BEPS project as a way to confer a brand new objective to the ALS.[750] In fact, this is implicitly recognized in the BEPS Action Plan: "transfer pricing rules serve to allocate income earned by a multinational enterprise among those countries in which the company does business."[751] The problem is that, once again, this "new" objective is far from

743. OECD (2011): Transfer pricing legislation: a suggested approach, p. 3, Baker, P. (2011), 9B.05 and Baistrocchi, E. (2005), p. 950 among others.
744. Navarro Ibarrola, A. (2016), pp. 62-63.
745. 2017 OECD TPG, paragraph 1.2: "the consideration of transfer pricing should not be confused with the consideration of problems of tax fraud or tax avoidance, even though transfer pricing policies may be used for such purposes."
746. Bizioli, G. (2014), p. 692.
747. Navarro Ibarrola, A. (2016), p. 65 and OECD (2011): Transfer pricing legislation: a suggested approach, p. 2: "at the theoretical level, the challenge (...) in the development of transfer pricing legislation is in essence (...) protecting their tax base."
748. Navarro Ibarrola, A. (2016), pp. 65-66.
749. Brauner, Y. (2012), p. 168.
750. Brauner, Y. (2016), p. 101: "the OECD expressed an intent to shift transfer pricing practice (...) to a more pragmatic business focused approach relying on the principle that profits should follow action or value creation" and in p. 107: "BEPS introduced a new principle: profits must follow value creation."
751. OECD (2013): BEPS Action Plan, p. 19.

evident and cannot be logically nor naturally inferred from the literal wording of the rule nor its final outcomes. What is more, the ALS as it currently stands is likely to bring outcomes that are not aligned with such objective.[752]

These observations suggest that the ALS may not be the most suitable instrument to satisfy the BEPS mantra on transfer pricing.[753] Indeed, pursuing this objective by means of the ALS entails a clear risk: it could eventually give rise to interpretations of the rule that substantially deviate from its literal scope, just as it has historically happened in the past with the other alleged objectives of the standard.[754]

Now we will proceed to evaluate whether the aforementioned risk has indeed materialized. In other words, we will assess whether the new guidance on transfer pricing resulting from the new "value creation" approach (i.e., the 2017 OECD TPG) can generally be regarded as consistent with the current legal configuration of transfer pricing rules following the ALS.

In essence, the ALS requires taxpayers and tax administrations to price transactions carried out between related parties as if such parties were unrelated, operating at arm's length and engaging in comparable transactions under similar conditions and economic circumstances. Taxpayers are the first ones that get to undertake this exercise and, in doing so, they enjoy a certain degree of freedom to choose the most appropriate methodology, set a transfer price for the transaction and further demonstrate that such price is consistent with the ALS.

In this context, transfer pricing methods are not expected to determine the price at which related parties would have indisputably traded but rather provide the price at which they would have presumably traded.[755] In other words, the methods may be regarded as establishing a rebuttable (legal) presumption that unrelated parties would have considered such transfer prices if they had found themselves in such situation. In principle, tax administrations could only contradict such presumption insofar they have convincing evidence that unrelated parties would most likely determine other prices.[756]

This being so, when related parties properly apply a transfer pricing method and derive from it a transfer price, such price would be presumably consistent with those that unrelated parties would have agreed upon in comparable circumstances, and therefore such parties should be theoretically protected from subsequent tax adjustments of the administration insofar the latter is not able to demonstrate that unrelated

752. Chapter 3 section §3.01[C]. Wittendorff notes that profit allocation in line with value creation may not be equal to profit allocation in line with third-party behavior. *See* Wittendorff, J. (2016), p. 333.
753. Schoueri notes that transfer pricing has incidentally become the "battleground" for broader reforms of the international tax regime. In fact, new approaches or suggested modifications to transfer pricing rules are more focused on "shifting taxing powers" than on solving real feasibility issues of transfer pricing. *See* Schoueri, L.E. (2015), p. 702. For his part, Wittendorff argues that the OECD should have retained the traditional ALS and combated BEPS by means other than transfer pricing rules, particularly by BEPS action 5 on harmful tax competition. *See* Wittendorff, J. (2016), p. 333.
754. Brauner, Y. (2012), p. 168.
755. Schoueri, L.E. (2015), p. 697. He argues that it is impossible to know how an independent party would have reacted in a specific transaction.
756. Schoueri, L.E. (2015), pp. 697-698.

parties would most likely determine other price. As we noted elsewhere,[757] the inherent subjectivity of the mandate based on the ALS gives rise to a wide range of prices that are "acceptable" from the perspective of the ALS,[758] a range within which taxpayers are theoretically entitled to move freely and legitimately without the interference and the subsequent tax adjustments of the administration.

The new approach on transfer pricing, resulting from the proposed new OECD TPG, intends to effectively limit the inherent subjectivity of the ALS by narrowing the afore mentioned range of acceptable prices on the grounds of the "profits must follow value creation" principle. In other words, the new guidance uses this principle to justify the restriction of the freedom to select the methodology that the taxpayer believes to be more appropriate considering the circumstances of the case and further set a transfer price that could be regarded as compliant with the ALS. In our opinion, this scenario appears to contradict the literal meaning of rules following the ALS.

This "restrictive effect" derived from the new OECD approach on transfer pricing is the logical outcome of the empowerment of certain transfer pricing methods (most notably the TPS) at the expense of others (e.g., C+) resulting from the 2017 OECD TPG.[759]

In the first place, the preeminence of certain transfer pricing methods over others appears to contradict the guideline enshrined in the OECD TPG according to which the selection of the relevant method should always aim at finding the "most appropriate method" considering the facts and circumstances of the case, a guideline that lies at the very heart of the ALS.[760] The OECD itself raised the question as to whether the preeminence of the TPS method constitutes an exception to the "most appropriate method" rule, as its use is recommended in certain scenarios without having to consider whether the use of the method is itself appropriate.[761]

The predetermination (and imposition) of the methodology to be used irrespective of the relevant circumstances not only confronts the "most appropriate method" rule, it leads to effectively restrict the freedom that the ALS supposedly grants the taxpayer to select the method he believes to be more appropriate and further demonstrate that the transfer prices resulting from such method are indeed consistent with the ALS.

757. *See* Chapter 3 section §3.01[C].
758. The 2017 OECD TPG defines arm's length range in its glossary as "a range of figures that are acceptable for establishing whether the conditions of a controlled transaction are arm's length and that are derived either from applying the same transfer pricing method to multiple comparable data or from applying different transfer pricing methods." *See* OECD TPG, p. 23. This notion reinforces the idea that there is not a single and indisputable arm's length price.
759. The same could be said of the American regime on CSA (Chapter 2 section §2.01[A][2]), which may be also regarded as inconsistent with the spirit of the ALS itself insofar it predetermines the use of a methodology based on C+.
760. 2017 OECD TPG, paragraph 2.2. The validity of this guideline is not only due to its presence in the OECD TPG and a great number of domestic transfer pricing regulations, it could be argued that it may be logically inferred from the own ALS.
761. OECD (2015): Final Report on BEPS Actions 8-10—Aligning transfer pricing outcomes with value creation, p. 58.

For example, by predetermining the TPS as the most suitable method in certain scenarios[762] irrespective of other circumstances, the OECD is in fact indirectly conditioning and limiting the range of acceptable transfer prices beyond what the ALS theoretically suggests. This position seems to contradict the literal meaning of rules following the ALS and the very *raison d'*être of the standard.

On the other hand, the outright rejection of the C+ method in certain cases[763] indirectly entails the dismissal of transfer prices that could arguably be within the ALS range of prices for the sole reason that they are based on a specific methodology that is deemed to inappropriate. Again, this stance is, to say the least, hard to reconcile with the ALS.[764]

Beyond the problems derived from the predetermination and rejection of certain transfer pricing methods (resulting in the so-called restrictive effect) from the perspective of the ALS, it should be noted that the TPS method itself raises concerns in this regard. Although it is commonly regarded as a halfway solution between the ALS and formulary apportionment,[765] some scholars have questioned whether the method either goes beyond the scope of the ALS[766] or may at least prompt an application of the rule that is inconsistent with the standard.[767]

In short, it seems that the intent of the OECD to counteract the subjectivity of the ALS by means of the ex-ante predetermination of the relevant method in fact collides with the ALS itself, the reason being that subjectivity is an inherent feature of this standard.[768]

Beyond the aforementioned concern, there are further aspects of the 2017 OECD TPG that may also be regarded as hard to reconcile with the ALS itself,[769] in the sense

762. Where the business operations are highly integrated and the parties of the transaction make unique and valuable contributions, in such a way that there are no reliable comparables. *See* Chapter 4 section §4.02[A][1] and OECD (2015): Final Report on BEPS Actions 8-10—Aligning transfer pricing outcomes with value creation, p. 58.
763. In cases in which what is being remunerated is the performance of R&D activities, particularly where significant residual profits are expected to arise. *See* Chapter 4 section §4.02[A][1] and OECD (2015): Final Report on BEPS Actions 8-10—Aligning transfer pricing outcomes with value creation, pp. 86 and 170 (2017 OECD TPG, paragraphs 6.79 and 8.26).
764. Brauner argues that the plain rejection of the C+ method when the time comes to value the contributions to a CSA is troublesome: "viewed from the literal arm's length perspective, it does not make sense since it would be easy to demonstrate that market ventures are often accounted for based on costs." *See* Brauner, Y. (2016), p. 124.
765. Chapter 4 section §4.02[A][1].
766. Brauner, Y. (2016), p. 110: "(the TPS method) is somewhat widely accepted as the best way for the OECD to abandon arm's length in the transfer pricing of intangibles without losing too much face." Schoueri believes that the TPS method is intended to be ALS-based method, as it intends to "mimic the allocation of profits that would be observed in a relation between independent parties if a comparable contribution to the success of the activity would occur" but has considerable doubts whether the method is ultimately compatible with the ALS. Indeed, he argues that the adoption of a consolidated approach rather than an entity approach may jeopardize the comparative exercises. *See* Schoueri, L.E. (2015), pp. 693, 695 and 696.
767. Ashley notes the tendency to use formulary concepts in disputes that are supposedly based on the TPS method in the context of transfer pricing rules. *See* Ashley, S. (2013), p. 18.
768. As it was already pointed out back in Chapter 3 section §3.01[C].
769. Robillard argues that the BEPS approach on transfer pricing denotes that the ALS is now "slowly but surely being related to the back seat" of the OECD TPG. *See* Robillard, R. (2015), p. 474.

that the new guidelines may well give rise to outcomes that differ from those that may have presumably occurred in the market.[770] This is attributed to various reasons. First, the fact that contractual risk allocation is disregarded.[771] Second, the overestimation of the market value of functions.[772] And third, the possibility to undertake *ex post* transfer pricing adjustments based on the *ex post* outcomes derived by the exploitation of the intangible.[773]

The aforementioned risks would however only materialize in practice to the extent that tax administrations go as far as to reject the pricing provided by the taxpayer (assuming it could arguably be within the ALS range of prices and this is in fact verifiable) on the sole grounds that it would not be consistent with the considerations comprised in the 2017 OECD TPG (e.g., the pricing is not based on the methodology that is regarded as appropriate by the guidelines).[774] Of course, this is more likely to happen in jurisdictions that tend to grant the OECD TPG a sort of authoritative status,[775] as the OECD TPG themselves suggest.[776]

---

770. Schoueri provides a very illustrative example in this regard. *See* Schoueri, L.E. (2015), pp. 714-715.
771. The approach was described in Chapter 4 section §4.02[A][1]. *See* Wittendorff, J. (2016), p. 333.
772. Wittendorff, J. (2016), p. 333.
773. Such possibility appears to exist in scenarios involving hard to value intangibles. This is how the 2015 report on actions 8-10 explains the new approach: "tax administrations can consider ex post outcomes as presumptive evidence about the appropriateness of the ex-ante pricing arrangements, and the taxpayer cannot demonstrate that the uncertainty has been appropriately taken into account in the pricing methodology adopted." *See* OECD (2015): Final Report on BEPS Actions 8-10—Aligning transfer pricing outcomes with value creation, p. 64. Schoueri believes that this may not be in accordance with the ALS. *See* Schoueri, L.E. (2015), p. 715.
774. This will also depend on the domestic rules on the allocation of the burden of the proof. According to the 2017 OECD TPG, preface, paragraph 18: "in most jurisdictions, the tax administration bears the burden of proof, which may require the tax administration to make a prima facie showing that the taxpayer's pricing is inconsistent with the arm's length principle. It should be noted, however, that even in such a case a tax administration might still reasonably oblige the taxpayer to produce its records to enable the tax administration to undertake its examination of the controlled transactions. In other jurisdictions the taxpayer may bear the burden of proof in some respects."
775. *See* Judgment by the Canadian Federal Court of Appeal, 2002, "Smithkline Beecham Animal Health Inc. v. The Queen": "it appears to be common ground that the OECD Guidelines inform or should inform the interpretation and application of subsection 69(2) of the Income Tax Act. The OECD Guidelines state the principles for determining international transfer prices and, where possible, the agreement among OECD members with respect to the practices to be followed." On the contrary, other courts do not share this view. *See* for example the judgment by the Australian Federal Court, 2011, "Commissioner of Taxation v. SNF Australia Pty Ltd":): "the Guidelines are just that—guidelines [...] The guidelines are not a legitimate aid to the construction of the double taxation treaties [...] they are, in any event, not permissible materials for interpreting tax treaties"; and the judgment by the Canadian Tax Court, 2013, "McKesson Canada Corporation": "OECD Commentaries and Guidelines are written not only by persons who are not legislators, but in fact are the tax collection authorities of the world. Their thoughts should be considered accordingly."
776. 2017 OECD TPG, preface, paragraphs 15-16: "The Guidelines are intended to help tax administrations (of both OECD member countries and non-member countries) and MNEs by indicating ways to find mutually satisfactory solutions to transfer pricing cases, thereby minimizing conflict among tax administrations and between tax administrations and MNEs and avoiding costly litigation (...) OECD member countries are encouraged to follow these

Throughout the present section, we first tried to demonstrate that the ALS is not the most suitable instrument to pursue the BEPS mantra on transfer pricing (i.e., the alignment between transfer pricing outcomes and value creation). In fact, we later confirmed that the proposed 2017 OECD TPG, inspired by the brand new "value creation" approach, is not consistent with the ALS itself, as it leads to effectively restrict its scope by narrowing the range of acceptable transfer prices that the taxpayer may provide in its transfer pricing assessment, particularly in cases in which the tax administrations blindly follows the guidance provided the OECD despite its soft law status.

This leads us to reconsider whether the new 2017 OECD TPG and the current normative configuration of the ALS should continue to coexist despite their divergences or, conversely, the proposed "value creation approach" requires a new legal basis, making it necessary to adopt new transfer pricing rules that go beyond the ALS.

This scenario was indeed envisaged by the OECD in the BEPS Action Plan,[777] explored in an interim discussion draft[778] and finally discarded by the final report, the supposed reason being that "the goals set by the BEPS Action Plan in relation to the development of transfer pricing rules have been achieved without the need to develop special measures outside the arm's length principle."[779] This being so, the OECD pretended that the new guidance merely constitutes a clarification (rather than an overcoming) of the current transfer pricing rules following the ALS.[780]

However, there are reasons to believe that the guidance on transfer pricing proposed by the OECD in fact goes beyond the *raison d'être* and the literal meaning of the rules following the ALS and, by extension, Article 9 of treaties following the MCs.[781] This would make it necessary to, at least, explore the adoption of domestic transfer pricing rules that are beyond the ALS but in turn are better aligned to the new alleged objective of transfer pricing rules and their new proposed guidance. For example, the adoption of domestic rules that in fact predetermine the use of certain transfer pricing methods in a transparent manner where certain conditions are met.

The adoption of domestic special measures in the context of transfer pricing rules may also need to be accompanied by the amendment of Article 9 of the tax treaties following the ALS. Such amendment would be necessary to ensure the potential application of these domestic rules in scenarios covered by tax treaties insofar we

Guidelines in their domestic transfer pricing practices, and taxpayers are encouraged to follow these Guidelines in evaluating for tax purposes."

777. BEPS Action Plan, p. 20: "special measures, either within or beyond the arm's length principle, may be required with respect to intangible assets, risk and over-capitalization to address these flaws."
778. OECD (2014): BEPS Actions 8, 9 and 10: Discussion draft on revision to chapter I of the transfer pricing guidelines (including risk, characterization and special measures), pp. 38-45.
779. OECD (2015): Final Report on BEPS Actions 8-10—Aligning transfer pricing outcomes with value creation, p. 12.
780. Wittendorff, J. (2016), p. 333.
781. Wittendorff states that the new OECD approach on transfer pricing, being out of the ALS, cannot be applied under existing tax treaties and may also require legislative action to incorporate it into domestic law. *See* Wittendorff, J. (2016), p. 333.

regard Article 9 of the treaty as a rule that demands the contracting States to respect the ALS insofar the conditions to apply the article are met.[782]

[B] Reconsideration of the Corporate Residence Definition for Tax Purposes

The tax residence of taxpayers is a paradigm of paramount importance in international taxation. It generally triggers a comprehensive tax liability that encompasses the worldwide income obtained by the taxpayer regardless of its sources, albeit this is typically mitigated by foreign tax credits or foreign income exemptions. Besides, it generally grants access to the benefits of the State's tax treaty network.

Chapter 3 demonstrated three fundamental facts regarding the traditional stance towards corporate tax residence. First, the absence of a true reflection on the particular role that corporate tax residence tests should play in the framework of CITs, considering the policy purposes the latter intend to achieve. Second, the fact that traditional tests do not generally guarantee a sufficient connection between the corporate taxpayer and its residence State and, in particular, cannot be regarded as consistent with the presumptive benefit principle. And finally, as a direct consequence of the previous conclusion, the fact that traditional residence tests are highly susceptible to manipulations, thereby generating the so-called residence electivity phenomenon along with profit shifting and treaty shopping opportunities.

We will depart from these three conclusions reached in Chapter 3 section §3.02 to put forward in the following sections a few proposals. In particular, our ultimate goal would be to ensure a better consistency between the notion of corporate tax residence and the presumptive benefit principle in line with what was exposed in Chapter 2 section §2.02 (section §4.02[B][3]).

[1] The Imperative Need to Rethink the Corporate Tax Residence Tests and Align Them with the Policy Purposes of the CIT (Whatever They Are)

The analysis of the most common types of corporate residence tests used in domestic tax legislations and their respective origins and alleged rationales revealed various significant findings that were pointed out in Chapter 3 section §3.02. In general, we noted that the inception and subsequent development of these residence tests have not been driven by clear policy purposes and lacked a thorough consideration on the supposed goals they were supposed to achieve in the framework of the CITs. First, because most of them were directly inherited from private international law (Chapter 3 section §3.02[A][2][a]). Second, because they are frequently implemented with the sole purpose of counteracting the shortcoming of the preexisting tests (Chapter 3 section §3.02[A][2][b]). And third, because jurisdictions are often reluctant to accept

782. Navarro Ibarrola, A. (2016), p. 99. This is the result of considering tax treaties as instruments that restrict the application of the relevant domestic tax rules (Vogel, K. (1997), p. 467).

the logical outcomes of their respective residence tests, precisely because they adopt these tests without really knowing, understanding and accepting their supposed rationale (Chapter 3 section §3.02[A][2][c]).

In a nutshell, all these reflections lead us to conclude that not much thought has been given to how corporate tax residence should be defined for tax law purposes. It seems that few have wondered why a company incorporated in a jurisdiction should be taxable therein for its worldwide income. Or why a company whose directors regularly meet within its jurisdiction should be equally liable to tax for its worldwide income in such jurisdiction.[783] Or similarly, why a company should be taxable in the territory in which the majority of its shareholders live or where its business activity is mainly located.

It is true that we tried to provide an answer to these questions and point out the supposed rationales behind each one of the categories of residence tests.[784] However, we observed that these considerations were largely absent from the explanatory memoranda to the bills, the governmental policy reports or the case law that supported the respective choice of the State concerned. Couzin arrived at the sad conclusion that "residence-based taxation of corporations was not designed having regard to any policy analysis,"[785] while Marian attributed the failure of corporate tax residence to the fact that "the discussion on corporate tax residence is disengaged from the discussion of the policy justifications for the taxation of corporate entities."[786] In the same vein, and after analyzing the most common residence tests, Nikolakakis concluded that "it remains unclear in policy terms why any of these connecting factors really justifies taxation."[787]

783. According to Schön, W. (2009), p. 103: "the basic concept of decision making as a starting point for tax allocation is a flawed one. Decisions are mental processes which do not lend themselves to a territorial fixation. Thus, it makes no sense to focus on the location of the person making that decision."

784. *See* Chapter 3 section §3.02[A][1] and more specifically the sections entitled "the rationale behind them."

785. Couzin, R. (2002), p. 17. More generally, Bird expressed his pessimistic view in this respect: "tax policy, like all public policy, is the product of attempts to achieve often partly conflicting goals in a heavily constrained and changing economic, political and institutional context." *See* Bird, R. (2002), p. 201.

786. Marian, O. (2013b), p. 475. What he intends to do in this article is precisely to force such engagement by means of proposing a different definition or definitions of corporate tax residence for each one of the four traditional policy purposes of corporate income taxes.

787. Nikolakakis, A. (2009), pp. 917-918. Then, he posed the question as to whether the location of the meetings of the directors should justify taxation, insofar the company's income does not really belong to the directors: "why the location of the meetings of the directors should justify taxation? It is simply not their income! That is, the directors are not the economic beneficiaries of the corporation's income (...) and the directors will presumably be paid for the value they add to the enterprise and that income will presumably be taxed where they are resident or perform their functions." Although Nikolakakis and some other scholars have been perfectly aware of this fact, some others have contributed to perpetuate this problem by promoting changes in the residence tests intended to counteract the manipulation of the preexisting ones but without considering their respective policy purposes. For example, Shaviro suggested the adoption of a new tax residence test in the US domestic legislation, alternatively: place of central management and control, place of listing (the treatment of companies publicly traded in prominent US securities markets as resident companies) or place of residence of the company's shareholders. However, we miss in his presentation a careful consideration on the

Considering all the above, it seems appropriate to stop for a while and reconsider whether current tax residence tests make any sense at all. In the first instance, efforts should be made to rethink the residence tests bearing in mind the particular nature and specificities of tax law and the functions it performs. That is to say, residence tests ought to define a bond between the taxpayer and the jurisdiction concerned that proves to be appropriate, meaningful and purposeful in the context of taxation.

Subsequently, once this is done, States should ask themselves a few questions of a more fundamental nature regarding corporate income taxation. In particular, they should consider why they are taxing companies for in the first place. That is, the policy objectives they pretend to achieve by means of their CITs and the role these are expected to play in their jurisdictions. Once the States have defined the policy purposes of their respective CITs (whatever they are) they will be in a better position to design their CITs accordingly.

For the purposes of the current section, the policy objectives of the CIT should inspire the delimitation of its subjective scope and thus the identification of the companies that should be subject to it. This way, the definition of corporate tax residence will be appropriately aligned to the objective of the CIT and will thus contribute to serve its purposes. We will subsequently provide a few examples departing from the tax residence tests analyzed in Chapter 3 section §3.02[A][1], although we will equally make reference to other categories of tests.

When a State regards its own CIT as a compensation for the benefits derived from the incorporation (the granting of limited liability, the transferability of interests, the centralization of management, etc.), it would certainly be coherent to adopt a POI test whereby all companies incorporated in accordance with the domestic laws will be subject to tax therein.[788] On the other hand, when a State intends to exert control over the accumulation of power held by the managers by means of its CIT, it would be logical to implement the POEM as a residence test and thus subject the company to tax wherever its managers meet to take decisions.[789] In the case a State regards its CIT as

purposes he expected to achieve with each one of these tests. Instead, his sole objective was to make the US residence rules "harder and costlier to avoid." *See* Shaviro, D. (2011), pp. 137-139.

788. *See* Chapter 3 section §3.02[A][1][a] (in particular the "rationale behind them" part) and Avi-Yonah, R. (2004), pp. 1205-1206. This idea seems equally present in Prof's Shaviro discourse, where he refers to the US taxation imposed upon foreigners incorporating a company in the US as "a fee for US incorporation," enumerating some of its advantages. Besides, he points out that some companies may consider that the US incorporation "brands them legally, reputationally, and otherwise as real company with high standards." *See* Shaviro, D. (2011), pp. 130-132. In the same vein, Avery Jones provided an example to justify this sort of tests: "if Italian subjects, who may not think their investments are safe in Italian companies, become shareholders in a company and receive an income under the protection of the laws of this country, I do not know why they should not be under the obligation of paying the tax." *See* Avery Jones, J.F. (2009), p. 451. On the other hand, Marian does not believe that formal tests are consistent with the policy purposes of CITs, and he warns that they "pose the risk of defeating the policy purpose for which we seek to tax corporations in the first place." *See* Marian, O. (2013b), pp. 473 and 476.

789. *See* Chapter 3 section §3.02[A][1][b] (in particular the "rationale behind them" part). Avi-Yonah has traditionally defended that CITs assists in curbing undesirable power accumulations by corporate management: "the imposition of the corporate tax will enable the government, the shareholders, and the public to obtain information that will serve as the basis for restricting

a vehicle for reaching the pockets of the individual shareholders that are behind the corporate veil, it seems only natural to link the tax residence status to the place where most of the shareholders reside.[790] On the contrary, if the State deems its CIT as a fee for the use or the enjoyment of public services by the corporate taxpayers, granting the tax residence status to the companies that effectively carry out their business within its territory would seem consistent with the purpose of its CIT.[791] Lastly, "place of listing" would be the most appropriate test for States which regard their CIT as an instrument to either charge for the access to liquidity in the domestic market[792] or to reduce agency costs arising out of the nonalignment of interests between managers and shareholders in publicly traded companies.[793]

A genuine alignment between the policy objectives behind the CIT and the tax residence tests would bring significant advantages. First of all, residence tests will become instrumental in reaching the policy objectives pursued by the State by means of its CIT and will thus greatly contribute to achieve them. Second, States will be at last willing to accept the logical outcomes of their respective residence tests, as they will be perfectly consistent with what they expect for their CITs. Therefore, the problem identified in Chapter 3 section §3.02[A][2][c] is likely to be finally overcome, as States will certainly be far less inclined to resort to anti-avoidance measures to correct the outcomes of their own tests.

In a nutshell, what we advocate for is to stop adopting traditional residence tests by inertia and instead conceive a test or a set of tests that departs from the specific policy purposes pursued by each State by means of its CIT, whatever these policy purposes are. This way, corporate tax residence would serve as an instrument to support the policies underlying CITs.[794]

---

such managerial abuses of power." *See* Avi-Yonah, R. (2007b), p. 383 and, in the same vein, Avi-Yonah, R. (2004) and Marian, O. (2013b), p. 477.

790. *See* Chapter 3 section §3.02[A][1][c] (in particular the "rationale behind them" part). Kleinbard stated that "the strongest justification for the existence of a corporate income tax is that it serves as a substitute for the imposition of current tax on the firm's owners." *See* Kleinbard, E.D. (2012b), p. 684, Auerbach, A. J. (2006), Bank, S.A. (2007), p. 393, Marian, O. (2013), p. 1628 and Marian, O. (2013b), pp. 474 and 477. In this latter article, Marian states that "assuming that corporate taxation is intended to reach shareholders' pockets, the logical functional residence test is a residence-of-majority-of-shareholders rule."

791. *See* Chapter 3 section §3.02[A][1][d] (in particular the "rationale behind them" part) and Antonini, M. (2008), p. 153.

792. Marian, O. (2013b), p. 479: "Liquidity provides a significant benefit, and corporate tax can be justified as a fee on liquidity."

793. Marian, O. (2013b), pp. 478-479: "In the absence of corporate-level tax, a corporate manager who also holds equity in the corporation is likely to prefer her own tax interest when making corporate-level decisions that shareholder-level tax consequences. Once a tax is imposed at the entity level, it creates alignment of interests, because managers and shareholders alike have an interest in reducing entity-level tax, regardless of their individual tax interests."

794. This is the objective pursued by scholars as Marian and Loomer. *See* Marian, O. (2013b) and Loomer, G.T. (2015).

[2] The Appropriateness of Abandoning Residence Tests That Merely Require a Weak Connection Between the Company and the State

For the purposes of this section, tests that do not demand a truly close connection between the company and the State concerned will be labeled as weak residence tests. This is particularly the case for the formal tests analyzed in Chapter 3 section §3.02[A][1][a], as the POI (the incorporation of a company in accordance with the domestic legislation of such jurisdiction), the registered office or the legal/statutory seat (as indicated in the bylaws of the company). However, some of the considerations presented here will similarly apply—to some extent—to the tests based on the place where the company is ultimately run (Chapter 3 section §3.02[A][1][b]).

From our perspective, the only valid argument to support the subsistence of a formal test as the POI would be the fact that the State in question regards its CIT as a "fee" for the benefits derived from the incorporation (the granting of limited liability, the transferability of interests, the centralization of management, etc.) in line with the arguments exposed in the previous section. Still, the prize for the scarce benefits that incorporation entails would seem disproportional at first sight, as the residence status generally triggers an unlimited tax liability on the worldwide income of the company.

Beyond the policy considerations that could eventually uphold the subsistence of these tests, there are compelling reasons not to maintain tests that do not require a substantial, genuine and sufficient connection between the corporate taxpayer and the State concerned. Such a policy option will be desirable from the two different perspectives that will be exposed below.

[a] A Better Alignment with the Presumptive Benefit Principle

An assessment of current corporate tax residence tests from the perspective of the presumptive benefit principle should lead us to reject all tests that become instrumental in detaching taxable profits from the jurisdictions where the relevant economic activities take place or the market of customers is (just as this principle would demand)[795] and instead book them in the jurisdiction of choice.

We already evaluated the profit shifting risks that each category of tests poses in Chapter 3 section §3.02[A][1].[796] We then reached the conclusion that two categories were particularly troublesome in this regard: formal tests and those relying on the place where the company is run. This is so for two main reasons.

First, both sets of tests rely on factors that are within the direct control of the taxpayer, so they enable him to basically select the jurisdiction in which it wishes to be tax resident irrespective of the place(s) where its real ties are. One may think at first glance that formal tests pose greater risks than substantive tests as the POEM, but this is not necessarily true. The truth is that companies may establish their board meetings in the jurisdiction of their choice and, what is more, they are free to transfer it

795. According to the role we proposed for this principle back in Chapter 2 section §2.02.
796. *See* Chapter 3 section §3.02[A][1] (in particular the "potential profit shifting risks they pose" part).

somewhere else at a later point. As we warned back in Chapter 3 section §3.02[A], jurisdictions relying on these tests should be prepared to accept that any genuine transfer of managerial functions would effectively cause the end of the residence status in their country. Therefore, as long as the jurisdictions concerned follow this sort of tests, companies may easily capture the tax residence status wherever they wish, either from its inception or at a later point in their life.

Second, both categories of tests rely on factors that bear no relation whatsoever to the place where the company is carrying out its economic activities or else has its market of customers.[797] The fact that the company conducts its physical economic activities or has its market in the same jurisdiction where it was incorporated, keeps its registered office or where its board of directors meets would be purely coincidental. As a result, the residence State of the company may not necessarily be the State providing the greatest part of the public services from which the company is benefiting.

For all the reasons outlined above, we believe that the progressive abandonment of both sets of tests may contribute to ameliorate the opportunities for profit shifting risks. Thus, such a decision would be welcome as a positive step towards a greater consistency between corporate residence tests and the presumptive benefit principle according to the considerations exposed in Chapter 2 section §2.02.

Although our claim seems to be sufficiently substantiated, it is true that neither the OECD nor any other international organization has traditionally got involved in the decision of the jurisdictions regarding their corporate residence tests.[798] In fact, when analyzing the causes allowing BEPS to happen, the OECD/G20 chose not to evaluate the role played by corporate tax residence tests, despite its evident contribution to the phenomenon. In this respect, the BEPS Monitoring Group expressly pointed out the profit shifting risks that both sorts of tests tend to pose,[799] requesting the OECD to revise these tests and suggest and standardization.

---

797. In Chapter 3 section §3.02[A][2][c] we noted that most residence tests, by their own nature, do not specifically require an economic attachment between the company and the country concerned.
798. Loomer, G. (2015), p. 99: "The OECD says very little about corporate residence formulations or their potential for exploitation (...) In my view, corporate residence is one matter that should be addressed, not least because it underlies many of the avoidance strategies and necessary responses that the OECD has identified." The only exception to this trend may be found in the report on Harmful tax competition, where the OECD called for a revision of the corporate residence rules to "better address harmful tax competition." It then suggested extending the domestic definition of corporate residence to cover companies incorporated abroad but effectively controlled by domestic taxpayers. In a nutshell, the OECD advocated for the adoption of corporate residence tests based on the residence of the shareholders (a category analyzed in Chapter 3 section §3.02[A][1][c]) *in lieu* of international transparency regimes as the CFC rules, even though both approaches produce similar outcomes. *See* OECD (1998): Harmful tax competition: an emerging global issue, p. 60.
799. *See* https://bepsmonitoringgroup.files.wordpress.com/2015/02/ap5-htps-modified-substance.pdf (last accessed on January 10, 2019): "For those jurisdictions that include one or more forms of management and control within their residency definition, it is fair to say that the combination of taxpayers' abilities to factually control where they take various corporate actions, and the difficulty for tax authorities to look for and identify indices of management and control for companies organized elsewhere, means that many companies established in convenient jurisdictions can practically escape residency in any country where they might have operations or from which their operations are directed (...) For those jurisdictions that use

[b] *Mitigation of Treaty Shopping Risks*

Residence tests that do not demand a close link to the State are equally prone to pose problems from a "treaty shopping" perspective. As we know, Article 1 of the MCs makes the application of the tax treaty to a taxpayer subject to its condition of tax resident of one of the Contracting States. However, jurisdictions observe that taxpayers that formally comply with domestic tax residence rules may be entitled to treaty benefits in circumstances in which they are not sufficiently attached to their Residence State. As we warned back in Chapter 3 section §3.02[C][3], this was the direct consequence of the weakness of most residence tests.

Consequently, a progressive abandonment of "weak" corporate residence tests along with a greater reliance on "strong" tests would lead to diminish the opportunities for treaty shopping and the dependency on anti-treaty shopping measures as the LOB clauses.[800]

[3] *The Convenience of Adopting Corporate Tax Residence Tests That Are Strong and Aligned with the Presumptive Benefit Principle*

In the previous section we advocated for the progressive abandonment of "weak" corporate residence tests (primarily those relying on formal criteria). Such decision should be however accompanied by the adoption of corporate tax residence tests that, by contrast, ensure a substantive, genuine and sufficient connection between the corporate taxpayer and the State concerned. It goes without saying that, as a general rule, "strong" corporate residence tests would effectively overcome the risks that "weak" tests tend to pose, particularly those we identified in the previous section.

First, tests requiring a sufficient connection would be less prone to give rise to profit shifting risks. Typically, these tests tend to rely on factors that reveal a profound, enduring and deeply rooted connection between the company and the jurisdiction concerned. These factors are normally beyond the direct control of the taxpayer, but even if they were under its control, they would rarely be susceptible to overnight alterations and manipulations.

Second, as long as residence tests demand a close, long-standing relationship between the company and the territory concerned, treaty shopping opportunities would tend to diminish and, by extension, measures to counteract them would be less and less necessary.

Naturally, the biggest challenge is how to define such connection and, above all, how to translate it into an efficient and easy to administer rule.

---

solely the place of incorporation to establish residency (most notably the U.S.), multinationals have blatantly conducted significant operations through tax haven subsidiaries while openly managing those operations from within the U.S."

800. Wheeler, J.C. (2011), p. 294: "In the current treaty framework the policy clash in respect of the place of incorporation as a connecting factor has led to the adoption of limitation-on-benefits provisions in an increasing number of treaties."

Throughout the present thesis we have advocated for the use of the presumptive benefit principle as a guiding principle for rules identifying the taxpayers that would become subject to a State's tax jurisdiction, corporate tax residence tests among them.[801] This way, residence tests would contribute to place tax bases wherever the corporate taxpayer is presumably benefiting from the local services and infrastructures defrayed by the State concerned and thus serve to compensate for the economic effort made by such State. A presumption may be made wherever the corporate taxpayer carries out physical economic activities or else accesses a market of customers of a State.[802]

The following section intends to reveal that the presumptive benefit principle already inspires the vast majority of residence tests in place in PITs while the subsequent section intends to put forward a number of suggestions for a new corporate tax residence that is indeed aligned with this principle.

[a] The Valuable Precedent of Personal Residence Tests

The search of the origins of the notion of corporate tax residence brings us directly to personal income taxation, as CITs borrowed from PITs some of their structural principles. By the time income taxation extended its scope to companies, these inherited from individuals the ability to "reside" in a certain jurisdiction for tax purposes.[803] However, we should depart from an undeniable fact: companies are mere legal fictions and, contrary to individuals, do not reside anywhere. The residence of individuals is an inherent aspect of its nature and may be deduced from its own circumstances: it is the place where the person develops his/her life, where he/she ordinarily lives, works and sleeps. Naturally, the same cannot be said about companies. In the words of Huddlestone B.: "the use of the word residence is upon the habits of a natural man and is therefore inapplicable to the artificial and legal person whom we call a corporation."[804]

As a consequence of this fact, jurisdictions face the challenge of conceiving an artificial notion of residence that could be assigned to these artificial persons for the purposes of applying their income tax systems to them.[805] This way, every time a company fulfills the requirements set in the corporate residence test, it would automatically be deemed to "reside" within the frontiers of the State concerned and,

801. Chapter 2 section §2.02.
802. Chapter 2 section §2.02[B][2].
803. The example of the UK explained in Chapter 3 section §3.02[A][1] is particularly illustrative. British courts were asked to apply the British Income Tax Act (designed for individuals) to corporations long before the introduction of a statutory corporate tax residence test in 1988. In the meantime, they had no other option but to force the application of the notion of "residence" to corporations. *See* Couzin, R. (2002), pp. 28-33 and Loomer, G.T. (2015), p. 102.
804. Judgment by the UK High Court (Exchequer Division), 1876, "The Cesena Sulphur Co Ltd v. Nicholson" and "The Calcutta Jute Mills Co Ltd v. Nicholson."
805. In the same vein, *see* Kleinbard, E.D. (2012), p. 517: "Because a corporation in the first instance exists only as a legal construct, not a natural one, the concept (of residence) piles one false analogy on top of another."

consequently, it would find its worldwide income subject to tax therein, just as it occurs with individuals.

The exercise of extrapolating the notion of residence from individuals to companies is certainly tricky. The process is aptly described by Graetz as "an effort to put flesh into fiction," an attempt to "find economic and political substance in a world occupied by legal niceties."[806] The reason is that companies do not only not reside anywhere: they may develop deep bonds with different jurisdictions simultaneously and thus be present in different territories at a time.[807] In this context, defining a nexus between a company and a territory that is analogous to the level of connection that an individual maintains with the territory where he resides constitutes a major challenge.

We intend to take up the challenge of extrapolating the notion of tax residence from individuals to companies, but to do so we will depart from the analysis of personal tax residence tests and, most notably, the principles underlying them. We will begin by analyzing the most widespread tax residence tests for individuals thanks to the comparative study conducted by the OECD on seventy-eight different jurisdictions.[808] Once this evaluation is over, we will proceed to infer the principle(s) that supposedly underlie these tests. After that, we will question current corporate residence tests in the light of such principle(s) and we will try to derive a few practical guidelines that may be useful to rethink and (eventually) redefine such tests.

The analysis of the most widespread residence tests leads us to distinguish between two broad categories: substantive and formal ones.

The vast majority of tests can be regarded as "substantive," as they tend to reflect a present close relationship between the person and the State concerned, either stable or temporary. They may be classified in four different subcategories:

- Physical presence. 92% of the countries reviewed follow purely quantitative residence tests that rely on the number of days that the taxpayer physically spends within the territory of the country concerned at a given period of time.[809] The time threshold is almost invariably set to 183 days or 6 months within a 12-months period.[810] However, a small number of countries demand either a shorter[811] or a longer[812] period of physical presence.

806. Graetz, M.J. (2001), p. 320.
807. Avi-Yonah, R. (1997), p. 520: "multinationals are not part of a single society and their income does not belong to any particular society for distributive purposes" and Zornoza Pérez, J. (2013), p. 7.
808. http://www.oecd.org/tax/automatic-exchange/crs-implementation-and-assistance/tax-residency (last accessed to data on January 10, 2019). Another comparative study of the residence tests in place in twelve countries may be consulted in Nikolakakis, A. (2010), pp. 75-83.
809. Seventy out of the seventy-eight countries reviewed.
810. Although Turkey finds itself in this group, the rule does not apply in cases in which the person's stay exceeds a period of 183 days as a consequence of a professional mission (scientists, businessmen, specialists, press), medical treatment, studies, rest, travel, detention, conviction or illness.
811. This is, for example, the case for Switzerland (thirty days in case the taxpayer participates in a gainful activity and 90 days in the remaining cases), South Africa (91), Isle of Man and Jersey (visits exceeding an average of 90 days in a period of 4 years), US (183 days in 3 years' time), Chile (183 days in 2 years' time), Faroe Islands (180), Hong Kong (180), India (182), Azerbaijan (182), Norway (270 days in 3 years' time), Israel (425 days in 3 years' time) and Ireland (280

- Availability of a dwelling that is habitually and/or currently in use with or without the need to demonstrate the intention to keep using it in the future. 46% of the surveyed countries grant the resident status to the individuals that have their home,[813] dwelling,[814] principal or habitual abode,[815] domicile[816] or residence[817] within the territory of the State. All these tests seem to require, either explicitly or tacitly, an actual use of the dwelling during the corresponding tax period[818] or, at least, the intention to return to it in the near future.
- Center of vital interests. 39% of the surveyed countries grant the residence status to persons that are regarded as sufficiently attached to them by reason of their economic, personal and/or social circumstances.[819] Most tests seek a balance between the different spheres of life of the individual, but a few of them only regard either the economic[820] or the personal[821] connections with

days in 2 years' time). Some of these jurisdictions, however, complement these tests (most notably the "look back" ones) with a 183-days rule. Strangely enough, Isle of Man grants the tax resident status to any person who reside therein for 183 days in a year time but also to those who have the "intention" to visit the country for more than 90 days per year on average, irrespective of the fact that they eventually do so.

812. Only Argentina, China, Japan require a longer period of time, as all three countries establish a twelve-months threshold.

813. Czech Republic (permanent home and intention to permanently stay at it), Faroe Islands, Mexico, Portugal (home with the intention to occupy it as the taxpayer's permanent residence, the rule does not explicitly demand its effective use but it does require the physical presence in Portugal for a period of time) and South Africa (the taxpayer has his/her "real" home in the country, in the sense that he/she will, naturally and as a matter of course, return to it after his/her wanderings).

814. Germany (indicia that the taxpayer maintains and uses the dwelling).

815. Austria, Canada ("where the individual regularly, normally or customarily lives in the usual mode of life"), Croatia ("place in which the taxpayer stays under circumstances based on which it may be concluded that he does not reside in that place only temporarily"), Finland, France ("main place of abode"), Greece, Italy ("habitual abode"), Japan ("where he ordinarily resides"), Lithuania, Luxembourg, Malta, New Zealand ("permanent place of abode"), San Marino and Slovenia.

816. Domicile is interpreted differently depending on the country: Austria (having a dwelling under circumstances that show that the taxpayer will keep and use the dwelling), Chile (current residency in Chile and the intention to keep it, as deduced from the taxpayer's activities and relationships), Belgium (having the actual residence or living quarters located in Belgium), China (habitual residence on account of domiciliary registration, family ties or economic interests), Luxembourg (permanent home available to the person that he uses and intends to maintain) and Switzerland (place where the person currently lives with the intention of staying permanently). For Luxembourg *see* https://www2.deloitte.com/content/dam/Deloitte/lu/Documents/tax/lu-en-wp-essentialguideindividuals-18062014.pdf (last accessed on January 10, 2019).

817. Croatia (habitual residence), Hungary (permanent residence) and Liechtenstein (person resides in a place at Liechtenstein with the intention of staying there permanently).

818. For example, in the case of Azerbaijan, the "normal residence test" only applies wherever the individual effectively uses their residence but his/her stay in the country does not exceed 182 days during the taxable year.

819. The most common factors that are taken into account the residence of the family members, the place of work and the location of the property or assets. Occasionally, tests make reference to other minor indicators as the place of birth (e.g., Malta), where the taxpayer attends the doctor, where his/her kids' school is (Curaçao) or where he/she has his/her insurance (e.g., Netherlands).

820. A third of the countries following this sort of test only regard the economic ties the taxpayer has with the territory concerned, irrespective of its personal circumstances. This is the case for

the State concerned irrespective of the other. These tests are of a purely qualitative nature, granting the resident status to persons that maintain close ties to the State. Even though they do not demand a minimum physical presence in the State concerned,[822] one could expect that the taxpayer makes frequent visits (despite not complying with a minimum time threshold at the moment the test is applied) or will return to the State in the near future as a consequence of the close ties that link him to it.

- Public employment. At least 18% of the surveyed countries[823] confer the tax resident status to the individuals (sometimes only nationals) employed by the government of the country regardless of the fact that they may be temporarily or permanently residing abroad, as it may be the case of diplomatic, consular, government and military personnel. Just as in the previous case, these tests do not demand a minimum period of physical presence but still allow us to assume that the taxpayer is likely to visit or eventually return to the territory of the country for which he works. Furthermore, in the cases of diplomats and consuls, if the taxpayer was also treated as tax resident in the State where he actually works and lives, tax treaties following the OECD MC would only regard the employer State as its Resident State for the purposes of the treaty.[824]

On the other hand, formal tests merely rely on factors that do not reveal a present nor a strong relationship with the State concerned.[825] In most cases, these tests operate as "deeming provisions," meaning that they do not automatically grant the tax resident status in all circumstances but instead establish a legal presumption that that may be rebutted in case the taxpayer do not effectively reside in the country or is not sufficiently attached to it (in the sense that he is not expected to make frequent visits

Andorra, Belgium (seat of wealth), Brazil (hired by a resident company), France (carrying on a professional activity therein, salaried or not), Italy (principal place of business), Mexico (deriving more than 50% of the income from its territory or having its main center of professional activities therein), Slovenia (location of the property and financial/economic interests) and Spain (main center of economic activities and interests).

821. Only Switzerland limits itself to the assessment of facts that pertain to the personal life of the taxpayer, as their personal relationships, the place where he spends its non-working hours, where he fosters friendships and family ties and where they take part in the social life of the community. On the other hand, the place of work is not considered as a relevant factor for the purposes of this rule.

822. In fact, the Italian test expressly states that an individual will be considered as Italian resident to the extent it has his/her place of business or interests therein irrespective of its effective presence within the Italian territory.

823. This is for example the case for Canada, Croatia, Denmark, Greece, Latvia, Lithuania, Portugal and Turkey among others, although we have reasons to believe that the number of countries is much greater than what the OECD survey suggests.

824. The reason is that Article 4.1 of the OECD MC denies residence under the treaty to taxpayers that are only liable to tax on income from sources in that country, and diplomats/consuls have their official salary and offshore income exempt in the receiving State under Article 34 of the Vienna Convention on Diplomatic Relations (1961) and Article 49 of the Vienna Convention on Consular Relations (1963), while Article 28 of the OECD MC respects the fiscal privileges granted by International Law to these collectives. *See* Dirkis, M. (2010), pp. 149-150.

825. Nikolakakis, A. (2010), p. 76: "civil law countries do tend to rely more than common law countries on certain somewhat formalistic conceptions of residence."

or return soon).[826] Only occasionally, these tests will grant the tax resident status to the individual straightaway regardless of his/her present circumstances. As a consequence, we will only regard as purely "formal" the tests that fall under the scope of this latter type, as they assign the tax resident status on the sole basis of a formal attachment to the State concerned, regardless of the fact that the taxpayer may well be physically present and/or have stronger personal/economic ties with any other State. These are the four subcategories of formal tests:

- Domicile without demanding its actual use. 11% of the surveyed countries make use of tests that require the existence of a dwelling or domicile within the territory of the State concerned without requiring, either explicitly or tacitly, the taxpayer to effectively use it.[827]
- Nationality. Only four States (representing just a 5% of the surveyed ones) automatically confer the tax residence status to its citizens regardless their present circumstances and the territory where they ordinarily live.[828] The most paradigmatic example may be found in the US legislation. For its part, the Hungarian rule uses an "escape clause" according to which dual citizens without a permanent or habitual residence in Hungary will not be regarded as residents for tax purposes therein. Azerbaijan only resorts to this test in a subsidiary manner in cases where the length of the stay of the individual in its

826. We will now enumerate and briefly comment the "deeming provisions" we observed in the OECD survey:

(i) Domicile. The tests in force in Australia, Mauritius and Seychelles grant the resident status to individuals having their domicile in their territories unless they have their "permanent place of abode" outside the country.

(ii) Personal and domicile registration. Belgium confers the tax residency to any individual listed in the National Registry of Individuals "unless evidence to the contrary con be provided."

(iii) i) Nationality. There are three countries that depart from the presumption that their nationals are tax residents but allow evidence to the contrary. For example, Argentine citizens lose their resident status when they become permanent residents in the foreign country or when they stay uninterruptedly in a foreign country for at least twelve months. On the other hand, Colombian citizens will only be treated as tax residents to the extent further substantive requirements are met (e.g., underage children resident in Colombia, 50% of the income sourced in Colombia, 50% of the assets administered in Colombia, etc.). Finally, Finland establishes that Finnish citizens who leave the country and its main abode therein will continue to be treated as tax residents for three more years unless there is evidence that they do not maintain substantial ties with Finland any more.

827. This is the case for Croatia (the taxpayer must own or have "in his/her possession" an apartment for at least 183 days in one or two calendar years, but the actual use of the apartment is not required), Jersey (the taxpayer maintains a "place of abode" in Jersey although he merely needs to stay therein for one night per year), Slovak Republic (the taxpayer must have a "permanent address" in the country) and the UK (the assessment of the UK domicile often requires the consideration of a person's life story and long-term intentions rather than his/her actual stay in the country). For their part, Greenland, Romania and Turkey require the presence of a "domicile" in the State without expressly requiring the taxpayer to effectively use it. The meaning of "domicile" for UK tax purposes is explained in: Lemos, M. (2010), p. 611.

828. This is the case for Azerbaijan, Hungary, the United Arab Emirates and the US.

territory does not exceed 182 days and other tests (as normal residence or vital interests) do not apply.

- Personal or domicile registration. For their part, 4% of the surveyed countries grant the tax resident status to individuals that are either registered as inhabitants or have an address registered in a public registry of the State concerned. The rule would apply irrespective of any other considerations of a substantive nature.[829]
- Reliance on other formal documents. For example, Brazil treats any individual with a Brazilian permanent visa as resident for income tax purposes without explicitly requiring the taxpayer to be physically present or at least have a dwelling available for him in the country, while the United Arab Emirates treats non-national individuals with a valid Emirates ID and a valid Residency Visa as tax residents in their country (Table 4).

829. This is the case for Italy (individuals registered in the municipal population registry for a certain period of time will be deemed to be residents in Italy), Latvia (individuals having the registered place of residence in Latvia) and San Marino (its test demands a registered residency in San Marino for most of the tax period).

Table 4 Criteria Used by Seventy-Eight Jurisdictions to Establish Personal Tax Residence in Their Respective Domestic Legislations (2019)[830]

	Substantive Tests				*Formal Tests*			
	Physical Presence	*Habit. Abode/ Home in Use*	*Vital Interests*	*Public Employm.*	*Domicile/House Not Requiring Use*	*Registration*	*Nationality*	*Other*
Andorra	X		X (E)					
Argentina	X (*)							
Aruba			X					
Australia	X		X		RP			
Austria		X						
Azerbaijan	X (*)	X	X	X			X	
Belgium		X	X (E)			RP		
Belize	X	X						
Brazil	X		X (E)					X
Brunei	X							
Bulgaria	X		X					
Canada	X	X	X	X				
Chile	X (*)	X						

830. The source of the information belongs to the OECD (*see* http://www.oecd.org/tax/automatic-exchange/crs-implementation-and-assistance/tax-residency, last accessed to data on January 10, 2019). Physical presence tests requiring a period shorter or longer than 183 days are marked with an (*). Vital interests' tests that focus on economic links are marked with an (E) and those focusing on personal ones with a (P). Boxes marked with a (RP) mean that the rule operates as a mere rebuttable presumption.

	Substantive Tests				*Formal Tests*			
	Physical Presence	*Habit. Abode/ Home in Use*	*Vital Interests*	*Public Employm.*	*Domicile/House Not Requiring Use*	*Registration*	*Nationality*	*Other*
China	X (*)	X	X					
Colombia	X				RP			
Cook Islands	X				X			
Costa Rica	X							
Croatia		X		X	X			
Curaçao	X	X	X					
Cyprus	X							
Czech Republic	X	X						
Denmark	X			X				
Estonia	X							
Faroe Islands	X (*)	X						
Finland	X	X						
France		X	X (E)					
Germany	X	X						
Gibraltar	X							
Greece	X	X	X	X				
Greenland	X				X			
Hong Kong	X (*)	X		X				
Hungary	X	X	X	X			X	

	Substantive Tests				*Formal Tests*			
	Physical Presence	*Habit. Abode/ Home in Use*	*Vital Interests*	*Public Employm.*	*Domicile/House Not Requiring Use*	*Registration*	*Nationality*	*Other*
Iceland	X							
India	X (*)							
Indonesia	X							
Ireland	X (*)							
Isle of Man	X (*)							
Israel	X (*)		X					
Italy		X	X (E)			X		
Japan	X (*)		X					
Jersey	X (*)				X			
Korea	X		X					
Latvia	X			X		X		
Lebanon	X	X	X					
Liechtenstein	X	X						
Lithuania	X	X		X				
Luxembourg	X	X						
Malaysia	X							
Malta	X	X	X					
Mauritius	X				RP			
Mexico		X	X (E)					

	Substantive Tests				*Formal Tests*			
	Physical Presence	*Habit. Abode/ Home in Use*	*Vital Interests*	*Public Employm.*	*Domicile/House Not Requiring Use*	*Registration*	*Nationality*	*Other*
Monstserrat	X	X						
Netherlands	X		X					
New Zealand	X	X						
Norway	X (*)							
Poland	X		X					
Portugal	X	X		X				
Romania	X		X	X	X			
Russia	X							
Saint Lucia	X							
Saint Vincent	X	X						
Samoa	X	X		X				
San Marino	X	X	X			X		
Saudi Arabia	X	X						
Seychelles	X	X			RP			
Singapore	X							
Slovak Republic	X				X			
Slovenia	X	X	X (E)					
South Africa	X (*)	X						
Spain	X		X (E)	X				

	Substantive Tests				Formal Tests			
	Physical Presence	*Habit. Abode/ Home in Use*	*Vital Interests*	*Public Employm.*	*Domicile/House Not Requiring Use*	*Registration*	*Nationality*	*Other*
Sweden	X		X					
Switzerland	X (*)	X	X (P)					
Trinidad & Tobago	X							
Turkey	X			X	X			
United Arab Emirates							X	X
United Kingdom	X		X		X			
United States	X (*)						X	
Uruguay	X		X					
TOTAL	70	35	30	14	8	3	4	2
78 States	92%	46%	39%	18%	11%	4%	5%	3%

Once the most common tests have been analyzed and classified, we will try to draw some preliminary conclusions:

(1) All States, without exception, rely on "substantive" tests. What is more, 80% of the surveyed countries solely use this sort of tests:[831] either one of them[832] or a combination of two or three. On the other hand, there is no single country that follows solely purely formal tests.[833] The remaining 20% combine both sorts of tests.[834]

(2) What the substantive tests have in common is that the fulfillment of their requirements normally reveals the effective presence of the taxpayer in the territory or, at least, allows us to assume his/her frequent visits and/or his/her imminent return to the country concerned after a temporary absence (the habitual abode, center of vital interests and public employment tests).[835] In any case, they all require an ongoing substantial and intimate relation between the individual and the State concerned, in a way that one could assume that, during the period concerned, the person finds himself/herself in a position to effectively benefit from the relevant public goods and services provided by the State, just as the presumptive benefit principle would require.[836] This is particularly evident in the case of an individual spending the greater part of the taxable year in the territory of the State.[837] But it also holds true, although to a lesser extent, for individuals who do not meet the minimum physical presence threshold but either keep their family, social relations, job, habitual abode and/or other important properties in the territory of the State or work as public servants for such State. In these latter

831. Sometimes such tests may be accompanied by formal tests that operate as "deeming provisions." This is the case for Australia or Colombia.

832. For example, Argentina, Colombia, Costa Rica, Estonia, Iceland, India, Isle of Man, Norway and Singapore only use physical presence tests, while countries as Austria and Belgium only use the "habitual abode" test.

833. United Arab Emirates is the only doubtful case. It confers the residence status to nationals but also to non-nationals who "reside" in its territory with a valid local ID and visa. In the latter scenario, individuals are required to "reside" in its territory to be regarded as tax residents, so their stay in the Emirates should be effective and present in the tax year concerned. However, such effective residence does not need to express itself by means of the fulfillment of any of the substantive tests here under review (e.g., 183-days rule, center of vital interests, etc.).

834. Countries following purely formal tests (Brazil, Croatia, Greenland, Italy, Jersey, Latvia, Luxembourg, San Marino, Slovak Republic, Turkey and the US, for example) always accompany them with substantial tests.

835. Nikolakakis believes that most conceptions of residence that are currently in use share a common feature: "they all tend to put the spotlight on elements of personal physical presence." While the physical presence tests do so directly, habitual abode and center of vital interests tend to cover certain gaps in physical presence and seek to cover situations involving physical presence in multiple locations. *See* Nikolakakis, A. (2010), p. 78.

836. *See* Chapter 2 section §2.02 and Decision by the King's Bench Division, 1904, "Goerz & Co v. Bell": "a person who is resident in the United Kingdom takes the benefit of the government of the country, of the security afforded to his life and liberty, and of the opportunity of conducting his business in the way in which the government of a settled and civilized country enables it to be conducted; he accordingly has to pay, like other inhabitants of the country, his full share towards the expenses of that government."

837. And therefore complying with the physical presence or the habitual abode tests.

cases, the taxpayer is still likely to make use of the public services of the State concerned either directly (as a result of his/her visits during the tax year concerned) or remotely. For example, diplomats or members of the military are generally entitled to benefits under their country's social program irrespective of its temporary or permanent absence. On the other hand, formal tests do not seem to have this conception in mind, as we cannot infer from them an effective enjoyment of benefits, neither remotely or directly. Naturally, the fact that the individual keeps an unused dwelling in the territory of the State, maintains his/her citizenship, is listed in a national or municipal registry or has visa does not per se imply that he would be in the position to effectively enjoy the public benefits granted by the State, at least in the tax year concerned. In fact, the most common and powerful argument against formal tests is precisely this one.[838]

(3) The combination of conclusions I and II leads us to make the next assertion: all States, without exception, have personal residence tests in place whose fulfillment allows us to assume that the tax resident finds himself/herself in a practical position to effectively benefit from the relevant public goods and services provided by the State, either directly (as a result of his/her actual physical presence or his/her frequent visits) or remotely.[839] In other words,

838. The US residence test based on the citizenship of the individual has been historically precisely on benefit grounds. This is because non-resident US citizens keep enjoying a number of benefits while being abroad, namely the right to vote in federal elections, travel on a US passport, pass on the US citizenship to their children born abroad, gain access to the US for certain noncitizen family members, re-enter the US at will, work in the US, receive personal and property protection from the US while abroad, apply for diplomatic and consular services and even request evacuation in emergencies. For further description of these benefits, *see* Kirsch, M.S. (2007), pp. 470-477 and Mason, R. (2015), p. 189. Even the US Supreme Court argued back in 1924 that "government by its very nature benefits the citizen and his property wherever found" (*see* judgment by the United States Supreme Court "Cook v. Tait" of May 5, 1924). However, this test is commonly regarded by the public opinion as undesirable, insufficient unjustifiable and anachronistic (*see* Von Bar, L. (1889), p. 319, Kemmeren, E.C.C.M. (2001), p. 21 and Christie, J.H. (1982), pp. 138 et seq. *inter alia*). But if we were to draw a principle underlying most attacks towards the nationality principle, we would surprisingly encounter the very same principle used by the Court to justify its existence: the benefit principle. There are three powerful counterarguments that equally rest on the benefit principle and yet call into question this weak rationale behind US citizenship taxation: (a) other States massively provide these same benefits to their non-resident nationals abroad and yet, do not conclude that access to such benefits justify on their own taxation on their worldwide income (Mason, R. (2015), pp. 191 and 193); (b) sometimes the US ask for the reimbursement of the costs (e.g., emergency evacuations) or charge a fee for providing it (e.g., passport renewal and departure assistance services), thus dismantling the justification for an additional (and extensive) income tax liability to compensate the US for the costs incurred in providing such benefits (*see* Kirsch, M.S. (2014), pp. 217-221 and Mason, R. (2015), p. 192); and (c) US citizens forgo a massive number of public benefits as they leave their country (e.g., use of public schools, roads, police and fire protection, many welfare programs (Mason, R. (2015), pp. 193-194 and Patton, B.L. (1975), pp. 699 et seq.).

839. Nikolakakis states that individual residence tests would only be "appropriate" to the extent they rely on proxies that allow us to assume that the individual concerned is in the position to enjoy the services and benefits provided by his/her Residence State. *Sensu contrario*, he states that "non-residents are either not entitled or not in a practical position to enjoy the same public benefits as residents." *See* Nikolakakis, A. (2010), pp. 81-83.

all States have personal residence tests that are perfectly consistent with the presumptive benefit principle pursuant to the considerations exposed back in Chapter 2 section §2.02. In a nutshell, the presumptive benefit principle seems to underlie the vast majority of the personal tax residence tests that are currently in place.[840]

While the presumptive benefit principle has clearly become the principle guiding personal tax residence tests, the same cannot be said of the corporate tax residence tests, just as Chapter 3 section §3.02[A] tried to demonstrate.[841] It appears that, in the adaptation of the notion of personal tax residence to corporate income taxation, the principle that theoretically inspired such notion (the presumptive benefit principle) has been completely neglected. The reason is that only one category of corporate residence tests (those relying on the location of the business activity of the company) may be regarded as consistent with such principle. This is perhaps best illustrated by the following revealing fact: while 100% of the States make use of personal residence tests according to which the (resulting) resident may find himself/herself in the position to use and enjoy the services provided by the State,[842] only 3% of the States do likewise in the context of corporate income taxation.[843]

840. Schön argues that the benefit principle does not only justify source-based taxation but also residence-based taxation, at least in the case of individuals, as "an individual taxpayer will also in his or her private life take advantage of some of the amenities provided for by government institutions (schooling, public security, cultural institutions, etc.)." *See* Schön, W. (2009), p. 75.

841. We will very briefly summarize the conclusions reached in this section in relation to each type of corporate residence test. As regards formal tests, it seems clear that the fact that a company was incorporated pursuant to the domestic legislation of a State or maintains its registered/statutory seat/office therein does not necessarily mean that the company has kept an ongoing relationship with such State and the enjoyment of its services is within its reach. As regards tests based on the governance of the company (e.g., POEM tests), a company whose board of directors regularly meet within the territory of one State in order to take the relevant decisions to run the company may not necessarily be in the position to access the benefits provided by such State. As regards the tests relying on the residence of the shareholders, the fact that the majority of the company's shareholders are residents for tax purposes in a particular State does not automatically put the company in the position to use and enjoy the public services provided by such State (only if we regard the shareholders behind the corporate veil as the ultimate taxpayers of CITs, we could reach the conclusion that the majority of them would be in fact in the position to enjoy the services provided by the State of Residence of the company they own as long, in turn, the residence tests according to which they are regarded as tax residents are consistent with the presumptive benefit principle). Lastly, only tests relying on the location of economic activities may be regarded as consistent with the presumptive benefit principle, although we will have the chance to further elaborate on this idea in the following section.

842. As we noted above, all surveyed countries without exception follow one or more of the so-called substantial personal tax residence tests.

843. *See* Table 1 in Chapter 3 section §3.02[A][1][e]. Only two States (Italy and Australia) follow this sort of tests.

[b] *Proposal for a Corporate Tax Residence Test Aligned with the Presumptive Benefit Principle*

In the previous section we confronted current corporate residence tests with the principle that supposedly underlie the vast majority of personal residence tests (the presumptive benefit principle). We reached the conclusion that only one category of corporate residence tests, namely those that grant the resident status to companies which carry on business activities within their territory, is consistent with this principle.

The objective of the present section is to analyze the advantages and disadvantages that the implementation of such tests in the domestic tax legislations may entail to further make a few suggestions. First, we will briefly make reference to the background in which they arose. Second, we will refer to the general advantages that the implementation of these tests may bring, particularly from the perspective of the policy considerations exposed in Chapter 2 section §2.02. Third, we will point out a few general challenges that this sort of tests tends to pose considering the experience in Italy and Australia. Fourth, we will put forward a few suggestions that could help to overcome the identified risks and challenges.

[i] Background

In the IFA general report on the fiscal residence of companies, Rivier raised the following question: where is a company's center of vital interest? Subsequently, he ventured to provide an answer to it: "(it) consists of a combination of elements which all contribute to its existence and smooth running: corporate status consented by the law of a State, management and administration, operational activity, running of the business, shareholders."[844] Naturally, there is no doubt that a company has its vital interests in the country where all these elements coexist. The problem comes when these elements are spread among different territories and different States are in the position to claim, on different grounds, that they are the State of Residence of a particular company.[845]

Tests granting the residence status to companies whose economic activities take place within the territory of the State concerned are rare[846] and relatively new. However, it was surprising to learn that the debate that resulted in the birth of the tests relying on the POEM (that took place in the British courts back in the second half of the nineteenth century) was on the verge of concluding that that the residence status should be conferred instead on the basis of the location of the economic activity. At this point we should go back to Chapter 3 section §3.02[A][1][b], where we explained that the UK courts faced a private international law rule according to which the UK had jurisdiction over persons dwelling or carrying on a business on the UK. The House of Lords concluded in *Cesena* that the rule referred to the place where "the real trade and

844. Rivier, J.-M- (1987), p. 74 and Loomer, G.T. (2015), p. 100.
845. Rivier, J.-M- (1987), p. 74.
846. Only Italy and Australia follow this category of tests. *See* Chapter 3 section §3.02[A][1][d].

business is carried on" or "le centre de l'enterprise."[847] Indeed, the House of Lords observed in its subsequent decisions that the term "resident" was exceedingly unsuited to describe a legal entity, as companies do not have to ability to reside at a certain place as individuals do.[848] In both *De Beers* and *Egyptian Delta*, the House of Lords concluded that the only possible way to extrapolate the notion of residence to companies was to look at the place where they were conducting their business.[849] However, and against all odds, the House of Lords finally concluded that this expression should be interpreted as the "place of intellectual control of the business,"[850] i.e., the place where the central management and control is found instead of the place where the productive operations take place.[851] For instance, Lord Loreburn stated in De Beers that "a company resides where its 'real' business is carried on and that the real business is carried on where the central management and control actually abides."[852]

We should however read these judgments in the context in which they arose. First of all, in the age of British colonialism (nineteenth and twentieth century), the approach taken helped the UK to retain its taxing rights on profits derived by companies controlled from the UK but operating offshore. As Loomer points out, the prevalence of "head and brain" over "hands and feet" was logically defensible, albeit not theoretically ideal in his opinion.[853] Second, the wording of the income tax regulations of that time did not permit the courts to equate residence with the notions of "trade" or "business" to the extent that this would have conflated residence-based and source-based taxation as understood at that time.[854]

847. Judgment by the High Court (Exchequer Division), 1876, "The Cesena Sulphur Co Ltd v. Nicholson" and "The Calcutta Jute Mills Co Ltd v. Nicholson."
848. Decision by the House of Lords of the United Kingdom, 1928, "Egyptian Delta Land and Investment Co. Ltd. V, Todd (Inspector of Taxes)," pp. 12-15.
849. Decision by the House of Lords of the United Kingdom, 1905, "De Beers Consolidated Mines Ltd. v. Howe (Surveyor of Taxes)", p. 458: "in applying the conception of residence to a company we ought, I think, to proceed as nearly as we can upon the analogy of an individual." Lord Loreburn recognized that companies do not eat or sleep at any place, but they do indeed "keep house and do business." Decision by the House of Lords of the United Kingdom, 1928, "Egyptian Delta Land and Investment Co. Ltd. V, Todd (Inspector of Taxes)," pp. 12-15: "the only analogy that is really possible between a natural person and a company is that of carrying on a business at a place."
850. Avery Jones, J.F. (2009), p. 129.
851. Huddlestone B. explained the reason behind the decision: "No doubt the manufacturing part was done in Italy, and the company might have found sulphur in another country, and carried on the manufacturing part of the business in that other country, but the administrative part were carried on at the place from which all the orders flowed, where officers and agents were appointed and recalled, where their powers were granted and revoked, where whatever money was sent was received, and where the dividends were declared and were payable" (Judgment by the High Court (Exchequer Division), 1876, "The Cesena Sulphur Co Ltd v. Nicholson" and "The Calcutta Jute Mills Co Ltd v. Nicholson," *see* excerpt in Avery Jones, J.F. (2009), p. 136) In the same vein, Lord Halsbury argued that, even though the company dealt with land, goods and clients in another country, "the person who governs the whole commercial adventure (and) makes the profits by his skill or industry, however distant may be the field of his adventure" is the manager (*See* Decision by the House of Lords of the United Kingdom, 1895, "San Paulo (Brazilian) Railway Company Limited v. Carter (Surveyor of Taxes)").
852. Decision by the House of Lords of the United Kingdom, 1905, "De Beers Consolidated Mines Ltd. v. Howe (Surveyor of Taxes)."
853. Loomer, G.T. (2015), p. 113.
854. Couzin, R. (2002), pp. 28-29.

Australia pioneered the implementation of a test of this nature back in 1936[855] and was later followed by Canada in 1961[856] and Italy in 1986.[857] Back in Chapter 3 section §3.02[A][1][d] we referred to the specific content and scope of the only two tests of this nature that remain in place, namely the Italian and the Australian rules. The experience in these States will undoubtedly help us to better identify the advantages and challenges that this sort of tests tends to pose to further make a proposal to this effect.

[ii] General Advantages

The potential adoption of residence tests relying on the location of the corporate business activity in the domestic legislations would pose notable advantages on many levels.

First and foremost, we analyzed back in Chapter 2 section §2.02 the principle we believe should inspire the rules that ultimately identify the taxpayers that would become subject to a State's tax jurisdiction, residence tests among them. From our point of view, this sort of residence tests would be perfectly consistent with the presumptive benefit principle due to the reasons we will now proceed to note.

In the first place, we concluded that the presumptive benefit principle should guide the identification of the members of the community that ought to contribute to the financial support of the government.[858] This being so, corporate tax residence tests should cover companies which find themselves in a position to (effectively or potentially) use and enjoy the State's services and infrastructures that are in fact susceptible to be used and enjoyed by them.[859]

The idea that corporate residence-based taxation should be inspired by the benefit principle is not entirely new. In fact, many scholars have actively advocated for it,[860]

855. Kashyap, A.; Shaflender, L. (2004), p. 189, footnote 2.
856. Canada amended its domestic legislation in 1961 to deem a company to be resident in Canada if it was incorporated in Canada and if it "carries on business" in Canada at any time of the year. This latter requirement was later removed in 1965. *See* Loomer, G.T. (2015), p. 107.
857. Apparently, Japan also used to have a test relying on the "principal place of business" but it no longer does. *See* Marian, O. (2013b), p. 473 (footnote 10).
858. Chapter 2 section §2.02[A].
859. Chapter 2 section §2.02[B]. Couzin suggests that residence tests should ideally require a strong connecting between the person and the State concerned, a connection that "warrants, indeed, demands a high level of contribution to the public finances." *See* Couzin, R. (2002), p. 2.
860. Couzin suggests that residence tests should ideally require a strong connecting between the person and the State concerned, a connection that "warrants, indeed, demands a high level of contribution to the public finances" (Couzin, R. (2002), p. 2). *See also* Mössner, M. (2006), p. 505 and Zornoza Pérez, J. (2013), p. 5, who share the idea that the unlimited taxation of residents is better justified by the benefit principle, taking into account the actual or potential benefits that the taxpayers attain from government-supplied goods and services. In the same vein, Musgrave argues that the home country's taxation of worldwide income may be justified by the benefit theory "as a payment for productivity enhancing benefits provided by the country of residence to its own factors of production prior to transfer abroad" (Musgrave, P.B. (1997), p. 450). For his part, Loomer understands that residence-based taxation can only be justified as "a sort of residual home source (...) if it represents a substantial economic interest in the home State." *See* Loomer, G.T. (2015), p. 95 and Loomer, G.T. (2011), Chapters 2 and 3

although they do not seem to agree on how best this could be achieved.[861] Surprisingly, the OECD itself, despite its well-known neutral position towards the configuration of domestic tax residence tests, literally stated back in 2001 that "it could be argued that if the State provides certain facilities and infrastructure for its residents, those who benefit most from such facilities and infrastructure ought to contribute to the State via residence-based taxes."[862]

In our opinion, residence tests ought to rely on certain *indicia* or factors whose presence in the territory concerned is visible and easily ascertainable and further allows us to assume that the company complying with those factors is in fact in the aforementioned position. We concluded back in Chapter 2 section §2.02 that we could only assume that a company would only find itself in such position to the extent that it is effectively carrying on a physical economic activity within the borders of the State concerned or else has a market of customers therein.[863] Accordingly, only this sort of tests would be consistent with the presumptive benefit principle[864] (in line with the vast majority of personal residence tests), as they are the only ones that effectively contribute to bring the taxable bases wherever the economic activities take place.[865]

Beyond their consistency with the presumptive benefit principle, we believe that these tests would be appropriate and desirable from other perspectives.

(his thesis). For his part, Brown departs from the general assumption that the State of residence provides public benefits to its taxpayers (e.g., a legal system that governs its rights and obligation, a court system, military protection and agencies that are responsible for relationships with other nations, etc.,) even though he does not refer to specific residence tests that may guarantee this outcome, contrary to what this thesis intends to do. *See* Brown, F.B. (2011), p. 611. On the contrary, other authors do not agree on the premise that residence-based taxation should be inspired by the benefit principle. For example, Bird believes that companies should however pay taxes in accordance with the public benefits they have access to by means of "user charges" of a local character and a low rate and, at the most, a small registration fee in consideration for the benefits that incorporation entails (e.g., limited liability, perpetual life, easy transfer of ownership, access to capital markets, etc.). *See* Bird, R.M. (2002), pp. 196-197.

861. Couzin, who departs from the benefit rationale, puts forward several alternatives. First, the adoption of tests relying on the location of the main business operations but also tests relying on the governance of the company, particularly those that refer to the effective management (rather than strategic one). Second, the strengthening of source-based taxation at the expense of residence-based taxation. *See* Couzin, R. (2002), pp. 262-263 and 268-269. For his part, Loomer advocates for "a test or a series of tests that focuses on where the practical, daily management or principal business operations exist (...) or where the real centre of management is situated." *See* Loomer, G.T. (2015), p. 132. Marian believes that all substantive tests (including POEM and tests relying on the location of employees and assets) serve the benefit rationale. *See* Marian, O. (2013b), p. 473.

862. The OECD reaches this conclusion when discussing new tie-breaker rules in the context of Article 4.3 of the OECD MC. *See* OECD (2001): The impact of the communications revolution on the application of "place of effective management" as a tie breaker rule (Discussion Paper), p. 12.

863. Chapter 2 section §2.02[B][2].

864. In fact, when discussing the Italian residence tests, Antonini pointed out that "the ratio of this connecting factor is the fact is justified by the greater use of the economic, legal, finance and infrastructure resources of the State in which the activity is carried out." *See* Antonini, M. (2008), p. 153 and Chapter 3 section §3.02[A][1][d] (the "rationale behind them" part).

865. And therefore contribute to ameliorate the gap between the economic and the tax presence of the companies, a gap we illustrated by means of a real case in Chapter 2 section §2.01[A][1].

To begin with, these tests deserve to be labeled as "strong" insofar they demand a substantive, close and ongoing connection between the company and the State concerned. Therefore, they offer the advantages that are commonly inherent in any sort of strong tests, advantages that were already enumerated in the introduction of the section §4.02[B][3]. In short, they are unlikely to cause multiple residence (and double taxation) issues, profit shifting risks and treaty shopping opportunities.

Furthermore, Rust noted that the normative concept of residence should ideally be equitable, difficult to manipulate and administrable.[866] We believe that this sort of tests could easily comply with the first two conditions. As regards the first one, it is clear that these tests tend to produce fair outcomes for all reasons mentioned above. As regards the second, they would be difficult to manipulate insofar they cannot be easily given up in one country and established in another one[867] unlike other categories of tests (most notably, the formal ones). With respect to the third one, we will subsequently refer to the risks that these tests may pose in this regard and then proceed to make a few suggestions to minimize such risks.

[iii] Major Challenges

Despite the evident benefits that the adoption of this residence test would bring, it poses significant challenges and risks that should be taken into consideration and, when possible, minimized. Some of these challenges have already become visible in the States using these tests (Italy and Australia) while some others are merely intuitively foreseeable.

First, we will note the difficulties arising from the application and administration of the tests. Second, we will refer to their natural tendency to distort the taxpayer's behavior. And finally, we will highlight their troublesome coexistence with other rules, most notably residence tests based on the governance of the company and the PE threshold.

In the first place, we will proceed to discuss the issues related to the application and manageability of this sort of tests. Rust argues that a test would be administrable insofar it is easy to apply and furthermore the residence State disposes of the necessary information to assess the worldwide income of the taxpayer and is furthermore able to collect the tax revenue.[868] As regards the first question, the response would greatly depend on the specific wording of the test. Chapter 3 section §3.02[A][1][d] evidenced that the interpretation of the Italian and the Australian tests ("oggetto principale dell'attività" and "carries on business" respectively) was far from unambiguous, thereby granting the administrative and judiciary bodies a great power (and by extension a wide margin of discretion) to interpret the rule with the consequent high degree of legal uncertainty. Naturally, this problem could be minimized if the wording of the rule was more univocal. As regards the second question, we believe that the adoption of these tests should be necessarily accompanied by the imposition of formal

866. Rust, A. (2010), p. 85.
867. Rust, A. (2010), p. 86.
868. Rust, A. (2010), p. 86.

obligations, such as certain documentation requirements and disclosure obligations. This being so, the resulting residence State would have the necessary information entirely at its disposal.

As for the second aforementioned challenge, the domestic implementation of these tests would entail a hidden risk. By granting the residence status on these grounds, jurisdictions face the risk of distorting the taxpayer's economic behavior, as taxpayers may feel tempted to place their economic activities in certain territories for reasons other than purely business ones.[869] This being so, companies may decide not to establish a business activity in an otherwise optimal jurisdiction for the simple fact that they wish to avoid the tax residence status therein and conversely do so in other jurisdiction which follows other categories of tests despite the fact it does not provide the perfect environment for their business in terms of workforce, infrastructures or legal system. Although CITs, by their very nature, always generate distortion in the taxpayer's economic decisions,[870] we fear that these residence tests are prone to exacerbate such distortions. We therefore believe that the potential significance of this risk justifies a careful assessment of their possible impact, a task that goes beyond the scope of the present study.

Finally, we will note the challenges derived from the coexistence between this category of tests and other preexisting rules, most notably the residence tests based on the governance of the company (e.g., POEM tests) and the PE threshold, due to the evident risk of overlap and confusion.

We will start with their coexistence with the first set of rules, namely the residence tests relying on the governance of the company. As these problems have already become visible in the States having these tests in place, we will illustrate them by means of real cases decided by the courts in both States. We should recall that both States follow a wide interpretation of "oggetto principale" and "business,"[871] thus integrating activities of control and management of assets, immovable property or stock portfolios among others. What happens in case it is established that the functions of management and control carried out by a company constitutes precisely its "oggetto principale" or main business? Would not these tests produce the same outcome than POEM tests do? This scenario may be more frequent than expected, particularly as regards holdings, real estate investment trusts (REITs), investment funds and a long etcetera. As we will see below, each State has addressed the issue differently.

For its part, Italy departs from the fact that concept "oggetto principale dell'attività" covers management and control activities and therefore may produce the same effects than residence tests as the POEM. The Italian Supreme Court concluded

869. On one hand, companies may decide not to establish a business activity in an otherwise optimal jurisdiction for the simple fact that they wish to avoid the tax residence status therein. On the other hand, taxpayers may choose to bring their business in a jurisdiction which follows other categories of tests despite the fact it does not provide the perfect environment for their business in terms of workforce, infrastructures or legal system.

870. In particular, CITs are likely to condition decisions concerning the choice of the business sector, the organizational form (the incorporation decision), the location of the activities, the company's capital structure (the debt: equity ratio), the policy dividend, etc. *See* Bird, R. (2002), p. 194.

871. Chapter 3 section §3.02[A][1][d].

that a real estate management company did not have its "oggetto principale dell'attività" in Italy insofar it carried out its management functions outside the country, irrespective of the fact that all its immovable assets were located in Italy. In the same vein, the Italian Tax Administration reached the conclusion that a holding company which managed its portfolio in a country other than Italy did not have its "oggetto principale dell'attività" in Italy even though it owned Italian subsidiaries. This approach was heavily criticized by De Broe, as these lines of reasoning lead, in his view, to subordinate the "oggetto principale" test to the place of management test.[872]

The case of Australia is certainly more complicated. The reason is that its residence test relies on two supposedly separate and distinct requirements: the company must both carry on a business in Australia and have its central management and control therein. From the wording of the rule and the use of the conjunction "and" it may be inferred that both conditions should be given different meaning and effects.

This is the reason why the renowned "Malayan Shipping" judgment ruled by the High Court of Australia[873] was so controversial at the time. The Court concluded that Malayan Shipping could be regarded as tax resident in Australia for concentrating both its central management and business in Australian soil: "if the business of the company carried on it Australia consists of or includes its central management and control, then the company is carrying on a business in Australia and its central management and control is in Australia."[874] Accordingly, it appeared that, provided that a company's central management and control was deemed to be in Australia, it would automatically follow that the company was equally carrying on a business therein. This redundant interpretation essentially led to render the phrase "carrying on business" superfluous[875] and hence significantly broaden the scope of the test.[876]

In order to put an end to the discussion, the ATO decided to issue a draft tax ruling in 2004[877] where it intended to provide a separate meaning to both requirements as a way to ensure a more consistent interpretation of the wording of the rule.[878] By

872. De Broe, L. (2009), p. 119.
873. Judgment by the High Court of Australia, 1946, "Malayan Shipping Company Limited v. Federal Commissioner of Taxation." The judgment is commented and analyzed by Kashyap, A.; Shaflender, L. (2004). Basically, the company (Malayan Shipping) was incorporated in Singapore upon the instructions of Mr. Sleigh, who carried on business in Australia as an importer, shipping agent and general merchant. Mr. Sleigh owned 2,500 shares, while the two remaining shares where owned by two nominees in Singapore which were also appointed as directors of the company. The only business carried out by the company was to charter a Norwegian tanker and sub-charter it to Mr. Sleigh on ten voyage charters.
874. The Court concluded that "the essence of the business was (Mr. Sleigh's) decision in Melbourne to charter and sub-charter the tanker. It was this decision which in every substantial sense gave rise to the profits which the company made out of the sub-charters." *See* Kashyap, A.; Shaflender, L. (2004). p. 186.
875. Kashyap, A.; Shaflender, L. (2004). p. 186.
876. Opinion of the Australian Treasury in consultation paper quoted by Kashyap, A.; Shaflender, L. (2004). p. 186.
877. Australian Taxation Office (2004): Draft Taxation Ruling: "Residence of companies not incorporated in Australia—carrying on business in Australia and central management and control."
878. Australian Taxation Office (2004): Draft Taxation Ruling: "Residence of companies not incorporated in Australia—carrying on business in Australia and central management and control," paragraph 6.

means of an example, the ruling concluded that the functions of management and decision-making are included within the ordinary activity of the Board, but do not necessarily take part of the business of the company as such.[879] Further, the ATO revisited the "Malayan Shipping" case to confirm its conclusion but clarify the rationale behind it.[880] It stated that the judgment could not be interpreted as setting the general principle that if a company's central management and control is located in Australia then this necessarily means that the company is equally carrying on a business therein. Instead, the ATO considered that, in the case concerned, the two separate requirements happened to be incidentally fulfilled by "the same set of facts and activities," the reason being that "the nature of the business and the managing director's complete management and control over the business operations and internal administration of the company resulted in a situation where his powers and actions evidenced CM&C (and) the carrying on of a business."[881]

As regards to the second challenge that these test pose (i.e., their coexistence with the PE threshold), we have noted that the issue has been generally overlooked by the consulted judgments and academic papers. We nonetheless believe it deserves further study.

In our opinion, a partial overlap is expected to happen between the terms "oggetto principale"/business and the domestic definition of PE. The degree of overlap would depend on the precise scope of the terms concerned in the corresponding domestic legislation and case law. However, we are in a position to put forward a few general considerations in this regard taking the PE concept of the OECD MC as a reference point.[882]

First, both the Australian and Italian tests are wide enough to cover certain business activities that go beyond the ordinary meaning that may be assigned to the terms of the PE clause. For example, we stated back in Chapter 3 section §3.03[E][2] that the PE clause largely equates physical and stable presence with taxable presence, a common pattern shared by all the four modalities of PEs set out in the MCs. We then noted that this fact automatically leads to leave untaxed all other significant business

879. Trade Co is incorporated in Papua New Guinea, its board of directors holds its meetings in Australia (where decisions on contracts entered by the company, finance, major policies and strategic directions are made) and all its trading activities are undertaken in Papua New Guinea. As a consequence of the ATO's approach to both tests, it concluded that Trade Co was not carrying any of its own business activities in Australian soil and therefore could not be regarded as tax resident therein. *See* Australian Taxation Office (2004): Draft Taxation Ruling: "Residence of companies not incorporated in Australia—carrying on business in Australia and central management and control," paragraph 68.

880. Australian Taxation Office (2004): Draft Taxation Ruling: "Residence of companies not incorporated in Australia—carrying on business in Australia and central management and control," paragraphs 30-38.

881. Australian Taxation Office (2004): Draft Taxation Ruling: "Residence of companies not incorporated in Australia—carrying on business in Australia and central management and control," paragraph 33. Even though the Australian courts and the ATO may coincide in the resolution of the "Malayan Shipping" case, it is still true that their reasoning may be interpreted as divergent. So, to the extent they may potentially lead to contradictory outcomes, the amendment of the Australian residence rule seems to be the only way to clear the uncertainty and clarify the distinct content of both tests. *See* Kashyap, A.; Shaflender, L. (2004), p. 187.

882. Article 5 of the 2017 OECD MC.

activities that occur in the source jurisdiction either physically (but without reaching the necessary level of temporal permanence and geographical stability) or remotely. This would be the case, for example, of commercial activities and/or sales conducted through remote means (call centers, websites, smartphone "apps") or the remote provision of services. On the other hand, one may argue that this sort of activities may eventually fall under the scope of the both Australian and Italian tests.

Second, none of these clauses would *a priori* enable a State to tax the profits of a controlling company incorporated and managed from another State whose only attachment to the State concerned is the fact that it controls a subsidiary that is resident therein.[883] As we noted above, neither Italy nor Australia would consider that the controlling company has an "oggetto principale dell'attività" or a business in their respective territories to the extent that the management functions are exercised elsewhere. On the other hand, the controlling company would not necessarily be considered to have a PE in such State on the sole ground that it controls a company that is resident therein. As a matter of principle, a subsidiary would only be deemed to be its parent's PE to the extent that it effectively carries out the parent's business besides its own one.[884]

Third, in case the activities of a company fall under the scope of both the corporate residence test and the PE clause, the question arises as to whether the company should be subject to tax by the State concerned as a resident taxpayer or as a PE. We believe that, as a matter of principle, the application of the residence test should prevail and hence the company should be treated for tax purposes as a resident of the company. The reason is that, typically, only non-resident taxpayers would be in a position to have a PE in a territory and therefore a company that fulfills a residence test would not be in such position. In any case, the definitive answer to this question necessarily depends on the precise content of the domestic tax legislation of the State concerned.

Lastly, we would like to point out the distinct effects of considering that the company is a resident taxpayer or have a PE in the State concerned. The definitive response would again depend on the domestic tax rules, although residence-based taxation generally triggers taxation on the taxpayer's worldwide profits while taxation based on the existence of a PE would be confined to the (worldwide) profits that are attributable to the PE. It is however true that the general tendency is to grant PEs with a tax treatment equivalent to that of resident taxpayers, partly due to the effect of the non-discrimination principles established in both tax treaties and EU Law, but we noted that equivalent treatment did not mean absolute neutrality and homogeneity.[885]

883. Antonini, M. (2008), pp. 154-156 referring to the Italian Supreme Court case law.
884. At least this is the logical consequence of Article 5.7 of the 2017 OECD MC: "The fact that a company which is a resident of a Contracting State controls or is controlled by a company which is a resident of the other Contracting State, or which carries on business in that other State (whether through a permanent establishment or otherwise), shall not of itself constitute either company a permanent establishment of the other."
885. Chapter 3 section §3.03[D].

[iv] Suggestions for a Proposal

Now that we have gone through some of the risks and challenges that these residence tests may potentially pose (some of them are already visible in Australia and Italia), we are in a better position to put forward a few recommendations for States that choose to adopt a similar corporate residence test.

In essence, these tests are (and should continue to be) factual-based. However, they could depart from paper-based indicia, as the corporate purpose reflected in the act of incorporation or the bylaws.[886] Such an approach would certainly contribute to save time and efforts, as the activities of the company are likely to be consistent with them. However, if paper-based factors were adopted, they should solely operate in the form of rebuttable presumptions, in a way that they could be easily overcome by the observation of the business activities that are effectively carried out by the company within the territory of the State.

One way to mitigate the high degree of legal certainty that these tests tend to pose (as any other substance-over-form approach) is to come up with a test that relies on quantitative factors. The selection of the relevant factor(s) would be up to the State concerned. However, the fulfillment of the factors included in the test should reveal the performance of significant business activities (either physically or remotely) in the territory of the State and, at the same time, should ideally enable us to assume that the company finds itself in a position to enjoy and use the public services provided by the State in accordance with the presumptive benefit rationale.[887] Examples of factors might include (but are not limited to) the presence of a large number of infrastructures and assets in the territory, the presence of an important number of employees therein, a significant level of revenue obtained from sources present in the State concerned[888]

886. This is the case for both the Italian and the Australian tests (*see* Chapter 3 section §3.02[A][1][d]). The Italian rule specifically indicates that the assessment should start from the object of the entity as determined on the law, the act of incorporation or the bylaws. The *oggetto principale dell'attività* is presumed to be the one that may be regarded as "essential to directly achieve the primary goals of the company as laid down in the law, act of incorporation or bylaws." For its part, Australian courts equally begin with the statutory definition of the corporate business.

887. In line with the ideas expressed primarily in Chapter 2 section §2.02. We then admitted that the presumptive benefit principle justifies the imposition of taxes by the State where the company's economic activities take place and also by the State providing the market, although to a lesser extent in this latter case. This is the reason why the market factor should ideally be given a relatively inferior weight in the proposed residence test.

888. This idea was originally put forward by the OECD in the context of the new nexus based on "significant economic presence," which was theoretically intended to coexist with the current PE threshold in the tax treaties. *See* OECD (2015): Final Report on BEPS Action 1—Addressing the tax challenges of the digital economy, pp. 107-108: "as a general matter, revenue that is generated on a sustained basis from a country could be considered to be one of the clearest potential indicators of the existence of a significant economic presence." The selection of this factor (and the next one) would be consistent with the considerations exposed in Chapter 2 section §2.02[B][2][b], where we concluded that the presence of a considerable number of customers in one State allowed us to assume that the company could be in the position to benefit from its services and infrastructures irrespective of the presence of a physical economic activity in that territory. According to Gadžo, S. (2016), p. 270: "the total amount of revenue taxpayer derives from a specific country is probably a good proxy for both public benefits

or the supplies of a notable level of goods or services to local customers.[889] The selection of the corresponding proxy (or group of proxies) should be preceded by a careful assessment on its manageability and potential implications, a study that, once again, goes beyond the scope of the present research.

Irrespective of the selected factor, we believe it would be convenient to demand a very significant amount of economic activity in the territory concerned. One way to achieve this is to adopt a quantitative threshold in the form of a percentage. Requiring the presence of a high percentage of the relevant factor(s) within the territory concerned would guarantee the presence of an adequate relative weight of the corresponding factor(s) in relation to the global figures of the company. This option would however pose two important challenges. First, groups may avoid reaching the high quantitative thresholds in force in the relevant jurisdictions by fragmenting the selected factor(s) among their subsidiaries. This concern should be however accepted, as the outcome would be, after all, consistent with the presumptive benefit principle. Second, the gathering of the relevant information to apply the test (e.g., the worldwide revenue obtained by the company or its global number of employees) may be troublesome. However, States are likely to have domestic disclosure requirements already in place that cover (or may potentially cover) this sort of information. In addition, the country-by-country report is expected to provide a great amount of relevant information (both consolidated and broken down separately by jurisdiction) on MNCs exceeding a certain revenue threshold.[890]

The reasons why we believe the residence test should demand a very significant amount of economic activity in the territory concerned (revealed by the presence of a high relative quantity of factors therein) are many and varied. However, the most powerful argument in favor of this approach rests on the presumptive benefit principle itself. We argued elsewhere[891] that this principle should theoretically help us to identify which companies ought to become subject to a State's tax jurisdiction while it should not get involved in the calculation of the resulting tax liability. This does not mean that we should forget about the fact that the residence status commonly triggers an

related to the market access therein and for the amount of value created for the enterprise on the demand side." We should recall at this time that Mexico follows a personal tax residence test according to which a person would be considered as tax resident in Mexico to the extent more than 50% of his/her total revenue arises from sources within the country. *See* http://www.oecd.org/tax/automatic-exchange/crs-implementation-and-assistance/tax-residency/Mexico-Residency.pdf (last accessed on January 10, 2019).

889. This is the position followed by the UK in its so-called Diverted profits tax, in force since April 2015. It led to subject to tax the profits derived by a non-resident company carrying on an activity in the UK "in connection with the supply of goods, services or other property." *See* British HM Revenue & Customs (2015): Guidance on the Diverted Profits Tax, pp. 17-18. This position would be aligned with the considerations made back in Chapter 2 section §2.02[B][2][b].

890. Groups with annual consolidated group revenue in the immediately preceding fiscal year of less than EUR 750 million or a near equivalent amount in domestic currency as of January 2015 would be obliged to comply with this documentation standard. The country-by-country report template includes information on revenue, number of employees, tangible assets, stated capital, etc. *See* OECD (2015): Final Report on BEPS Action 13—Transfer pricing documentation and country-by-country reporting, pp. 21 and 29-30.

891. Chapter 2 section §2.02[A].

unlimited tax liability that encompasses the worldwide income obtained by the company irrespective of its source (albeit generally mitigated by foreign tax credits or foreign income exemption). This being so, we believe that the effective presence of the company required by the test in the territory concerned should be of such magnitude that it could on its own justify the generation of an unlimited tax liability on the grounds of the supposed high quantify of public benefits that the company would be, presumably, in a position to enjoy. This means that the test should preferably cover only the companies whose business activities are concentrated solely or mostly in the territory concerned, as opposed to those which spread their activities between different countries. Otherwise, residence tests would capture companies that are economically present in a considerable number of States, thus giving rise to an unjustifiable high level of taxation in the State concerned and multiplying the risk of double taxation.[892] In these cases, residence tests based on the location of the economic activity should not come into play, and the State should rely instead on the eventual tax liabilities it could impose to the non-resident company by means of source-based taxation.

We also warned above about the probable overlapping effects between other rules, most notably residence tests based on the governance of the company and the PE threshold. Naturally, the possibility of an overlap would depend on the specific wording of the corresponding rules.

As regards the possible overlap with residence tests based on the governance of the company, it would occur insofar States adopt residence tests that resemble the ones already in place in Italy and Australia and furthermore follow a broad interpretation of the notion of economic activity for the purposes of their residence tests, thus covering the mere management of activities, assets, immovable property, stock portfolio, etc. This being so, a company may well be regarded to conduct its business or economic activity wherever it performs its management functions, in a way that both sets of tests would lead to the same outcome. Contrary to the opinion of certain scholars,[893] we believe that this result is not troublesome and should be accepted.[894] The only alternative to prevent such overlap would be to deny that passive activities may qualify as economic activities, an alternative that we do not consider as appropriate.

As regards the coexistence between these residence tests and the PE threshold, we warned about the fact that the potential implementation of corporate residence tests based on the location of the economic activities is likely to generate an overlap between the "new" residence-based taxation and the "traditional" source-based taxation in its current form: the PE. Hence, a company conducting a substantial economic activity in State X may well fall under the scope of both the domestic tax residence test and the PE clause. We do not perceive this overlap as a problem but rather as an opportunity to finally overcome the inherent limitations of the PE clause,[895] in particular, the fact that

892. Double taxation that could be the consequence of either multiple residence issues or the overlap between residence and source-based taxation.
893. De Broe, L. (2009), p. 119.
894. We do however understand the concerns this overlap generates in Australia (commented above), as the Australian rule encompasses both a "carry on business" and a POEM test, tests with a supposedly different meaning and effects.
895. Chapter 3 section §3.03[E][2].

it is solely fitted to encompass economic activities that entail a physical presence that is stable over time and takes place in a particular (tangible) geographical spot. As we noted above, a wide corporate tax residence test of this sort would cover significant business activities that occur in the territory of the State either physically (but without reaching the necessary level of temporal permanence and geographical stability required by the PE clause) or remotely (e.g., remote provision of services or conclusion on sales).

Beyond the few general suggestions pointed out above, we believe we are not yet in the position to provide a definitive legislative proposal. It seems clear that this matter deserves a more thorough study due to the enormous impact that a change of the residence paradigm might have and the significant risks and challenges it poses. We limited ourselves to intuitively foresee some of these risks and challenges but we believe a study should be carried out to better identify these issues (most notably, distortions in the economic decisions the taxpayer, an expected high degree of legal uncertainty and the troublesome coexistence with other tax rules), try to minimize or neutralize them when possible and furthermore assess whether the benefits of these tests compensate for such problems.

In case such study does not conclude that it is possible to draft a residence test of these characteristics that is equitable, manageable and precise and furthermore does not cause significant distortions, we should begin to conceive residence as a residual and secondary proxy[896] that does not absorb a significant amount of taxable base and instead devote ourselves to strengthening and updating source-based taxation to ensure that the presumptive benefit principle is effectively observed and complied with by means of this latter form of taxation.[897] This is precisely what we will intend to do later in section §4.02[C]. The following proposal related to corporate residence in the context of tax treaties can still be set into motion irrespective of the decision of the States as regards the amendment of their domestic tests.

[4] *New Tie-Breaker Rule to Resolve Double Residence Issues Considering the Economic Presence of the Company in Both Contracting States*

We observed in Chapter 3 section §3.02[D] that the great variety of domestic residence tests used by States, along with the different ways to interpret them, is likely to generate situations in which the same company is regarded as resident for domestic tax purposes in two or more jurisdictions. A risk that would be, by the way, mitigated if States abandoned the use of weak residence tests.[898]

896. Based on other residence tests, either those already in place that were analyzed in Chapter 3 or new ones. In any event, we suggest States to take into consideration the observations we noted back in Chapter 4 sections §4.02[B][1] and §4.02[B][2].

897. Graetz, M.J. (2001), p. 323: "the fragility and manipulability of the residence of corporations suggests to me that US international tax policy, to the extent possible, should reduce the tax consequences of determinations of residence for corporations. There are several policy implications that flow from this judgment. First and foremost, it implies priority of taxation of business income at source." *See also* Shaviro, D. (2011), Marian, O. (2013b), p. 474.

898. Chapter 4 section §4.02[B][2].

In cases in which two of those residence States have signed a tax treaty patterned after one of the most influential MCs, the double residence issue (and by extension the double taxation this entails) would be a priori solvable by means of the "tie-breaker" rules contained in the treaty, whose function is to discern which contracting State will perform the role of "residence State" and which one would eventually perform the role of the "source State" for the purposes of the application of the treaty.

After analyzing the tie-breaker rules contained in the MCs and their supposed respective justifications,[899] we concluded that there does not seem to be a clear rationale behind the choice of the corresponding tie-breaker rule.[900] In other words, there does not seem to be a clear principle underlying the criteria according to which the residence status of a company in one State should prevail over its residence status in the other contracting State for treaty purposes.

In this context, we would like to put forward a proposal to amend the tie-breaker rule concerning the double residence status of persons other than individuals. We have defended throughout the present study that the most appropriate way to define a sufficient and strong connection between a company and a State is to demonstrate the presence of a relevant economic activity carried out by the company within the territory of the State concerned on the basis of the presumptive benefit principle. Accordingly, we propose that the tie-breaker rule indeed tips the balance in favor of the residence State to which the corporate taxpayer is more closely connected in terms of economic presence. A rule that may be compared to the "centre of vital interest" tie-breaker rule that tax treaties provide for cases of double residence concerning individuals.[901]

This is not new, as the OECD itself alluded to the idea of amending Article 4.3 in this same direction back in 2001.[902] They justified such proposal precisely on the grounds of the benefit principle: "it could be argued that if the State provides certain facilities and infrastructure for its residents, those who benefit most from such facilities and infrastructure ought to contribute to the State via residence-based taxes. So, if a company uses the legal infrastructure, consumes or uses the facilities in that State, there is a case that it ought to be treated as a resident."[903]

899. Chapter 3 section §3.02[D].
900. Chapter 3 section §3.02[D][3].
901. OECD (2001): The impact of the communications revolution on the application of "place of effective management" as a tie breaker rule (Discussion Paper), p. 12.
902. OECD (2001): The impact of the communications revolution on the application of "place of effective management" as a tie breaker rule (Discussion Paper), pp. 11-12. The OECD did not provide a specific wording for its proposal, but it did suggest that the tie-breaker should tip the balance in favor of the contracting State "where the economic nexus is strongest."
903. OECD (2001): The impact of the communications revolution on the application of "place of effective management" as a tie breaker rule (Discussion Paper), p. 12.

The proposed Article 4.3 reads as follows:

> Proposed Article 4.3 for tax treaties[904]
>
> "3. Where by reason of the provisions of paragraph 1 a person other than an individual is a resident of both Contracting States, the competent authorities of the Contracting States shall endeavour to determine by mutual agreement the Contracting State of which such person shall be deemed to be a resident for the purposes of the Convention, ~~having regard to its place of effective management, the place where it is incorporated or otherwise constituted and any other relevant factors~~ **considering the State to which the person maintains a strongest economic connection**. In the absence of such agreement, such person shall not be entitled to any relief or exemption from tax provided by this Convention except to the extent and in such manner as may be agreed upon by the competent authorities of the Contracting States."

We choose to adhere to the general tendency, revealed by the recent practice followed by a great number of States,[905] according to which the tie-breaker rule directly leaves the resolution of the dual residence issue in the hands of the competent authorities of the Contracting States, albeit listing the factors they must necessarily consider when the time comes to fulfill their task.[906] This should ideally be accompanied by an arbitration clause which establishes the submission of the case to an arbitrator in case the competent authorities are unable to reach an agreement within the given time period.[907]

The current proposed wording is however too broad. We believe that the definitive wording should be as precise as possible and should ideally specify as much as possible the criteria that should guide the competent authorities when the time comes to fulfill their duty.[908] The selection of the relevant criteria should be assessed in a more profound study that goes beyond the scope of the present thesis.

---

904. Words in bold and strike-through indicate the variations from Article 4.3 of the 2017 OECD and the UN MC.
905. *See* the introduction to Chapter 3 section §3.02[D] (showing the tendency of the newest versions of the MCs to resort to MAP to resolve double taxation issues) Chapter 3 and section §3.02[D][2].
906. However, as Sanghavi points out, the explicit reference to the MAP provides no guarantee that a taxpayer's dual residence would be resolved, as it is possible that the authorities are unable to reach an agreement. In fact, he argues that this reference is redundant, as Article 25.3 of the OECD MC already obliged the competent authorities to "endeavor to resolve by mutual agreement any difficulties of doubts arising as to the interpretation or application of the Convention" (e.g., the case of the tie-breaker of Article 4.3.). *See* Sanghavi, D. (2016), p. 522.
907. *See* Article 25.5 of the 2017 OECD MC. *See also* OECD (2015): Final Report on BEPS Action 14—Making dispute resolution mechanisms more effective, p. 41 and OECD (2016): Multilateral convention to implement tax treaty related measures to prevent base erosion and profit shifting, p. 29.
908. For example, the OECD suggested that the economic connection may be characterized by "the extent that land, labor, capital and enterprise (the factors of production) are used by the

[C] Reconsideration of the Permanent Establishment Threshold

The PE has become the most widespread threshold allowing source-based taxation of business profits in both domestic law and tax treaties. Its relevance should not be underestimated, as the presence of a PE within the territory of a State generally triggers its entitlement to tax all the worldwide profits that could arguably be attributed to such PE under conditions equivalent to those taxpayers that are deemed to be tax resident therein.[909]

In Chapter 3 we had the opportunity to analyze the PE concept in detail[910] and further dissect the causes that explain why it cannot be regarded as aligned with the presumptive benefit principle and has even become, to some extent, a tool to detach taxable profits from the jurisdictions where the corporate taxpayer may presumably have access to public benefits (i.e., wherever it carries out relevant economic activities or have its market of customers).[911]

We then reached the conclusion that a literal interpretation of the PE clause prevented States from taxing profits obtained by non-resident taxpayers in cases in which they have a relevant economic activity therein due to a number of reasons, some derived from deficiencies in its wording[912] and some others of a more fundamental nature concerning the scope of the clause.[913] In this context, we strongly opposed the propensity of States to address these deficiencies by means of either eccentric or substance-based interpretations or an overuse of anti-avoidance rules, a tendency that has been further promoted by the OECD itself via its soft law documents.[914] Instead, we advocated for the direct amendment of the rule as the best and most straightforward way to address its inherent shortcomings, an approach we intend to explore in the present section.

We will first evaluate the objectives of the BEPS project as regards the PE concept and their consistency with the presumptive benefit principle (section §4.02[C][1]). Subsequently, we will assess the PE clause resulting from the project, particularly in the light of its alleged objectives and the aforementioned principle (section §4.02[C][2]). Lastly, we will explore the possibility of adding a new provision to the clause so as to ensure a better consistency with this principle (section §4.02[C][3]). Some conclusions will finally be drawn.

---

company in deriving its profits" (*see* OECD (2001): The impact of the communications revolution on the application of "place of effective management" as a tie breaker rule (Discussion Paper), p. 11).

909. The reasons and rationale behind this assertion may be found in Chapter 3 section §3.03[D] and §3.03[F][1].
910. Chapter 3 sections §3.03[A] to §3.03[D].
911. Chapter 3 section §3.03[E].
912. Chapter 3 section §3.03[E][1].
913. Chapter 3 section §3.03[E][2].
914. Chapter 3 section §3.03[F][2]. The reason is that this approach is prone to compromise the principle of legal certainty and the respect for the rule of law.

[1] Evaluation of the Purpose of BEPS as Regards the Permanent Establishment Concept: Consistent with the Presumptive Benefit Rationale but Inconsistent with the PE Clause in Its Current Form

We made reference above to the general policy objective pursued by the BEPS project in section §4.01[A] (the so-called BEPS mantra: i.e., the alignment between the allocation of taxable income and the economic activity that generates that income) and further noted that Actions 1 and 6 to 10 were entrusted with the task to achieve it. However, the BEPS mantra does not remain static and unaltered throughout the different work streams, as it is rather subject to specifications when the time comes to put forward the particular objectives and scope of each of these work streams.[915] The same occurs with the actions concerning the PE concept (Actions 1 and 7), as we will now proceed to explain.

A closer look at the Action Plan and the corresponding reports on Actions 1 and 7 reveals that BEPS does not intend to bring the tax bases to wherever the "economic activities" take place by means of the PE, as one may intuitively presuppose. Instead, it seems that the OECD intends to use the PE to bring the taxable profits to wherever the market is. Such an objective was not made explicit but could be easily inferred from the wording used in the Action Plan as regards Actions 1[916] and 7[917] and, most clearly, from the final reports, where the OECD came to recognize that it sought to ensure taxation at the level of the market jurisdiction and that Actions 1 and 7 were instrumental for these purposes.[918]

The question now arises as to whether the new OECD approach towards the PE may be considered as consistent with the presumptive benefit rationale. The question should be responded positively: the ambition of the OECD to ensure taxation at the level of the market jurisdiction by means of the PE clause may be regarded as aligned with this principle insofar as corporate taxpayers may be deemed to be benefiting from

915. For example, we already noted that the purpose of Actions 8-10 was to ensure that transfer pricing outcomes were aligned with "value-creating activities." *See* Chapter 4 section §4.02[A].
916. For example, one of the functions of Action 1 was to assess "the ability of a company to have a significant digital presence in the economy of another country without being liable to taxation due to the lack of nexus under current international rules" (BEPS Action Plan, p. 14). In other words, the objective was to consider whether the scope of the PE clause could be modified to further cover the "digital presence" of non-resident companies in their respective market jurisdictions.
917. The Action Plan expressed its concern about the recurrent replacement of distributors with "commissionaires," as it allegedly resulted in a "shift of profits out of the country where the sales take place without a substantive change in the functions performed in that country" (BEPS Action Plan, p. 19).
918. There are constant references (a total of 34) to the "market jurisdiction" along the 202-pages final report on Action 1. *See* OECD (2015): Final Report on BEPS Action 1—Addressing the tax challenges of the digital economy, p. 88: "the treaty definition of PE may limit the application of domestic law rules applicable to the taxation of the business profits of non-resident companies derived from sources in the market country. The work done with respect to Action 7 was aimed at preventing the artificial avoidance of the treaty threshold below which the market country may not tax." The report acknowledged that the structures addressed in Action 7 (e.g., commissionaire arrangements, fragmentation of operations to qualify for the PE exceptions, etc.) precisely resulted in the avoidance of tax liabilities at the level of the market jurisdiction (*see* pp. 79, 80, 86 and 88).

the services and infrastructures defrayed by the jurisdictions that host their customers.[919]

However, this sudden desire to bring the PE threshold closer to where the consumers are constitutes a major novelty in the discourse of the OECD, even though it is not presented as such.[920] In fact, the OECD has historically disdained the significance of the market when the time comes to determine the source of profits and legitimize the potential tax claims of the State providing the market (at least before the advent of the BEPS project),[921] contrary to the position held by certain scholars for a long time.[922]

As a matter of fact, we find a discrepancy between the new alleged objective of the PE and the current form of the clause. We believe that the PE clause was not originally conceived to ensure taxation at the level of the market jurisdiction: it was rather designed to encompass situations in which the non-resident company was carrying out a significant (value-adding) economic activity within the territory of a State, measured in terms of physical presence and continuity in time.[923] The fact that the PE-State and the market State tended to coincide was casual or, to be more precise, it was the natural consequence of the economic context in which the PE arose. An economic context in which the physical presence, continuous in time—precisely that required by the PE clause—was critical to reach the market. Changes in business models, communications and technology have resulted in the increasing possibility to reach the consumers resident in a certain jurisdiction by remote means.[924] In these scenarios, the State where a PE arises and the State providing the market are less likely to coincide.[925] This confirms our hypothesis: the PE clause as it currently stands is inherently unable to ensure taxation at the level of the market jurisdiction since it does not necessarily bring the taxable bases wherever the consumers are, even though this may incidentally occur (more frequently in the past).

919. Chapter 2 section §2.02[B][2][b].
920. Escribano, E. (2015), p. 11.
921. OECD (2003): Are the current treaty rules for taxing business profits appropriate for e-commerce? Final report, p.14: "economic literature suggests that there are two possible approaches to determining a proper allocation of business profits: the supply-based and supply-demand based views. Under the supply-based approach, profits originate from where the factors that produce the profits operate (...) Under the 'supply-demand' view, however, the interaction of supply and demand is what creates business profits (...) The TAG's approach was therefore in line with the supply-based approach of considering that business profits should be viewed as originating from the location of the factors that allow the enterprise to realize business profits. It therefore rejected the suggestion that the mere fact that a country provides the market where an enterprise's goods and services are supplied should allow that country to consider that a share of the profits of the enterprise is derived therefrom."
922. *See* for example Skaar, A.A. (1991), p. 23 and Vogel, K. (1988c).
923. *See* Chapter 3 sections §3.03[C] and §3.03[E]. *See* Hongler, P.; Pistone, P. (2015), pp. 9-10 and 15 for a very divergent opinion.
924. Chapter 3 section §3.03[E][2].
925. McLure notes: "increasing amounts of sales being made by firms that lack a permanent establishment in market nations." *See* McLure, C.E. (Jr) (2000), 6:2.

In addition, we have good reasons to believe that the current methodology to attribute profits to the PEs promoted by the OECD (the so-called AOA)[926] was not designed either to allocate taxable profits to the market jurisdictions. The reason is that the allocation of profits between the head office and the PE (i.e., the resident and the host State) is fundamentally guided by the determination of who performs the "significant people functions," that is, the functions[927] carried out by people[928] which may be regarded as significant, in the sense that they are economically relevant and prone to generate profits.[929] This means that the AOA will ultimately allocate profits to wherever the persons carry out the relevant economic activity (either in the Residence or the PE-State), irrespective of the place where automated functions are performed (e.g., servers)[930] or where the customers are.[931]

In short, we may conclude that the "new" mission assigned to the PE in the context of BEPS (despite its alignment with the presumptive benefit principle) is not intrinsic in the PE in its current form, as it cannot be inferred from either the literal wording of the clause or the methodology to attribute profits. This means that the OECD seems to be once again pursuing an objective by means of an instrument that is unsuitable for the objective.[932]

Once the objective of the BEPS project as regards the PE threshold has been identified and evaluated, the time comes to review the conclusions reached in the two work streams dedicated to this clause, namely Actions 1 and 7.

926. *See* Chapter 3 section §3.03[D] and OECD (2010): Attribution of profits to permanent establishments.
927. Kamphuis argues that a function encompasses at least three elements: the duty to perform the assigned tasks (responsibility), the allocation of decision-making powers (authority) and the competencies (e.g., knowledge and skills) required to perform the task. *See* Kamphuis, E. (2008), p. 302. The attribution of risks and assets, along with the remuneration they trigger under the ALS, will depend on this first exercise. In other words, the identification of these functions ultimately conditions the level of profits that could arguably be attributable to the PE. *See* Chapter 3 section §3.03[D].
928. As opposed to non-people functions, as automated ones performed by robots or machines, which would be insignificant for the purposes of profit attribution. *See* Kamphuis, E. (2008), p. 302.
929. Kamphuis, E. (2008), p. 302.
930. We made reference to the potential existence of server-PEs in Chapter 3 Section §3.03[F][2]. According to the OECD "the automated nature of the functions means that the assets or risks attributed to the PE are only likely to be those directly associated with the server hardware. In fact, since a server-PE will not be carrying out any significant people functions relevant to the attribution of economic ownership of assets and/or the assumption of risks in the absence of personnel acting on behalf of the enterprise, no asset or risk could be attributed to it under the authorized OECD approach, supporting the conclusion that little or no profit would be attributed to such a PE" (OECD (2010): Attribution of profits to permanent establishments, p. 26).
931. The Spanish courts have sometimes attributed to a PE located in Spain all the income derived from sales in the country (*see* the last part of Chapter 3 section §3.03[F][2], concerning the "PE Spanish approach") but this outcome results from a non-orthodox interpretation of the rules for attributing profits to PEs. Schön rightly notes that the place of physical presence (as required by the PE clause) and the place where the "significant people functions" are performed may well bear no relation at all with the place where the customers are (Schön, W. (2009), p. 103).
932. Just as we denounced above in the context of the BEPS Actions concerning transfer pricing rules, *see* Chapter 4 section §4.02[A][2].

First of all, we believe that the willingness of the OECD to finally amend the PE clause should be welcomed in any case, as it implies the final abandonment of its longstanding and unfortunate tendency to force the interpretation of the clause beyond the literal meaning of its terms.[933] The BEPS project wished to address the reform of the PE at two different levels. On the one hand, it devoted Action 7 to preventing the use of certain common "tax avoidance" strategies resulting in the circumvention of the clause.[934] On the other hand, Action 1 explored the possibility to reconsider the scope of the clause in the light of the challenges posed by the digital economy.[935] We will first refer to the measures proposed by Action 7, where consensus was indeed reached.

[2] The Advantages and Shortcomings of the Amendments to the PE Clause Envisaged in the New 2017 OECD MC

In the present section we will first briefly describe the proposed changes to the PE clause comprised in the final report on Action 7, which ultimately lead to the update of Article 5 in the 2017 OECD MC. Subsequently, we will evaluate their actual impact in terms of tax revenue by hypothesizing the expected profits that could be attributable to the renovated PE clause. Finally, a few conclusions will be drawn.

[a] The Strengthening of the Agency Clause

In Chapter 3 we identified three important weaknesses in the agency clause (as drafted in the 2014 OECD MC) that were prone to generate profit shifting risks.[936] The first two arise due to the relative ease with which two expressions of Article 5.5 may be circumvented, as they rely on objective formal concepts that make the threshold very vulnerable to tax planning.[937] In the view of them, some amendments were introduced to the 2017 OECD MC: [938]

933. This approach was described and severely criticized back in Chapter 3 section §3.03[F][2].
934. BEPS Action Plan, p. 19 and OECD (2015): Final Report on BEPS Action 7—Preventing the artificial avoidance of permanent establishment status.
935. BEPS Action Plan, pp. 14-15. We will later make reference to one of the proposals (*see* Chapter 4 section §4.02[C][3]).
936. Chapter 3 section §3.03[E][1][c].
937. Eisenbeiss, J. (2016), p. 487.
938. Words in bold and strike-through indicate the variations from Article 5.5 of the 2014 OECD MC.

5. Notwithstanding the provisions of paragraphs 1 and 2 **but subject to the provisions of paragraph 6**, where a person ~~other than an agent of an independent status to whom paragraph 6 applies~~ is acting **in a Contracting State** on behalf of an enterprise and ~~has, and habitually exercises, in a Contracting State, an authority to conclude contracts~~, **in doing so, habitually concludes contracts, or habitually plays the principal role leading to the conclusion of contracts that are routinely concluded without material modification by the enterprise, and these contracts are**

a) in the name of the enterprise, or
b) for the transfer of the ownership of, or for the granting of the right to use, property owned by that enterprise or that the enterprise has the right to use, or
c) for the provision of services by that enterprise,

that enterprise shall be deemed to have a permanent establishment in that State in respect of any activities which that person undertakes for the enterprise, unless the activities of such person are limited to those mentioned in paragraph 4 which, if exercised through a fixed place of business, would not make this fixed place of business a permanent establishment under the provisions of that paragraph.

First, the "conclusion of contracts" requirement was avoidable by the simple expedient of authorizing or finalizing the contract in a jurisdiction other than that in which the agent substantially negotiated it. In this context, the OECD added an alternative requisite according to which an agent who habitually plays "the principal role leading to the conclusion" of a contract[939] would still constitute a DAPE to the extent that the principal limits itself to routinely conclude it without material modification (the so-called rubber-stamp approvals).

Second, the requirement to conclude contracts "in the name of the enterprise" was also easily avoidable by means of a commissionaire arrangement (as evidenced in the Apple case).[940] In view of this, the OECD decided to add two new alternative requisites which did not relate to a formality in the contract but rather to its effects, in both cases demanding the subsequent performance of the principal, either by providing a service or transferring the ownership or the right to use a property. This being so, the agency clause would apply to contracts that create rights and obligations that are legally enforceable between the principal and the third party (for being concluded "in

939. This wording replaces the "negotiates the material elements of contracts" expression originally suggested by the OECD (2015): Revised Discussion Draft on BEPS Action 7: prevent the artificial avoidance of PE status. *See* OECD (2015): Final Report on BEPS Action 7—Preventing the artificial avoidance of permanent establishment status, pp. 19-20. *See* new addition to Article 5.5 of the 2017 OECD MC and Commentary on Article 5 of 2017 OECD MC, paragraph 83.

940. Chapter 2 section §2.01[A][2] and, more generally, Chapter 3 section §3.03[E][1][c]. A commissionaire arrangement may be defined as "an arrangement through which a person sells products in a given State in its own name but on behalf of a foreign enterprise that is the owner of these products" according to OECD (2015): Final Report on BEPS Action 7—Preventing the artificial avoidance of permanent establishment status, p. 15.

the name" of the former) but also to contracts that create obligations that will effectively be performed by the principal (as results from the addition of the new two requirements).[941] Accordingly, a commissionaire would typically constitute a DAPE under the new agency clause, thus finally overcoming the unjustified disparate treatment of commissionaires in common and civil law jurisdictions.[942] However, it should be noted that other much simpler alternatives could have been selected in order to cover these scenarios, most notably the agency clause comprised in the US MC[943] or other proposals that were discarded in the course of the BEPS project.[944]

The basic premise upon which both proposals are based is that "where the activities that an intermediary exercises in a country are intended to result in the regular conclusion of contracts to be performed by a foreign enterprise," such enterprise should be deemed to have a DAPE in the jurisdiction where the activities of the intermediary take place.[945] In view of this, it could be concluded that the intention of the new Article 5.5 goes far beyond counteracting the aforementioned "rubber-stamp" approval cases and commissionaire arrangements.[946] On the contrary, the proposals result in a substantial extension of the scope of the clause that may potentially encompass a variety of diverse activities in the source State. For example, scenarios in which the agent limits itself to convince the customer to accept a predetermined contract that the agent is not authorized to negotiate nor modify, or where a marketing service companies provides local marketing and sales support to the principal, ultimately leading to the conclusion of contracts even though it lacks the authority to conclude them.[947]

---

941. Article 5.5.b and c of the 2017 OECD MC and OECD (2015): Final Report on BEPS Action 7—Preventing the artificial avoidance of permanent establishment status, p. 20. Martín Jimenez states that, what is now relevant is whether the actions of the commissionaire end up with a factual effect on the principal to sell gods or services to the client. *See* Martín Jiménez, A. (2016), p. 468.
942. This disparity has never been justified on the basis of the alleged rationale behind the agency-PE (*see* Chapter 3 section §3.03[E][1][c]) as the question whether or not the foreign principal is legally bound becomes conceptually irrelevant where the agent has the authority to involve the principal in local business activities. *See* Eisenbeiss, J. (2016), pp. 489 and 492, Skaar, A.A. (1991), pp. 487-490 and Oyama, H. (2014), pp. 1167-1168.
943. The American clause refers to contracts "that are binding on the enterprise" irrespective of the name that appears in the contract. We already noted the reasons behind the divergence in both MCs in Chapter 3 section §3.03[E][1][c] (*see* Avery Jones, J.F.; Lüdicke, J. (2014), p. 206).
944. The BEPS discussion draft considered two other proposals that referred to contracts "which, by virtue of the legal relationship between that person and the enterprise are on the account and risk of the enterprise." *See* OECD (2014): BEPS Action 7: public discussion draft: preventing artificial avoidance of the PE status, pp. 13 and 14.
945. OECD (2015): Final Report on BEPS Action 7—Preventing the artificial avoidance of permanent establishment status, p. 15.
946. Hoor, O.R.; O'Donnell, K. (2015), pp. 933 and 936: "the proposals regarding commissionaire arrangements seem overbroad and would undermine the current rules on dependent agents."
947. Cunningham, K. M. (2016), p. 506, Eisenbeiss, J. (2016), p. 489 and Hoor, O.R.; O'Donnell, K. (2015), p. 933. According to Eisenbeiss, the latter case should be assessed on a case-by-case basis, as it may not always give rise to a PE. For his part, Cunningham believes that sellers of goods may rapidly be found to have a taxable presence in countries where they deploy marketing teams. Lastly, Hoor and O'Donnell believe that all local support services may

The third weakness we identified was the fact that companies could easily avoid the application of the agency clause by resorting to a related entity to which the exception of Article 5.6 of the MC applies to the extent that it carries on a business as an independent agent and is in fact acting in the ordinary course of that business. Of the face of it, the 2017 OECD MC incorporated some amendments:[948]

> 6. ~~An enterprise shall not be deemed to have a permanent establishment in a Contracting State merely because it carries on business in that State through a broker, general commission agent or any other agent of an independent status, provided that such persons are acting in the ordinary course of their business.~~
>
> a) **Paragraph 5 shall not apply where the person acting in a Contracting State on behalf of an enterprise of the other Contracting State carries on business in the first-mentioned State as an independent agent and acts for the enterprise in the ordinary course of that business. Where, however, a person acts exclusively or almost exclusively on behalf of one or more enterprises to which it is closely related, that person shall not be considered to be an independent agent within the meaning of this paragraph with respect to any such enterprise.**
>
> b) **For the purposes of this Article, a person is closely related to an enterprise if, based on all the relevant facts and circumstances, one has control of the other or both are under the control of the same persons or enterprises. In any case, a person shall be considered to be closely related to an enterprise if one possesses directly or indirectly more than 50 per cent of the beneficial interest in the other (or, in the case of a company, more than 50 per cent of the aggregate vote and value of the company's shares or of the beneficial equity interest in the company) or if another person possesses directly or indirectly more than 50 per cent of the beneficial interest (or, in the case of a company, more than 50 per cent of the aggregate vote and value of the company's shares or of the beneficial equity interest in the company) in the person and the enterprise.**

The OECD chose to presume that agents who are "closely related" to the principal and furthermore act "exclusively or almost exclusively" on its behalf[949] would never

---

potentially constitute a PE regardless of the pricing of the support services, a fact that demonstrates that the BEPS proposal goes far beyond commissionaire arrangements.

948. Words in bold and strike-through indicate the variations from the 2014 OECD MC.

949. Commentary on Article 5 of the 2017 OECD MC, paragraphs 112-113: "this means that where the person's activities on behalf of enterprises to which it is not closely related do not represent a significant part of that person's business, that person will not qualify as an independent agent. Where, for example, the sales that an agent concludes for enterprises to which it is not closely related represent less than 10 per cent of all the sales that it concludes as an agent acting for other enterprises, that agent should be viewed as acting 'exclusively or almost exclusively' on behalf of closely related enterprises." The only apparent reason behind this amendment does not seem to go beyond the apparent ease to circumvent the clause in the context of corporate groups. *See also* OECD (2015): Final Report on BEPS Action 7—Preventing the artificial avoidance of permanent establishment status, p. 26.

have independence status without admitting evidence that could eventually demonstrate that such agent in fact complies with the definition of independent agent considering the specific facts and circumstances of the case.[950] However, establishing a rebuttable presumption of dependence would have been a more coherent approach.[951]

[b] The Enhancement of the PE Exemption Clause

Article 5.4 of the OECD MC includes a list of exceptions according to which a PE is deemed not to exist where a POB is used solely for the activities listed in the paragraph. In Chapter 3 we already mentioned and briefly described the two profit shifting risks resulting from the prior version of this clause,[952] both addressed by the BEPS project.

First, prior version of Article 5.4 presumed that all the activities listed in the paragraph were of preparatory or auxiliary nature without admitting evidence to the contrary.[953] Consequently, a POB would never be treated as a PE for the purposes of the treaty insofar it only carries one of the listed activities irrespective of any further considerations. This gives rise to the question as to whether such activities, in the context of certain recent business models, may play a prominent role in practice and may thus become significant in their respective value chains.[954] This being so, the 2017 OECD MC chose to subject the listed activities to the extra condition that they are of a preparatory or auxiliary character having regard to what may be regarded as the essential and significant part of the activity of the enterprise as a whole:[955]

950. Even though the final report refers to the amendment as a mere assumption ("independent status is less likely if the activities of the person are performed wholly or almost wholly on behalf of only one enterprise"), neither the new proposed Article 5.6 nor its Commentaries seems to admit evidence to the contrary. *See* OECD (2015): Final Report on BEPS Action 7—Preventing the artificial avoidance of permanent establishment status, pp. 25-26. According to Pleijsier, the non-rebuttable presumption is correct, to the extent these agents could hardly be considered as "economically independent" from the principal. *See* Pleijsier, A. (2015), p. 152.

951. Suggestion made by Collier and the International Bar Association. *See* Collier, R. (2015), pp. 63-64 and OECD (2015): Comments received on the Revised Discussion Draft on BEPS Action 7: prevent the artificial avoidance of PE status, p. 196.

952. Chapter 3 section §3.03[E][1][a].

953. This conclusion may be inferred from the wording of Article 5.4 of the 2014 OECD MC. The OECD itself confirmed it in 2012. *See* OECD (2012): OECD Model Tax Convention: revised proposals concerning the interpretation and application of Article 5 (permanent establishment), pp. 24 and 26: "the question was raised as to whether the activities that are mentioned in subparagraphs a) to d) of paragraph 4 are automatic exceptions or whether these exceptions are conditional on the activities being of a preparatory or auxiliary nature (...) the Working Party agreed that the wording of subparagraphs a) to d) did not support the view that the application of these subparagraphs was subject to the additional condition that the relevant activity be of a preparatory or auxiliary character, which was a condition that was expressly included in subparagraphs e) and f)."

954. This could be, for example, the case for a server intended to gather relevant information about a group of users (Article 5.4.d of the 2014 OECD MC) or an Internet retailer which operates a warehouse to promptly deliver goods to its customers (Article 5.4.a) (*see* Cunningham, K.M. (2016), p. 507). *See also* OECD (2015): Final Report on BEPS Action 7—Preventing the artificial avoidance of permanent establishment status, p. 28.

4. Notwithstanding the preceding provisions of this Article, the term "permanent establishment" shall be deemed not to include:

a) the use of facilities solely for the purpose of storage, display or delivery of goods or merchandise belonging to the enterprise;
b) the maintenance of a stock of goods or merchandise belonging to the enterprise solely for the purpose of storage, display or delivery;
c) the maintenance of a stock of goods or merchandise belonging to the enterprise solely for the purpose of processing by another enterprise;
d) the maintenance of a fixed place of business solely for the purpose of purchasing goods or merchandise or of collecting information, for the enterprise;
e) the maintenance of a fixed place of business solely for the purpose of carrying on, for the enterprise, any other activity of a preparatory or auxiliary character;
f) the maintenance of a fixed place of business solely for any combination of activities mentioned in subparagraphs *a)* to e), ~~provided that the overall activity of the fixed place of business resulting from this combination is of a preparatory or auxiliary character,~~
provided that such activity or, in the case of subparagraph f), the overall activity of the fixed place of business, is of a preparatory or auxiliary character.

This amendment is no trouble-free. In the first place, making all the exceptions subject to the "preparatory or auxiliary" condition reduces certainty and increases the number of disputes, as exceptions would cease to apply automatically and rather require an individual assessment on a case-by-case basis.[956] Furthermore, it could be argued that the addition of this supplementary requirement questions the sense of maintaining the list of exceptions (subparagraphs a through d) to the extent that all kinds of activities would now need to pass this test,[957] unless the listed activities are considered to be subject to some sort of presumption that they are in fact preparatory and auxiliary.[958]

Second, the OECD equally addressed the fragmentation of activities that deliberately or inadvertently results in the application of the exemption clause. MNCs may

955. OECD (2015): Final Report on BEPS Action 7—Preventing the artificial avoidance of permanent establishment status, p. 30. Words in bold and strike-through indicate the variations from the 2014 OECD MC.
956. These are the reasons why the OECD discarded this alternative back in 2012. *See* OECD (2012): OECD Model Tax Convention: revised proposals concerning the interpretation and application of Article 5 (permanent establishment), p. 24 "the alternative option to make all the exceptions subject to the 'preparatory or auxiliary' condition would reduce certainty by subjecting the existing exceptions that currently apply automatically and therefore provide a bright line test to a condition that is inherently more subjective. The change would therefore increase the potential for disputes between taxpayers and tax authorities." *See also* Hoor, O.R.; O'Donnell, K. (2015), p. 934.
957. Cunningham, K.M. (2016), p. 507.
958. Which is clearly not the position of the OECD. *See* Commentary on Article 5 of the 2017 OECD MC: "the examples listed in subparagraphs a) to d) being merely common examples of activities that are covered by the paragraph because they often have a preparatory or auxiliary character" and OECD (2015): Final Report on BEPS Action 7—Preventing the artificial avoidance of permanent establishment status, p. 34.

easily split their activities in a certain jurisdiction into geographically separate places of business (under the responsibility of either one enterprise or two or more related parties) which, on their own, qualify for the exemption envisaged in Article 5.4.[959] The fact that such activities are not carried out altogether in the same POB but in separate ones would render ineffective Article 5.4.f, as this subparagraph merely combines the activities of a sole POB for the purposes of evaluating whether the combination effectively exceeds the threshold. This phenomenon is typically referred to as "fragmentation of activities" and eventually allows MNCs to have a substantial economic presence in a jurisdiction without incurring in tax liabilities therein.[960] In this context, the OECD suggested the adoption of a new proviso (Article 5.4.1) that is precisely intended to deny the exemption of Article 5.4 to a fixed POB (that would otherwise constitute a PE) where the activities carried on at that place and other activities of the same enterprise or of closely related enterprises[961] exercised at that place or another place within the relevant territory constitute complementary functions that are part of a cohesive business operation:

4.1 Paragraph 4 shall not apply to a fixed place of business that is used or maintained by an enterprise if the same enterprise or a closely related enterprise carries on business activities at the same place or at another place in the same Contracting State and

a) that place or other place constitutes a permanent establishment for the enterprise or the closely related enterprise under the provisions of this Article, or

b) the overall activity resulting from the combination of the activities carried on by the two enterprises at the same place, or by the same enterprise or closely related enterprises at the two places, is not of a preparatory or auxiliary character,

provided that the business activities carried on by the two enterprises at the same place, or by the same enterprise or closely related enterprises at the two places, constitute complementary functions that are part of a cohesive business operation.

959. OECD (2015): Final Report on BEPS Action 7—Preventing the artificial avoidance of permanent establishment status, p. 39. The risk was already foreseen in the Commentary on Article 5 of the 2014 OECD MC, paragraph 27.1.

960. Martín Jiménez, A. (2014), p. 7.

961. The new rule combines both branch activities of various related enterprises taking place in the Source state and residence-based activities conducted by related subsidiaries. Cunningham warns that this position is likely to give rise to an explosion of PEs, as the combined activities will almost never be regarded as preparatory and auxiliary: "the affiliate's activities will always fail to be preparatory and auxiliary and the affiliate will always have a PE." *See* Cunningham, K.M. (2016), p. 509.

Once again, the amendment is prone to multiply disputes between taxpayers and administrations and give rise to a certain degree of legal uncertainty,[962] while its effectiveness may be questionable in certain cases.[963]

[c] *Rules for Attributing Profits to the New PE Clause Questions the Actual Impact of the Proposals*

It is an undeniable fact that the 2017 OECD MC has effectively led to lower the PE threshold, in such a way that the number of PEs is expected to rapidly grow in the following years insofar as tax treaties adopt these suggested amendments. However, the efforts of the OECD would be fruitless unless the amendment of the clause in fact prompts increased tax revenues in the States where the new PEs arise.

This makes it necessary to evaluate the rules and guidelines that govern the attribution of profits to PEs—an exercise we already made in Chapter 3, with a particular focus on the AOA methodology[964] and further hypothesize their potential application to the renovated PE clause envisaged in the 2017 OECD MC. We will first refer to the attribution of profits to the new DAPEs resulting from Article 5.5 of the 2017 OECD MC and, subsequently, to the attribution of profits to the new PE resulting from Article 5.4 of the 2017 OECD MC.[965]

As regards the attribution of profits to DAPEs, we should first make reference to a long-standing discussion that dates back for decades, long before the advent of the BEPS project. The peculiarity of DAPEs, contrary to the rest of the PE fictions, is that they necessarily arise behind a person. In other words, it is always a person, either natural or legal, related or unrelated, the one performing the functions of dependent agent. This being the case, the host State would be *a priori* entitled to tax the profits of both that person (the dependent agent enterprise (hereinafter "DAE")), which may qualify as tax resident therein, and those attributed to the DAPE (i.e., the PE of the non-resident enterprise). In calculating the profits attributable to the DAPE it would be necessary to first determine and deduct an arm's length reward to the DAE for the services provided to the non-resident enterprise.[966] The question arises as to whether, once the arm's length remuneration is deducted, there would remain any further profits to be attributed to the DAPE.[967] On the one hand, it has been argued that the net profit attributable to the DAPE should be zero to the extent that the compensation paid to the

962. Hoor, O.R.; O'Donnell, K. (2015), p. 935.

963. Martín Jiménez observes that the new clause would not apply in case the MNC ultimately avoids the formation of a fixed POB in the territory concerned, as this is a necessary requirement to be able to accumulate the activities of the group in the territory. *See* Martín Jiménez, A. (2016), p. 470.

964. Chapter 3 section §3.03[D].

965. The OECD itself is working on an update to the 2010 report on attribution of profits considering the amendments proposed to the PE clause. Up until now, it has published a discussion draft on the issue, *see* OECD (2016): Discussion Draft on BEPS Action 7—Additional guidance on the attribution of profits to permanent establishments.

966. OECD (2010): Attribution of profits to permanent establishments, paragraph 234.

967. This very same question has been recently addressed by Dziurdz, K. (2014) and Jiménez-Valladolid, D.J. (2016) among many others.

DAE is considered to adequately reward the agent for the functions performed, assets used, and risks assumed under Article 9 of the OECD MC.[968] On the other hand, the OECD claims that the DAPE could be expected to obtain further profits under Article 7.2 beyond those corresponding to the DAE under Article 9.[969]

However, even if we adhere to the OECD's position (i.e., the "dual taxpayer approach"), the reality is that the amount of profits that would remain in the DAPE's tax base will often be zero or virtually zero.[970] The same observations apply to the profits attributable to the new DAPEs resulting from Article 5.5 of the 2017 OECD MC, as it may be inferred from the OECD draft itself.[971] This ultimately means that the

968. This is commonly referred to as the "single taxpayer" or "zero-sum" approach. According to Dziurdz, the reason behind this position is that there would no other functions performed, assets used and risks assumed in the source State, therefore no further profits could be attributable (Dziurdz, K. (2014)). In this context, the host State would not be entitled to any additional revenue as a result of the presence of a PE (Hoor, O.R.; O'Donnell, K. (2015), p. 933). An argument against this approach is that it would render Article 5.5 meaningless and thus infringe the principle that one should not assume law to be redundant (Eisenbeiss, J. (2016), p. 500). *See* the observations exposed in this regard on Chapter 2 section §2.01[A][2] concerning the Apple case.

969. This is called "dual taxpayer approach." *See* OECD (2010): Attribution of profits to permanent establishments, part I, paragraph 234 and Dziurdz, K. (2014), pp. 137-138. Jiménez-Valladolid notes three arguments to uphold the OECD's position. In the first place, an employee may act as a dependent agent of its own firm and his/her remuneration is very likely to be inferior to that he would have obtained in an arm's length scenario considering the functions he/she performs, the assets he/she uses and the risks he/she assumes. This circumstance justifies on its own the fact that they may be two separate taxable bases: that of the employee and that of the DAPE. Second, the principal may deploy its own or subcontracted staff to the PE and this fact would also give rise to the possibility to attribute profits to the PE beyond those attributed to the DAE. And third and most importantly, in the context of transfer pricing rules, functions may not necessarily be accompanied with the assumption of risks and the use of assets, as these concepts may well be dissociated. This being so, remuneration under Article 9 may only compensate for the function performed but not for the other concepts. On the contrary, under Article 7.2 (as interpreted by the AOA), risks and assets necessarily follow functions. In this context, the profit attributable to the PE would not be zero, as it would include compensation for the risks assumed and the assets used, concepts that were excluded from the arm's length remuneration of the subsidiary under Article 9. *See* Jiménez-Valladolid, D.J. (2016), pp. 27-34. The OECD provides one example as regards the third scenario noted by Jiménez-Valladolid. From a strictly legal perspective, both the inventory risk and the credit risk in respect of the customer receivables are necessarily assumed by the non-resident enterprise. However, it might be the case that the DAPE effectively performs the significant people functions relevant to the assumption and/or management of these risks, reason why the DAPE would be attributed the economic ownership of these risks under the AOA and thus the profits derived from those risks. These profits would not be attributable to the DAE but only to the DAPE. *See* OECD (2010): Attribution of profits to permanent establishments, part I, paragraphs 243-245 and OECD (2016): Discussion Draft on BEPS Action 7—Additional guidance on the attribution of profits to permanent establishments, pp. 14-18. Under the so-called PE Spanish approach, DAPEs were also attributed a significant amount of profits as a result of a complete disregard of the functional analysis required by Article 7.2 of the OECD MC and the AOA. *See* Chapter 3 section §3.03[F][2] and Martín Jiménez, A. (2016), pp. 468-469.

970. Jiménez-Valladolid, D.J. (2016), p. 34.

971. The 2016 Draft on the topic provided four examples involving the attribution of profits to new DAPEs. In the first case, the profit of the DAPE after the payment of an arm's length remuneration to the DAE, is zero. In the next three examples, the DAPE is merely attributed a minimal profit. *See* OECD (2016): Discussion Draft on BEPS Action 7—Additional guidance on the attribution of profits to permanent establishments, pp. 7-26.

expected increase in the number of DAPEs will not be necessarily accompanied by an increase in tax revenues in the PE-States.

As regards the attribution of profits to the new PEs resulting from Article 5.4 of the 2017 OECD MC, the situation would be very similar. The amendment to Article 5.4 will result in a significant increase of PEs whereas only very limited profits would be attributable to such PEs on the basis of the AOA.[972] The reason is that all the activities listed in this paragraph (as well as any other activity that may be labeled as "preparatory" or "auxiliary") are low value adding activities that could hardly expect a significant remuneration at arm's length, this being precisely the reason why they were originally excluded from the scope of the PE in the first place.[973]

[d] Interim Conclusions

In view of the above, we will now proceed to draw a few general conclusions.

First of all, the proposed amendments respect the original sense of the clause. They do not entail a substantial alteration of the scope of the clause but rather the introduction of a number of patches with the idea of restoring its alleged original effects, in line with the expectations set out by the own Action Plan.[974]

Second, the title given to Action 7 (i.e., "preventing the artificial avoidance of permanent establishment status") is erroneous and misleading. The reason is that the practices and structures addressed by the Action can hardly be regarded as cases of "artificial avoidance."[975] For example, in the context of the agency clause, it should not be presumed that the replacement of distributors with commissionaires is necessarily artificial or abusive, as the latter offer notable (non-tax) advantages over the former ones.[976] It should neither be assumed that the "rubber-stamp" approval of contracts—previously negotiated by an agent—by the non-resident principal necessarily constitute abuse.[977] The same is true for the use of a closely related company as an agent, whose dependent character is now presumed.[978] In other words, it seems that Action 7 simply wishes to extend the notion of the PE concept irrespective of the "abusive" intention of the taxpayer.[979]

Third, the amendments made to Article 5.5 of the 2017 OECD MC entail the replacement of objective and formalistic criteria with substance-focused ones. This

972. Hoor, O.R.; O'Donnell, K. (2015), p. 935.
973. This may be inferred from the Commentary on the 2014 OECD MC on Article 5.4, paragraphs 21-30.
974. *See* Chapter 4 section §4.01[B] and BEPS Action Plan, p. 11: "actions to address BEPS will restore both source and residence taxation in a number of cases."
975. We already denounced this tendency in Chapter 3 section §3.03[F][2].
976. For example, commissionaire arrangements allow MNCs to reduce costs where operations in the market jurisdiction are small as well as compliance costs (TP documentation or VAT filing), while they allow the centralization of the control over the value chain and the delegation of the authority. *See* Eisenbeiss, J. (2016), p. 492, Hoor, O.R.; O'Donnell, K. (2015), p. 931 and Pleijsier, A. (2015), P. 152.
977. Pleijsier, A. (2015), P. 147.
978. Eisenbeiss notes that the amendment to Article 5.6 goes beyond the "narrow goal" of preventing artificial avoidance of PE status. *See* Eisenbeiss, J. (2016), p. 493.
979. Schön, W. (2018), section 4.

new agency clause has the virtue of making the threshold less vulnerable to tax planning,[980] although this comes at a relatively high price. The new clause is now comprised by more subjective and broader criteria, thus giving rise to a wider scope of discretion when the time comes to interpret and apply the rule.[981] This ultimately results in a decreased degree of clarity and legal certainty,[982] a higher number of PEs and a proliferation of disputes[983] and an increment of administrative costs[984] together with a probable increased sense of legitimacy for "creative" PE assertions.[985] It is essential to acknowledge and accept these costs before taking a decision on the adoption of the proposed amendments in actual tax treaties.

Fourth, the potential adoption of the amendments suggested by Action 7 would finally put an end to a long history of unfortunate interpretations of the PE clause. In Chapter 3, we identified the habit of certain States to counteract the weaknesses of the PE clause by resorting to either eccentric interpretations, substance-over-form approaches and anti-avoidance rules, being the "PE Spanish approach" the greatest exponent of this tendency.[986] We then recognized that the outcome of these approaches may be regarded as desirable and legitimate, but denounced that the means employed were unacceptable, as they led to compromise the principle of legal certainty and the respect for the rule of law. In this context, we advocated for the direct amendment of the PE clause, and Action 7 has finally provided a response to our plea. It should be noted that the proposed amendments do not come out of thin air, as they were clearly inspired by either preexisting Commentaries on older versions of the OECD MC[987] or certain interpretations followed by domestic tax courts.[988] And lastly, we would like to draw attention to the elimination of most of the Commentary on Article 5 of prior versions of the OECD MC that promoted interpretations of the PE clause either contradicting or going beyond the literal meaning of its terms;[989] although we still find a few reminiscences of this unfortunate habit in the new Commentaries.[990]

980. Indeed, these amendments put an end to the most obvious PE-related tax planning techniques commonly used by MNCs.
981. Eisenbeiss, J. (2016), p. 487 and Cunningham, K.M. (2016), p. 508 ("the PE analysis was always factual by nature and after those changes will become even more factual").
982. Eisenbeiss, J. (2016), pp. 489 and 495.
983. Cunningham, K.M. (2016), p. 510.
984. Hoor, O.R.; O'Donnell, K. (2015), p. 935.
985. Also favored by the strong "anti-tax planning" rhetoric that has been present in the BEPs project. Eisenbeiss, J. (2016), p. 494.
986. Chapter 3 section §3.03[F][2].
987. We noticed the tendency of the BEPS project to upgrade Commentaries on the MC into the MC itself (*see* Chapter 4 section §4.01[B]). For example, one of the changes proposed to Article 5.4 was retrieved from the Commentary on Article 5 of the 2014 OECD MC, paragraph 27.1, while one of the changes suggested for Article 5.5 was already present in the Commentary on Article 5 of the 2014 OECD MC, paragraph 32.1.
988. Martín Jiménez demonstrated that there are good reasons to regard the PE Spanish approach as a prequel of Action 7 (*see* Martín Jiménenz, A. (2016), pp. 467-472), although he anticipates that such approach is likely to survive in the post-BEPS world, as it has "more far reaching effects" than the changes brought by Action 7 (*see* p. 473).
989. A tendency we identified and denounced also in Chapter 3 section §3.03[F][2].
990. *See* the Commentaries on the 2017 OECD MC, paragraph 93: "the reference to contracts in 'the name of' in subparagraph a) does not restrict the application of the subparagraph to contracts

Fifth, the ultimate impact of the recommendations fostered by Action 7 can only be measured by quantifying the increase (or decrease) of tax revenues that the PE-States are expected to collect as a consequence of the adoption of such recommendations. In the previous section, we reached the conclusion that Article 5 of the 2017 OECD MC will undoubtedly give rise to a greater number of PEs but this will probably not result in an increment of tax revenues in the PE-States. This discovery ultimately calls into question the practical relevance of the measures recommended by Action 7, unless the methodology to attribute profits to PEs along with Article 7.2 of the OECD MC is revised.[991] For the time being, it could be argued that the implementation of these measures would hardly pass a cost-benefit test, considering the great administrative burden for both taxpayers and tax administrations and the scarce additional profits that could be attributable to the new PEs.[992]

Last but not least, the effectiveness of the proposed amendments should be also evaluated in the light of the alleged objective of Action 7, i.e., ensuring taxation at the level of the market jurisdiction. We noted above that the PE clause (along with the methodology used to attribute profits to it), at least before the advent of BEPS, was inherently unable to ensure this outcome.[993] The potential adoption of the renovated version of Article 5 does not change this situation much, as the proposed amendments do not alter the scope of the clause but rather introduce a number of patches intended to restore its alleged original effects. It is true, however, that the expected increased number of PEs may incidentally bring taxable bases to the market jurisdictions.[994]

All in all, the amendments to the PE clause recommended by Action 7 should be welcomed, as they provide normative solutions to many of the weaknesses present in the clause, as opposed to the unfortunate past tendency to force its interpretation beyond reasonable limits, thus ensuring a greater degree of legal certainty. However, it should not be forgotten that governments must acknowledge and accept the risks that their implementation entail, and also understand that the practical effect of these changes is expected to be minimal in terms of tax revenues (unless the methodology to attribute profits to PEs is revised) and that they do not effectively ensure taxation at the market jurisdiction.

---

that are literally in the name of the enterprise; it may apply, for example, to certain situations where the name of the enterprise is undisclosed in a written contract").

991. In fact, Hellerstein proposed back in 2014 a set of amendments to the PE clause (similar to that recommended in Action 7) coupled by the "force of attraction" principle (in line with that followed by the UN in its Model), intended to capture any profits obtained by the non-resident company from digital activities within the PE-State. *See* Hellerstein, W. (2014), pp. 348-349.
992. Hoor, O.R.; O'Donnell, K. (2015), pp. 933 and 937.
993. Chapter 4 section §4.02[C][1].
994. New PEs are likely to result from the revision of Articles 5.4 and 5.5 and, insofar the location of the new PEs coincide with the location of the market of the non-resident enterprise, the objective of the BEPS project may incidentally be achieved. For example, online retailers are likely to use storage facilities for a quick delivery of products to their customers. This being so, if these facilities are deemed to constitute a PE (e.g., for not being preparatory or auxiliary), a PE will arise in the market jurisdiction and profits that may arguably be attributed to it will fall under the scope of the market State's tax jurisdiction.

[3] *Proposal for a Remote-Sales PE*

We concluded in Chapter 3 that the current scope of the PE clause was inherently unable to exhaust all situations in which access to public benefits could be assumed. In particular, situations in which the corporate taxpayer accesses the market of customers by remote means and without having a physical and stable presence in the territory of the host jurisdiction.[995] In the previous section, we argued that the amendments to the clause fostered by the BEPS project do not have any true impact in this regard, however desirable their adoption may be considered to be for other policy reasons. In particular, they proved to be useless in ensuring taxation at the level of the market jurisdictions despite their legitimate demands under both the presumptive benefit principle and the own postulates of the BEPS project.[996]

In this section we will proceed to suggest a normative proposal intended to ensure a greater level of consistency between the PE and the presumptive benefit principle, in the light of the considerations exposed above. In doing so, we will incidentally contribute to achieve the objective of the BEPS project as regards the PE threshold, i.e., taxation at the level of the market jurisdiction.[997]

The finding that the current PE clause may generally be regarded as consistent with the presumptive benefit principle[998] leads us to advocate for the preservation of the current threshold at both the treaty and the domestic level. Incidentally, it cannot be denied that the PE has historically served well in transactions involving cross-border scenarios, having given rise to an already established and consolidated 120-years history doctrine and jurisprudence enlightening its interpretation, along with a variety of tailor-made methodologies to attribute profits to it. This results in the direct rejection of proposals involving the replacement by current Article 5 with an entirely brand new standard.[999]

In the present section we will assess the advisability (along with the technical feasibility) of adopting a new PE deeming rule aimed at supplementing the current threshold, thus adding a new paragraph to current Article 5 of the MCs. This approach

995. Chapter 2 section §2.02[B][2][b].
996. Chapter 4 section §4.02[C][2][d].
997. Chapter 4 section §4.02[C][1].
998. Chapter 3 section §3.03[E][1].
999. Most notably, the "significant presence test" suggested by the OECD itself in the course of the BEPS project. The proposal sought to replace the existing PE concept with a new test based on three possible alternative proxies: (a) relationships with customers or users extending over six months combined with a certain degree of physical presence (through a POB or a DAPE); (b) sale of goods or services to customers in the country, e.g., through a website in local language; and (c) supplying goods or services to customers in the country resulting from or involving systematic data-gathering or contributions of content from persons in the country. *See* OECD (2014): BEPS Action 1: addressing the tax challenges of the digital economy, p. 146. Along the same lines, Schön suggests the replacement of the PE clause by a quantitative threshold based on gross revenues obtained from sales and provision of services to customers in a given jurisdiction (Schön, W. (2009), pp. 99-104.

is consistent with the traditional tendency to respond to structural changes in international business by aggregating new fictions to the clause, i.e., deemed inclusions in the definition of a PE despite the basic conditions not being satisfied.[1000]

We believe the new rule should ideally target remote sales made by a supplier resident in one of the Contracting States to customers located in the other contracting State in scenarios where the gross annual receipts derived from such sales exceed a certain quantitative threshold. To date, this approach has already been explored and advocated by a considerable number of scholars[1001] and organizations.[1002] While our proposal is undeniably inspired by the ideas expressed by this notable group of academics and institutions, we intend to identify their respective shortcomings and further provide a few possible solutions to counteract them.

[a] Justification under the Presumptive Benefit Principle

The primary objective we intend to pursue by means of this new PE fiction is a better consistency between the presumptive benefit principle and the PE threshold in the light of the conclusions reached throughout the present study.

The proposed rule essentially relies on the level of revenues derived by remote transactions which, by their own nature, do not require physical presence for their conclusion. As we argued elsewhere,[1003] having a market in a certain State automatically makes the non-resident supplier a presumable beneficiary to the benefits defrayed by such State, either directly or indirectly. A presumption that tends to be stronger as revenues get higher.[1004]

1000. Skaar, A. (1991), pp. 15-16 and Pinto, D. (2003), pp. 80, 193-194. The most prominent examples being the clauses targeting construction projects (*see* Chapter 3 section §3.03[E][1][b]) or the petroleum-related industries.

1001. Although the first comprehensive proposal may be found in Avi-Yonah, R. (1997), it has impregnated subsequent recommendations, e.g., Hellerstein, W. (1997), pp. 497-502 (US domestic income tax level), McLure, C.E. (Jr.) (2000), Cockfield, A. (2003), Pinto, D. (2003), pp. 207-231, Schön, W. (2009), pp. 92 and 99-104 (although he prefers the replacement of the PE clause by this test), AVI-Yonah, R.; Halabi, O. (2014) and Gadžo, S. (2016), pp. 289-302.

1002. Although the OECD has not provided a definite proposal in this regard, its "significant economic presence" test may be regarded as somehow consistent with our approach, as it relies on factors we believe to be relevant. *See* OECD (2015): Final Report on BEPS Action 1—Addressing the tax challenges of the digital economy, pp. 107-111. However, the OECD appears to be at a dead end now, as it has postponed a consensus-based solution on the matter for 2020 while at the same time admitting the very diverse positions of the States participating in the debate (*see* OECD (2018): Tax challenges arising from digitalisation: interim report). More recently, the EU proposal on PE based on significant digital presence has also served as inspiration. *See* EU Commission (2018): Proposal for a Council Directive laying down rules relating to the corporate taxation of a significant digital presence.

1003. Chapter 2 section §2.02[B][2][b].

1004. Gadžo, S. (2016), p. 270: "the total amount of revenue taxpayer derives from a specific country is probably a good proxy for both public benefits related to the market access therein and for the amount of value created for the enterprise on the demand side" and p. 290: "the total amount of revenue non-resident derives from customers located in a country signals that he enjoys significant benefits linked with the existence of the market therein." Along the same lines, albeit not mentioning explicitly the benefit principle, *see* OECD (2015): Final Report on BEPS Action 1—Addressing the tax challenges of the digital economy, pp. 107-108: "as a

The proposal may be challenged on the basis that it grants distinct tax treatment to e-commerce and traditional commerce, thus compromising the principle of neutrality and giving rise to distorting effects.[1005] The generation of distortions is inherent in any kind of tax and CITs are no exception, as they are likely to condition a considerable number of business decisions. Undoubtedly, either the adoption or the non-adoption of the new proposed PE fiction is prone to give rise to distortive effects, thus conditioning the choice as to how to approach the market of a certain State.

The non-adoption of the new threshold along with the preservation of the PE clause as it currently stands entails the infringement of the neutrality principle, as the clause would merely affect companies reaching the market of a State by means of a physical presence therein, thus exempting from source-based taxation competing companies in a comparable situation which, on the contrary, choose to access the market by remote means.[1006] On the other hand, the adoption of the new fiction may equally infringe the principle, as it would ensure that both types of companies are subject source-based taxation but in a distinct manner. This is because the first company would immediately become subject to tax therein—irrespective of its level of sales—insofar as profits could be attributed to its PE, while the second one would only be subject to tax at source once its gross sales exceed a certain quantitative threshold.

Departing from the self-evident fact that both options are likely to prompt distortions, the second one is preferable on the basis of the presumptive benefit principle. This principle does not only entitle the market jurisdiction to tax in both situations but also justifies the asymmetry identified above on the basis that the presumption of enjoyment of public benefits is weaker in cases the company access a market by remote means.[1007] This being so, it seems desirable to make traditional sellers subject to source-based taxation irrespective of its level of sales (on the basis that the presumable use and/or enjoyment of public benefits is always greater when the company is physically present in the State) while requiring e-sellers to reach a *de minimis* sales threshold (as e-sellers not reaching such threshold may have presumably enjoyed the benefits of the State to a very limited extent).

---

general matter, revenue that is generated on a sustained basis from a country could be considered to be one of the clearest potential indicators of the existence of a significant economic presence."

1005. Back in 1998 the OECD included neutrality among a set of principles that should inspire a potential tax reform targeting e-commerce scenarios, along with efficiency, certainty/simplicity, effectiveness/fairness and flexibility. *See* OECD (2015): Final Report on BEPS Action 1—Addressing the tax challenges of the digital economy, p. 20: "taxation should seek to be neutral and equitable between forms of business activities (...) In this sense, neutrality also entails that the tax system raises revenue while minimizing discrimination in favor of, or against, any particular economic choice."

1006. Hongler, P.; Pistone, P. (2015), p. 42.

1007. Chapter 2 sections §2.02[B][2] and §2.02[B][3].

[b] Objective Scope

The new PE fiction should ideally cover "remote transactions"[1008] involving the conclusion of contracts for the sale of goods or services between two or more parties by remote means.[1009] These goods and services can be either tangible or intangible and thus be delivered through conventional channels (e.g., tangible goods ordered online) or completely electronically (e.g., digital goods or electronically supplied services).[1010] The remote booking or order of services to be furnished physically will be left out of the scope of the clause for one main reason. The obligation to pay can be (in fact it is likely to be) postponed until the time the service is effectively provided, a fact that can generate unjustified distortions in the context of the tax collection system we will later propose.

The expression should encompass transactions carried out by all sort of remote means, including but not limited to the Internet, telephone (e.g., conclusion of contracts through call centers) and ordinary mail (e.g., catalogue shopping).[1011] A clause solely relying on digital transactions[1012] would give rise to certain risks, as companies may feel tempted to circumvent it by using their digital platforms to display

1008. Avi-Yonah's 2014 proposal explicitly refers to "remote sales," although we believe the definitions suggested for Article 3.1.f and 3.1.o of the MC are manifestly insufficient ("the term 'remote sale' means a sale into a Contracting State (...) the term 'a sale into a Contracting State' means a sale in which the location where the product or service sold is received by the purchaser, based on the location indicated by instructions for delivery that the purchaser furnishes to the seller, is within that Contracting State"). *See* Avi-Yonah, R.; Halabi, O. (2014). For his part, Gadžo endorses Avi-Yonah's 2014 proposal but fails to provide any useful guidance on how to interpret the expression (Gadžo, S. (2016), pp. 289-302).

1009. OECD (2015): Final Report on BEPS Action 1—Addressing the tax challenges of the digital economy, p. 108. For its part, the EU proposal on the PE based on significant digital presence solely would solely capture "digital services," meaning those "delivered over the internet or an electronic network and the nature of which renders their supply essentially automated and involving minimal human intervention." This presupposes, for example, the immediate exclusion of sales of tangible goods that by nature need to be delivered physically, even in cases where the order and processing is previously carried out electronically. *See* EU Commission (2018): Proposal for a Council Directive laying down rules relating to the corporate taxation of a significant digital presence, p. 14 (Article 3 of the proposed Directive) and Escribano E. (2019b), pp. 571-572.

1010. The first phenomenon is commonly referred to as "indirect" or offline e-commerce while the latter is known as "direct" or "online" e-commerce. *See* OECD (2015): Final Report on BEPS Action 1—Addressing the tax challenges of the digital economy, p. 55. The second one is gaining weight over the years: "through digitization of information, including text, sound, and visual images, an increasing number of goods and services can be delivered digitally to customers increasingly remote from the location of the seller." A long list of examples of electronically supplied services may be found in EU Commission (2014): Explanatory notes on the EU VAT changes to the place of supply of telecommunications, broadcasting and electronic services that enter into force in 2015, pp. 83-88.

1011. OECD (2015): Final Report on BEPS Action 1—Addressing the tax challenges of the digital economy, pp. 107-108.

1012. The following proposals only target digital/electronic transactions: Avi-Yonah, R. (1997), pp. 535-541, McLure, C.E. (Jr.) (2000), Pinto, D. (2003), pp. 207-231 and EU Commission (2018): Proposal for a Council Directive laying down rules relating to the corporate taxation of a significant digital presence.

the products and further route their customers to make a call to perform the final purchase.[1013]

The provision should be drafted in deliberately broad terms, thereby omitting further qualitative specifications intended to ring-fence its scope in an unjustified manner. We believe it is necessary to make this clarification due to the widespread tendency to include this sort of extra requirements of qualitative nature in the clauses proposed by both the academia and the OECD,[1014] commonly based on the belief that the volume of sales does not per se proves a regular, purposeful and sustained participation in the host jurisdiction.[1015] What the majority of these requisites do is predetermine the means through which remote sales ought to be conducted in order to fall under the scope of the PE fiction. We will now proceed to explain the three reasons why we believe this approach is unfortunate.

First, the only reason why we suggest the adoption of this new PE fiction is the fact that we believe market jurisdictions should be entitled to a share on the non-resident's taxable income on the basis that the latter is presumably benefiting directly or indirectly from their governments' public investments. In this context, the means used to reach such market (e.g., website, software smartphone app, telephone, ordinary mail) are of no concern and thereby should not play any role when the time comes to draft the rule. While it is true that the use of certain communication systems may presumably entail a slightly greater use and/or enjoyment of public benefits than others, we believe this does not justify asymmetries in the rule.

Second, the inclusion of references to certain traits of today's digital business models may first give the impression that the clause is conveniently up-to-date. However, it goes without saying that the digital economy is an ever-evolving reality: what is popular today may fall into oblivion tomorrow. This means that references to these features may render the clause obsolete overnight. While domestic tax regulations may be amended with relative ease, the same cannot be said of tax treaties, which tend to remain in force for decades until further negotiations take place. In this context, it is important to draft an enduring rule that is capable of fulfilling its function for a relatively long period of time. These arguments bring us to advise against references to, for example, electronic applications (the "apps")[1016] or the existence of a website in local language and/or with local domain.[1017]

1013. OECD (2015): Final Report on BEPS Action 1—Addressing the tax challenges of the digital economy, p. 108.
1014. Hellerstein, W. (1997), p. 501, Hinnekens, L. (1998), pp. 195-199 (suggesting a facts-and-circumstances test), OECD (2014): BEPS Action 1: addressing the tax challenges of the digital economy, pp. 143-145 (the "significant digital presence" test targeting solely enterprises engaged in "fully dematerialized digital activities"), OECD (2015): Final Report on BEPS Action 1—Addressing the tax challenges of the digital economy, pp. 109-111 (suggesting the supplementation of the quantitative threshold with digital and user-based factors) and Hongler, P.; Pistone, P. (2015), pp. 23-26, among many others.
1015. Hinnekens, L. (1998), p. 197 and OECD (2015): Final Report on BEPS Action 1—Addressing the tax challenges of the digital economy, pp. 107 and 111 ("total revenue, however, may not by itself suffice to evidence a non-resident enterprise-s regular and sustained participation in the economic life of a country").
1016. Hongler, P.; Pistone, P. (2015), pp. 25-26 and EU Commission (2018): Proposal for a Council Directive laying down rules relating to the corporate taxation of a significant digital presence,

Third, the insertion of requirements of a qualitative nature in the clause entails a higher level of complexity when the time comes to interpret and apply the clause along with a higher expected number of tax disputes, while a quantitative threshold has the virtue of being straightforward and certain.[1018]

Lastly, we would like to refer to a specific group of qualitative factors that are commonly used in the tests proposed by the academia and the OECD. We are referring to user-based factors, e.g., the number of users of a digital platform,[1019] the amount of time they spend in such platform[1020] or the volume data collected from them.[1021] This set of factors responds to one of the most lucrative business opportunities that the digital economy offers to enterprises: the ability to collect personal[1022] and non-personal data about their users/customers and further monetize it by means of, *inter alia*, improving or customizing existing products and services, conceiving new ones that better suit the needs identified in the market or offering the possibility to place targeted digital advertising to potential advertisers.[1023]

Data is often the invisible price users pay for seemingly free digital services. In this context, one may observe that this reality is in fact not much different from the sale of an electronically supplied service comprised in our proposed clause, the only difference being that the user is not paying directly for the service but rather providing his/her data, whose exploitation is very likely to ultimately end up in profits. Both

p. 14 (Article 3.2 of the proposed directive). However, this latter proposal only includes a reference to "apps" as an illustrative example of the digital interfaces through which the covered digital services may be supplied. Statistics reveal the unstoppable growth in cell phone usage, resulting in greater time spent in "apps" and increased expenditure in them. However, there is no guarantee that their popularity is going to last. *See* for example: http://www.smartinsights.com/mobile-marketing/mobile-marketing-analytics/mobile-marketing-statistics/ (last accessed on January 10, 2019).

1017. OECD (2015): Final Report on BEPS Action 1—Addressing the tax challenges of the digital economy, p. 109. The OECD departs from the assumption that having a website using a local domain, translated into local language, or displaying prices in local currency, etc. constitute sufficient evidence of an adequate level of integration of the non-resident enterprise in the local market. The fact is that these factors may have lost their relevance over the decades. For example, in-built translation services in search platforms and websites (e.g., Google translate) make it increasingly unnecessary to make use of a local domain or translate the website. This reveals that reference to this sort of factors may be considered as already obsolete.

1018. Cockfield criticizes Hinnekens' facts-and-circumstances test on the basis that the US experience on a similar domestic test produced countless problems. *See* Cockfield, A. (2003), pp. 10-11.

1019. OECD (2015): Final Report on BEPS Action 1—Addressing the tax challenges of the digital economy, p. 110, Hongler, P.; Pistone, P. (2015), pp. 24-26 and EU Commission (2018): Proposal for a Council Directive laying down rules relating to the corporate taxation of a significant digital presence, p. 16 (Article 4.3.b of the proposed Directive).

1020. Hongler, P.; Pistone, P. (2015), p. 25.

1021. OECD (2015): Final Report on BEPS Action 1—Addressing the tax challenges of the digital economy, pp. 110-111.

1022. Personal data may be provided voluntarily, observed or inferred. For further information, *see* OECD (2015): Final Report on BEPS Action 1—Addressing the tax challenges of the digital economy, pp. 40-41.

1023. Task Force on Taxation of the Digital Economy (2013): Report to the French Minister for the Economy and Finance and the Minister for Industrial Recovery (popularly known as the Collin & Colin report), pp. 33-60 and OECD (2015): Final Report on BEPS Action 1—Addressing the tax challenges of the digital economy, pp. 68-70.

situations may also be regarded as comparable from the perspective of the presumptive benefit principle, in the sense that the State where the users are located are not only providing a "market" (in a broad sense) but also the necessary infrastructures to facilitate the access to the relevant platform.[1024]

However, while fully acknowledging this reality, we believe references to these factors should be left out of the wording of the clause for the time being, as the potential application and enforcement of a threshold relying on these factors is likely to generate countless practical issues.[1025]

[c] Subjective Scope

The proposed clause necessarily requires the identification of the two persons involved in the remote transaction, namely the supplier and the customer. This is one of the major challenges that the drafting of the new PE fiction poses, and we suspect this is reason why all the proposals on the table tend to be (either deliberately or inadvertently) particularly ambiguous in this respect.

As regards the taxpayer, it must be a (natural or legal) person resident in one of the Contracting States for the purposes of the relevant tax treaty and further carrying on a business activity,[1026] thereby excluding C2C transactions. The remote seller should be the person which concludes the remote sale of the good/service.[1027] The rule may be however easily circumvented by a number of strategies. First, the taxpayer may fragment its selling activities with customers in a given State among a number of related parties resident in different States so as to ensure that the quantitative threshold of the respective treaties is never surpassed.[1028] Second, the taxpayer may equally resort to a related party resident in a State with which the Market State has a treaty in force that lacks the new PE fiction, thus impeding the latter State to exercise its taxing

1024. Hongler, P.; Pistone, P. (2015), p. 25 and Chapter 2 section §2.02[B][2][b].

1025. E.g., computing users that are not genuine ones but rather bots or users managing multiple or fraudulent accounts. *See* OECD (2015): Final Report on BEPS Action 1—Addressing the tax challenges of the digital economy, p. 110.

1026. Article 7 of the MCs applies to an "enterprise of a Contracting State," which in turn mean, according to Article 3, an enterprise/business carried on by a person (individual, company or any other body of persons) that is resident of a Contracting State. For its part, the European Commission only intends to apply its PE based on significant digital presence to entities (thus excluding individuals) carrying out a business, although considering the high quantitative thresholds set out by the draft Directive, individual businesspersons would rarely exceed them. *See* EU Commission (2018): Proposal for a Council Directive laying down rules relating to the corporate taxation of a significant digital presence, p. 14 (Article 2 of the proposed Directive).

1027. Article 3.1.k of the MC suggested in Avi-Yonah, R.; Halabi, O. (2014) (p. 11) defines "remote seller" as a "person that makes remote sales."

1028. OECD (2015): Final Report on BEPS Action 1—Addressing the tax challenges of the digital economy, p. 108.

rights.[1029] Third, the taxpayer may also channel its sales through an unrelated entity acting as distributor or reseller.[1030]

There are at least a couple of options to address the first scenario. First, the clause can be applied on a related-group basis rather than on a separate-entity basis. The aggregation rule may operate in all circumstances,[1031] as a rebuttable presumption[1032] or merely under specific conditions in the form of a SAAR.[1033] We believe the first option is preferable. Even though one could expect this would be unjustifiably burdensome, we believe the group will be in the position to calculate the consolidated amount of gross sales with relative ease assuming that one of the two proposed collection systems[1034] is finally implemented. In the absence of an anti-fragmentation rule of this kind, the recently suggested principal purpose test rule (Article 29 of 2017 OECD MC) is equally suited to confront these risks.[1035]

As regards the customer, it is the person (either an individual or entity, business or final consumer) purchasing the good or service. Be that as it may, either the customer or the act of consumption should be somehow related to the territory of the other contracting State of the treaty. Proposals under review define this connection in different ways, *inter alia*, the place where the goods or services sold are consumed/used[1036] or otherwise received by the purchaser,[1037] or where the consumer is physically present at the time of the consumption.[1038]

1029. A situation that may, at best, be addressed by means of a LOB clause insofar the related party does not constitute a qualified person for the purposes of the treaty. *See* Chapter 3 section §3.02[C][2].
1030. Avi-Yonah, R. (1997), p. 537. Some of these distributors have ultimately turned into huge cybermalls offering a vast catalogue of products provided by small-sized suppliers. Amazon, EBay and AliExpress find themselves between the major worldwide e-distributors.
1031. Pinto, D. (2003), pp. 215-216 and EU Commission (2018): Proposal for a Council Directive laying down rules relating to the corporate taxation of a significant digital presence, p. 16 (Article 4.3 of the proposed Directive).
1032. OECD (2015): Final Report on BEPS Action 1—Addressing the tax challenges of the digital economy, p. 108: "this aggregation rule could be introduced as a rebuttable presumption, with the taxpayer being able to demonstrate that it did not artificially fragment the distance selling activities in order to manipulate the revenue threshold."
1033. Likewise, the BEPS project suggested the addition of an anti-fragmentation rule (Article 5.4.1 of the 2017 OECD MC), intended to prevent an enterprise and its closely related enterprises from fragmenting a "cohesive business operation" into several small operations in order to qualify for the PE-exemption envisaged in Article 5.4. The clause does not allow always allow the aggregation of activities, as it is restricted to cases where these enterprises conducted "complementary functions" part of a "cohesive business operations." *See* OECD (2015): Final Report on BEPS Action 7—Preventing the artificial avoidance of permanent establishment status, p. 39. This is the option preferred by Gadžo, S. (2016), p. 270.
1034. *See* Chapter 4 section §4.02[C][3][e].
1035. OECD (2015): Final Report on BEPS Action 6: Preventing the granting of treaty benefits in inappropriate circumstances. The clause is drafted in p. 55 while example J in the Commentaries to the clause (p. 64) refers to a comparable situation that falls under the scope of the anti-abuse rule.
1036. Avi-Yonah, R. (1997), p. 536. Hongler and Pistone use the term "domicile" but in fact intend to refer to the place where the user "uses" the relevant digital service. *See* Hongler, P.; Pistone, P. (2015), p. 26 and footnote 55.
1037. Avi-Yonah, R.; Halabi, O. (2014), p. 11.
1038. This is the approach we infer from the proposals suggested by the OECD ("in-country customers"; "transactions concluded with customers in the country concerned"), Schön

Although we believe the place where the consumer is located at the time of the purchase can be regarded as a reasonable starting point for our analysis, the explicit reference of this proxy in the PE proviso would technically entail the case-by-case assessment of the relevant facts and circumstances involving every separate remote transaction which, on top of this, tend to be numerous and relatively unimportant in amount.[1039]

To avoid an unnecessarily high compliance burden, the clause should rely instead on an indicator which could guide us, to the extent possible, towards the State where the consumer is located at the time of the act of consumption while at the same being straightforward, manageable and relatively easy to enforce by the pertinent operator. In this context, we will put forward three indicators that should ideally apply in consecutive order:

(a) Digital certificate of residence.[1040] Tax administrations may issue a digital ID card on an annual basis certifying the residence status of the relevant taxpayer. The card can initially trust the ordinary place of residence of the taxpayer as declared in its own annual tax return, although the tax Administration should always be entitled to rebut the presumption considering the domestic tax residence tests in place along with the facts and circumstances surrounding the case. This being so, the tax Administration may always revoke the digital certificate denying the residence status of the relevant taxpayer in its jurisdiction or else issue a new one with a different content.

We believe this indicator should be the first to be considered, as it is in our view the most suitable one. The main reason is that the State of residence of the consumer is very likely to coincide, in the case of individuals, with the State where they are physically present at the time of the consumption[1041] and, in the case of entities, with the State to which they are deemed to be somehow linked. Apart from this, the certificate is ultimately endorsed by a government and therefore will tend to be up-to-date, relatively trustworthy and less susceptible to self-interested manipulations than other indicators we could use. The major challenge this rule would entail is certainly its implementation. In this regard, States adopting the new PE proviso in their treaties

("customers in a given jurisdiction"), Pinto ("country where a customer is located") and Gadžo ("where the customer base for goods and services of an enterprise is located"). *See* OECD (2015): Final Report on BEPS Action 1—Addressing the tax challenges of the digital economy, p. 108, Schön, W. (2009), p. 100, Pinto, D. (2003), pp. 220-222 and Gadžo, S. (2016), p. 290.

1039. *See* OECD (2015): Final Report on BEPS Action 1—Addressing the tax challenges of the digital economy, p. 100.

1040. Also suggested, albeit in different terms, by Avi-Yonah, R. (1997, p. 537 and Pinto, D. (2003), pp. 221-222. While Avi-Yonah merely makes a general reference to this idea, Pinto argues that a trusted third party—as a government agency- should be responsible for ensuring its veracity.

1041. Chapter 4 section §4.02[B][3][a] revealed that 92% of the 78 surveyed jurisdictions use residence tests in their PITs based on the effective physical presence of the individual within their respective territories. This means that an individual who is granted the residency status on these grounds is very likely to find himself/herself in his/her State of Residence when he/she makes an online purchase throughout the year.

ought to mutually undertake to set up the necessary domestic administrative procedures to make it possible.[1042]

In scenarios where States do not have this system in place or where customers lack a valid digital certificate (either due to its stateless status or other reasons), the following indicator would apply.

(b) Address of the customer as specified in the payment instrument.[1043] Remote sales rely on a number of payment methods. The following figure indicates an estimation of the most widely used in online transactions.

Figure 5 Estimated Percentage of Use of Different Payment Methods in E-Commerce Worldwide (2018)[1044]

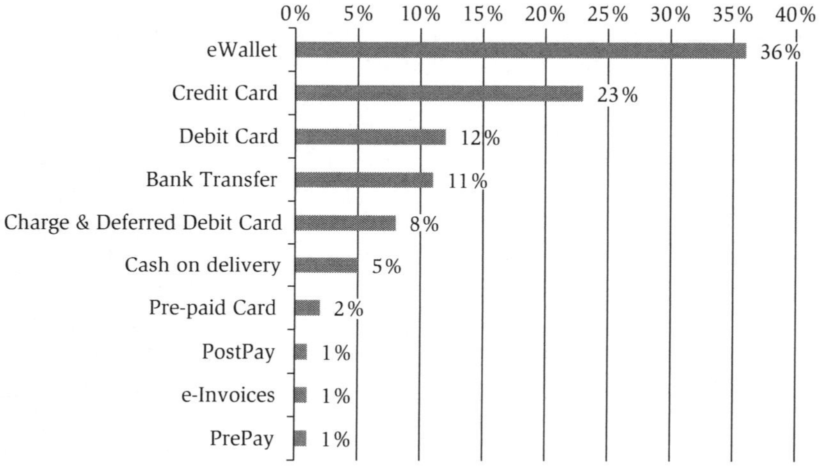

Figure 5 reveals that banks are behind a considerable volume of the payment methods used worldwide to purchase online. In other words, if we aggregate the percentages corresponding to eWallet (e.g., PayPal, Alipay),[1045] credit/debit cards, bank transfers, charge and deferred debit cards (e.g.,

1042. In case the new proviso is added to the Multilateral Convention to Implement tax treaty measures to prevent BEPS (promoted by the G20 and the OECD as a result of the BEPS project), these procedures may be discussed and negotiated on a multilateral basis. *See* http://www.oecd.org/tax/treaties/multilateral-convention-to-implement-tax-treaty-related-measures-to-prevent-BEPS.pdf (last accessed on January 10, 2019).

1043. Avi-Yonah and Halabi suggest using this indicator solely in scenarios where the seller has no other means to know the customer's address (by means of, e.g., the billing address or the delivery address). *See* Avi-Yonah, R.; Halabi, O. (2014), p. 11.

1044. *See* the Global Payments Report 2018 issued by Worldpay (p. 9), accessible upon subscription in this link: https://worldpay.globalpaymentsreport.com/#/ (last accessed on January 10, 2019). The definitions for each payment method are comprised in p. 107 of the report.

1045. PayPal and its competitors (e.g., Google Wallet or WePay *inter alia*) are platforms that allow the customer to use their funding sources (bank account and credit/debit card) to buy online in a streamlined and safe way. *See* https://www.paypal.com/uk/webapps/mpp/ua/servicedescription-full (last accessed on January 10, 2019).

American Express) and pre-paid cards, we shall conclude that the payment process of 92% of online purchases is ultimately run by a financial institution in which the customer has a bank account. Any person willing to open a bank account is commonly expected to supply certain personal information to do so, including its postal address.

The customer's address in the hands of the financial institution is certainly not as trustworthy and convenient as the first suggested proxy for various reasons. First, it is unlikely to be up-to-date, as the client has few incentives to report its changes of address to the bank. Second, the day will come when the customer's postal address will be literally of no concern to the banks, as their clients are increasingly demanding to be contacted online. This tendency may ultimately render this indicator obsolete in just a few decades.

Lastly, a solution still needs to be found for the remaining 8% of remote sales which are conducted outside the radar of financial institutions and to which this indicator cannot apply. We are referring to cases where customers choose to pay in cash (5%), PostPay (1%), e-invoices (1%), PrePay (1%) or virtual currencies as Bitcoin, which may well be anonymous. It is in these scenarios where the following indicator comes into play.

(c) Address explicitly provided by the customer to the remote seller.[1046] Customers are often required to submit a postal address when setting up a new user account in a website (where sales may eventually take place) and, most likely, during the purchase process (e.g., billing address or delivery address).

This indicator is ideally suited for the so-called offline e-commerce, where tangible goods are ordered online and subsequently delivered by regular mail. In these cases, the indicator will fulfill its function perfectly, as it will guide us directly to the place where the customer is physically located. The same cannot be said, however, for online e-commerce concerning digital goods and electronically supplied services, where the customer's postal address has no relevance whatsoever. As a result, purchasers may not be required to provide a postal address at all or, even if they do, they will have little or no incentive to do it correctly.[1047] Indeed, they may potentially feel tempted to provide a false address wherever the application of the new PE proviso has an impact on the price of the transaction, which could be the case depending on the method used to collect the tax revenue.[1048]

The potential adoption of the new PE-deeming rule must be necessarily accompanied by adjustments in the remote purchase processes to guarantee its effective enforceability. In other words, States implementing this rule should strive to ensure, by means of the necessary domestic regulations, that purchase platforms effectively require the submission of the digital certificate of residence—where applicable—and,

1046. Avi-Yonah, R. (1997), p. 536, Pinto, D. (2003), p. 221 and Avi-Yonah, R.; Halabi, O. (2014), p. 11.
1047. Pinto, D. (2003), pp. 221-222.
1048. *See* Chapter 4 section §4.02[C][3][e].

in any event, the customer's postal address, as this latter indicator would operate as a sort of closing clause in cases where the first two indicators cannot apply.

We are fully aware of the fact that these three indicators may not always guide us to the State we intend them to do, i.e., that where the customer is located at the time of the purchase. We however take this risk, as we feel compelled to sacrifice accuracy in favor of practicability and enforceability.

States may wish instead to rely on more accurate indicators at the expense of compliance costs. In this context, proxies suggested by the European Commission in the framework of the new Value-Added Tax (hereinafter "VAT") regime on electronic services may well serve as inspiration.[1049]

1049. EU Commission (2014): Explanatory notes on the EU VAT changes to the place of supply of telecommunications, broadcasting and electronic services that enter into force in 2015, pp. 54-73 and 89-91. Lamensch notes that the new VAT rules on electronic services result in legal uncertainty and an unacceptable compliance burden for e-suppliers. *See* Lamensch, M. (2012).

Figure 6 Proxies Aimed at Locating the Customer for the Purposes of the European VAT Regime on Telecommunications, Broadcasting and Electronic Services[1050]

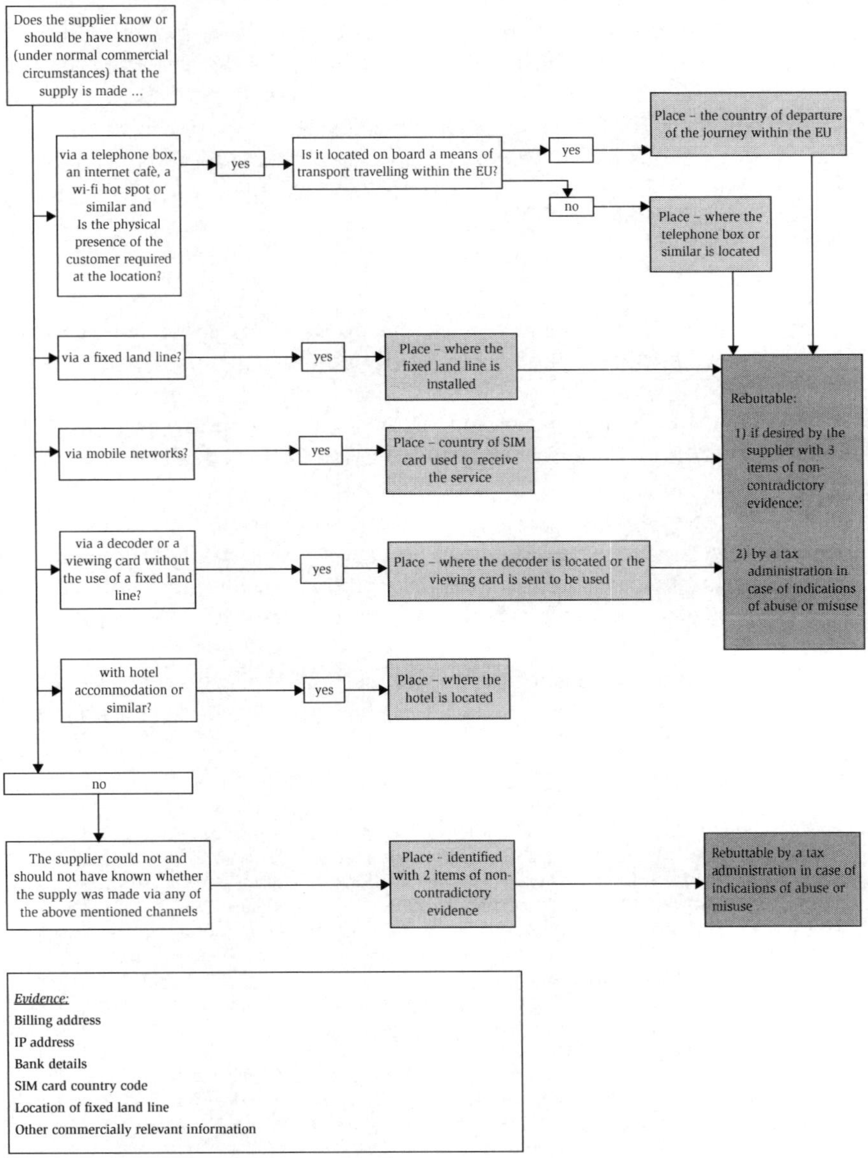

1050. EU Commission (2014): Explanatory notes on the EU VAT changes to the place of supply of telecommunications, broadcasting and electronic services that enter into force in 2015, p. 61.

IP addresses are one of the proxies used by the European VAT to locate the customer of electronic services and have also been considered in policy proposals dealing with the PE threshold.[1051] IP addresses are numerical labels that identify the devices, allowing them to communicate with other devices over the internet, and are nowadays one of the most common methodologies to ascertain the geographical location of a connected device and, by extension, the user behind the device. While its use is undoubtedly more straightforward and simple than others, it is equally true that they are increasingly becoming less accurate and reliable (e.g., programs called "anonymizers" can easily mask the real IP address of the users) and pose significant implementation challenges[1052] that ultimately discourages their use (Figure 6).

[d] Quantitative Threshold

The new PE fiction should apply only to the extent that remote sales conducted between the abovementioned parties are significant from a quantitative point of view. This can be measured by means of a quantitative threshold written in absolute terms—e.g., a yearly minimum amount of revenue[1053]—or relative terms—e.g., a minimum percentage in relation to either the MNC's consolidated sales[1054] or a national macroeconomic factor.[1055]

Either of these options appear to be equally consistent with the presumptive benefit principle, so we base our decision to opt for a fixed *de minimis* fixed revenue-based threshold primarily on simplicity grounds, as it is more straightforward than the rest of the options and further provides a considerable degree of legal certainty.[1056]

The threshold should be expressed in gross revenue terms, irrespective of the fact that income taxation (and PE taxation is not an exception) is commonly imposed on a

1051. OECD (2000): Report by the Technology Technical Advisory Group (TAG) on Tax and e-commerce and, most notably, EU Commission (2018): Proposal for a Council Directive laying down rules relating to the corporate taxation of a significant digital presence, p. 17 (Articles 4.4 and 4.7 of the proposed Directive).

1052. We already reviewed in detail the pros and cons of using IP addresses as proxies in proposals of digital PEs in Escribano, E. (2019b), pp. 586-589. *See also* Svantesson, D. (2007).

1053. Avi-Yonah, R. (1997), Hellerstein, W. (1997), pp. 497-502, Pinto, D. (2003), pp. 207-231, Gadžo, S. (2016), pp. 289-302 and EU Commission (2018): Proposal for a Council Directive laying down rules relating to the corporate taxation of a significant digital presence, p. 16 (Article 4.3 of the proposed Directive).

1054. This is the preferred approach of the Association Française de Femmes Fiscalistes. *See* OECD (2014): BEPS Action 1: comments received on public discussion draft, p. 7: "the PE definition could possibly be reviewed by introducing some materiality threshold based on the level of business of an MNE in a foreign country in which it has no reported corporate tax presence (subsidiary or branch). As an example, if more than x% of consolidated sales of an MNE headquartered in country A is realized in a foreign country B, and subject to meeting other criteria as per (revised) Article 5 of the OECD Model Convention, the MNE headquartered in country A could be deemed to have a permanent establishment in country B."

1055. Hongler/Pistone suggest a reference to the average income or a GDP in Hongler, P.; Pistone, P. (2015), p. 25.

1056. Arnold, B.J. (2003b), p. 94, Cockfield, A. (2003), p. 12 and Gadžo, S. (2016), pp. 271-272.

net basis.[1057] It seems unreasonable to compel all taxpayers conducting remote sales in a State to calculate the net profits derived from such in any event just to determine whether the relevant threshold is satisfied, as this involves a massive administrative burden. On the contrary, a gross revenue-based threshold would automatically exempt taxpayers not exceeding the threshold from the costs of complying with the market State tax regulations. Be that as it may, the calculation of the tax liability derived from this clause should ultimately rely on the net profits obtained by the taxpayer, as it will be later discussed.

The establishment of a monetary threshold in a treaty involves certain risks Arnold warns us about.[1058] First, reciprocity may not always be desirable for policy reasons[1059] and, even when it does, it may not always be easily achieved due to currency fluctuations.[1060] Second, monetary limits may soon lose their effectiveness due to the impact of inflation, unless adjustments are foreseen in the treaty itself. Third and lastly, States should try to be as consistent as possible when negotiating the quantity of the threshold in their respective treaties so as to ameliorate risks derived from treaty-shopping practices and the potential application of the most-favored-nation clause.

The amount of revenue to be included in the new proviso should ideally be relatively high for various reasons. First, this would ensure that income derived from the market jurisdiction exceeds the costs of complying with its tax laws.[1061] Second, it would be less prone to distort the business choices of the taxpayer.[1062] Last but not least, a relatively high amount of revenue would normally evidence a presumably greater direct/ indirect use and/or enjoyment of the public benefits defrayed by the market State. The definition of the exact threshold amount would be up to the States

1057. Avi-Yonah, R. (1997), p. 536 and Arnold, B.J. (2003b), p. 94. Pinto warns against the risk that gross sales may not correlate with the net income ultimately allocable to a jurisdiction (Pinto, D. (2003), P. 215), while the OECD is of the opinion that gross revenue in a reliable proxy for net income in the context of the digital economy, as e-retailers often need to make a substantial up-front investment of resources (including capital and labor) at the beginning of their activities but, once this is done, the provision the products and services online frequently requires only limited marginal costs (OECD (2015): Final Report on BEPS Action 1—Addressing the tax challenges of the digital economy, P. 114).

1058. Arnold, B.J. (2003b), pp. 94-95.

1059. Treaties between developed and developing States may place asymmetric thresholds considering their relative economic positions and different standards of living.

1060. Arnold refers to two thresholds comprised in the US-Canada treaty which illustrate two possible approaches in this regard. On one hand, the branch tax provision fixes an amount by reference to Canadian dollars when Canada is applying the treaty and by reference to the US equivalent of the Canadian dollar amount when the US is applying the treaty. This ensures reciprocity, although the amount relevant for the US will fluctuate from time to time. On the other hand, the thresholds for employees and entertainers apply irrespective of exchange rates, as amounts are expressed in both Canadian and US dollars.

1061. Avi-Yonah, R. (1997), p. 536, Pinto, D. (2003), p. 213 and Schön, W. (2009), p. 104.

1062. On the contrary, a low threshold creates a substantial incentive not to invest in a foreign country at all, a result which should be avoided at all costs according to Schön, W. (2009), p. 104.

concerned, although there is some agreement among scholars that USD 1,000,000 would be reasonable.[1063]

[e] Compliance and Enforcement

Beyond the abovementioned difficulties associated with the design of the new proviso, the most notable challenges surely rest in its enforceability. These challenges, if not conveniently addressed, can render the rule impracticable, no matter how desirable and theoretically justifiable is deemed to be.[1064]

A remote seller is likely to lack any sort of physical presence in its market jurisdictions, a circumstance that can seriously endanger the effective implementation of the rule due to two important barriers the local tax authority is expected to face: information deficit and extraterritorial enforcement.

As regards the first one, tax authorities need information to satisfactorily apply the rule. Information that would allow them to first identify the non-resident taxpayer along with its relevant remote transactions with in-country customers and, subsequently, assess its tax liability. However, tax authorities would face tremendous difficulties when the time comes to access such information. While the imposition of unilateral reporting obligations to taxpayers who have literally never set foot in its territory may prove to be laborious, if not illegal,[1065] tax authorities would rarely have the capacity and resources to obtain the information by their own means.[1066]

On top of this, even assuming that tax authorities manage to gather the relevant information and thus are in the position to conclude that the threshold has been overrun, the problem arises as to how to collect the resulting tax due. One could expect that a remote seller will normally not have any assets in the territory of the market State (e.g., tangible property, bank accounts, etc.) that may be subject to confiscation.[1067] This being so, the only possible way forward is to serve notice of assessment wherever the taxpayer is and ultimately seize its assets located abroad, a practice that may potentially compromise the International Court of Justice doctrine expressly prohibiting the extraterritorial enforcement of domestic rules (at least in the absence of authorization by the affected jurisdiction).[1068] On the other hand, Hellerstein suggests

1063. Avi-Yonah, R. (1997), p. 536, Avi-Yonah, R.; Halabi, O. (2014), pp. 15 and 18, Gadžo, S. (2016), p. 293 (he suggests expressing the amount in special drawing rights, whose value is determined with reference to the four major currencies, i.e., USD, GPR, EUR and JPY). For its part, the European Commission suggests a much higher quantitative threshold of EUR 7,000,000 (EU Commission (2018): Proposal for a Council Directive laying down rules relating to the corporate taxation of a significant digital presence, p. 16, Article 4.3.a of the proposed Directive).

1064. *See* Hellerstein, W. (2014) on the importance to align both substantive and enforcement jurisdiction.

1065. In the absence of international agreements on exchange of information (e.g., Intergovernmental agreements or IGAs), extraterritorial reporting requirements are prone to trigger serious conflicts of laws, *see* Parada, L. (2016), section 2.6.

1066. Gadžo, S. (2016), p. 272.

1067. Doernberg, R.L.; Hinnekens, L. (1999), pp. 341-342 and Gadžo, S. (2016), p. 274.

1068. Judgment by the International Court of Justice "S.S. Lotus" of September 7, 1927, pp. 18-19.

a number of domestic actions of limited scope that market States can take to ensure, or at least induce, enforceability within their reserved domains.[1069]

In this context, we will put forward two alternative courses of action. The first one entails the establishment of an ad-hoc collection system based on the practice of (refundable) withholding taxes while the second one relies on a greater level of bilateral and multilateral cooperation among States adopting the new PE proviso.

The aforementioned ad-hoc collection system has been proposed by some scholars and the OECD itself as an effective way to cope with the difficulties associated with both access to information and enforcement.[1070] Withholding taxes play a double role in this regard: they ensure the effective monitoring of the covered transactions—along with the collection of the information involving those transactions that is relevant for the purposes of the new rule—while forcing the taxpayer to comply with the tax rules of a State where it is not physically present.[1071]

We will now proceed to define the four different stages in which the process is divided:

(a) Imposition of a refundable withholding tax. As a matter of principle, the withholding tax should be imposed on the gross amount paid in consideration for any remote purchase covered by the new proviso (either business to business—hereinafter "B2B" or business to consumers—hereinafter "B2C"). This poses significant challenges, in particular those related to the determination of both the withholding agent and the applicable tax rate.

As regards the selection of the withholding agent, it seems logical to first assess whether the payer could be entrusted with this task. As a general rule, businesses are required to register in many countries (often granted a number or code that identifies them as such)[1072] and tend to be familiar with withholding tax liabilities. This being so, businesses located in the market State and making a remote purchase may reasonably be expected to serve as withholding agents in the context of the new proposed collection system.[1073] On the contrary, private consumers are typically inexperienced in record-keeping obligations and withholding tax liabilities, not to mention the

1069. Hellerstein, W. (2014), p. 348. For example, he wonders whether available technologies can block or interfere with the company's virtual presence in the country if the company fails to comply with its tax obligations (China does). If the answer is positive, he wonders whether countries may be willing to employ such technologies to enforce compliance with country's tax obligations. If the answer is negative, he raises the question as to whether companies are likely to comply with such obligations to avoid exposure to risk and unresolved tax debts. Alternatively, he suggests the imposition of indirect measures, such as withholding requirements, to induce compliance with the country's tax obligations.

1070. Avi-Yonah, R. (1997), pp. 537-541, Pinto, D. (2003), pp. 207-231, OECD (2015): Final Report on BEPS Action 1—Addressing the tax challenges of the digital economy, pp. 113-115 and Gadžo, S. (2016), pp. 276-282 and 293-294.

1071. Indeed, withholding taxes are typically used to tax income derived by non-residents who lack a permanent presence within their borders. *See* Simader, K. (2013), pp. 8-9.

1072. Brauner, Y.; Báez Moreno, A. (2015), p. 13.

1073. OECD (2015): Final Report on BEPS Action 1—Addressing the tax challenges of the digital economy, p. 114, Gadžo, S. (2016), pp. 293-294.

logistical nightmare that the imposition of such obligation would undoubtedly entail, reasons why no proposal to date has pursued this approach any further.[1074]

In view of the risks and disadvantages that the exclusion of B2C remote transactions of the proposed system would entail,[1075] alternatives involving third-parties as withholding agents started to be explored. In particular, it has been suggested that the agent should be an intermediary somehow involved in the purchase process, e.g., the financial institution behind the instrument of payment,[1076] the company ultimately operating the bank card (e.g., Visa, Mastercard, American Express)[1077] or even the web browser.[1078]

We believe financial institutions would be the least bad candidate to play this role for two main reasons. First, they find themselves behind 92% of the online purchases (*see* Figure 5) and may be reasonably expected to be also behind the vast majority of the other remote (non-digital) transactions. Second, they have an extensive experience in complying with withholding tax obligations.

The process should be as automated and streamlined as possible. The RTvat project,[1079] although originally conceived to counteract VAT carousel frauds, suggests the adoption of a technological process whose potential utility in the context of VAT online supplies has already been suggested.[1080] We believe it could also be of help in this context.

It is essential that the purchase platform allows the withholding agent to first check whether the payment falls under the scope of proposed clause and second, verify the residence of the remote seller and its status of business (e.g., via a digital certificate of residence) along with the presumable location of the customer according to the three indicators suggested above (i.e., the digital certificate of residence, the address linked to the payment instrument and the address explicitly provided to the seller). In this context, the secured

1074. There is a broad consensus on the fact that requiring withholding from a private customer is unreasonably burdensome and would give rise to an unimaginable level of costs of challenges (Pinto, D. (2003), p. 223, OECD (2015): Final Report on BEPS Action 1—Addressing the tax challenges of the digital economy, p. 114, Brauner, Y.; Báez Moreno, A. (2015), p. 17, Gadžo, S. (2016), p. 282) that would very rarely pass a cost-benefit test.
1075. This was indeed the decision taken by, for example Brauner, Y.; Báez Moreno, A. (2015) and Gadžo, S. (2016), pp. 281-282 and 293-294, being fully aware of its downsides, most notably those related to the loss of revenue potentially suffered by the market State and the lack of neutrality between B2B and B2C comparable transactions (Brauner, Y.; Báez Moreno, A. (2015), pp. 17-18 and Báez Moreno, A.; Brauner, Y. (2018), p. 12). While these outcomes were ultimately underestimated and even regarded as justified under the base-erosion approach in the case of Brauner/Báez, Gadžo viewed it as a clear policy-trade-off between the principles of equity and practicability.
1076. Pinto, D. (2003), pp. 223-224, Brauner, Y.; Báez Moreno, A. (2015), p. 18 and OECD (2015): Final Report on BEPS Action 1—Addressing the tax challenges of the digital economy, p. 114.
1077. Pinto, D. (2003), p. 223.
1078. Pinto, D. (2003), pp. 223-224.
1079. http://www.rtvat.eu/ (last accessed on January 10, 2019).
1080. This is at least the thesis defended by Lamensch, M. (2015), summed up in Lamensch, M. (2012).

payment area should contain the necessary functionalities to allow the submission of the aforementioned information.[1081]

Once the relevant information has been communicated by both parties, the system would automatically determine whether a withholding tax ought to be imposed and, if so, calculate the tax rate by virtue of the applicable tax treaty in place (that signed between the State where the remote supplier is resident and the market State, i.e., where the customer is presumably located) and the domestic tax law of the market State.

The customer would always make one single payment. In case it is deemed to be subject to withholding tax, the bank would transfer the net price to the remote seller while retaining the withholding tax, which would then be subsequently wired to the relevant tax authority in an automated way. In both cases, the agent would send the money along with the information concerning the transaction that is deemed to be relevant for the purposes of the new proviso (i.e., residency of the seller, location of the customer, amount of the payment, etc.).[1082]

While it is true that the process is automatic and the financial institution's cooperation would be minimal,[1083] certain implementation and compliance costs are expected to arise and may negatively impact the agent. This being so, we suggest the agent should be allowed to retain a fixed amount per transaction as a consideration for the costs of collecting and transferring the tax due, as these costs are expected to be correlated with the overall volume of transactions.[1084] Besides, such fee—if sufficiently high—may serve as a positive incentive to promote compliance by an otherwise disinterested institution. Either way, non-compliant financial institutions could also face monetary penalties.

Lastly, the selected tax rate should ideally lie somewhere between a low/minimal rate and the corporate tax rate in the market State. While low rates appear to be more consistent with gross taxation,[1085] high rates have the virtue of ensuring that the taxpayer will have the incentive to effectively comply with the tax rules of the market jurisdiction regarding this clause.[1086] We should recall at this time that the proposed withholding tax is not meant to be final but refundable, and its primary objective is no other but to ensure

1081. Lamensch, M. (2012), pp. 89-90.
1082. Lamensch, M. (2012), p. 89.
1083. Lamensch, M. (2012), p. 90.
1084. In our view, this solution is more equitable than Pinto's proposal (1% of the amount of the transaction) precisely because costs of compliance are correlated with the volume of transactions rather than their amounts. *See* Pinto, D. (2003), pp. 223-224.
1085. Pinto provides several arguments in favor of a relatively low rate while Brauner/Báez suggest rates of 10% and 15%. *See* Pinto, D. (2003), pp. 217-219 and Brauner, Y.; Báez Moreno, A. (2015), pp. 19-20.
1086. Avi-Yonah suggests a rate equal to the (nominal) corporate tax rate in the market jurisdiction while Gadžo proposes a "sufficiently high" rate as compared to the effective rates of CIT in the market State. *See* Avi-Yonah, R. (1997), pp. 537-538 and Gadžo, S. (2016), p. 281.

compliance. That said, we would advocate for a relatively high tax rate closer to the average effective net corporate tax rate in the market State.

(b) Calculation of the annual remote sales. Once the tax period concerned is over, the taxpayer will be required to determine whether the quantitative threshold of the proposed proviso has been exceeded. To this end, the taxpayer will consult the information sent by the different withholding agents as regards the (covered) remote transactions conducted throughout the year with customers presumably located in each one of the relevant States and subsequently aggregate the gross revenues arising from such transactions. Tax authorities may easily cross-check the outcome of this calculation against the information they have at their disposal.

In case the taxpayer belongs to a MNC, the calculation must be done on a related-group basis. To this end, one of members of the group (hereinafter the "qualifying taxpayer") should be entrusted with the task of aggregating the gross amounts derived by all remote transactions carried out between entities belong to its group and customers presumably located in the relevant State. The "qualifying taxpayer" may be, for example, the one which obtained the greatest amount of gross revenues resulting from its remote sales.[1087] Again, the calculation should be relatively easy to make, as the remote sellers already have the information sent by the withholding agents at their disposal.

Whenever the annual gross sales remain below the threshold, the qualifying taxpayer would be entitled to file a return in the Market State to claim for a full refund of the withheld amounts.[1088] In case the *de minimis* threshold is met, the following stage would come into play.

(c) Submission of a tax return on a net basis.[1089] The qualifying taxpayer would be required to file a tax return on the basis of the net profits that are deemed to be attributable to the new PE fiction in accordance with the treaty in place and the domestic tax laws of the market State (pursuant to the guidelines we will put forward in the next section), deducting thereupon the withheld amounts. In view of the result, the taxpayer would be entitled to a refund or else be required to pay the remaining tax due.

(d) Alleviation of double taxation at the level of the Residence State. The State where the taxpayer(s) reside(s) would be compelled to provide relief from double taxation by virtue of the relevant domestic and treaty provisions.

1087. Hongler/Pistone argue that the qualifying company should never be a mere shelf company but one which is deemed to render "significant people functions" so as to avoid the risk of "accounting rules shopping" (*see* Hongler, P.; Pistone, P. (2015), pp. 37-38). From our perspective, we believe it is much more straightforward and unambiguous to identify the qualifying company by reference to the total amount of gross revenues derived from their remote sales.

1088. Avi-Yonah, R. (1997), p. 538, Pinto, D. (2003), p. 210, Gadžo, S. (2016), p. 294. In case withholding taxes were imposed on the payments made to two or more related taxpayers, the qualifying company shall split the refund among them.

1089. Avi-Yonah, R. (1997), p. 538, Pinto, D. (2003), pp. 219-220, Gadžo, S. (2016), p. 294.

Both the design of this collection system and its implementation procedure should be subject to negotiation at a bilateral level to ensure standardization and enforceability. Ideally, interested States could foster the inclusion of this discussion in the potential future negotiations of the Multilateral Convention to Implement Tax treaty related measures to prevent BEPS.[1090]

Beyond the unquestionable virtues of this proposed collection system, it entails great risks that should be identified and, eventually, accepted or addressed. First, an approximate 8% of the remote sales occur outside the radar of financial institutions according to Figure 5. We are referring to payments made through cash at delivery, PostPay, PrePay, e-invoices or virtual currencies. While the collection of the information relevant for the purposes of the new proviso may still be possible, the imposition of the withholding tax is likely to be severely compromised, not to say impossible. Second, the identification by the withholding agent of the transactions that fall within the scope of the clause may prove to be troublesome.[1091] Third, domestic regulations of the market State are likely to prompt compliance obligations on financial institutions which are likely to be resident abroad,[1092] a fact that may hinder and endanger compliance and enforcement unless positive incentives and/or penalties prove to be effective. Fourth, prices for the products and services displayed by the remote vendor will inexorably be subject to changes depending on the applicable withholding tax rate, thus creating an incentive for customers to manipulate the information concerning their postal address under the third proposed rule intended to indicate their presumable location, as it was anticipated above. Fifth, companies not reaching the threshold (e.g., SMCs) would bear the negative consequences of the imposition of withholding taxes, as they would have no alternative but to wait until the end of the tax period to receive the refund of the amounts withheld.[1093]

The aforementioned risks may deter States from implementing the proposed collection system. In this context, challenges concerning information and enforcement would need to be addressed in some other ways.

At this point, the alternative course of action would rely on a greater level of cooperation among States adopting the new proviso.

States can commit to set up a register for resident taxpayers that wish to conduct remote sales.[1094] Registration should be compulsory and may be conceived as a prerequisite to acquire an official license as remote seller in the absence of which the taxpayer would face penalties. Upon registration, sellers would be required to identify their related parties (either resident or non-resident ones) and open a domestic bank account whose sole function would be to accrue the revenues derived from their

1090. http://www.oecd.org/tax/treaties/multilateral-convention-to-implement-tax-treaty-related-measures-to-prevent-beps.htm (last accessed on January 10, 2019).
1091. OECD (2014): BEPS Action 1: addressing the tax challenges of the digital economy, p. 254 and OECD (2015): Final Report on BEPS Action 1—Addressing the tax challenges of the digital economy, p. 114.
1092. OECD (2015): Final Report on BEPS Action 1—Addressing the tax challenges of the digital economy, p. 114.
1093. Pinto, D. (2003), pp. 225-226.
1094. Brauner, Y.; Báez Moreno, A. (2015), p. 13. For his part, Wagh recommends establishing a registry for websites through which sales are conducted. *See* Wagh, S. (2013), pp. 12-15.

subsequent remote sales. Once the relevant tax period is over, the "qualifying taxpayer" (e.g., the one who obtained the greatest amount of gross revenues resulting from its remote sales throughout the year) would be expected to submit a form reflecting both the overall gross revenues derived from the consolidated remote sales conducted by the group and a breakdown of such revenues per market jurisdiction (Figure 7).[1095] The financial institutions where each of the related sellers have their respective accounts would disclose account movements to their respective tax authorities to enable them to challenge the calculations made by the qualifying taxpayer.

Figure 7 Functioning of a Registry of Remote Sellers Operating in Various Market Jurisdictions

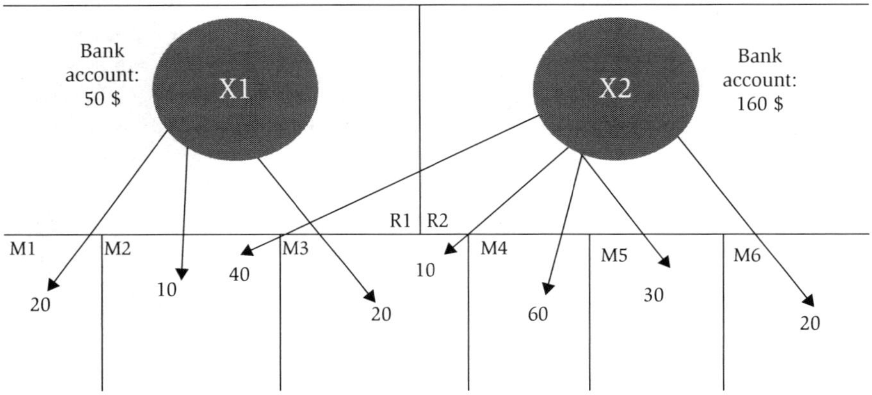

Market jurisdiction	Seller X1	Seller X2
M1	20	
M2	10	40
M3	20	10
M4		60
M5		30
M6		20
Total per seller (as reflected in bank account)	50	160
Total per group	210	

Whenever the quantitative threshold is reached with respect to the customers located in a specific jurisdiction, the qualifying taxpayer would then need to file a tax return on a net basis and subsequently calculate the resulting tax due in the market State in accordance with the treaty in place and its domestic tax rules. Tax authorities of the residence State would collect this tax on behalf of the authorities of the market State

1095. Remote sellers would apply the indicators suggested in the Chapter 4 section §4.02[C][3][c] to identify the presumed location of their customers.

and subsequently wire the payment to such State pursuant to a preexisting ad-hoc agreement to ensure assistance in tax collection.[1096]

This alternative framework contributes to overcome the risks posed by the collection regime based on the withholding tax, but its primary downside is its heavy reliance on a close collaboration among States.

[f] Attribution of (Deemed) Profits to the New PE

Once it has been ascertained that either a taxpayer or a group of related taxpayers have obtained annual gross revenues above the quantitative threshold as a result of the remote sales conducted with customers presumably located in a jurisdiction, the second question is how—and most notably to what extent—this latter jurisdiction should exert its taxing rights. In particular, how it should configure its domestic taxable base.

It goes without saying that the market jurisdiction should not be entitled to impose taxes on the total amount of gross receipts derived from these sales, regardless of the fact that the new proviso is expressed in gross terms.[1097] Such a stance not only defies common sense but may also infringe the ability to pay principle, deeply rooted in the constitutional and legal framework of the international community (and most probably in that of the market jurisdiction). This principle, in its different modalities, typically compels the legislator to levy income taxes solely on the (net) income that is genuinely at the disposal of the relevant taxpayer, that is, revenues obtained during a certain period less the expenses that enabled those revenues to be obtained.[1098] Indeed, (net) income is commonly regarded as the most direct measure of the taxpayer's ability to pay and has thus become a widely accepted yardstick by which taxpayers are compared for tax purposes to ensure inter-individual equity.

This being so, we believe it is essential to confer the taxpayers exceeding the threshold the possibility to submit a tax return on a net basis, as we have suggested in both proposed enforcement regimes.

1096. The most notable precedent would be the Rubik agreements signed by Switzerland with Austria and the UK, which establish collection and subsequent remittance of taxes due to the residence State to the source State. *See* Hongler, P.; Pistone, P. (2015), pp. 36-37 and Gadžo, S. (2016), pp. 274-275. However, there are already a number of legal instruments in place intended to foster cooperation in the collection of taxes, e.g., tax treaties (*see* Article 26 of the OECD MC), regional instruments (e.g., EU Council Directive 2010/24/EU), the multilateral Convention on mutual administrative assistance in tax matters, etc.

1097. Avi-Yonah, R. (1997), pp. 537-540 and Pinto, D. (2003), pp. 219-220.

1098. There is however not a single, pure definition of (net) income, as it is rather an arbitrary figure resulting from a number of assumptions regarding revenues and expenses made by the legislator providing the definition (Fernández, P. (2015)). Herrera Molina argues that there a number of different techniques that States may use to reach this figure. For example: (i) allowing the deduction of all expenses that are deemed to be necessary to obtain the revenue (the most widespread system); (ii) allowing the deduction of all expenses resulting from the entrepreneurial activity or else; (iii) making a direct remission to the accounting profit (Herrera Molina, P. (1998), p. 96). The choice of the applicable technique responds to the specific policy objectives of the State concerned (Brooks, J.R. (2017) and Herrera Molina, P. (1998), p. 96).

The problem comes with the fact that the clause enables the eventual accumulation of gross revenues obtained by two or more related remote sellers resident in different States. Each of these related taxpayers may make separate expenses linked to their respective remote transactions (e.g., marketing initiatives, IT) which, in turn, are likely to receive a distinct tax treatment in their respective domestic tax regimes (e.g., as deductible or non-deductible). In this context, it does not seem reasonable to compel the "qualifying taxpayer" (i.e., the entity responsible for the submission of the consolidated tax return) to identify the different expenses incurred by each of the relevant parties and subsequently apply a distinct tax treatment to each one of them pursuant to the corresponding domestic legislation.

This being so, it seems advisable to make use of a presumption method to arrive at a "deemed profit." This would entail the application of a fixed ratio of presumed expenses to the taxpayer(s)'s gross revenue derived from the transactions covered by the new clause. The OECD itself evaluated the possibility of resorting to this mechanism in the context of the proposed significant economic presence test on the basis of the expected practical difficulties to audit expenses that are incurred overseas.[1099]

The ratio should ideally reflect the reasonably expected level of expenses in an average market situation, which would in turn depend on a number of factors, *inter alia*, the industry/sector concerned, the degree of integration of the enterprise and the type of product or service provided.[1100] Under no circumstances should it mimic the ratio of expenses that would be appropriate for an equivalent traditional retail enterprise[1101] for the simple reason that they do not find themselves in a comparable situation in terms of expected costs, as remote sellers are likely to bear an ostensibly lower level of expenses.[1102]

The ratio(s) may be established either in the treaty or in the market State's domestic legislation. While the first option ensures reciprocity and prevents the risk of unilateral revenue-motivated increases, the second alternative has the virtue of flexibility. The fact that the ratio should ideally be updated on a regular basis and should vary depending on the circumstances of the taxpayer may make it necessary to resort to the second alternative. Either way, the provision should ideally take the form of a rebuttable presumption to prevent flagrant breaches of the ability to pay principle, thus enabling the qualifying taxpayer to demonstrate, for example, that its/their actual

---

1099. OECD (2015): Final Report on BEPS Action 1—Addressing the tax challenges of the digital economy, pp. 108 and 112-113. We should recall at this time that the OECD equally intended to apply its proposed test on a related-group basis.
1100. OECD (2015): Final Report on BEPS Action 1—Addressing the tax challenges of the digital economy, p. 112.
1101. OECD (2015): Final Report on BEPS Action 1—Addressing the tax challenges of the digital economy, p. 112: "one possible approach would thus be to regard the presence to be equivalent to a physical presence from which non-resident is operating a commercial business and determine the deemed net income applying a ratio of presumed expenses."
1102. The OECD argues that e-retailers often face a substantial investment of resources at the beginning of their activities but, once this is done, the provision the products and services online frequently requires only limited marginal costs. *See* OECD (2015): Final Report on BEPS Action 1—Addressing the tax challenges of the digital economy, p. 114.

amount of expenses was considerably higher than that presumed by the ratio or that it/they find(s) itself/themselves in a loss-making position.[1103]

Once the deemed (net) income has been calculated (by discounting either a ratio or the actual amount of expenses incurred), the question arises as to how to split it between the residence and the market States. In this context, the presumptive benefit principle would *a priori* favor an equitable allocation between both States, considering that the former is presumably providing public benefits necessary for the taxpayer's economic activity while the latter offers a market of consumers.[1104] Naturally, this involves the outright rejection of methods which lead to either deprive the market State of any profit at all[1105] or else ensure its exclusive rights over it.[1106]

Now the challenge lies in identifying an equitable balance between the legitimate taxing claims of the residence and the market States and further determining the most appropriate manner to translate it into a rule.

At this point, there are two general courses of action. The first one involves the introduction of amendments to preexisting rules and/or guidance governing the allocation of profits to PEs while the second advocates for more ground-breaking measures.

1103. OECD (2015): Final Report on BEPS Action 1—Addressing the tax challenges of the digital economy, p. 113. Hongler, P.; Pistone, P. (2015), p. 27.

1104. Both situations allow us to presume that the taxpayer finds itself in the position to access the State's public benefits as we argued back in Chapter 2 section §2.02[B][2]. We are however assuming that the taxpayer is carrying out some sort of economic activity in its State of Residence, which may not be the case considering the nature of the most widespread corporate residence tests (Chapter 3 section §3.02[A][1]). For their part, Hongler/Pistone arrive at the same conclusion by means of the sourcing theory (Hongler, P.; Pistone, P. (2015), pp. 17-19 and 33-34). In the same vein, *see* Cockfield, A. (2003), p. 14.

1105. Existing methodologies to attribute profits to PEs (and most notably the AOA referred to in Chapter 3 section §3.03[D]) tend to put emphasis on the functions performed, risks assumed and assets used by the PE. A remote seller will hardly ever perform functions, assume risks and use tangible assets—at least in the traditional sense- in the market jurisdiction. Therefore, it follows that only minimal profits (if any) would finally be attributable to the remote-sales PE and, by extension, to the market State. Indeed, we noted back in Chapter 4 section §4.02[C][1] that this methodology was never meant to allocate profits to the market jurisdictions. *See* Schön, W. (2009), p. 103 (he notes that the place where the significant people functions are performed may well bear no relation at all with the place where the customers are), LI, J. (2014), p. 41, OECD (2015): Final Report on BEPS Action 1—Addressing the tax challenges of the digital economy, p. 111, Hongler, P.; Pistone, P. (2015), p. 32 and Gadžo, S. (2016), pp. 295-296. For example, the adoption of Avi-Yonah/Halabi's first proposal of a remote-sales PE (Avi-Yonah, R.; Halabi, O. (2014), p. 15) would inexorably give rise to a PE completely devoid of profits insofar it is not accompanied by amendments to the methodology to attribute profits.

1106. Avi-Yonah/Halabi's second alternative proposal (Avi-Yonah, R.; Halabi, O. (2014), p. 18) leads to grant the full amount of profit to the State in which the remote-sales PE arises. This may be inferred from the suggested wording for Article 7.1 of the treaties: "profits of an enterprise of a Contracting State shall be taxable only in that State unless the enterprise carries on business in the other Contracting State through a permanent establishment situated therein [Alternative 2 for Remote Sales] [or unless the income is of a remote seller, in whatever capacity, which has gross annual receipts in total remote sales in the other Contracting States in the preceding calendar year exceeding $1,000,000.] If the enterprise carries on business as aforesaid, the profits that are attributable to the permanent establishment in accordance with the provisions of paragraph 2, [or the profits of a remote seller,] may be taxed in the other Contracting State." This is also the approach defended by Wagh, S. (2013), pp. 17-21.

As regards the first alternative, adjustments may be made either in the first step of the attribution process (i.e., the functional analysis aimed at hypothesizing the PE as if it were a separate enterprise) and/or in the second (i.e., the determination of profits based on a comparability analysis):[1107]

- First step. The functional analysis departs from the identification of the functions ("significant people functions" according to the AOA) performed by the PE and subsequently proceeds to equip it with the enterprise's assets, risks and capital it would have/need if it were a separate entity performing the same functions. This analysis would however be doomed to failure in the context of the proposed clause insofar as the resulting PE does not perform any significant function within the territory of the market State, which is indeed the most probable scenario.

  Two solutions have been proposed to overcome this obstacle and hence enable the allocation of certain functions to the new PE: either regarding automated functions as relevant ones for the purposes of this analysis or treating customers and users as performing certain functions on behalf of the enterprise.[1108] As for the first solution, it was explored by the OECD back in 2001 in the context of the potential attribution of profits to server-PEs[1109] and rightly discarded later in 2010,[1110] while the European Commission has recently adopted this stance in its proposal on a PE based on a significant digital presence.[1111] As for the second, it was never examined in depth beyond the brief observations made by the OECD on the fact that data collected from

1107. The content of which was briefly outlined back in Chapter 3 section §3.03[D].
1108. OECD (2015): Final Report on BEPS Action 1—Addressing the tax challenges of the digital economy, p. 111.
1109. OECD (2001): Attribution of profit to a permanent establishment involved in electronic commerce transactions (Discussion paper). The paper made a huge effort to shoehorn this new reality into preexisting rules but, when doing so, incurred in numerous inconsistencies. *See* Cockfield, A. (2002) for further information and criticism.
1110. In fact, no other conclusion could have been reached under the AOA, as automated functions carried out by the server-PE would hardly qualify as significant people functions insofar they are neither human (but performed by robots or machines) nor economically significant (i.e., prone to generate profits). *See* Kamphuis, E. (2008), p. 302 and OECD (2010): Attribution of profits to permanent establishments, p. 26: "the automated nature of the functions means that the assets or risks attributed to the PE are only likely to be those directly associated with the server hardware. In fact, since a server-PE will not be carrying out any significant people functions relevant to the attribution of economic ownership of assets and/or the assumption of risks in the absence of personnel acting on behalf of the enterprise, no asset or risk could be attributed to it under the authorized OECD approach, supporting the conclusion that little or no profit would be attributed to such a PE."
1111. The proposed Directive deviates from the traditional OECD approach (reliant on "significant people functions") and opts for the expression "economically significant activities" instead. The most visible and notorious novelty is the removal of the word "people" so as to capture automated functions such as those that its digital PE would predictably perform. *See* EU Commission (2018): Proposal for a Council Directive laying down rules relating to the corporate taxation of a significant digital presence, pp. 17-18 (Article 5 of the proposed Directive) and a critical analysis of this profit attribution methodology in Escribano, E. (2019b), pp. 594-598.

users and customers is likely to generate value for the enterprise.[1112] However, it should not take for granted that all remote sellers collect and monetize data from their customers, as the lucrative collection of data is more likely to occur in the context of "seemingly" free digital services.[1113]

Lastly, Cockfield suggests analogizing the new PE with a traditional retail outlet conducting an equivalent business.[1114] Undoubtedly, this approach has its virtues. For example, it ensures a tax treatment that is concordant that to that conferred to traditional PEs. Nonetheless, the question remains as to whether we are somehow overusing the mechanism of fictions, as we would need to hypothesize the functions that a retail outlet in a comparable situation would perform and further attribute these nonexistent functions to the PE. We should recall at this time that this approach would entail adding a brand new fiction (i.e., treating the remote-sales PE as if it were a traditional retail outlet) on top of three preexisting fictions:[1115] the company (treating it as if it were a person), the PE itself (treating it as if it were a company), and the ALS (treating the PE and the head office as if they were separate and unrelated parties).

Either way, once functions have been properly attributed to the new remote-sales PE (as a result of any of the aforementioned proposals) along with the corresponding assets, risks and capital, the second step of the process will come into play. That is to say, determining the profits that the hypothesized separate enterprise—the PE—would obtain in an arm's length situation.

- Second step. Alternatively, adjustments could be made in the second phase of the attribution process. In this context, it has been proposed to amend the TPS method in the OECD TPG so as to ensure an upfront allocation of profits to the market State wherever a remote-sales PE is deemed to arise therein.[1116] While the exact amount of such allocation should be a matter of further study and negotiation, it has been suggested to save one third of profits for the PE-State while splitting the remaining two thirds pursuant to the general principles envisaged in the OECD TPG. Its advocates claim that this solution is consistent and compatible with the ALS as embedded in Article 7.2 of tax treaties,[1117] but

1112. OECD (2015): Final Report on BEPS Action 1—Addressing the tax challenges of the digital economy, pp. 102-104 and Hongler, P.; Pistone, P. (2015), p. 33.
1113. As it was noted above in Chapter 4 section §4.02[C][3][b].
1114. Cockfield, A. (2003), p. 14.
1115. Petrucci, R. (2010), p. 10, footnote 44.
1116. Hongler, P.; Pistone, P. (2015), pp. 34-35 and Gadžo, S. (2016), pp. 295-296. In both papers, the initiative is justified on the grounds that value creation occurs in the market jurisdiction. This is also the position followed by the EU Commission (2018): Proposal for a Council Directive laying down rules relating to the corporate taxation of a significant digital presence, p. 18, Article 5.6 of the proposed Directive).
1117. Hongler, P.; Pistone, P. (2015), pp. 34-35 ("such approach should not be misunderstood as an introduction of a formulary apportionment and therefore the denial of the arm's length principle. But it is the intention of the authors to bring more formula elements into the profit-based methods endorsed by the PE") and Gadžo, S. (2016), p. 296. Article 7.2 of the OECD MC: "the profits that are attributable (...) to the permanent establishment (...) are the

we have serious doubts about it for the following reasons. First, the predetermination of a particular transfer pricing method (i.e., the TPS method) irrespective of the relevant circumstances confronts the "most appropriate method" rule and unjustifiably narrows the range of acceptable arm's length prices contrary to what the ALS theoretically permits.[1118] Second, the predetermination of the result of applying the TPS method regardless of the specific circumstances of the case prevents the taxpayer and the tax administration from using other (equally) economically valid criteria to split the profits insofar they lead to a different outcome, even though this would be allowed under the ALS.[1119] Third, the upfront attribution of one third of the profits to the remote-sales PE on the basis that the market "adds value"[1120] is incongruous and inconsistent with the ALS. It is evident that customers are of paramount importance for any business, as no profits would ultimately arise in their absence.[1121] But this does not mean that customers are per se in a position to add value and should thus be entitled to a remuneration in an arm's length situation, as they merely place value on the offered product by way of its willingness to purchase it and its ultimate acceptance of the offer.[1122]

The main advantage of the aforementioned proposals is that none of them involve the amendment of Article 7 of current tax treaties but solely changes to the OECD's soft law guidance (i.e., the OECD TPG and/or the AOA report), ideally complemented by changes in the domestic tax regulation of the relevant State(s). On the other hand, we believe these are illustrative examples of an unfortunate tendency noted by Graetz back in 2001. He argued that States struggle to keep their income taxes intact come what may, and further strive to shoehorn modern transactions into their preexisting regulations.[1123] Indeed, it seems that we are pushing preexisting rules and methodologies to attribute profits to PEs too far, as they are being used to face realities and pursue objectives other than those they were conceived for.[1124] As a result, these

---

profits it might be expected to make, in particular in its dealings with other parts of the enterprise, if it were a separate and independent enterprise engaged in the same or similar activities under the same or similar conditions, taking into account the functions performed, assets used and risks assumed by the enterprise through the permanent establishment and through the other parts of the enterprise."

1118. We reached the same conclusion back in Chapter 4 section §4.02[A][2] when assessing the BEPS proposals on transfer pricing rules. Gadžo suggests a change of the OECD TPG so as to "ensure usage of profit split method to cases where the enterprise has newly defined revenue-based nexus in a country" (Gadžo, S. (2016), p. 296).

1119. As a matter of principle, taxpayers and tax administrations should be allowed to split the combined profits pursuant to any set of economically valid criteria that approximates the division of profits that would have been anticipated and reflect in an agreement made at arm's length. *See* OECD TPG, paragraph 2.108.

1120. Hongler, P.; Pistone, P. (2015), p. 34 and Gadžo, S. (2016), p. 296.

1121. Schoueri, L.E.; Galendi, R.A. (2017).

1122. Escribano, E. (2019b), p. 568.

1123. Graetz, M.J. (2001), pp. 264 and 270.

1124. They were designed for a rule that demanded a physical and stable presence in the territory concerned (Chapter 3 section §3.03[E][2]) with the ability to perform relevant value-adding functions on behalf of its enterprise. Both the clause and the methodology to attribute profits have traditionally followed the "supply approach" and are thus unable to allocate any profits

approaches are prone to give rise to outcomes that are inconsistent and/or even contrary to the literalism of the relevant rule in place.

In view of all this, we now intend to put forward a proposal that effectively overcomes the aforementioned risks and problems. We believe the automatic allocation of a fixed percentage of the profits to the remote-sales PE is a reasonable solution, in line with what was suggested by Hongler/Pistone. States would need to negotiate the exact proportion, although that proposed by Hongler/Pistone (i.e., one third for the remote-sales PE and two thirds to be attributed according to the methodology in force) appears to be a sensible option.[1125] Nonetheless, this cannot be disguised as a sort of specification of the ALS for the reasons explained above. On the contrary, Article 7.2 of the MCs should be amended in order to ensure the upfront allocation of the relevant fraction of the profits wherever a remote-sales PE is deemed to arise,[1126] thus leaving the remaining fraction at the mercy of preexisting attribution rules. This implies the implicit recognition of the inherent limits of the ALS, in particular wherever States wish to ensure the attribution of profits to a type of PE that, by its very nature, is inherently unable to perform functions that would give rise to a compensation in an arm's length scenario.[1127]

Lastly, in case States choose to adopt a fixed ratio of presumed expenses (so as to calculate the taxpayer's deemed net profits) along with an equally fixed percentage of profit to be automatically attributed to the remote-sales PE, the easiest solution would be to impose withholding taxes—whose rate reflects the aforementioned proportions[1128] on the transactions covered by the clause[1129] and further grant the refund of the withheld amounts or else make them final depending on whether the taxpayer reaches the annual quantitative threshold or not. This provision should ideally include an escape clause so as to prevent loss-making taxpayers from being subject to tax in the PE-State.

---

to a type of PE that does not carry out any value-adding activities and merely reflects the presence of a market (*see also* Chapter 4 section §4.02[C][1]).

1125. Hongler, P.; Pistone, P. (2015), pp. 34-35. Furthermore, this proportion is consistent with that proposed in the framework of the EU CCCTB proposal. *See* EU Commission (2011): Proposal for a Council Directive on a Common Consolidated Corporate Tax Base, p. 49: "Article 38. The consolidated tax base shall be shared between the group members in each tax year on the basis of a formula for apportionment. In determining the apportioned share of a group member, the formula shall take the following form, giving equal weight to the factors of sales, labour and assets."

1126. The OECD itself has assessed this possibility in the context the proposed "significant economic presence test" in OECD (2015): Final Report on BEPS Action 1—Addressing the tax challenges of the digital economy, p. 112.

1127. Indeed, Musgrave came to recognize back in 1984 that the supply-demand approach (*see* Chapter 3 sections §3.03[C] and §4.02[C][1]) could only be pursued by means of formulary measures. *See* Musgrave, P.B. (1984), pp. 231 and 240-241.

1128. Let us assume that States agree to apply a fixed ratio of 10% as deemed expenses and attribute an equally fixed percentage of 33% to the remote-sales PE. This being the case, they may agree to impose a withholding tax of 29.7% on the gross amount of transactions covered by the clause.

1129. In line with the procedure depicted in Chapter 4 section §4.02[C][3][e].

[g] Role Within the Treaty

The new proposed PE proviso could be introduced in a new paragraph at the end of Article 5 of the OECD MC (i.e., as paragraph number 8). In principle, it will coexist with the preexisting modalities of PEs, although its interaction should be a matter of further study.[1130]

The clause should make it clear that this PE fiction would only be relevant for the purposes of the taxation of the business profits governed by Article 7 of the MCs. This is key because PEs play a wide role within tax treaties that go beyond enabling the jurisdiction where the PE is located to tax the business profits that arise from it by virtue of Article 7.[1131] On one hand, the PE-State is entitled to tax other types of income (covered by Articles of the MC other than 7) as long as they are attributable to the PE by virtue of Article 7.4 of the 2017 OECD MC. This is the case for income dealt with in Articles 10.4, 11.4, 12.3, 13.2 and 21.2 which may be found attributable to the PE to the extent that the underlying right, asset or property giving rise to such income is "effectively connected" to it.[1132] While this was a plausible scenario in the context of the traditional PEs, it seems difficult to imagine a dividend or interest having a close connection to a remote-sales PE.[1133] This being so, it seems preferable to automatically exclude the new PE proviso from the objective scope of all these articles so as to avoid unnecessary confusion. On the other hand, Article 24.3 of the 2017 OECD MC seeks to ensure that a PE is not treated by the PE-State less favorably than enterprises resident in such State and carrying on the same activities. The nature of the new proposed PE fiction severely hampers the applicability of the non-discrimination principle in this context, reason why we prefer to rely solely on the aforementioned ratio of presumed expenses (in the form of a rebuttable presumption) so as to ensure taxation on a net basis just as enterprises resident therein.[1134]

Another option, and probably much less troublesome, would be to allow the taxation of remote transactions directly through Article 7 of the treaty while keeping the PE clause intact. This way, the potential application of the non-discrimination principle (Article 24) and the PE provisos (contained in Articles 10, 11, 12 and 21) would be eluded at a single stroke.

[h] Interim Conclusions

Along the present section, we have endeavored to strike a balance between equity (here understood in terms of benefit) and practicability in the form of a new PE-fiction.

1130. Hongler, P.; Pistone, P. (2015), pp. 38-39.
1131. Chapter 3 section §3.03[D].
1132. Chapter 3 section §3.03[D] and Haller, B. (2003), pp. 227-250. Furthermore, Article 15.2 of the 2017 OECD MC treats PEs and residents as interchangeable categories for the purposes of this allocation rule.
1133. Hongler, P.; Pistone, P. (2015), p. 39. Dissenting opinion in Wagh, S. (2013), p. 20.
1134. However, it is clear that a remote-sales PE would never be granted a tax treatment similar that to that conferred to a traditional PE located therein or a taxpayer residing for tax purposes in the same State.

The most balanced (and least bad) solution we could reach is the remote-sales PE based on a quantitative threshold explored in this section. Despite its consistency with the presumptive benefit principle,[1135] it poses a considerable amount of risks and challenges (some of which have already been noted above) from a number of perspectives.

As regards its legal configuration, the rule must accurately identify both parties of the remote transaction, contrary to the majority of the evaluated proposals. For example, it must specify the scope of the definition of group of companies for the purposes of the clause so as to prevent tax-motivated fragmentations of selling activities with customers in a given State among a number of related parties that are resident in different States. Likewise, the clause must define a connection point between the customer and a State by means of straightforward and manageable rules, as we sought to do.

The effective enforceability of the rule raises significant challenges we tried to overcome by means of two alternative strategies: an ad-hoc collection system based on the imposition of refundable withholding taxes and a registration-based system for remote sellers. Nonetheless, the implementation of both approaches entails considerable costs that first need to be estimated and evaluated. For example, governments would need to put into place and start issuing a digital certificate of residence so that vendors and customers can adequately identify themselves at the time of conclusion of the remote transaction. In parallel, adjustments to the functionalities of remote payment platforms would need to be introduced to ensure that the information relevant for the purposes of the application of the rule is submitted therein.[1136] For its part, the practice of refundable withholding taxes in this context is not only costly but may also pose further problems of their own, as we noted above. For example, a solution must be sought for remote transactions that occur outside the radar of the proposed withholding agents (i.e., the financial institutions) (8% of worldwide remote transactions according to Figure 5). Second, it must be ensured that withholding agents are in a position to properly identify the transactions that fall within the scope of the clause so that they can set into motion the corresponding procedure. And lastly, positive incentives and/or penalties should be put in place so that financial institutions cooperate in the collection process, especially in cases where they are tax resident in States other than the market State.

Furthermore, the proposed rules may potentially conflict with preexisting legal and/or constitutional rules. For example, the suggested ratio of presumed expenses, if not accompanied by an effective escape clause, may infringe the ability to pay principle as set out in the domestic constitution or legislation.

However, the most important risk to be considered when exploring the possibility to adopt the proposed set of rules lies in the apparent ease with which they can be

1135. Explained in the Chapter 4 section §4.02[C][3][a].

1136. Most importantly, information concerning the identification of both parties. In case States choose to adopt the collection system based on the imposition of withholding taxes, the purchase platform would need to be prepared to apply automatically the relevant withholding tax rate according to the domestic legislation of the market jurisdiction and further transfer the amount to its tax Administration.

circumvented unless they are widely and homogeneously adopted. We will illustrate these risks by means of the following example.

Let us assume that company S (tax resident in State SS), dedicated to the development, manufacture and sales of smartphone batteries, earns a gross amount of USD 1,050,000 in State MM throughout the year 2016 as a result of the sales conducted through its website. States SS and MM have a remote-sales PE clause in their treaty in place along with the corresponding domestic tax regulation on the matter. Further, they agree to implement one of the two proposed strategies to ensure the enforcement of the clause. This being so, State MM would be entitled to tax—and effectively collect the tax due arising from such PE.

However, let us imagine that company S decides to constitute a wholly owned subsidiary (company X) that qualifies as tax resident in State XX by virtue of its domestic tax legislation.[1137] For its part, State XX has never expressed any interest in adopting a remote-sales PE neither in its treaty network nor its domestic legislation, reason why the government has never taken the steps necessary to track the remote sales concluded by its residents.

As of 2017, company X begins to sell on its own an entire range of batteries by means of a website (using a local domain) to which company S's website automatically redirects once the user clicks on any of the displayed products pertaining to this group. Companies S and X obtain USD 1,200,000 as a result of the online sales conducted with customers located in State MM, USD 800,000 and 400,000 respectively.

Theoretically, State MM would continue to be entitled to tax the profits arising from these transactions in the year 2017 as long as the requirements set out in the remote-sales provision envisaged in the treaty SS-MM and its domestic legislation are met. However, the advent of company X on the scene gives rise to a number of risks that could however thwart the legitimate tax claims of this State.

First, the question arises as to whether the actions of State MM may entail the infringement of Article 7 of the treaty XX-MM, as they may be regarded as the imposition of a tax on the profits of a non-resident company (X) in the absence of a PE in the territory of State MM.[1138] In this respect, it could be argued that MM would be technically taxing the profits of company S according to the treaty SS-MM, while merely quantifying the revenues derived from the sales carried out by company XX for the purposes of applying the PE proviso of the aforementioned treaty.

But, even assuming that the tax claim of MM is consistent with the legal framework in place, the question remains as to whether it is enforceable or not. We should recall at this time that State XX lacks any kind of registration for remote sellers, does not require them to have an ad-hoc bank account for their remote sales, does not issue any sort of digital certificate of residence to identify and locate the seller and does not ensure either that purchase platforms are conveniently adjusted to track the

1137. This is extremely easy to achieve to the extent the most widespread corporate residence tests (most notably those covered in Chapter 3 sections §3.02[A][1][a] and §3.02[A][1][b]) are kept in place. We made reference to the "residence electivity" phenomenon in Chapter 3.

1138. We assume the relevant treaty follows Article 7 of the MCs: "profits of an enterprise of a Contracting State shall be taxable only in that Sate unless the enterprise carries on business in the other Contracting State through a permanent establishment situated therein."

information relevant for the purposes of the proposed clause and eventually enable the practice of a withholding tax. In this context, State MM would hardly be in a position to track the remote sales made by company X so as to challenge the tax return submitted by company S, which may well limit itself to report its own sales, not having any incentive to do the same with company X's untraceable transactions. What is more, even if State MM had the means to check whether the requirements of the proviso are fulfilled and further quantify the amount of tax due, its collection would be an ordeal to the extent that withholding taxes are not imposed at the time of the payment and no cooperation on the collection of taxes is agreed between States XX and MM.

As noted above, only a widespread and consistent implementation of this regime can contribute to mitigate the risks illustrated in the aforementioned example. For example, by including the remote-sales PE proviso along with all the necessary procedural rules to support it in the Multilateral Convention to Implement Tax treaty related measures to prevent BEPS.[1139] Nonetheless, as long as there is a single non-cooperative State using corporate residence tests which are in turn vulnerable to manipulations and remote vendors continue to be able to establish a subsidiary in that State so as to conduct its sales through it, these risks will inexorably remain.

In view of all the challenges, costs and risks that the adoption of the proposed proviso is expected to give rise to, we believe more thought should be given to the proposal before considering its implementation. In particular, future studies should endeavor to provide a response to the challenges here identified, conceive measures that serve to mitigate the anticipated risks (particularly those related to the use of a subsidiary resident in a non-cooperative State) and ultimately carry out a cost-benefit analysis to assess whether the expected outcomes can arguably offset all the costs and efforts.

States may instead opt for a rule whose implementation is less troublesome. Of all the proposals on the table, the withholding tax system put forward by Brauner/Báez[1140] stands out for its technical feasibility, pragmatism and apparent simplicity. It involves the practice of withholding taxes on every business-deductible payment made by residents or PEs of a contracting State to a person resident in the other Contracting State to the extent that it falls under the scope of Article 7 (as a business profit) and does not qualify for any of the proposed exemptions. The ultimate goal of its proponents is to capture solely the payments connected with the digital economy, although they prefer to achieve this by means of a long list of exemptions rather than by a positive definition of digital transactions.[1141]

1139. http://www.oecd.org/tax/treaties/multilateral-convention-to-implement-tax-treaty-related-measures-to-prevent-beps.htm (last accessed on January 10, 2019).

1140. Brauner, Y.; Báez Moreno, A. (2015). In Báez Moreno, A.; Brauner, Y. (2018), pp. 13-27, the authors put forward a number of convincing arguments supporting this proposal *vis-á-vis* other policy options suggested by the OECD/EU (e.g., the PEs based on a significant economic presence or a significant digital presence respectively, which are relatively similar to our remote-sales PE) from the perspective of its design, implementation and legal consistency with other legal orders (e.g., tax treaties, WTO and EU Law).

1141. For example, they suggest to provide exemptions for, *inter alia*: (i) low-risk payments to identifiable taxpayers that are already taxed on a net basis (e.g., wages and deductible

Nonetheless, practicability comes at a high price: equity. For example, the proposal can be questioned from the perspective of the ability to pay principle, as the proposed withholding taxes are imposed on a gross basis and are not refundable.[1142] But, most importantly, it would be inconsistent with the presumptive benefit principle. We reached the conclusion that this principle justifies the imposition of taxes by the State providing the market regardless of any further considerations.[1143] However, this rule fails to ensure this to the extent that it solely captures deductible payments made by businesses, thereby giving rise to asymmetries between BC2/B2B transactions and deductible/non-deductible payments that cannot be sustained from a benefit perspective.[1144] Furthermore, the taxpayer would become subject to tax in the market jurisdiction from the very first transaction, irrespective of its overall level of integration in the State.[1145]

All in all, States should evaluate all the options on the table assuming that the perfect balance between practicability and equity (here understood in terms of benefit) is probably a utopia, or at the very least, hard to achieve.

[4] Preliminary Conclusions

First, we noted that the BEPS project intended to bring the taxable profits to wherever the market is by means of the PE (section §4.02[C][1]). While the objective can be perceived as legitimate from the perspective of the presumptive benefit principle, we concluded that it is inconsistent with the current wording of the PE clause as well as the methodology to attribute profits to it, as the PE was never conceived to ensure taxation at the level of the market jurisdiction but rather to ensure taxation in territories where non-residents were carrying out a significant value-adding economic activities.

Second, we analyzed the proposed amendments introduced to the PE clause of the 2017 OECD MC resulting from the BEPS project and further reached a few conclusions (section §4.02[C][2]). In general, we welcomed all the proposals due to the fact that they contribute to make the threshold less vulnerable to tax planning and further put an end to a long history of unfortunate interpretations of the clause that seriously compromised the principle of legal certainty, as very well illustrated by the

---

payments made to PEs); (ii) dividends/interests (already dealt with in other articles of the MC), (iii) capital gains from the sale of shares and d) payments made in consideration for non-digital goods or services (e.g., rental or purchase of equipment, land or business; payments for material and services entailing individuals present on-site), etc. For its part, royalty payments would be subject to this regime (in fact, they recommend the elimination of Article 12 of the OECD MC). *See* Brauner, Y.; Báez Moreno, A. (2015), pp. 20-21 and 23.

1142. Brauner, Y.; Báez Moreno, A. (2015), pp. 21-22.

1143. Chapter 2 sections §2.02[B][2][b] and §2.02[B][3].

1144. Gadžo, S. (2016), pp. 283-284. Indeed, the proposal is in turn theoretically justified on the grounds of the base-erosion principle (Brauner, Y.; Báez Moreno, A. (2015), pp. 8-10).

1145. Indeed, we explained above that a *de minimis* threshold is more coherent with benefit considerations (*see* Chapter 4 section §4.02[C][3][a]). In the same vein, *see* Gadžo, S. (2016), p. 283. This approach would be however welcomed by Schön, who advocates for a limited tax liability in the market jurisdiction "starting from the first market contact, gradually moving up with intensified market penetration" as opposed to the distorting "all-of-nothing" effect commonly triggered by the traditional PE (Schön, W. (2009), p. 100).

so-called PE Spanish approach. Nonetheless, we equally noted the expected inconveniences that their adoption would entail and anticipated that they will not result in a significant increment of tax revenues in the PE-States as a result of the current rules guiding the methodology to attribute profits to PEs. Last but not least, we concluded that the proposed amendments do not contribute to effectively accomplish the objective of BEPS as regards the PE (i.e., ensuring taxation at the level of the market jurisdiction) and, by extension, meet the demands required by the presumptive benefit principle.

In view of the fact that the new mission assigned to the PE is not inherent at all in the current clause, the only way forward was to reevaluate its overall scope and explore the possibility of introducing a significant amendment to its wording (section §4.02[C][3]). In this context, we considered the option of adopting a new PE fiction so as to ensure that the market State can exercise its tax jurisdiction under certain circumstances, in line with what the presumptive benefit principle demands. Thus, we brought forward and defined the key characteristics of the "remote-sales PE" with regard to its subjective/objective scope, methodology to attribute profits as well as two alternative strategies intended to ensure its enforceability. All in all, we warned against certain risks that the proposal would give rise to along with a few challenges that still remain unsolved, thereby calling for further research on the matter before considering the adopting of the proposed clause.

§4.03 THE DEPARTURE FROM CURRENT PARADIGMS

We choose not to explore in depth more disruptive measures that involve the departure of these paradigms considering that they require a degree of international coordination and political agreement that is today unattainable. We do so in the knowledge that some of these measures may be precisely the most adequate and straightforward way to achieve the policy objective set out in Chapter 2 section §2.02 and, incidentally, overcome some of the long-standing structural problems of CITs (some of which have been noted in Chapter 3). However, we wish to make a very brief reference to two of them.[1146]

The first proposal is the CCCTB, an EU project that suggests group consolidation for tax purposes and a subsequent distribution of the profits according to a formula based on sales, labor and assets.[1147] The second proposal is the destination-based

1146. The present section is based on the conclusions reached in a previous publication, *see* Escribano, E. (2017), pp. 257-258.

1147. EU Commission (2011): Proposal for a Council Directive on a Common Consolidated Corporate Tax Base (CCCTB). The European Commission has recently revived this project after its initial failure in 2011, although with two important novelties noted in Maguire, T. (2015). First, the new project is not conceived any more as an elective regime, at least not for MNCs whose global turnover exceeds EUR 750 million a year. Second, the Commission has proposed a progressively phased implementation, thereby putting into motion the first two steps (common tax base and consolidation) and postponing the negotiation of the formula apportionment. One of the most outstanding academic contributions in the topic is Wilde, M.F. de (2017).

corporate tax (hereinafter "DBCT"),[1148] which advocates for the replacement of current CITs for an entirely new model. The tax would depart from the company's cash flow (thereby including net financial inflows and allowing the immediate expensing of all investment expenditure) and would secure that the State of destination (wherever the final customer is resident) is ultimately entitled to exercise its taxing rights.

Both proposals entail a substantial departure from the paradigms that have been called into question here. This is because taxation would no longer arise wherever a company is deemed to be located for tax purposes (i.e., the State in which it is tax resident or where its PE is located) and these factors would cease to determine which State would be entitled to tax its profits. This should be welcomed as good news, considering the increasing irrelevance and inappropriateness of the notions of corporate tax residence and PE (Chapter 3) and the subsequent disadvantages of making taxation heavily dependent on them.

Finally, and most importantly, both regimes would contribute to accomplish both the so-called BEPS mantra (section §4.01[A]) and the presumptive benefit principle (Chapter 2 section §2.02). Taxation would arise wherever assets are kept, employees work, sales are conducted (CCCTB) or where the final customer resides (DBCT). And, as long as we understand these are valid indicators of where value is generated (the "BEPS mantra") or where the company is presumably using/enjoying the State's public benefits (the presumptive benefit principle), it can be concluded that their outcomes would be aligned with both policy objectives.

In view of the above, we nonetheless believe that the CCCTB would be a much more balanced option from the perspective of both policy guidelines, as it does not neglect the legitimate taxing rights of the State(s) where economic activities are presumably occurring, contrary to what the DBCT does. With regard to the BEPS mantra, value can be deemed to be added wherever economic activities take place (being assets and employees adequate indicators of them) and consumers are.[1149] As for the presumptive benefit principle, we already concluded in Chapter 2 section §2.02[B][2] that both carrying out a physical economic activity within a territory and the access to customers located therein allow us to assume that the corporate taxpayers find themselves in a position to use/enjoy the public benefits defrayed by such State.[1150] Indeed, the proportion of the allocation (i.e., two thirds to indicators of

1148. Auerbach, A.J.; Devereux, M.P.; Keen, M.; Vella, J. (2017), although originally suggested in Avi-Yonah, R. (2000). In June 2016 the House Republicans of the US submitted a comprehensive tax reform plan proposing the implementation of a DBCT. *See* https://taxfoundation.org/understanding-house-gop-border-adjustment/ (last accessed January 10, 2019).

1149. This is so if we believe the demand is as essential as the supply in the value-creation process, as argued by Schoueri, L.E.; Galendi, R.A. (2017).

1150. Brown equally argues that formulary apportionment is by far the most suitable alternative from the perspective of the benefit principle (Brown, F.B. (2011), pp. 612-615). This is so because there may be various States providing benefits to the corporation and the option to merely indicate one (the "single-source approach") as the "greatest contributor" may lead to disproportionate or arbitrary outcomes. He suggests the implementation of a formula that allocates the taxable profits among: (i) the destination of services/property, (ii) the location of the activities giving rise to the income and (iii) the residence of the person receiving the income due to the fact that all these States "has the potential for contributing significantly to the earning and enjoyment of income." We cannot fully agree with his proposal insofar we

physical economic activity and one third to indicators of market) would be consistent with the view that the number of benefits within the reach of the company is expected to be greater when the company physically performs an economic activity in the State concerned than in cases in which it reaches its market through remote means.[1151]

§4.04 PRELIMINARY CONCLUSIONS

We will now briefly summarize the main conclusions of the present chapter.

First of all, we concluded that the primary goal of the BEPS project (i.e., to provide domestic and international instruments aiming at better aligning rights to tax with real or actual economic activity) appears to be consistent with our understanding of the benefit principle (Chapter 2 section §2.02) but the scope of its Action Plan is unduly limited to be able to achieve the aforementioned goal satisfactorily (section §4.01[B])

Second, we welcomed the "value-creation" approach promoted by BEPS in the framework of transfer pricing rules along with the corresponding changes to the 2017 OECD TPG, considering they are likely to prompt outcomes more aligned with the presumptive benefit principle (section §4.02[A][1]). However, we noted that such approach is hard to reconcile with provisions following the ALS and further provided a number of arguments and examples to prove our point (section §4.02[A][2]). Accordingly, we finally concluded that this approach requires the adoption of domestic special measures in the context of transfer pricing rules that go beyond the ALS and a possible amendment of Article 9 of tax treaties.

Third, we put forward a number of suggestions concerning the definition of the corporate tax residence in view of the conclusions reached in Chapter 3. We first called for the reconsideration of the corporate tax residence tests in place in the light of the policy objectives the States pretend to achieve by means of their respective CITs, whatever they are (section §4.02[B][1]). Later, we advocated for the abandonment of "weak" residence tests (most notably the formal ones) on the grounds that they tend to be troublesome from the perspective of the presumptive benefit principle (section §4.02[B][2]). Furthermore, we explored the possibility of formulating a new type of corporate tax residence test that was aligned with the presumptive benefit principle (section §4.02[B][3]), just as the vast majority of the residence tests in place in PITs are (section §4.02[B][3][a]). We argued that the only type of tests that can arguably meet this standard are those demanding the presence of a significant economic activity in the territory concerned, just as those in place in Italy and Australia. To this end, we assessed their advantages and disadvantages and further posed a number of suggestions, although we finally recognized that the matter undoubtedly deserves a more thorough study before considering the widespread adoption of this type of tests. Lastly,

believe the State where the company is tax resident may not necessarily be in the position to provide benefits to it (Chapter 3 section §3.02[A][1]). In the same vein, Kaufman links formulary apportionment with the principles of inter-nation equity (Chapter 2 section §2.02[A]), economic allegiance and benefit (*see* Kaufman, N.H. (1988), pp. 200-201).

1151. Chapter 2 section §2.02[B][3].

we suggested the adoption of a new tie-breaker rule in Article 4.3 of tax treaties that would tip the balance in favor of the residence State where the corporate taxpayer has strongest economic bounds (section §4.02[B][4]).

Fourth, we put forward a number of proposals related to the definition of the PE concept in view of the conclusions reached in Chapter 3. First of all, we welcomed the objective of the BEPS project as regards the PE threshold (i.e., to ensure taxation at the level of the market jurisdiction) from the perspective of the presumptive benefit principle, although we noted its inconsistency with the current wording of the PE clause as well as the methodology to attribute profits to it (section §4.02[C][1]). Subsequently, we evaluated the proposals concerning the PE recently introduced in the 2017 OECD MC (section §4.02[C][2]) to finally conclude that they should be welcomed insofar they are expected to put an end to unfortunate interpretations of the clause, as illustrated by the "PE-Spanish approach." However, we also noted the risks that their adoption might entail and the fact that they are unlikely to result in a significant increment of tax revenues in the PE-States due to current rules guiding the methodology to attribute profits to PEs. Also, we concluded that the proposed amendments do not contribute to effectively accomplish the objective of BEPS as regards the PE and, by extension, the presumptive benefit principle. Finally, we chose to reevaluate the current scope of the clause, considering this was the only way to ensure its consistency with both the objective of BEPS and the presumptive benefit principle (section §4.02[C][3]). In this context, we explored the possibility of introducing a new PE fiction (a "remote-sales PE") aimed at targeting remote sales made by a business supplier resident in one of the contracting States to customers presumably located in the other contracting State in scenarios provided that the gross annual receipts derived from such sales exceeded a certain quantitative threshold). However, we concluded that more thought should be given to the proposal before considering its implementation in view of the expected costs and challenges (some of which were identified in the text) it entails.

Finally, we explained the reasons why we decided not to examine in detail the policy and academic proposals that entail the departure for the three paradigms under review in the present thesis (section §4.03). Nonetheless, we concluded that the CCCTB made by the European Commission, which entails group consolidation and a subsequent distribution of the profits according to a formula based on sales/labor/assets, contributes to overcome some of the structural problems of these paradigms and is expected to give rise to outcomes that are better aligned with the presumptive benefit principle.

CHAPTER 5

General Conclusions

In view of the discoveries made during the research, the following conclusions may be drawn. Please note that arguments supporting each statement may be found in the indicated section.

I. Profit Shifting Is a Real but Troublesome Phenomenon from a Tax Policy Perspective (Chapter 2)

In Chapter 2 we succeeded to empirically demonstrate that profit shifting (i.e., the ability of companies to shift their taxable profits out of the jurisdictions where economic activities take place and instead book them in the jurisdictions of their choice) is real by means of a real-life case study. Subsequently, we provided some tax policy reasons that justify why this phenomenon ought to be addressed and mitigated globally.

II. The Profit Shifting Phenomenon Is Severe in the Case of Apple (Section §2.01[A][1])

Throughout Chapter 2 section §2.01[A][1] we endeavored to collect relevant data on the economic, corporate and tax presence of Apple across the globe. We chose to focus on nine indicators we deemed to be particularly illustrative of the essential aspects of the company: its direction, value creation process and markets. Subsequently, we superimposed in a single graphic the economic and tax data concerning the same fiscal period (2011) and broken down by geographical operating segments (*see* Figure 1, depicted below). The graphic evidences a clear lack of correlation between the location of the tax bases and the location of the indicators revealing the presence of a significant (either managerial, business or sales) activity in the region concerned. This ultimately reveals, both from a qualitative and quantitative perspective, a severe breach between the economic and the tax presence of this MNC across the globe.

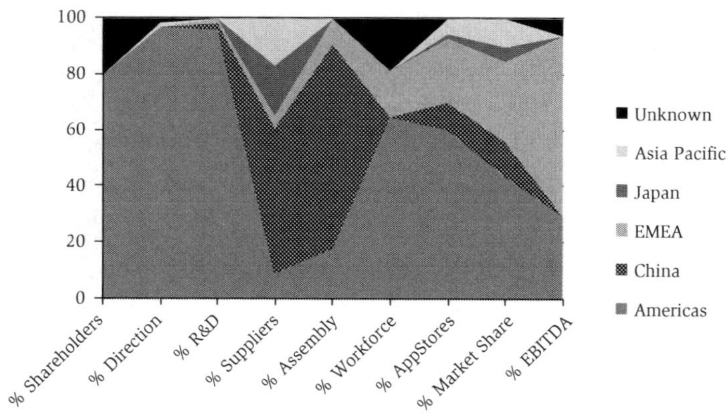

A more exhaustive examination of the data disaggregated by States brings to light the particular role played by two jurisdictions: the US and Ireland (*see* Figure 2, depicted below). For its part, the US did not only witness the birth of Apple in 1976 but continue to play a decisive role in terms of shareholding ownership, direction and management, contribution to R&D activities, number of employees and stores and market share. In this scenario, an approximate 30% of the group's global EBITDA ended up within its territory, a percentage that is, in turn, proportionate to its market share (39%). On the other hand, Ireland does not contribute whatsoever to the management of the group nor its R&D activities and barely contributes to the production process with a small manufacturing facility in Cork and a component provider (out of a total of 817). The insertion of Apple products in the Irish market is very modest, since there are no Apple stores in its territory and its market share scarcely represents 1%. Despite the foregoing, Ireland surprisingly captured 64% of the group's global EBITDA in 2011. The data concerning Ireland constitutes the clearest evidence of the profit shifting phenomenon.

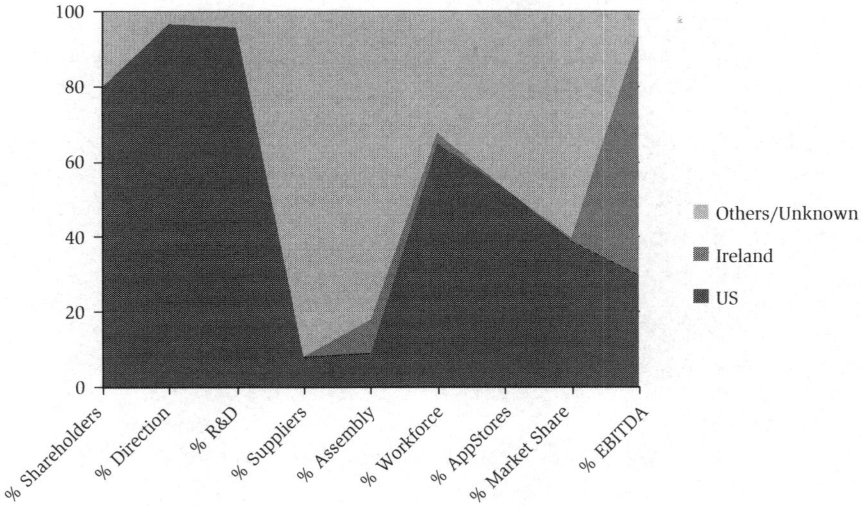

III. The Profit Shifting Phenomenon in Apple Is Primarily due to US Domestic Tax Rules but Also to Certain Structural Problems Related to Corporate Income Taxation (Section §2.01[A][2])

The analysis of the tax planning strategy followed by Apple along with the most relevant applicable rules allowed us to conclude that Apple managed to book their profits in jurisdictions where economic activities are virtually nonexistent by fully and scrupulously complying with the tax laws of the States involved, without traces of any sort of abusive behavior. This suggests that the profit shifting phenomenon is not a problem of tax compliance but rather a problem of rules.

On the question of which specific rules ought to be blamed in the particular case of Apple, we identified two major groups. The first group comprises two very specific regimes that pertain to the US domestic tax legislation (the regimes on CSAs and CFCs along with the check-the-box provisions). As for the regime on CSAs, it allowed the Irish subsidiaries to become entitled to substantial profits derived by the exploitation of Apple's intangibles in exchange for an extremely low price (for bearing part of the costs of its development) and without requiring the transfer of any sort of activities to Ireland. As for the CFC regime, the so-called check-the-box rules together with the exceptions provided by the own regime bear the greatest responsibility for rendering the CFC regime virtually ineffective and thus thwarting the possibility of imposing US taxation on the offshore income perceived by the Irish subsidiaries. For its part, the second group of rules involves those that reproduce two fundamental structural paradigms underlying CITs: residence and source. Our conclusions suggest that the profit shifting phenomenon may be, to some extent, the result of the misguided and out-of-date legal configuration of these two paradigms. These revelations led us to study the origins and rationale behind each of these paradigms, along with the profit shifting risks they tend to pose in Chapter 3.

IV. The Profit Shifting Phenomenon Is Widespread and Commonly Regarded as a Global Concern (Section §2.01[B])

Profit shifting appears to be a widespread phenomenon that goes well beyond the case here under review. There is also a broad political consensus on the fact that this phenomenon is harmful and ought to be addressed and mitigated as a matter of urgency. But surprisingly, the same international organizations (OECD and EU) that have recently opened fire on profit shifting, have failed to provide solid policy reasons to uphold and justify their belligerent attitude towards it. In other words, they fail to explain in tax policy terms why corporate profits ought to be taxed wherever the company carries out its economic activities.

V. The Presumptive Benefit Principle Provides Both a Consistent Theoretical Rationale Against Profit Shifting and a New Guideline to Counteract It (Section §2.02)

In the light of the aforementioned, we intended to put forward a specific tax policy guideline that aims to provide both a consistent theoretical rationale that may help sustain the discourse of rejection towards the profit shifting phenomenon and, at the same time, a new guideline whose observance may help counteract profit shifting risks (Chapter 2 section §2.02). To this effect, we called for the recovery of a long-standing principle (the benefit principle) but advocated for a very peculiar understanding of this policy guideline that largely deviates from its conventional sense ("the presumptive benefit principle") (Chapter 2 section §2.02[A])

We concluded that the benefit principle should help identify the members of the community that ought to contribute to the financial support of the government (Chapter 2 section §2.02[A]). There are two main reasons why we believe that the benefit principle is an appropriate standard to guide the determination of a State's community of taxpayers. First, the benefit principle provides justification for the imposition of taxes on persons who presumably benefit from the relevant public goods, services and infrastructures provided by the State concerned, as they would be the most suitable candidates for assuming the responsibility to financially support the maintenance of such services. And second, the use of the benefit principle helps to underline the mutual "quid pro quo" commitment between the State concerned and its respective taxpayers. On one hand, taxpayers are likely to feel part of the community and thereby understand and accept the reason why they ought to contribute to its preservation and development. In fact, they will generally be able to witness first-hand the correlation between their economic effort and the quantity and quality of the public goods, services and infrastructures. On the other hand, the State would feel committed towards its own community of taxpayers and endeavor to provide the highest possible quality of services and infrastructures, just as if they were its clients.

If we accept the fact that the benefit principle ought to play this role, then we should make sure that the tax rules that ultimately identify the taxpayers that would become subject to a State's tax jurisdiction (i.e., the "tax connecting factors") are somehow inspired by this principle. These rules should not however demand a case-by-case empirical demonstration of the effective use and enjoyment of the State's public services by the taxpayer and a correlation to his subsequent realization of profits, as such exercise would be unrealistic. On the contrary, they should merely rely on certain *indicia* or factors whose presence in the territory concerned is visible and easily ascertainable and further allows us to assume that the taxpayer is in a position to (effectively or potentially) use and enjoy the State's services and infrastructures (Chapter 2 section §2.02[A]). The fact that the access of benefits does not need to be effective but should rather be presumed justifies coining the new expression "presumptive benefit principle" to differentiate this specific understanding of the benefit principle from its common understanding.

Subsequently, we sought to define the role that the benefit principle should play in the framework of corporate income taxation (Chapter 2 section §2.02[B]). Assuming that companies are treated as separate legal persons for all purposes, if the identification of the taxpayers of CITs was to be guided by the presumptive benefit principle, the relevant benefits to be considered would be those used/ enjoyed by the company itself irrespective of those used/enjoyed by its shareholders. In this context, we enumerated a considerable number of public benefits that are susceptible to be used/enjoyed by legal entities (Chapter 2 section §2.02[B][1]) and further endeavored to identify a number of *indicia* whose presence in the territory of a State allowed us to assume that the company finds itself in a position to use/enjoy such public benefits (Chapter 2 section §2.02[B][2]). At this stage, we reached two conclusions. First, that companies performing a physical economic activity in the territory concerned would be presumably in such position (Chapter 2 section §2.02[B][2][a]). Second, that companies reaching the market of a State by remote means would be similarly potential beneficiaries of the State's services and infrastructures, although to a lesser extent (Chapter 2 section §2.02[B][2][b]). This is because we may infer from the presence of a considerable market of customers in a certain territory that the State has contributed financially to build this market and further make it possible the relevant (remote) transaction that would ultimately give rise to the profit.

VI. Corporate Income Taxation Is Not Appropriately Aligned with the Presumptive Benefit Principle and Thus Tend to Trigger Profit Shifting Outcomes (Chapter 3)

Chapter 3 confirmed our hypothesis according to which CITs cannot be regarded as generally consistent with the presumptive benefit principle and thus tend to trigger profit shifting outcomes. In particular, the main purpose of this chapter was to ascertain to what extent three long-standing paradigms underlying CITs (the separate-entity approach and the definitions of corporate residence and source for tax purposes) have effectively contributed to make it possible for taxpayers to book their tax bases in jurisdictions other than those where they presumably derive their public benefits (i.e., wherever they carry out their relevant economic activities, either physically or remotely), contrary to what the presumptive benefit principle would require.

Besides, we also took the opportunity to examine and reflect on the origins and supposed rationales behind those three traditional paradigms so as to reach further conclusions that go beyond the main purpose of the chapter.

VII. The Separate-Entity Approach Gives Rise to Certain Profit Shifting Risks that the Arm's Length Standard Is Inherently Unable to Impede (Section §3.01)

States have mostly followed the tendency to impose CITs and further regard companies as opaque tax subjects, separate and autonomous from both their own shareholders (Chapter 3 section §3.01[A]) and the related parties belonging to its group (Chapter 3 section §3.01[B]). This approach gives rise to what might be considered the simplest strategy to shift profits: related parties can easily manipulate the conditions of its intra-group transactions in a way that results in the transfer of profits to subsidiaries resident in low-tax jurisdictions. To counteract this risk, States have commonly relied on the ALS, thus adjusting the conditions of intra-group transactions so that the tax base of the entity concerned includes the profits it would have obtained if the transaction had occurred with an unrelated entity (Chapter 3 section §3.01[C]).

Although the ALS should be theoretically capable of fully preventing the profit shifting risks derived from transfer pricing manipulation, the truth is that it has proven to be far from infallible in the accomplishment of this task (Chapter 3 section §3.01[C]). Its fundamental flaw lies precisely in its eminently subjective nature. It enables taxpayers to equally advocate for the compatibility of two different transfer prices—significantly distant from each other—with the ALS, thus admitting a broad range of acceptable transfer prices within which taxpayers and administrations are entitled to move freely and legitimately. We argued that taxpayers can exploit this feature to shift profits out the jurisdictions where economic activities take place, for example by simply choosing the transfer pricing method that best suits their interests in each case. This is particularly troublesome in transactions involving intangible assets, as the conclusions derived from the Apple case already suggested.

VIII. Corporate Tax Residence Tests Are Not the Fruit of a Thorough Reflection in Policy Terms and Are Not Consistent with the Presumptive Benefit Principle. They Also Give Rise to Severe Profit Shifting and Treaty Shopping Risks (Section §3.02)

After the analysis of the most common types of corporate tax residence tests (Chapter 3 section §3.02[A][1]) used by a sample of jurisdictions, we realized that some of them were inherited from private international law (Chapter 3 section §3.02[A][2][a]). At this point, we warned against the risks derived by a mere extrapolation of terms from a legal order whose function and purpose had little to do with those of tax law, noting that this ultimately revealed that the gestation process of current tax residence tests lacked a serious policy assessment. In addition, we noted that, historically, the implementation of new residence tests was primarily driven by the desire of closing the loopholes of the preexisting tests rather than by clear policy purposes (Chapter 3 section §3.02[A][2][b]).

The main purpose of Chapter 3 section §3.02 was however to discern whether the way corporate tax residence is currently defined is somehow aligned with the presumptive benefit principle. In essence, the question on the table was whether the definition of corporate tax residence contributes to make taxpayers book their taxable profits in the jurisdictions where they presumably enjoy public benefits (i.e., wherever they carry out their relevant economic activities, either physically or remotely) or else facilitate its shift to the jurisdiction(s) of their choice where no relevant business is occurring. The vast majority of States (97%) make use of corporate residence tests that rely on factors that bear no relation whatsoever to the presence of an economic activity in the territory concerned with the sole exception of Italy and Australia (Chapter 3 section §3.02[A][1][e]). This means that most States grant the tax residence status (and further subject them to tax on their worldwide income) to companies which may well not be carrying out any sort of economic activity (neither physically nor remotely) in their territories (Chapter 3 section §3.02[A][1]). This being so, residence tests may well be instrumental in tax planning schemes intended to shift profits to selected jurisdictions where no relevant business is occurring.

The fact that jurisdictions have adopted residence tests without really knowing, understanding and accepting their supposed rationale and meaning (Chapter 3 sections §3.02[A][2][a] and §3.02[A][2][b]) commonly results in their unwillingness to accept the logical outcomes of their own residence tests (Chapter 3 section §3.02[A][2][c]). Particularly when the tests lead to consider a State in which the company does not have "economic substance" as its residence State, a situation that is in turn the natural consequence of applying the vast majority of residence tests in place (as noted above). When this is the case, States tend to reject the outcome of their tests and resort to anti-avoidance rules. We criticized this approach for giving rise to an unacceptable level of legal uncertainty and advocated instead for considering alternative residence tests.

The lack of coordination in the definition of the respective domestic corporate tax residence tests along with the manipulability of the majority of them results in an additional (and severe) opportunity for profit shifting (Chapter 3 section §3.02[B]). We are referring to the "stateless companies," i.e., companies that are not regarded as tax resident by any jurisdiction and thus may enable the taxpayer to make taxable profits disappear from the face of the Earth for tax purposes (as evidenced in the Apple case in Chapter 2 section §2.01[A][2]). The same asymmetry observed in the case of Apple between the US and Ireland is present in a total sum of 135 combinations of States (within a sample of solely seventy-three) and are thus equally vulnerable to exploitation by taxpayers.

We also concluded that treaty shopping opportunities are a direct consequence of the weakness of corporate tax residence tests (Chapter 3 section §3.02[C]). In this context, anti-treaty shopping measures (e.g., LOBs) become necessary to compensate such deficiencies and further require a sufficient and substantive connection between the corporate taxpayer and the relevant State, as most residence tests are inherently unable to do so. LOB clauses often rely on two main groups of indicators (similar to those used by the SAARs analyzed in Chapter 3 section §3.02[A][2][c]): those related to the location of the company's owners (publicly traded companies, ownership, base-erosion and derivative benefits tests) and those related to the location of the company's business (active trade or business test). This confirms once again the tendency of States to cope with the dissatisfaction associated with traditional residence tests with a layer of anti-avoidance rules. Naturally, a greater use of residence tests relying on the residence of the corporate shareholders (Chapter 3 section §3.02[A][1][c]) or the location of the business activity of the company (Chapter 3 section §3.02[A][1][d]), which per se demand this sort of connection to the State concerned, would in practice render unnecessary LOB provisions (Chapter 3 section §3.02[C][3]).

We believe the proliferation of dual residence cases equally signals the malfunction of corporate tax residence tests (Chapter 3 section §3.02[D]). The reason being that most tests do not demand a genuine and strong connection between the corporate taxpayer and the jurisdiction concerned and are thus prone to cause overlapping attributions of residence. As for the treaty tie-breaker rules intended to resolve dual residence issues, we reached two additional conclusions (Chapter 3 section §3.02[D][3]). First, these clauses merely tip the balance in favor of one the contracting States that regard the taxpayer as resident therein but are inherently unable to deal with stateless companies. Second, the choice of the relevant tie-breaker criteria does not seem to follow any sort of thoughtful logic.

IX. The Permanent Establishment Concept Is Clearly the Result of the Economic and Political Context in Which It Arose and Is Not As Consistent with the Presumptive Benefit Principle as It Could Be Expected, So It Is Prone to Pose Profit Shifting Risks (Section §3.03)

We began by recognizing that there is not a self-defining and unambiguous concept of source we may infer from the nature of things (Chapter 3 section §3.03[A]). This being so, rules defining source for tax purposes cannot aspire to become more than legal conventions. Yet, States tend to draft their respective source rules in a quite homogeneous way, the probable reason being that they generally rely on the same theoretical justifications, e.g., economic allegiance, capital import neutrality or base erosion (Chapter 3 section §3.03[B]). In this context, we focused on one of the most widespread legal conventions in this respect: the PE.

We concluded that the PE evidenced a clear preference for the so-called supply-based approach—as opposed to the supply-demand approach—insofar it intends to lead us to wherever the production factors are located irrespective of the location of the market (Chapter 3 section §3.03[C]). Second, we argued that the PE is undoubtedly the result of the economic context where it originally arose, where physical presence was critical to perform any kind of business activity. Third, we believe it responded to the particular needs and wishes of the capital exporting jurisdictions, whose fiscal interests were ultimately preserved by the adoption of a high source threshold capable of minimizing the chances of taxation at source.

We stated that the PE has ultimately become a sort of "functional" resident, as there is an increasing tendency to equate the tax treatment of PEs to those of resident subsidiaries (Chapter 3 sections §3.03[D] and §3.03[F][1]), the primary reason being that the PE-State is *a priori* entitled to tax the worldwide income attributable to the PE a non-resident enterprise has within its territory. Further, tax treaties give precedence to the taxing rights of the PE-State over those of the Residence State, thus emptying the tax base of the latter in favor of the former. A preference that may be justified on the grounds that residence tests rarely guarantee a substantive connection between the taxpayer and the territory, while the PE concept does (Chapter 3 section §3.03[F][1]).

The primary purpose of Chapter 3 section §3.03 was however to ascertain whether the legal configuration of source—by means of the PE concept as drafted in the 2014 OECD MC—could be regarded as aligned with the presumptive benefit principle. In other words, whether the definition of PE contributes to make taxpayers book their profits in the jurisdictions where they presumably enjoy public benefits (i.e., wherever they physically carry out their relevant economic activities or access a market of customers) or else facilitate its shift to the jurisdiction(s) of their choice where no relevant business is occurring. To this end, we analyzed each one of the modalities of PE separately (Chapter3 section §3.03[E]). We first concluded that some of the modalities are perfectly consistent with the aforementioned principle (e.g., Chapter 3 sections §3.03[E][1][a] and §3.03[E][1][b]) while the existence of others may not be that justified on the grounds of this principle (Chapter 3 section §3.03[E][1][e]). However, we also arrived at the conclusion that there are situations well beyond the scope of the clause where access to benefits can similarly be assumed, e.g., the remote supply of goods and/or services that allow the corporate taxpayer to access the market of customers of the host jurisdiction and thereby indirectly benefit from its local services and infrastructures (Chapter 3 section §3.03[E][2]). Finally, we denounced that States that showed dissatisfaction with the outcomes derived by the literal wording of Article 5 tended to counteract its limitations and weaknesses by means of substance-based interpretations and anti-avoidance rules (Chapter 3 section §3.03[F][2]) instead of admitting the deficiencies of its wording and the limitations of its scope and further promote its direct amendment, an option that was later evaluated and explored in Chapter 4.

X. The Presumptive Benefit Principle Should Ideally Inspire Tax Connecting Factors in Corporate Income Taxation and This Requires a Number of Significant Legal Reforms (Chapter 4)

We believe the presumptive benefit principle should ideally underlie the tax rules that identify the taxpayers that would become subject to a State's tax jurisdiction (i.e., the tax connecting factors) (Chapter 2) but the reality is that, in general terms and except for a few notable exceptions, current tax connecting factors in CITs are not only not aligned with the aforementioned principle but they are actually prone to give rise to opposed outcomes (Chapter 3). In Chapter 4, we submitted a number of few policy proposals that are generally intended to ensure the consistency of CITs with the presumptive benefit principle and further counteract profit shifting risks by bringing taxable profits to the jurisdictions where the company's economic activities are taking place and to those that provide a market of customers, departing from the assumption that these jurisdictions are effectively or potentially providing the services and infrastructures from which the corporate taxpayer is presumably benefiting.

XI. The Objective of the BEPS Project Is Compatible with the Presumptive Benefit Principle, but Its Scope Is Inadequate to Reach Its Alleged Goals (Section §4.01)

The primary goal of the BEPS project is to provide domestic and international instruments aiming at better aligning rights to tax with real or actual economic activity (the "BEPS mantra"). We noted that this objective appears to be aligned with the presumptive benefit principle, since the State where the company carries out its economic activities is very likely to be the State whose services and infrastructures have better contributed to the profitability of the activity (Chapter 4 section §4.01[A]).

Despite the aforementioned, we soon realized that the scope of the project was unduly narrow and thus inherently limited to reach its alleged goals satisfactorily. In particular, we criticized the fact that the Action Plan had renounced to open a serious discussion on the pertinence of keeping the separate-entity approach, the ALS or the traditional configuration of residence and source (most notably the PE threshold), despite their very probable contribution to the problems observed by the Project, most notably the profit shifting phenomenon (Chapter 4 section §4.01[B]). As such contribution was brought to light in Chapter 3, we chose to put forward a number of amendments to these paradigms that sought to ensure a greater consistency with the presumptive benefit principle, in doing so, we also evaluated some of the proposals derived from the BEPS project.

XII. The BEPS "Value-Creation" Approach as Regards the ALS Is Consistent with the Presumptive Benefit Principle but Does Not Accord with Transfer Pricing Rules Following the ALS (Section §4.01[B]).

The main objective the BEPS project wishes to pursue in the framework of transfer pricing rules is to ensure that their outcomes are aligned with value creation, i.e., that the taxable bases ultimately end up wherever the value creating activities occur. This objective is compatible with the presumptive benefit principle, insofar the performance of value-adding activities in the State concerned generally allow us to assume that the company carrying out such activities may be in the position to effectively or potentially use the benefits provided by such State (Chapter 4 section §4.02[A][1]). However, we also observed that BEPS neglected the role that the market may arguably be considered to play in the process of value creation, thus preventing the market States from getting a portion of the taxable profits, contrary to what the presumptive benefit principle would suggest.

Subsequently, we reached the conclusion that such approach is not entirely consistent with the current legal configuration of transfer pricing rules following the ALS (Chapter 4 section §4.02[A][2]). First, we argued that the ALS lacks a specific objective, as it is a mere legal convention that serves to assign profits between related parties and should be applied in an aseptic way following the literal wording of the rule. In this context, conferring an artificial brand new objective (the "value-creation" approach) to the ALS entails a clear risk: it could eventually give rise to interpretations of the rule that substantially deviate from its literal scope and the possible meaning of its terms, just as it has historically happened in the past with the other alleged objectives of the standard (i.e., the ability to pay and the anti-avoidance objectives). In fact, we indicated that this risk is prone to materialize if the proposals put forward by BEPS are finally implemented. For example, we realized that this new approach effectively limits the inherent subjectivity of the ALS by narrowing the range of acceptable prices on the grounds of the "profits must follow value creation" principle (by, for example, predetermining ex-ante the transfer pricing method to be used in certain scenarios, as the 2017 OECD TPG do). Additionally, we noted three examples that show that the 2017 OECD TPG may well give rise to outcomes that differ from those that may have presumably occurred in the market.

Departing from the fact that the value-creation approach is desirable but, at the same time, hard to reconcile with provisions following the ALS, we finally concluded that the possibility to adopt domestic special measures in the context of transfer pricing rules that go beyond the ALS should be explored, along with the possible amendment of Article 9 of tax treaties (Chapter 4 section §4.02[A][2]).

XIII. Proposals Concerning the Definition of Corporate Tax Residence Tests for a Better Consistency with the Presumptive Benefit Principle (Section §4.02[B]).

As it became apparent in Chapter 3 that residence-based taxation of companies was not designed having regard to any policy analysis, we first called for the reconsideration of the corporate tax residence tests in place in the light of the policy objectives the States pretend to achieve by means of their respective CITs, whatever they are (Chapter 4 section §4.02[B][1]). This way, corporate tax residence would be appropriately aligned to the objective of the CIT concerned and would thus contribute to serve its purposes. To this end, we briefly reviewed the policy objectives that preexisting residence tests can contribute to achieve.

Later, we concluded that the abandonment of weak residence tests (i.e., those requiring a weak connection between the company and the State concerned) is desirable (Chapter 4 section §4.02[B][2]). By weak tests we are mostly referring to formal tests (e.g., POI tests) but also, to a certain extent, to those based on the place where the company is run (e.g., POEM tests). The reasons are manifold. First, the proposed stance is advisable from the perspective of the presumptive benefit principle, as weak tests rely on factors that are within the direct control of the corporate taxpayer, thus allowing it to basically select the jurisdiction in which it wishes to be tax resident irrespective of the place(s) where access to public benefits may be presumed (Chapter 4 section §4.02[B][2][a]). Second, the abandonment of this sort of domestic tests would equally mitigate treaty shopping risks and thus reduce the dependency on anti-treaty shopping measures as LOB clauses (Chapter 4 section §4.02[B][2][b]).

We advocated for the adoption of corporate tax residence tests that, by contrast, ensure a substantive, genuine and sufficient connection between the corporate taxpayer and the State concerned, ideally aligned with the presumptive benefit principle (Chapter 4 section §4.02[B][3]). To this end, we first analyzed tax residence tests currently in place in PITs (Chapter 4 section §4.02[B][3][a]). Such study allowed us to conclude that all surveyed States, without exception, have personal residence tests in place whose fulfillment allows us to assume that the tax resident finds himself/herself in a practical position to effectively benefit from the relevant public goods and services provided by the State, either directly (as a result of his/her actual physical presence or frequent visits) or remotely. In other words, we observed that the common principle underlying the vast majority of residence tests in PITs appears to be the presumptive benefit principle. However, we noted that, while 100% of the States make use of personal residence tests according to which the (resulting) resident may find himself in the position to use and enjoy the services provided by the State, only 3% of the States do likewise in the context of CITs.

We argued that the only sort of corporate tax residence tests that can be deemed to be consistent with the presumptive benefit principle are those that demand the presence of a significant economic activity in the territory concerned (Chapter 4 section §4.02[B][3][b]). This being so, we departed from the analysis of the experience of Italy and Australia as a way to foresee the main advantages and disadvantages these tests tend to have in practice. In particular, we identified two major challenges that need to be overcome or mitigated: their potential distorting effects and the practical difficulties arising from their application and administration.

Finally, we set out a number of suggestions for a proposal de *lege ferenda* on a new corporate tax residence standard based on the presence of significant economic activity in the territory of the State concerned. We proposed the use of a quantitative threshold based on the presence of a minimum amount of certain factors in the territory. The selection of the relevant factor(s) would be up to the State concerned. Be that as it may, they should always reveal the performance of significant business activities (either physically or remotely) in the territory of the State and thus enable us to assume that the company finds itself in a position to enjoy and use the public services provided by the State in accordance with the benefit rationale. Examples of factors might include (but are not limited to) the presence of a large number of infrastructures and assets in the territory, the presence of an important number of employees therein, a significant level of revenue obtained from sources present in the State concerned or the supplies of a notable level of goods or services to local customers. The selection of the corresponding proxy (or group of proxies) should be preceded by a careful assessment on its manageability and potential implications, a study that, once again, goes beyond the scope of the present research.

Irrespective of the selected factor, we believe it would be convenient to demand a very significant amount of activity in the territory concerned, for example by requiring the presence of a (high) percentage of the relevant factor(s) within the territory concerned in relation to the global figures of the company. The reason behind this decision is that residence-based taxation commonly triggers an unlimited tax liability that encompasses the worldwide income obtained by the company (albeit this is generally mitigated by the grant of certain foreign income exemptions or foreign tax credits). This being so, we believe that the bond between the company and the State concerned should be of such magnitude that it could on its own justify the generation of such an extensive tax liability on the grounds of the benefits presumably enjoyed therein. Hence, these tests should solely the companies whose business activities are concentrated solely or mostly in the territory concerned, as opposed to those which spread their activities between different countries. In these latter cases, residence tests based on the location of the economic activity should not come into play, and the State should rely instead on the eventual tax liabilities it could impose to the non-resident company by means of source-based taxation.

All in all, we finally recognized that we are not yet in the position to provide a definitive legislative proposal, as it is clear that the matter deserves a more thorough study due to the enormous impact that a change of the residence paradigm might have and the significant risks and challenges it poses.

Finally, we suggested the adoption of a new tie-breaker rule in Article 4.3 of tax treaties that would tip the balance in favor of the residence State to which the corporate taxpayer is more closely connected in terms of economic presence (Chapter 4 section §4.02[B][4]), as we have defended countless times that the most appropriate way to define a sufficient connection between a company and a State is to demonstrate the presence of an economic activity carried out by the company in the territory concerned, just as the presumptive benefit principle would demand.

XIV. Proposals Concerning the Definition of the Permanent Establishment Concept for a Better Consistency with the Presumptive Benefit Principle (Section §4.02[C])

We first evaluated the specific objectives that the BEPS project intended to accomplish as regards the PE concept (Chapter 4 section §4.02[C][1]). Although it was not made explicit, we learned that BEPS sought to ensure taxation at the level of the market jurisdiction by means of the PE and its corresponding Actions (1 and 7). While the objective can be perceived as legitimate from the perspective of the presumptive benefit principle, we concluded that it is inconsistent with the current wording of the PE clause as well as the methodology to attribute profits to it, as the PE was never conceived to ensure taxation at the level of the market jurisdiction (although this may have incidentally occurred sometimes) but rather to ensure taxation in territories where non-residents were carrying out a significant value-adding economic activities.

Subsequently, we assessed the advantages and disadvantages of the amendments to the PE clause recommended by Action 7 of the BEPS Project and implemented in the 2017 OECD MC (Chapter 4 section §4.02[C][2]). In general, we welcomed all the proposals, as they contribute to make the threshold less vulnerable to tax planning and further put an end to a long history of unfortunate interpretations of the clause and overuse of anti-avoidances rules which seriously compromised the principle of legal certainty, as very well illustrated by the so-called PE Spanish approach. However, we also warned against the expected inconveniences and risks that their adoption would entail. For example, the fact that the rule is now comprised by broader and more subjective criteria gives rise to a wider scope of discretion and a decreased degree of clarity and legal certainty. Additionally, we anticipated that the amendments are not expected to result in a significant increment of tax revenues in the PE-States due to current rules guiding the methodology to attribute profits to PEs. Last but not least, we concluded that the proposed amendments do not contribute to effectively accomplish the objective of BEPS as regards the PE (i.e., ensuring taxation at the level of the market jurisdiction) and, by extension, meet the demands required by the presumptive benefit principle.

In view of the fact that the PE clause as it currently stands does not seem to be perfectly consistent with the presumptive benefit principle (Chapter 3 section §3.03[E]) and the new amendments introduced in the 2017 OECD MC do not have any true impact in this regard, we chose to reevaluate its scope in the light of such principle.

In the light of the aforementioned, we chose to explore the possibility of introducing a new PE fiction (a "remote-sales PE") that would coexist with the other preexisting provisos (Chapter 4 section §4.02[C][3]) and would ensure a greater consistency between the PE clause and the presumptive benefit principle (Chapter 4 section §4.02[C][3][a]).

The new PE fiction should ideally cover "remote transactions," i.e., contracts for the sale of goods or services conducted through remote means (Chapter 4 section §4.02[C][3][b]). These goods and services can be either tangible or intangible and thus be delivered through conventional channels (e.g., tangible goods ordered online) or completely electronically (e.g., digital goods or electronically supplied services). The clause should encompass transactions carried out by all sorts of remote means, including but not limited to the Internet, telephone (e.g., conclusion of contracts through call centers) and ordinary mail (e.g., catalogue shopping). The reason why all remote sales should equally fall under the scope of the new clause is the fact that the presumable accessibility to the benefits provided by the market States is equivalent in all these scenarios.

The proposed clause necessarily requires the identification of the two persons involved in the remote transaction, namely the supplier and the customer (Chapter 4 section §4.02[C][3][c]). As regards the taxpayer, it must be a person resident in one of the Contracting States for the purposes of the relevant tax treaty and further carrying on a business activity, thereby excluding C2C transactions. As regards the customer, it would be the person (either business or final consumer) purchasing the good or service. Be that as it may, either the customer or the act of consumption should be somehow connected to the territory of the other contracting State of the treaty (the "market State"). To avoid an unnecessarily high compliance burden, the clause should rely instead on an indicator which could guide us, to the extent possible, towards the State where the consumer is located at the time of the act of consumption while at the same being straightforward, manageable and relatively easy to enforce by the pertinent operator. To this end, we proposed three indicators that should ideally apply in consecutive order: (a) a digital certificate of residence issued by the tax Administration and certifying the residence status of the customer; (b) address of the customer as specified in the payment instrument; and (c) address explicitly provided by the customer to the remote seller.

The potential adoption of the new PE-deeming rule must be necessarily accompanied by adjustments in the remote purchase processes so as to guarantee its effective enforceability. In other words, States implementing this rule should strive to ensure, by means of the necessary domestic regulations, that purchase platforms effectively require the submission of the digital certificate of residence—where applicable—and, in any event, the customer's postal address, as this latter indicator would operate as a sort of closing clause in cases where the first two indicators cannot apply.

The new clause should only apply to the extent that remote sales conducted between the abovementioned parties are significant from a quantitative point of view (Chapter 4 section §4.02[C][3][d]). This can be measured by means of a quantitative threshold written in absolute terms—e.g., a yearly minimum amount of revenue—or relative terms—e.g., a minimum percentage in relation to either the MNC's consolidated sales or a national macroeconomic factor. Either of these options appear to be equally consistent with the benefit principle, so we based our decision to opt for a fixed *de minimis* fixed revenue-based threshold primarily on simplicity grounds, as it is more straightforward than the rest of the options and further provides a considerable degree of legal certainty. The threshold should be expressed in gross revenue terms either way, irrespective of the fact that the calculation of the tax liability derived from the clause would ultimately rely on the net profits obtained by the taxpayer.

Beyond the abovementioned difficulties associated with the design of the new proviso, we realized that the most notable challenges lied in its enforceability. In view of the significant obstacles concerning the access to the relevant information for the purposes of applying the rule and its effective enforcement and collection, we concluded that the adoption of the new clause would necessarily need to be accompanied by a set of treaty and/or domestic rules aimed at overcoming such obstacles (Chapter 4 section §4.02[C][3][e]). In this context, we suggested two alternative courses of action.

First, the establishment of an ad-hoc collection system based on the practice of (refundable) withholding taxes. The financial institution behind the instrument of payment used in the transaction would be required to withhold a percentage of the payment and further transfer it to the market State. The process should be as automated and streamlined as possible so as to minimize the compliance burden for the withholding agent. To this end, the remote purchase platform should be in a position to automatically determine whether the remote transaction falls under the remote-sales PE clause on the basis of the information provided by the parties and subsequently calculate the withholding tax to be retained by the financial institution. This mechanism would help to track the covered transactions and further calculate the annual remote sales so as to determine whether the threshold has been passed. Whenever the annual gross sales remain below the threshold, the taxpayer would be entitled to file a return in the market State to claim for a full refund of the withheld amounts. In case, the *de minimis* threshold is met, the taxpayer would be required to submit a tax return on a net basis.

Alternatively, States can commit to set up a register for resident taxpayers that wish to conduct remote sales. Registration should be compulsory and may be conceived as a prerequisite to acquire an official license as remote seller. Upon registration, sellers would be required to identify their related parties (both resident and non-resident ones) and open a domestic bank account whose sole function would be to accrue the revenues derived from their subsequent remote sales. Once the relevant tax period is over, the taxpayer would be expected to submit a form reflecting both the overall gross revenues derived from the consolidated remote sales conducted by the group and a breakdown of such revenues per market jurisdiction. The financial institutions where each of the related sellers have their account would disclose account movements to their respective tax authorities to enable them to challenge the calculations made by the taxpayer. Whenever the quantitative threshold is reached with respect to the customers located in a specific jurisdiction, the taxpayer would then need to file a tax return on a net basis and subsequently calculate the resulting tax due in the market State in accordance with the treaty in place and its domestic tax rules.

Once it has been ascertained that the quantitative threshold has been passed, either by means of the withholding tax mechanism or the registry of remote sales, the ultimate tax liability should be calculated on a net basis in accordance with the ability to pay principle (Chapter 4 section §4.02[C][3][f]). Two major challenges lie head in this regard. First, the determination of the actual expenses that may be regarded as specifically connected to the remote sales. Second, the ability to audit expenses that are likely to be incurred overseas. In this scenario, it seems advisable to make use of a presumption method to arrive at a "deemed profit." This would entail the application of a fixed ratio of presumed expenses to the taxpayer's gross revenue derived from the transactions covered by the new clause.

Once the deemed net income has been calculated, the question arises as to how to split it between the residence and the market States (Chapter 4 section §4.02[C][3][f]). In this context, the presumptive benefit principle would a priori favor an equitable allocation between both States, considering that the former is presumably providing public benefits necessary for the taxpayer's economic activity while the latter offers a market of consumers. We first wondered whether such allocation could be guided by the present rules (Article 7.2 of the MC) and methodology to attribute profits to PEs and finally discarded this option, as there were clearly not conceived for a PE of this nature. Instead, we advocated for the direct amendment of Article 7.2 so as to establish the automatic allocation of a fixed percentage of the gross revenues arising from remote sales to the PE (e.g., one third).

Throughout this last section, we endeavored to strike a balance between equity (here understood in terms of benefit) and practicability in the form of a new PE-fiction, but we were aware that its implementation poses a considerable amount of costs risks and challenges (some of which were identified) (Chapter 4 section §4.02[C][3]h]). In this context, we concluded that more thought should be given to the proposal before considering its implementation. In particular, future studies should endeavor to provide a response to the challenges here identified, conceive measures that serve to mitigate the anticipated risks and ultimately carry out a cost-benefit analysis to assess whether the expected outcomes can arguably offset all the costs and efforts.

XV. Formulary Apportionment Is the Most Optimal Solution from the Perspective of the Presumptive Benefit Principle but Is Today a Political Utopia (Section §4.03)

We chose not to examine in depth disruptive measures that involve the departure of the paradigms here under review (i.e., the separate-entity approach, the ALS, corporate tax residence and the PE) considering that they require a degree of international coordination and political agreement that is today unattainable.

However, we concluded that the proposal on the CCCTB made by the European Commission, which entails group consolidation and a subsequent distribution of the profits according to a formula based on sales/labor/assets, contributes to overcome some of the structural problems of these paradigms and is likely to give rise to outcomes that are better aligned with the presumptive benefit principle. This is so because the formula would ensure that taxation arise wherever physical economic activates take place (being assets and employees adequate indicators of them) and customers are located (sales). Indeed, the proportion of the allocation (i.e., two thirds to indicators of physical economic activity and one third to indicators of market) would be consistent with the view that the number of benefits within the reach of the company is expected to be greater when the company physically performs an economic activity in the State concerned than in cases in which it reaches its market through remote means (Chapter 2 section §2.02[B][3]).

References

Allix, E. (1937): La condition des étrangers au point de vue fiscal (Collected Courses of the Hague Academy of International Law, vol. 61, pp. 540-636).

Antonini, M. (2008): Brevi riflessioni in merito alle interrelazioni tra rapporti di controllo, oggetto principale e stabile organizzazione (Rivista di diritto tributario, vol. 18, n. 6, pp. 142-161).

Arnold, B.J.; Dibout, P. (2001): General report on limits on the use of low-tax regimes by multinational businesses: current measures and emerging trends (IFA Cahiers de droit fiscal international, vol. 86b).

Arnold, B.J. (2003): A tax policy perspective on corporate residence (Canadian Tax Journal, vol. 51, n. 4, pp. 1599-1566).

Arnold, B.J. (2003b): Threshold requirements for taxing business profits under tax treaties, in Arnold, B.J.; Sasseville, J.; Zolt, E.M. (eds.): *The taxation of business profits under tax treaties* (Toronto: Canadian Tax Foundation).

Arnold, B.J. (2011): The taxation of income from services under tax treaties: cleaning up the mess—expanded version (Bulletin for International Taxation, vol. 65, n. 2, pp. 59-68).

Ashley, S. (2013): The BEPS Action Plan and its impact on global transfer pricing principles (International Tax Review, vol. 24, n. 7, pp. 16-18).

Auerbach, A. J. (2006): Who bears the corporate tax? A review of what we know (Tax Policy and the Economy, vol. 20, n. 1, pp. 1-40).

Auerbach, A.J.; Devereux, M.P.; Keen, M.; Vella, J. (2017): Destination-based cash flow taxation (Oxford University Centre for Business Taxation, working paper 17/01). Available at: http://eml.berkeley.edu/~auerbach/CBTWP1701.pdf.

Ault, H.J.; Bradford, D.F. (1990): Taxing international income: an analysis of the US system and its economic premises, in Razin, A.; Slemrod, J. (eds.): *Taxation in the global economy* (Cambridge: National Bureau of Economic Research).

Avery Jones, J.F. (2009): Corporate residence in Common Law: the origins and current issues, in Maisto, G. (ed.): *Residence of companies under tax treaties and EC Law* (Amsterdam: International Bureau of Fiscal Documentation).

Avery Jones, J.F.; Lüdicke, J. (2014): The origins of article 5(5) and 5(6) of the OECD Model (World Tax Journal, vol. 6, n. 3, pp. 203-241).

Avi-Yonah, R. (1997): International taxation of electronic commerce (Tax Law Review, vol. 52, pp. 507-555).

Avi-Yonah, R. (2000): Globalization, tax competition and the fiscal crisis of the welfare state (Harvard Law Review, vol. 113, n. 7, pp. 1573-1676).

Avi-Yonah, R. (2004): Corporations, society and the State: a defense of the corporate tax (Virginia Law Review, vol. 90, n. 5, pp. 1193-1255).

Avi-Yonah, R. (2007): *International tax as international law: an analysis of the international tax regime* (Cambridge: Cambridge University Press).

Avi-Yonah, R. (2007b): Why was the US corporate tax enacted in 1909?, in Avery Jones, J.F.: *Studies in the history of tax law* (Oxford: Oxford Hart).

Avi-Yonah, R. (2007c): The rise and fall of arm's length: a study in the evolution of US international taxation (Public Law and Legal Theory Working Paper Series, Working Paper, n. 92, pp. 1-62). Available at: https://papers.ssrn.com/sol3/papers.cfm?abstract_id=1017524.

Avi-Yonah, R.; Panayi, H.J.I. (2010): Rethinking treaty shopping: lessons from the European Union, in Barthel, F (ed.): *Tax treaties: building bridges between law and economics* (Amsterdam: International Bureau of Fiscal Documentation).

Avi-Yonah, R.; Benshalom, I. (2011): Formulary apportionment: myths and prospects (World Tax Journal, vol. 3, n. 3, pp. 371-398).

Avi-Yonah, R.; Halabi, O. (2014): A model treaty for the age of BEPS (University of Michigan Public Law and Legal Theory Research Paper series, n. 411). Available at: https://papers.ssrn.com/sol3/papers.cfm?abstract_id=2400024.

Báez Moreno, A. (2015): The taxation of technical services under the United Nations Model Double Taxation Convention: a rushed—yet appropriate—proposal for (developing) countries? (World Tax Journal, vol. 7, n. 3, pp. 267-328).

Báez Moreno, A.; Zornoza Pérez, J.J. (2017): Corporate residence and mobility: Spanish report (EATLP Congress Report Series). Available at: http://eatlp.org/uploads/public/2017/National%20Report%20Spain.pdf.

Báez Moreno, A.; Brauner, Y. (2018): Policy options regarding tax challenges of the digitalized economy: making a case for withholding taxes. Available at: https://papers.ssrn.com/sol3/papers.cfm?abstract_id=3167124.

Baistrocchi, E. (2005): The transfer pricing problem. A global proposal for simplification (Tax Lawyer, vol. 59, n. 4, pp. 941-979).

Baker, P. (2011): *Double taxation conventions: a manual on the OECD Model Tax Convention on income and capital* (London: Sweet & Maxwell).

Bank, S.A. (2007): Entity theory as a myth in the US corporate excise tax of 1909, in Avery Jones, J.F. (ed.): *Studies in the history of tax law* (Oxford: Oxford Hart).

Bardini, C. (2010): The fine line between anti-abuse measures and the delimitation of a Member State's tax jurisdiction: the Italian case (European Taxation, vol. 50, n. 8, pp. 374-382).

Barna, T. (1945): *Redistribution of income through public finance in 1937* (London: Oxford University Press).

Bates, J.D. (et al.) (2013): Limitation on benefits articles in income tax treaties: the current state of play (Intertax, vol. 41, n. 6/7, pp. 395-404).

Behrens, P. (2009): General principles of residence of companies, in Maisto, G. (ed.): *Residence of companies under tax treaties and EC Law* (Amsterdam: International Bureau of Fiscal Documentation).

Bennet, M. (2008): The attribution of profits to permanent establishments: the 2008 Commentary on article 7 of the OECD Model Convention (European Taxation, vol. 6, n. 1, pp. 467-471).

Bird, R. (2002): Why tax corporations? (Bulletin for international fiscal documentation, vol. 56, n. 5, pp. 194-203).

Bizioli, G. (2014): Considerazioni critiche in merito all'orientamento giuriusprudenziale in tema di transfer pricing (Rivista della Guardia de Finanza, n. 3, pp. 691-711).

Brauner, Y. (2008): Value in the eye of the beholder: the valuation of intangibles for transfer pricing purposes (Virginia Tax Review, vol. 28, pp. 79-164).

Brauner, Y. (2008b): The non-sense tax: a reply to new corporate income tax advocacy (Michigan State Law Review, vol. 2008, n. 2, pp. 591-636).

Brauner, Y. (2009): United States, in Maisto, G. (ed.): *Residence of companies under tax treaties and EC Law* (Amsterdam: International Bureau of Fiscal Documentation).

Brauner, Y. (2010): Cost sharing and the acrobatics of arm's length taxation (Intertax, vol. 38, n. 11, pp. 554-567).

Brauner. Y. (2012): Formula based transfer pricing, in Brauner, Y.; Mcmahon, M.J. (eds.): *The proper tax base. Structural fairness from an international and comparative perspectives. Essays in honor of Paul McDaniel* (Alphen aan den Rijn: Kluwer Law International, pp. 149-176).

Brauner, Y. (2014): What the BEPS (Florida Tax Review, vol. 16, n. 2, pp. 55-115).

Brauner, Y. (2014b): Formula based transfer pricing (Intertax, vol. 42, n. 10, pp. 615-631).

Brauner, Y.; Báez Moreno, A. (2015): Withholding taxes in the service of BEPS Action 1: address the tax challenges of the digital economy (IBFD White papers). Available at: https://www.ibfd.org/sites/ibfd.org/files/content/WithholdingTaxesintheServiceofBEPSAction1-whitepaper.pdf.

Brauner, Y. (2016): Transfer pricing aspects of intangibles, in Lang. M.; Storck, A.; Petruzzi, R. (eds.): *Transfer pricing in a post-BEPS world* (Alphen aan den Rijn: Kluwer Law International).

Brauner, Y.; Pistone, P. (2017): Adapting current international taxation to new business models: two proposals for the European Union (Bulletin for International Taxation, vol. 71, n. 12, pp. 681-687).

Brooks, J.R. (2017): The definitions of income (Tax Law Review, vol. 71, pp. 253-309). Available at: https://papers.ssrn.com/sol3/papers.cfm?abstract_id=2928972.

Brown, F.B. (2011): An equity-based multilateral approach for sourcing income among nations (Florida Tax Review, vol. 11, n. 7, pp. 565-641).

Brown, P.A. (2014): What makes a Dutch company Dutch? The evolution of limitation on benefits provisions (Canadian Tax Journal, vol. 2, n. 3, pp. 741-752).

Buchanan, J.M. (1960): *Fiscal theory and political economy: selected essays* (Raleigh: The University of North Carolina Press).

Burgers, I.J.J. (2009): The new OECD approach on profit allocation: a step forward towards neutral treatment of permanent establishments and subsidiaries (Florida Tax Review, vol. 10, n. 1, pp. 51-76).

Burke, J. (2011): Re-thinking first principles of transfer pricing rules (Virginia Tax Review, vol. 30, pp. 613-629).

Calderón Carrero, J.M.; Martínez-Matosas, E. (2012): Spanish court rules on permanent establishment in Dell (Tax Notes International, vol. 68, n. 4, pp. 385-387).

Carmona Fernández, N. (2007): La fiscalidad de los no residentes en España: elementos subjetivos, in Cordón Ezquerro, T. (ed.): *Manual de fiscalidad internacional* (Madrid: Instituto de Estudios Fiscales).

Carmona Fernández, N. (2013): The concept of permanent establishment in the Courts: operating structures utilizing commission subsidiaries (Bulletin for international taxation, vol. 67, n. 6).

Chan, C. (2014): Corporate residence: has Esquire Nominees stood the test of time? (Taxation in Australia, vol. 49, n. 5, pp. 253-257).

Christie, J.H. (1982): Citizenship as a jurisdictional basis for taxation: section 911 and the Foreign Source income experience (Brooklyn Journal of International Law, vol. 7, n. 1, pp. 109-158).

Clausing, K. (2011): The revenue effects of multinational firm income shifting (Tax Notes, pp. 1580-1586).

Clifton, J.; Díaz-Fuentes, D. (2011): From "club of the rich" to globalization à la carte? Evaluating reform at the OECD, in Lessage, D.; Van de Graff, T. (eds.): *Rising powers and multilateral institutions* (London: Palgrave Macmillan).

Cockfield, A. (2002): Computer servers and e-commerce profit attribution (Tax Notes, vol. 94, n. 6, pp. 761-767).

Cockfield, A. (2003): Reforming the permanent establishment principle through a quantitative economic presence test (Canadian Business Law Journal, vol. 38, n. 3, pp. 400-422). Available at: http://post.queensu.ca/~ac24/CanBusLJArticle.pdf.

Cockfield, A. (2006): The rise of the OECD as informal "world tax organization" through national responses to e-commerce tax challenges (Yale Journal of Law and Technology, vol. 8, n. 1, pp. 136-187).

Cockfield, A.; Hellerstein, W.; Millar, R.; Waerzeggers, C. (2013): *Taxing global digital commerce* (Alphen aan den Rijn: Kluwer Law International).

Collier, R. (2015): Revised BEPS PE proposals: indeterminate agents, principals and principles (Tax Notes International, vol. 76, n. 1, pp. 61-64).

Couzin, R. (2002): *Corporate residence and international taxation* (Amsterdam: International Bureau of Fiscal Documentation).

Cunningham, K.M. (2016): The post-BEPS world of permanent establishment (Tax Notes International, vol. 82, n. 5, pp. 503-510).

Darby, J.B. (2006): Commissionaire agreements are an important tool in international tax planning (Practical European Tax Strategies, vol. 8, n. 2, pp. 15-16).

De Boynes, N. (2009): France, in Maisto, G. (ed.): *Residence of companies under tax treaties and EC Law* (Amsterdam: International Bureau of Fiscal Documentation).

De Broe, L. (2009): Corporate tax residence in civil law jurisdictions, in Maisto, G. (ed.): *Residence of companies under tax treaties and EC Law* (Amsterdam: International Bureau of Fiscal Documentation).

De Broe, L. (et.al.) (2011): Tax treaties and tax avoidance: application of anti-avoidance provisions (Bulletin for international taxation, vol. 65, n. 7, pp. 375-389).

Dedrick, J.; Kraemer, K.L.; Linden, G. (2009): Who profits from innovation in global value chains?: a study of the iPod and notebook PCs (Industrial and Corporate Change, vol. 19, n. 1, pp. 81-116).

Dedrick, J.; Kraemer, K.L.; Linden, G. (2011): Capturing value in global networks: Apple's iPad and iPhone. Available at: http://pcic.merage.uci.edu/papers/2011/value_ipad_iphone.pdf.

Della Valle, E. (2016): Residenza e stabile organizzazione (Resegna Tributaria, n. 4, p. 871).

Desai, M.A.; Dharmapala, D. (2010): Do strong fences make strong neighbors? (National Tax Journal, vol. 63, n. 4, p. 1, pp. 723-740).

Devereux, M.; de la Feria, R. (2014): Designing and implementing a destination-based corporate tax (Oxford University Centre for Business Taxation, working paper 14/07). Available at: http://eureka.sbs.ox.ac.uk/5081/1/WP1407.pdf.

Dirkis, M. (2009): Australia, in Maisto, G. (ed.): *Residence of companies under tax treaties and EC Law* (Amsterdam: International Bureau of Fiscal Documentation).

Dirkis, M. (2010): The expression "liable to tax by reason of his domicile, residence" under article 4(1) of the OECD Model Convention, in Maisto, G. (ed.): *Residence of individuals under tax treaties and EC Law* (Amsterdam: International Bureau of Fiscal Documentation).

Dodge, J.M. (2004): Does the new benefit principle (or the partnership theory) of income taxation mandate an income tax at both the individual and corporate levels? (FSU College of Law, Public Law and Legal Theory Research Paper n. 118, pp. 1-29). Available at: https://papers.ssrn.com/sol3/papers.cfm?abstract_id=571826.

Dodge, J.M. (2005): Theories of tax justice: ruminations on the benefit, partnership and ability-to-pay principles (Tax Law Review, vol. 58, n. 4, pp. 399-461).

Doernberg, R.L.; Hinnekens, L. (1999): *Electronic commerce and international taxation* (The Hague: Kluwer Law International).

Doernberg, R.L.; Hinnekens, L.; Hellerstein, W.; Jinyan, L. (2001): *Electronic commerce and multijurisdictional taxation* (The Hague: Kluwer Law International).

Durst, M.C. (2014): Analysis of a formulary system, part VII: the sales factor (Tax Management Transfer Pricing Report, vol. 22, n. 22, pp. 1414-1422).

Dziurdz, K. (2014): Attribution of functions and profits to a dependent agent PE; different arm's length principles under articles 7(2) and 9? (World Tax Journal, vol. 6, n. 2).

Eisenbeiss, J. (2016): BEPS Action 7: evaluation of the agency permanent establishment (Intertax, vol. 44, n. 6/7, pp. 481-502).

Englisch, J. (2009): Germany, in Maisto, G. (ed.): *Residence of companies under tax treaties and EC Law* (Amsterdam: International Bureau of Fiscal Documentation).

Escribano, E. (2015): An opportunistic, yet appropriate, revision of the source threshold for the twenty-first century tax treaties (Intertax, vol. 43, n. 1, pp. 6-13).

Escribano, E. (2017): Is the OECD/G20 BEPS Initiative Heading in the Right Direction? Some Forgotten (and Uncomfortable) Questions (Bulletin for International Taxation, vol. 71, n. 5, pp. 250-258).

Escribano, E. (2019): La tributación de los beneficios de las empresas digitales: soluciones desde la (re)intepretación del concepto de establecimiento permanente y desde su enmienda. Un análisis comparado vis a vis de las propuestas de la OCDE y la Comisión Europea (Crónica Tributaria, n. 170).

Escribano, E. (2019b): A preliminary assessment of the EU proposal on significant digital presence: a brave attempt that requires and deserves further analysis, in Almudí, J.M.; Ferreras Gutiérrez, J.A.; Hernández González-Barreda, P.A. (eds.): *Combating tax avoidance in the EU: harmonization and cooperation in direct taxation* (Alphen aan den Rijn: Kluwer Law International).

Fernández, P. (2015): Cash flow is a fact: net income is just an opinion. Available at: https://ssrn.com/abstract = 330540.

Fleming, J.C. (Jr.); Peroni, R.J.; Shay, S.E. (2002): The David R. Tillinghast lecture: what's source got to do with it? Source rules and US international taxation (Tax Law Review, vol. 56, n. 1, pp. 81-155).

Fleming, J.C. (Jr.) (2012): Searching for the uncertain rationale underlying the US Treasury's anti-treaty shopping policy (Intertax, vol. 40, n. 4, pp. 245-253).

Foss, N.J. (1996): Knowledge-based approaches to the theory of the firm: some critical comments (Organization Science, vol. 7, n. 5, pp. 470-476).

Gadžo, S. (2016): Nexus requirements for taxation of non-residents' business income: a normative evaluation in the context of the global economy (Zagreb: Doctoral Dissertation presented at the University of Zagreb). Available at: https://www.academia.edu/31765430/Nexus_requirements_for_taxation_of_non-residents_business_income_a_normative_evaluation_in_the_context_of_the_global_economy.

Gadžo, S. (2018): The principle of nexus or genuine link as a keystone of international income tax law: a reappraisal (Intertax, vol. 46, n. 3, pp. 194-209).

García Prats, F.A. (1994): Triangular cases and residence as a basis for alleviating international double taxation. Rethinking the subjective scope of double tax treaties (Intertax, n. 11, p. 473-491).

García Prats, F.A. (1996): *El establecimiento permanente: análisis jurídico-tributario internacional de la imposición societaria* (Madrid: Tecnos).

González Sánchez, E. (2005): *Corporate tax harmonization in the European Union: harmonization of the tax connecting factors* (Bilbao: Servicio Editorial de la Universidad del País Vasco).

Graetz, M.J.; O'Hear, M.M. (1997): The "original intent" of US international taxation (Duke Law Journal, vol. 46, n. 5, pp. 1021-1109).

Graetz, M.J. (2001): The David R. Tillinghast lecture: taxing international income: inadequate principles, outdated concepts and unsatisfactory policies (Taw Law Review, vol. 54, n. 3, pp. 261-336).

Green, R.A. (1993): The future of source-based taxation of the income of multinational enterprises (Cornell Law Review, vol. 79, pp. 18-86).

Griziotti, B. (1929): *Principi di politica, diritto e scienza delle finance* (Padova: Cedam).

Gutiérrez de Gandarilla, F.A. (2010): *El concepto tributario de establecimiento permanente* (Granada: Comares).

Haller, B. (2003): The permanent establishment proviso 10(4), 11(4), 12(3) and 21(2) MC, in Aigner, H.J.; Zuger, M. (eds.): *Permanent establishments in international tax law* (Vienna: Linde).

Hamaekers, H.M.A.L. (1998): Transfer pricing and the arm's length principle: history, present situation, future (Skatterett, vol. 16, pp. 286-305).

Harris, P.A. (1996): *Corporate/shareholder income taxation and allocating taxing rights between countries* (Amsterdam: International Bureau of Fiscal Documentation).

Hellerstein, W. (1997): State taxation of electronic commerce (Tax Law Review, vol. 52, n. 3, pp. 425-505).

Hellerstein, W. (2014): Jurisdiction to tax in the digital economy: permanent and other establishments (Bulletin for International Taxation, vol. 68, n. 6/7, pp. 346-351).

Herrera Molina, P. (1998): *Capacidad económica y sistema fiscal (análisis de Derecho español, a la luz del ordenamiento alemán)*. Available at: https://www.academia.edu/6995484/Capacidad_Econ%C3%B3mica_y_Sistema_Fiscal_An%C3%A1lisis_de_Derecho_Espa%C3%B1ol_a_la_luz_del_Ordenamiento_Alem%C3%A1n_Marcial_Pons_Madrid_1998.

Hinnekens, L. (1998): Looking for an appropriate jurisdictional framework for source-state taxation of international electronic commerce in the twenty-first century (Intertax, vol. 26, n. 6/7, pp. 192-200).

Hirschböck, M. (2003): The force of attraction principle under the UN Model Convention, in Aigner, H.J.; Zuger, M. (eds.): *Permanent establishments in international tax law* (Vienna: Linde).

Hongler, P.; Pistone, P. (2015): Blueprints for a new PE nexus to tax business income in the era of the digital economy (IBFD White papers). Available at: https://www.ibfd.org/sites/ibfd.org/files/content/pdf/Redefining_the_PE_concept-whitepaper.pdf.

Hoor, O.R.; O'Donnell, K. (2015): BEPS Action 7: the attempt to artificially create a taxable nexus (Tax notes international, vol. 78, n. 10, pp. 929-937).

Hughes, D. (2013): *Corporate residence* (London: Bloomsbury Professional).

Jiang, Q. (2015): Treaty shopping and limitation on benefits articles in the context of the OECD base erosion and profit shifting project (Bulletin for international taxation, vol. 69, n. 3, pp. 139-148).

Jiménez-Valladolid, D.J. (2016): Atribución de beneficios al establecimiento permanente de agencia: ¿una reconsideración del criterio arm's length? (Revista de Contabilidad y Tributación, n. 403, pp. 5-38).

Kamphuis, E. (2008): Significant people functions and functional ownership: the new motto in transfer pricing (Tax management transfer pricing report, vol. 17, n. 7, pp. 300-310).

Kashyap, A.; Shaflender, L. (2004): Residence of companies not incorporated in Australia (Taxation in Australia, vol. 39, n. 4, pp. 185-189).

Kaufman, N.H. (1988): Fairness in the taxation of international income (Law and Policy in International Business, vol. 29, pp. 145-203).

Keightley, M.P. (2013): An analysis of where American companies report profits: indications of profit shifting (Report for the Congressional Research Service). Available at: https://www.fas.org/sgp/crs/misc/R42927.pdf.

Kelsen, H. (1946): *The general theory of law and State* (Cambridge: Harvard University Press).

Kemmeren, E.C.C.M. (2001): *Principle of origin in tax conventions: a rethinking of models* (Dongen: Pijnenburg vormgevers uitgevers).

Kendrick, M.S. (1939): The ability-to-pay theory of taxation (American Economic Review, vol. 29, n. 1, pp. 92-101).

Kleinbard, E.D. (2001): The lessons of stateless income (Tax Law Review, vol. 65, n. 1, pp. 99-171).

Kirsch, M.S. (2007): Taxing citizens in a global economy (New York University Law Review, vol. 82, pp. 443-530).

Kirsch, M.S. (2014): Revisiting the tax treatment of citizens abroad: reconciling principle and practice (Florida Tax Review, vol. 16, n. 3, pp. 117-222).

Kleinbard, E.D. (2011): Stateless income (Florida Tax Review, vol. 11, n. 9, pp. 699-774).

Kleinbard, E.D. (2012): Stateless income's challenge to tax policy—Part 1 (Tax Notes International, vol. 68, n. 5, pp. 499-518).

Kleinbard, E.D. (2012b): Stateless income's challenge to tax policy—Part 2 (Tax Notes International, vol.68, n. 7, pp. 671-687).

Kofler, G.W.; Mayr, G.; Schlager, C. (2017): Taxation of the digital economy: quick fixes of long-term solution? (European Taxation, vol. 57, n. 12, pp. 523-532).

Lamensch, M. (2012): Unsuitable EU VAT of supply rules for electronic services—proposal for an alternative approach (World Tax Journal, vol. 4, n. 1, pp. 77-91).

Lamensch, M. (2015): *European VAT in the digital era: a critical analysis and proposals for reform* (Amsterdam: IBFD).

Lang, M., Staringer, C. (2014): General report on qualification of taxable entities and treaty protection (IFA Cahiers de droit fiscal international, vol. 99b).

Lemos, M. (2010): United Kingdom, in Maisto, G.: *Residence of individuals under tax treaties and EC Law* (Amsterdam: International Bureau of Fiscal Documentation).

Li, J. (2014): Protecting the tax base in the digital economy (United Nations Papers on selected topics in Protecting the tax base of Developing Countries, paper n. 9). Available at: http://www.un.org/esa/ffd/tax/2014TBP/Paper9_Li.pdf.

Loomer, G.T. (2011): Reformulating corporate residence: a coherent response to international tax avoidance. Available at: http://ora.ox.ac.uk/objects/uuid:1f515456-3d87-4942-9600-b9cfe73c6662.

Loomer, G.T. (2015): The disjunction between corporate residence and corporate taxation: is improvement possible? (Canadian Tax Journal, vol. 63, n. 1, pp. 91-132).

Maguire, T. (2015): CCCTB: the sequel (Irish Tax Review, vol. 28, n. 3, pp. 107-113).

Maisto, G. (ed.) (2009): *Residence of companies under tax treaties and EC Law* (Amsterdam: International Bureau of Fiscal Documentation).

Maisto, G. (ed.) (2010): *Residence of individuals under tax treaties and EC Law* (Amsterdam: International Bureau of Fiscal Documentation).

Maisto, G. (2014): Controlled foreign company legislation, corporate residence and anti-hybrid arrangement rules (Bulletin for International Taxation, vol. 68, n. 6/7, pp. 327-331).

Manzitti, A. (1998): Commento alla sentenza n. 4992 del 1996 (Rivista di Diritto Tributario, part IV, n. 5, pp. 176 et seq.).

Marian, O. (2013): Jurisdiction to tax corporations (Boston College Law Review, vol. 54, n. 4, pp. 1613-1665).

Marian, O. (2013b): Meaningful corporate tax residence (Tax notes international, vol. 71, n. 8, pp. 471-480).

Martínez Giner, L.A. (2009): Spain, in Maisto, G. (ed.): *Residence of companies under tax treaties and EC Law* (Amsterdam: International Bureau of Fiscal Documentation).

Martín Jiménez, A. (2014): Preventing the artificial avoidance of PE status (United Nations Papers on Selected Topics in protecting the tax base of developing countries).

Martín Jiménez, A. (2016): The Spanish position on the concept of a permanent establishment: anticipating BEPS, beyond BEPS or simply a wrong interpretation of article 5 of the OECD Model? (Bulletin for international taxation, vol. 70, n. 8, pp. 458-473).

Mason, R. (2015): Citizenship taxation (Southern California Law Review, vol. 89, pp. 169-240).

Mason, R. (2017): Special report on State Aid: part 3 Apple (Tax Notes, vol. 154, pp. 735-751).

Masui, Y. (2004): General report on group taxation (IFA Cahiers de droit fiscal international, vol. 89b).

McLure, C.E. (Jr.) (2000): Source-based taxation and alternatives to the concept of permanent establishment, in VVAA: *2000 World Tax Conference Report* (Toronto: Canadian Tax Foundation).

McLure, C.E. (Jr.) (2000b): Implementing state corporate income taxes in the digital age (National Tax Journal, vol. 53, n. 4, pp. 1287-1305).

McLure, C.E. (Jr.) (2001): Globalization, tax rules and national sovereignty (Bulletin for international fiscal documentation, vol. 55, n. 8, pp. 328-341).

Mill, J.S. (1848): *Principles of political economy*. Available at: http://eet.pixel-online.org/files/etranslation/original/Mill,%20Principles%20of%20Political%20Economy.pdf.

Moerer, O.; Klaver, B. (2015): The AOA, PE status and BEPS, some reassurance in a time of change? (Tax Management Transfer Pricing Report, vol. 23, n. 24, pp. 1587-1594).

Montesquieu, C.L. (1747): *De l'espirit des lois*. Available at: https://fr.wikisource.org/wiki/De_l%E2%80%99esprit_des_lois_(%C3%A9d._Nourse).

Mössner, J.M. (2006): Source versus residence—an EU perspective (Bulletin for International Taxation, vol. 60, n. 12, pp. 501-506).

Mullis, K. (2011): Check-the-box and hybrids: a second look at the elective US tax classification for foreign entities (Tax Notes International, vol. 64, n. 5, pp. 371-380).

Musgrave, R.A. (1959): *The theory of public finance: a study in public economy* (York: McGraw-Hill Book Company).

Musgrave, P.B. (1963): Economic criteria, principles and policies of the taxation of foreign investment income, in Musgrave, P.B. (ed.): *Taxation of foreign investment income: an economic analysis* (Baltimore: Johns Hopkins Press).

Musgrave, P.B.; Musgrave, R.A. (1972): Inter-nation equity, in BIRD, R.; Head, J.G. (eds.): *Modern fiscal issues: essays in honor of C.S. Shoup* (Toronto: Toronto University Press).

Musgrave, P.B. (1984): Principles for dividing the state corporate tax base, in McLure, C.E. (ed.): *The state corporation income tax: issues in worldwide unitary combination* (Stanford: Hoover Institution Press).

Musgrave, P.B. (1997): Consumption tax proposals, in VVAA: *Tax conversations: a guide to the key issues in the tax reform debate* (The Hague: Kluwer Law International).

Navarro Ibarrola, A. (2016): *Los ajustes transaccionales en la normativa sobre precios de transferencia*. Available at: http://e-archivo.uc3m.es/handle/10016/23300.

Navarro Ibarrola, A. (2017): La modificación de las pautas sobre precios de transferencia (Acciones 8-10): ¿cambio o evolución?, in Almudí, J.M.; Ferreras, J.; Hernández, P. (dirs.): *El plan de acción sobre erosión de bases imponibles y traslado de beneficios (BEPS): G-20, OECD y Unión Europea* (Pamplona: Aranzadi).

Novara, G. (1990): "Residenza di enti e società nell'imposizione persone sui rediti" (Bollettino Tributario d'informazioni, n. 1).

Nikolakakis, A. (2009): The unbearable lightness of being incorporated: the diminishing relevance of corporate residence, in Maisto, G. (ed.): *Residence of companies under tax treaties and EC Law* (Amsterdam: International Bureau of Fiscal Documentation).

Nikolakakis, A. (2010): Civil Law and Common Law perspectives: a view from the left, in Maisto, G. (ed.): *Residence of individuals under tax treaties and EC Law* (Amsterdam: International Bureau of Fiscal Documentation).

Oakland, W.H., Testa, W.A. (1996): State-local business taxation and the benefits principle (Economic perspectives, vol. 20, n. 1). Available at: https://www.chicagofed.org/ ~ /media/publications/economic-perspectives/1996/epjan96 a-pdf.pdf.

Oestreicher, A., Spengel, C., Koch, R. (2011): How to reform taxation of corporate groups in Europe (World Tax Journal, vol. 2, n. 1, pp. 5-38).

Owens, J. (2005): Should the arm's length principle retire? (International Transfer Pricing Journal, vol. 12, n. 3, pp. 99-102).

Oyama, H. (2014): Countering BEPS: preventing abusive commissionaire arrangements (Tax Notes International, vol. 75, n. 13, pp. 1163-1170).

Panayi, H.J.I. (2013): The taxation of permanent establishments: selected issues (Bulletin for international taxation, vol. 67, n. 4/5, pp. 26-237).

Parada, L. (2015): Intergovernmental agreements and the implementation of FATCA in Europe (World Tax Journal, vol. 7, n. 2, pp. 201-240).

Patton, B.L. (1975): United States individual income tax policy as it applies to Americans resident overseas or, if I am paying taxes equal to 72 percent of my gross income I must be living in Sweden (Duke Law Journal, vol. 1975, pp. 691-740).

Penrose, E.T. (1959): *The theory of the growth of the firm* (Oxford: Oxford University Press).

Petrucci, R. (2016): The arm's length principle, in Lang. M.; Storck, A.; Petruzzi, R. (eds.): *Transfer pricing in a post-BEPS world* (Alphen aan den Rijn: Kluwer Law International).

Pinto, D. (2003): *E-commerce and source-based income taxation* (Amsterdam: International Bureau of Fiscal Documentation).

Pires, M. (1989): *International juridical double taxation of income* (Deventer: Kluwer Law and Taxation Publishers).

Pleijsier, A. (2015): The agency permanent establishment in BEPS action 7: treaty abuse or business abuse (Intertax, vol. 43, n. 2, pp. 147-154).

Pyrcz, O.A. (1973): The basis of Canadian corporate taxation: Residence (Canadian Tax Journal, vol. 21, n. 4, pp. 374-390).

Reimer, E. (2012): Permanent establishment in the OECD Model Tax Convention, in Reimer, E.; Urban, N.; Schmid, S. (eds.): *Permanent establishments: a domestic taxation, bilateral tax treaty and OECD perspective* (Alphen aan den Rijn: Kluwer Law International).

Ribes, A. (2012): Tax residence and the mobility of companies in the European Union: the desirable harmonization of connecting factors (Intertax, vol. 40, n. 11, pp. 606-615).

Rivier, J.-M. (1987): General report on the fiscal residence of companies (IFA Cahiers de droit international, vol. 72a).

Robillard, R. (2015): BEPS: is the OECD now at the gates of global formulary apportionment? (Intertax, vol. 43, n. 6/7, pp. 447-453).

Rosenbloom, D. (1983): Tax treaty abuse: policy and issues (Law and Policy in International Business, vol. 15, n. 3, pp. 763-831).

Rosenbloom, D. (1994): Derivative benefits: emerging US treaty policy (Intertax, vol. 22, n. 2, pp. 83-86).

Rosenbloom, D. (2000): The David R. Tillinghast Lecture: International tax arbitrage and the "International tax system" (Tax Law Review, vol. 53, n. 2, pp. 137-166).

Rust, A. (2010): The concept of residence in inheritance tax law in Maisto, G. (ed.): *Residence of individuals under tax treaties and EC Law* (Amsterdam: International Bureau of Fiscal Documentation).

Sachdeva, A.M. (2014): International tax and private international law: exploring and exploiting similarities (Tax Planning International Review, vol. 41, n. 4).

Sampay, A.E. (1951): *Derecho fiscal internacional* (Buenos Aires: Biblioteca Laboremus).

Sanchirico, C.W. (2015): As American as Apple Inc.: international tax and ownership nationality (Tax Law Review, vol. 68, n. 2, pp. 207-274).

Sanghavi, D. (2016): The proposed tiebreaker rule in OECD/G20 BEPS Action 6: a critical examination of the possible motives and means and a potential alternative (Bulletin for International Taxation, vol. 70, n. 9, pp. 520-525).

Schanz, G. (1892): Zur Frage der Steuerpflicht (FinanzArchiv, vol. 9, band II, p. 365).

Schindel, A.; Atchabahian, A. (2005): General report on source and residence, new configuration of their principles (IFA Cahiers de droit fiscal international, vol. 90a).

Schön, W. (2005): Playing different games? Regulatory competition in tax and company law compared (Common Market Law Review, vol. 42, n. 2, pp. 331-335).

Schön, W. (2009): International tax coordination for a second-best word (part I) (World Tax Journal, vol. 1, n. 1, pp. 67-114).

Schön, W. (2010): International tax coordination for a second-best word (part III) (World Tax Journal, vol. 2, n. 3, pp. 227-261).

Schön, W. (2018): Ten questions about why and how to tax the digitalized economy (Bulletin for international taxation, vol. 72, n. 4/5, pp. 278-292).

Schoueri, L.E.; Günther, O-C (2011): The subsidiary as a permanent establishment (Bulletin for international taxation, vol. 65, n. 2, pp. 69-74).

Schoueri, L.E. (2015): Arm's length: beyond the guidelines of the OECD (Bulletin for international taxation, vol. 69, n. 12, pp. 690-716).

Schoueri, L.E.; Galendi, R.A. (2017): Justification and implementation of the international allocation of taxing rights: can we take one thing at a time?, in Rocha, S.A.; Christians, A. (eds.): *Tax sovereignty in the BEPS era* (Alphen aan den Rihn: Kluwer Law International).

Shaviro, D. (2011): The David R. Tillinghast Lecture: The rising tax electivity of US corporate residence (Tax Law Review, vol. 64, n. 3, pp. 101-154).

Simader, K. (2009): Austria, in Maisto, G. (ed.): *Residence of companies under tax treaties and EC Law* (Amsterdam: International Bureau of Fiscal Documentation).

Simader, K. (2013): *Withholding taxes and the fundamental freedoms* (Alphen aan den Rijn: Kluwer Law International).

Skaar, A.A. (1991): *Permanent establishment: erosion of a tax treaty principle* (Deventer/Boston: Kluwer Law and Taxation Publishers).

Smith, A. (1776): *An inquiry into the nature and causes of the wealth of nations.* Available at: https://www.ibiblio.org/ml/libri/s/SmithA_WealthNations_p.pdf.

Staudt, N.C. (2002): Taxation without representation (Tax Law Review, vol. 55, pp. 555-600).

Sullivan, M. (2012): Apple reports high rate but saves millions on taxes (Tax Analysts, pp. 777-778).

Svantesson, D. (2007): E-commerce tax: how the taxman brought geography to the borderless internet (Revenue Law Journal, vol. 17, n. 1).

Tadmore, N. (2012): Source in the digital age (Clayton Utz). Available at: https://www.claytonutz.com/ArticleDocuments/178/Clayton-Utz-Taxation-Source-in-the-Digital-Age-2012.pdf.aspx?Embed = Y.

Tanzi, V. (1998): The impact of economic globalization on taxation (Bulletin for international fiscal documentation, vol. 52, n. 8/9, pp. 338-343).

Tavares, R.J.S. (2016): Multinational firm theory and international tax law: seeking coherence (World Tax Journal, vol. 8, n. 2, pp. 243-276).

Tenore, M. (2009): Italy, in Maisto, G. (ed.): *Residence of companies under tax treaties and EC Law* (Amsterdam: International Bureau of Fiscal Documentation).

Tillinghast, D.R. (1984): A matter of definition: foreign and domestic taxpayers (Berkeley Journal of International Law, vol. 2, n. 2, pp. 1-34).

Tillinghast, D.R. (1996): The impact of the internet on the taxation of international transactions (Bulletin for International Fiscal Documentation, vol. 50, n. 11/12, pp. 524-526).

Ting, A. (2014): iTax—Apple's International tax structure and the double non-taxation issue (British Tax Review, n. 1, pp. 40-71).

Ting, A. (2014b): Old wine in a new bottle: Ireland's revised definition of corporate residence and the war on BEPS (British Tax Review, n. 3, pp. 237-247).

Van Daele, J. (2011): Tax residence and the mobility of companies: borderline cases under private international law and tax law (European Taxation, vol. 51, n. 5, pp. 190-200).

Vann, R.J. (2003): Reflections on business profits and the arm's length principle, in Arnold, B.J.; Sasseville, J.; Zolt, E.M. (eds.): *The taxation of business profits under tax treaties* (Toronto: Canadian Tax Foundation, pp. 133-169).

Vann, R.J. (2010): Taxing international business income: hard-boiled wonderland and the end of the world (World Tax Journal, vol. 2, n. 3, pp. 291-346).

Van Weeghel, S. (2010): General report on tax treaties and tax avoidance: application of anti-avoidance provisions (IFA Cahiers de droit fiscal international, vol. 95a).

Vega Borrego, F.A. (2003): *Las cláusulas de limitación de beneficios en los convenios para evitar la doble imposición* (Madrid: Instituto de Estudios Fiscales). Available at: http://www.ief.es/documentos/recursos/publicaciones/libros/Investig_juridicas/InvJuridica01_03.pdf.

Vega Borrego, F.A. (2006): *Limitation on benefits clauses in double taxation conventions* (London: Kluwer Law International).

Vogel, K. (1988): Worldwide versus source taxation of income: a review and re-evaluation of arguments—part I (Intertax, n. 8/9, pp. 216-229).

Vogel, K. (1988b): Worldwide vs. source taxation of income: a review and re-Evaluation of arguments—part II (Intertax, n. 10, pp. 310-320).

Vogel, K. (1988c): Worldwide vs. source taxation of income: a review and re-evaluation of arguments—part III (Intertax, n. 11, pp. 393-402).

Vogel, K. (1988d): The justification for taxation: a forgotten question (American Journal of Jurisprudence, vol. 33, n. 1, article 2, pp. 19-61).

Vogel, K. (1997): *Klaus Vogel on Double Taxation Conventions* (London: Kluwer Law International).

Voget, J. (2010): Relocation of headquarters and international taxation (Journal of Public Economics, vol. 95, pp. 1067-1081).

Von Bar, L. (1889*): Theorie und Praxis des internationalen Privatrechts* (Hannover: Hahn).

Wagh, S. (2013): Digital permanent establishment: a road ahead for e-commerce taxation. Available at: https://www.academia.edu/3797885/Digital_Permanent_Establishment_Digital_PE_A_Road_Ahead_for_E-Commerce_Taxation.

Wardzynski, A. (2014): The limitation on benefits article in the OECD Model: closing abusive (undesired) conduit gateways (Bulletin for international taxation, vol. 68, n. 9, pp. 471-479).

Wheeler, J.C. (2011): The missing keystone of income tax treaties (World Tax Journal, vol. 3, n. 2, pp. 247-367).

Wilde, M.F. de (2017): *Sharing the pie: taxing multinationals in a global market* (Amsterdam: IBFD).

Williams, R.L. (2014): *Fundamentals of permanent establishments* (The Hague: Kluwer Law International).

Wittendorff, J. (2016): BEPS action 8-10: birth of a new arm's-length principle (Tax Notes International, vol. 81, n. 4, pp. 331-358).

Yuan, J.; Liu, R.; Chan, H. (2015): Profit splits in the context of global value chain and its impact from Greater and China and Hong Kong's perspective (Transfer Pricing International Journal, vol. 16, n. 3, p. 9).

Zapata, S. (1998): The Latin America approach to the concept of permanent establishment in tax treaties with developed countries (Bulletin for international fiscal documentation, vol. 52, n. 6, pp. 252-261).

Zornoza Pérez, J.; Báez Moreno, A. (2010): The 2003 revisions to the Commentary to the OECD Model on tax treaties and GAARs: a mistaken starting point, in Lang, M. et al. (eds.): *Tax treaties: building bridges between law and economics* (Amsterdam: International Bureau of Fiscal Documentation).

Zornoza Pérez, J. (2013): Changing residence as tax planning (Pricewaterhouse Coopers Chair on International Corporate Taxation Working Papers, n. 2). Available at: http://e-archivo.uc3m.es/handle/10016/18175.

Table of Cases

International

International Court of Justice

Judgment by the International Court of Justice, September 7, 1927, "S.S. Lotus.", 236

Domestic

Judgments classified by countries (in alphabetic order) and listed by chronological order.

Australia

Judgment by the High Court of Australia, 1946, "Malayan Shipping Company Limited v. Federal Commissioner of Taxation.", 196

Judgment by the Australian Federal Court, 2011, "Commissioner of Taxation v. SNF Australia Pty Ltd.", 167

Canada

Judgment by the Canadian Federal Court of Appeal, 2002, "Smithkline Beecham Animal Health Inc. v. The Queen.", 167

Judgment by the Canadian Tax Court, 2013, "McKesson Canada Corporation.", 167

Germany

Judgment by the Finanzgericht Baden-Württenmerg, April 13, 2000, 3 K 235/97., 92

France

Judgment by the French Supreme Administrative Court (Conseil d'État), March 31, 2010, "Zimmer Ltd v. Ministre d l'Économie, des Finances et de l'Industrie.", 137

Italy

Judgment by the Italian Supreme Court (Corte di Cassazione), December 10, 1974.

Resolution by the Italian Tax Administration, January 29, 2003, n. 18/E., 78

Judgment by the Italian Supreme Court (Corte di Cassazione), March 9, 2012, "Boston Scientific.", 137

Reports

Companies

Reports classified by companies (in alphabetic order) and listed by chronological order.

Apple Inc.

Apple Inc.'s Annual Reports (form 10-K). Available at: http://investor.apple.com/sec.cfm?ndq_keyword=&DocType=Annual.

Apple Inc.'s 2018 Supplier List. Available at: https://www.apple.com/supplier-responsibility/pdf/Apple-Supplier-List.pdf.

International Organizations

Reports classified by organizations (in alphabetic order) and listed by chronological order.

European Union

EU Commission (2011): Proposal for a Council Directive on a Common Consolidated Corporate Tax Base (CCCTB).

EU Commission Expert Group on Taxation of the Digital Economy (2014): Final report.

EU Commission (2014): Explanatory notes on the EU VAT changes to the place of supply of telecommunications, broadcasting and electronic services that enter into force in 2015. Available at: http://ec.europa.eu/taxation_customs/sites/taxation/files/resources/documents/taxation/vat/how_vat_works/telecom/explanatory_notes_2015_en.pdf.

EU Commission (2015): Communication from the Commission to the European Parliament and the Council: a fair and efficient corporate taxation in the European Union: 5 key areas for action.

EU Commission (2017): Communication from the Commission to the European Parliament and the Council: a fair and efficient tax system in the European Union for the Digital Single Market.

EU Commission (2018): Proposal for a Council Directive laying down rules relating to the corporate taxation of a significant digital presence.

EU Commission (2018): Proposal for a Council Directive on the common system of a digital services tax on revenues resulting from the provision of certain digital services.

League of Nations

Economic and Financial Commission for the League of Nations (1923): Report on Double Taxation.

Economic and Financial Commission for the League of Nations (1928): Report on Double taxation and tax evasion.

League of Nations (1929): Report on the Council on the work of the First Session of the Committee.

Organisation for Economic Cooperation and Development

OECD (1986): Double taxation and the use of conduit companies.

OECD (1998): Harmful tax competition: an emerging global issue.

OECD (1999): The application of the OECD Model Tax Convention to partnerships.

OECD (2000): Report by the Technology Technical Advisory Group (TAG) on Tax and e-commerce. Available at: http://www.oecd.org/tax/consumption/1923248.pdf.

OECD (2001): Attribution of profit to a permanent establishment involved in electronic commerce transactions (Discussion paper). Available at: http://www.oecd.org/ctp/treaties/1923312.pdf.

OECD (2001): The impact of the communications revolution on the application of "place of effective management" as a tie breaker rule (Discussion Paper).

OECD (2002): Issues arising under article 5 (permanent establishment) of the model tax convention.

OECD (2003): Are the current treaty rules for taxing business profits appropriate for e-commerce? Final report.

OECD (2003): Restricting the entitlement to treaty benefits.

OECD (2008): Attribution of profits to permanent establishments.

OECD (2008): Tax treaty issues related to REITs.

OECD (2010): Attribution of profits to permanent establishments.

OECD (2010): The granting of treaty benefits with respect to the income of collective investment vehicles.

OECD (2011): Corporate loss utilization through aggressive tax planning.

OECD (2011): Transfer pricing legislation: a suggested approach. Available at: http://www.oecd.org/tax/transfer-pricing/45765682.pdf.

OECD (2011): Tackling aggressive tax planning through improved transparency and disclosure.

OECD (2012): Hybrid mismatch arrangements: tax policy and compliance issues.

OECD (2012): OECD Model Tax Convention: revised proposals concerning the interpretation and application of article 5 (permanent establishment).

OECD (2013): Addressing base erosion and profit shifting (referred to as BEPS report). Available at: http://www.oecd.org/tax/beps/addressing-base-erosion-and-profit-shifting-9789264192744-en.htm.

OECD (2013): Action plan on base erosion and profit shifting (referred to as BEPS Action Plan). Available at: https://www.oecd.org/ctp/BEPSActionPlan.pdf.

OECD (2013): Co-operative compliance: a framework from enhanced relationship to co-operative compliance.

OECD (2014): BEPS Action 1: comments received on public discussion draft. Available at: http://www.oecd.org/ctp/comments-action-1-tax-challenges-digital-economy.pdf.

OECD (2014): BEPS Action 1: addressing the tax challenges of the digital economy. Available at: http://www.keepeek.com/Digital-Asset-Management/oecd/taxation/addressing-the-tax-challenges-of-the-digital-economy_9789264218789-en#.WQWu7lV9780.

OECD (2014): BEPS Action 7: public discussion draft: preventing artificial avoidance of the PE status.

OECD (2014): BEPS Action 8 deliverable: guidance on transfer pricing aspects of intangibles.

OECD (2014): BEPS Action 10: draft on the use of profit splits in the context of global value chains.

OECD (2014): BEPS Actions 8, 9 and 10: Discussion draft on revision to chapter I of the transfer pricing guidelines (including risk, characterization and special measures).

OECD (2014): Two-part report to G20: Developing working group on the impact of BEPS in low income countries. Available at: http://www.oecd.org/tax/tax-global/report-to-g20-dwg-on-the-impact-of-beps-in-low-income-countries.pdf.

OECD (2015): Comments received on the Revised Discussion Draft on BEPS Action 7: prevent the artificial avoidance of PE status. Available at: http://www.oecd.org/ctp/treaties/public-comments-revised-beps-action-7-prevent-artificial-avoidance-pe-status.pdf.

OECD (2015): Principles of corporate governance. Available at: http://www.oecd-ilibrary.org/docserver/download/2615021e.pdf?expires = 1497526948&id = id &accname = guest&checksum = E74A4A1AC9123F37FAE22B8DDCE9F1D6.

OECD (2015): Revised Discussion Draft on BEPS Action 7: prevent the artificial avoidance of PE status. Available at: https://www.oecd.org/tax/treaties/public-comments-revised-beps-action-7-prevent-artificial-avoidance-pe-status .pdf.

OECD (2015): Final Report on BEPS Action 1—Addressing the tax challenges of the digital economy. Available at: http://www.oecd.org/ctp/addressing-the-tax-challenges-of-the-digital-economy-action-1-2015-final-report-9789264241046-en.htm.

OECD (2015): Final Report on BEPS Action 3: Designing effective Controlled Foreign Company rules. Available at: http://www.oecd.org/tax/designing-effective-controlled-foreign-company-rules-action-3-2015-final-report-9789264241152-en.htm.

OECD (2015): Final Report on BEPS Action 6: Preventing the granting of treaty benefits in inappropriate circumstances. Available at: http://www.oecd.org/

tax/preventing-the-granting-of-treaty-benefits-in-inappropriate-circumstances-action-6-2015-final-report-9789264241695-en.htm.

OECD (2015): Final Report on BEPS Action 7—Preventing the artificial avoidance of permanent establishment status. Available at: http://www.oecd.org/ctp/preventing-the-artificial-avoidance-of-permanent-establishment-status-action-7-2015-final-report-9789264241220-en.htm.

OECD (2015): Final Report on BEPS Actions 8-10—Aligning transfer pricing outcomes with value creation. Available at: http://www.oecd.org/tax/aligning-transfer-pricing-outcomes-with-value-creation-actions-8-10-2015-final-reports-9789264241244-en.htm.

OECD (2015): Final Report on BEPS Action 11—Measuring and monitoring BEPS. Available at: http://www.oecd.org/tax/measuring-and-monitoring-beps-action-11-2015-final-report-9789264241343-en.htm.

OECD (2015): Final Report on BEPS Action 13—Transfer pricing documentation and country-by-country reporting. Available at: http://www.oecd.org/tax/transfer-pricing-documentation-and-country-by-country-reporting-action-13-2015-final-report-9789264241480-en.htm.

OECD (2015): Final Report on BEPS Action 14—Making dispute resolution mechanisms more effective. Available at: http://www.oecd.org/tax/making-dispute-resolution-mechanisms-more-effective-action-14-2015-final-report-9789264241633-en.htm.

OECD (2016): Discussion Draft on BEPS Action 7—Additional guidance on the attribution of profits to permanent establishments. Available at: https://www.oecd.org/tax/transfer-pricing/BEPS-discussion-draft-on-the-attribution-of-profits-to-permanent-establishments.pdf.

OECD (2016): Multilateral convention to implement tax treaty related measures to prevent base erosion and profit shifting. Available at: http://www.oecd.org/tax/treaties/multilateral-convention-to-implement-tax-treaty-related-measures-to-prevent-BEPS.pdf.

OECD (2017): Inclusive framework on BEPS: progress report July 2016-June 2017. Available at: http://www.oecd.org/tax/beps/inclusive-framework-on-BEPS-progress-report-july-2016-june-2017.pdf.

OECD (2018): Tax challenges arising from digitalisation: interim report. Available at: http://www.oecd.org/ctp/tax-challenges-arising-from-digitalisation-interim-report-9789264293083-en.htm.

United Nations

UN (2013): Practical manual on transfer pricing.

National Governments

Reports classified by companies (in alphabetic order) and listed by chronological order.

Australia

Australian Taxation Office (2004): Draft Taxation Ruling: "Residence of companies not incorporated in Australia—carrying on business in Australia and central management and control." Available at: http://law.ato.gov.au/atolaw/view.htm?docid = DTR/TR2004D7/NAT/ATO/00001#P4.

France

Task Force on Taxation of the Digital Economy (2013): Report to the French Minister for the Economy and Finance and the Minister for Industrial Recovery (popularly known as the Collin & Colin report). Available at: http://www.hldataprotection.com/files/2013/06/Taxation_Digital_Economy.pdf.

Luxembourg

Leaked tax ruling by Luxembourg Administration regarding Itunes S.à, r.l. Available at www.icij.org.

United Kingdom

British Inland Revenue (1981): Company residence: a consultative document.

British HM Revenue & Customs (2014): International Manual. Available here: https://www.gov.uk/hmrc-internal-manuals/international-manual.

British HM Revenue & Customs (2015): Guidance on the Diverted Profits Tax. Available here: https://www.gov.uk/government/uploads/system/uploads/attachment_data/file/480318/Diverted_Profits_Tax.pdf.

United States

Exhibits used in the hearing on "Offshore profit shifting and the US tax code—part 2 (Apple Inc.)," Available at: http://www.hsgac.senate.gov/subcommittees/investigations/hearings/offshore-profit-shifting-and-the-us-tax-code_-part-2.

Memorandum on "Offshore profit shifting and the US tax code—part 2 (Apple Inc.)" submitted before the US Senate—Permanent Subcommittee on Investigations. Available at: http://www.hsgac.senate.gov/subcommittees/investigations/hearings/offshore-profit-shifting-and-the-us-tax-code_-part-2.

Testimony of Apple Inc. submitted before the US Senate—Permanent Subcommittee on Investigations. Available at: http://www.hsgac.senate.gov/subcommittees/investigations/hearings/offshore-profit-shifting-and-the-us-tax-code_-part-2.

Testimony of Prof. Shay on "Offshore profit shifting and the US tax code—part 2 (Apple Inc.)" submitted before the US Senate—Permanent Subcommittee on Investigations. Available at: http://www.hsgac.senate.gov/subcommittees/investigations/hearings/offshore-profit-shifting-and-the-us-tax-code_-part-2.

Testimony of Prof. Harvey Jr on "Offshore profit shifting and the US tax code—part 2 (Apple Inc.)" submitted before the US Senate—Permanent Subcommittee on Investigations. Available at: http://www.hsgac.senate.gov/subcommittees/investigations/hearings/offshore-profit-shifting-and-the-us-tax-code_-part-2.

US Department of the Treasury (2016): United States Model Technical Explanation accompanying the United States Model Tax Convention of November 15 2016.

Available at: https://www.treasury.gov/press-center/press-releases/Documents/hp16802.pdf.
US Department of the Treasury (2017): Foreign portfolio holdings of US securities. Available at: http://ticdata.treasury.gov/Publish/shla2017r.pdf.
US Government Accountability Office (2008): Effective tax rates are correlated where income is reported. Available at: https://www.gao.gov/assets/280/279648.pdf.

Media

Spain

El País: "Apple factura en Irlanda el 99% de sus ventas en España," March 16, 2011. Available at: http://economia.elpais.com/economia/2011/03/16/actualidad/1300264382_850215.html.

El País: "La declaración de impuestos le sale a Apple a devolver en España," May 20, 2012. Available at: http://economia.elpais.com/economia/2012/05/20/actualidad/1337547016_498517.html.

United States

New York Times: "How Apple sidesteps billions in taxes," April 28, 2012. Available at: http://www.nytimes.com/2012/04/29/business/apples-tax-strategy-aims-at-low-tax-states-and-nations.html?_r = 3&.

Forbes: "The $ 1,250 iPhone XS Max costs Apple $ 450 to make, nearly a 200% profit margin," September 27, 2018. https://www.forbes.com/sites/jeanbaptiste/2018/09/27/the-1250-iphone-xs-max-costs-apple-450-to-make-nearly-a-200-profit-margin/#3b981c6a4966 (last accessed on January 10, 2019).

SERIES ON INTERNATIONAL TAXATION

1. Alberto Xavier, *The Taxation of Foreign Investment in Brazil,* 1980 (ISBN 90-200-0582-0).
2. Hugh J. Ault & Albert J. Rädler, *The German Corporation Tax Law with 1980 Amendments,* 1981 (ISBN 90-200-0642-8).
3. Paul R. McDaniel & Hugh J. Ault, *Introduction to United States International Taxation,* 1981 (ISBN 90-6544-004-6).
4. Albert J. Rädler, *German Transfer Pricing/Prix de Transfer en Allemagne,* 1984 (ISBN 90-6544-143-3).
5. Paul R. McDaniel & Stanley S. Surrey, *International Aspects of Tax Expenditures: A Comparative Study,* 1985 (ISBN 90-654-4163-8).
6. Kees van Raad, *Nondiscrimination in International Tax Law,* 1986 (ISBN 90-6544-266-9).
7. Sijbren Cnossen (ed.), *Tax Coordination in the European Community,* 1987 (ISBN 90-6544-272-3).
8. Ben Terra, *Sales Taxation. The Case of Value Added Tax in the European Community,* 1989 (ISBN 90-6544-381-9).
9. Rutsel S.J. Martha, *The Jurisdiction to Tax in International Law: Theory and Practice of Legislative Fiscal Jurisdiction,* 1989 (ISBN 90-654-4416-5).
10. Paul R. McDaniel & Hugh J. Ault, *Introduction to United States International Taxation* (3rd revised edition), 1989 (ISBN 90-6544-423-8).
11. Manuel Pires, *International Juridicial Double Taxation of Income,* 1989 (ISBN 90-6544-426-2).
12. A.H.M. Daniels, *Issues in International Partnership Taxation,* 1991 (ISBN 90-654-4577-3).
13. Arvid A. Skaar, *Permanent Establishment: Erosion of a Tax Treaty Principle,* 1992 (ISBN 90-6544-594-3).
14. Cyrille David & Geerten M.M. Michielse (eds), *Tax Treatment of Financial Instruments,* 1996 (ISBN 90-654-4666-4).
15. Herbert H. Alpert & Kees van Raad (eds), *Essays on International Taxation,* 1993 (ISBN 90-654-4781-4).
16. Wolfgang Gassner, Michael Lang & Eduard Lechner (eds), *Tax Treaties and EC Law,* 1997 (ISBN 90-411-0680-4).
17. Glória Teixeira, *Taxing Corporate Profits in the EU,* 1997 (ISBN 90-411-0703-7).
18. Michael Lang et al. (eds), *Multilateral Tax Treaties,* 1998 (ISBN 90-411-0704-5).
19. Stef van Weeghel, *The Improper Use of Tax Treaties,* 1998 (ISBN 90-411-0737-1).
20. Klaus Vogel (ed.), *Interpretation of Tax Law and Treaties and Transfer Pricing in Japan and Germany,* 1998 (ISBN 90-411-9655-2).
21. Bertil Wiman (ed.), *International Studies in Taxation: Law and Economics; Liber Amicorum Leif Mutén,* 1999 (ISBN 90-411-9692-7).
22. Alfonso J. Martín Jiménez, *Towards Corporate Tax Harmonization in the European Community,* 1999 (ISBN 90-411-9690-0).

23. Ramon J. Jeffery, *The Impact of State Sovereignty on Global Trade and International Taxation*, 1999 (ISBN 90-411-9703-6).
24. A.J. Easson, *Taxation of Foreign Direct Investment*, 1999 (ISBN 90-411-9741-9).
25. Marjaana Helminen, *The Dividend Concept in International Tax Law: Dividend Payments Between Corporate Entities*, 1999 (ISBN 90-411-9765-6).
26. Paul Kirchhof, Moris Lehner, Kees van Raad, Arndt Raupach & Michael-Rodi (eds), *International and Comparative Taxation: Essays in Honour of Klaus Vogel*, 2002 (ISBN 90-411-9841-5).
27. Krister Andersson, Peter Melz & Christer Silfverberg (eds), *Liber Amicorum Sven-Olof Lodin*, 2001 (ISBN 90-411-9850-4).
28. Juan Martín Jovanovich, *Customs Valuation and Transfer Pricing: Is It Possible to Harmonize Customs and Tax Rules?*, Second Edition, 2018 (ISBN 978-90-411-6134-5).
29. Stefano Simontacchi, *Taxation of Capital Gains under the OECD Model Convention: With Special Regard to Immovable Property*, 2007 (ISBN 978-90-411-2549-1).
30. Michael Lang, Josef Schuch, & Claus Staringer (eds), *Tax Treaty Law and EC Law*, 2007 (ISBN 978-90-411-2629-0).
31. Duncan Bentley, *Taxpayers' Rights: Theory Origin and Implementation*, 2007 (ISBN 978-90-411-2650-4).
32. Sergio André Rocha, *Interpretation of Double Taxation Conventions: General Theory and Brazilian Perspective*, 2008 (ISBN 978-90-411-2822-5).
33. Robert F. van Brederode, *Systems of General Sales Taxation: Theory, Policy and Practice*, 2009 (ISBN 978-90-411-2832-4).
34. John G. Head & Richard Krever (eds), *Tax Reform in the 21st Century: A Volume in Memory of Richard Musgrave*, 2009 (ISBN 978-90-411-2829-4).
35. Jens Wittendorff, *Transfer Pricing and the Arm's Length Principle in International Tax Law*, 2010 (ISBN 978-90-411-3270-3).
36. Marjaana Helminen, *The International Tax Law Concept of Dividend*, Second Edition, 2017 (ISBN 978-90-411-8394-1).
37. Robert F. van Brederode (ed.), *Immovable Property under VAT: A Comparative Global Analysis*, 2011 (ISBN 978-90-411-3126-3).
38. Dennis Weber & Stef van Weeghel, *The 2010 OECD Updates: Model Tax Convention & Transfer Pricing Guidelines - A Critical Review*, 2011 (ISBN 978-90-411-3812-5).
39. Yariv Brauner & Martin James McMahon, Jr. (eds), *The Proper Tax Base: Structural Fairness from an International and Comparative Perspective—Essays in Honour of Paul McDaniel*, 2012 (ISBN 978-90-411-3286-4).
40. Robert F. van Brederode (ed.), *Science, Technology and Taxation*, 2012 (ISBN 978-90-411-3125-6).
41. Oskar Henkow, *The VAT/GST Treatment of Public Bodies*, 2013 (ISBN 978-90-411-4663-2).
42. Jean Schaffner, *How Fixed Is a Permanent Establishment?*, 2013 (ISBN 978-90-411-4662-5).

43. Miguel Correia, *Taxation of Corporate Groups*, 2013 (ISBN 978-90-411-4841-4).
44. Veronika Daurer, *Tax Treaties and Developing Countries*, 2014 (ISBN 978-90-411-4982-4).
45. Claire Micheau, *State Aid, Subsidy and Tax Incentives under EU and WTO Law*, 2014 (ISBN 978-90-411-4555-0).
46. Robert F. van Brederode & Richard Krever (eds), *Legal Interpretation of Tax Law*, 2014 (ISBN 978-90-411-4945-9).
47. Radhakishan Rawal, *Taxation of Cross-border Services*, 2014 (ISBN 978-90-411-4947-3).
48. João Dácio Rolim, *Proportionality and Fair Taxation*, 2014 (ISBN 978-90-411-5838-3).
49. Paulo Rosenblatt, *General Anti-avoidance Rules for Major Developing Countries*, 2015 (ISBN 978-90-411-5839-0).
50. Gaspar Lopes Dias V.S., *Tax Arbitrage through Cross-Border Financial Engineering*, 2015 (ISBN 978-90-411-5875-8).
51. Geerten M.M. Michielse & Victor Thuronyi (eds), *Tax Design Issues Worldwide*, 2015 (ISBN 978-90-411-5610-5).
52. Oktavia Weidmann, *Taxation of Derivatives*, 2015 (ISBN 978-90-411-5977-9).
53. Chris Evans, Richard Krever & Peter Mellor (eds), *Tax Simplification*, 2015 (ISBN 978-90-411-5976-2).
54. Reuven Avi-Yonah & Joel Slemrod (eds), *Taxation and Migration*, 2015 (ISBN 978-90-411-6136-9).
55. Alexander Bosman, *Other Income under Tax Treaties: An Analysis of Article 21 of the OECD Model Convention*, 2015 (ISBN 978-90-411-6610-4).
56. John Abrahamson, *International Taxation of Manufacturing and Distribution*, 2016 (ISBN 978-90-411-6664-7).
57. Frederik Boulogne, *Shortcomings in the EU Merger Directive*, 2016 (ISBN 978-90-411-6713-2).
58. Angelika Meindl-Ringler, *Beneficial Ownership in International Tax Law*, 2016 (ISBN 978-90-411-6833-7).
59. Andreas Waltrich, *Cross-Border Taxation of Permanent Establishments: An International Comparison*, 2016 (ISBN 978-90-411-6832-0).
60. Sergio André Rocha & Allison Christians (eds), *Tax Sovereignty in the BEPS Era*, 2017 (ISBN 978-90-411-6707-1).
61. Peter Antony Wilson, *BRICS and International Tax Law*, 2018 (ISBN 978-90-411-9435-0).
62. Louise Otis, Brigitte Alepin & Blanca Moreno-Dodson (eds), *Winning the Tax Wars: Tax Competition and Cooperation*, 2018 (ISBN 978-90-411-9460-2).
63. Marta Castelon, *International Taxation of Income from Services under Double Taxation Conventions: Development, Practice and Policy*, 2018 (ISBN 978-90-411-9594-4).
64. D.M. Broekhuijsen, *A Multilateral Tax Treaty: Designing an Instrument to Modernise International Tax Law*, 2018 (ISBN 978-90-411-9872-3).

65. John Abrahamson, *International Taxation of Energy Production and Distribution*, 2018 (ISBN 978-90-411-9101-4).
66. Leopoldo Parada, *Double Non-taxation and the Use of Hybrid Entities: An Alternative Approach in the New Era of BEPS*, 2018 (ISBN 978-90-411-9991-1).
67. Richard Snoeij, *International Tax Aspects of Sovereign Wealth Investors: A Source State Perspective*, 2018 (ISBN 978-90-411-9431-2).
68. Aleksandra Bal, *Taxation, Virtual Currency and Blockchain*, 2019 (ISBN 978-94-035-0103-1).
69. Werner Haslehner, Georg Kofler, Katerina Pantazatou & Alexander Rust (eds), *Tax and the Digital Economy: Challenges and Proposals for Reform*, 2019 (ISBN 978-94-035-0361-5).
70. Eva Escribano, *Jurisdiction to Tax Corporate Income Pursuant to the Presumptive Benefit Principle: A Critical Analysis of Structural Paradigms Underlying Corporate Income Taxation and Proposals for Reform*, 2019 (ISBN 978-94-035-0640-1).